D0906479

SEXUAL DEVIANCE

This book is dedicated to the memory of Steve Hudson
January 18, 1950-November 1, 2001
He was a valued colleague,
a dear friend, and we miss him.

SEXUAL DEVIANCE
ISSUES AND CONTROVERSIES

TONY WARD
University of Melbourne, Australia

D. RICHARD LAWS
South Island Consulting, Victoria, BC, Canada

STEPHEN M. HUDSON

EDITORS

SAGE Publications
International Educational and Professional Publisher
Thousand Oaks ■ London ■ New Delhi

For information:

Sage Publications, Inc.
2455 Teller Road
Thousand Oaks, California 91320
E-mail: order@sagepub.com

Sage Publications Ltd.
6 Bonhill Street
London EC2A 4PU
United Kingdom

Sage Publications India Pvt. Ltd.
M-32 Market
Greater Kailash I
New Delhi 110 048 India

Printed in the United States of America

Library of Congress Cataloging-in-Publication Data

Sexual deviance : issues and controversies / edited by Tony Ward, D. Richard Laws, Stephen M. Hudson.
     p. cm.
Includes bibliographical references and index.
ISBN 0-7619-2732-8 (cloth)
   1. Sexual deviation. 2. Deviant behavior. 3. Psychosexual disorders. 4. Child sexual abuse. 5. Sex offenders-Psychology. 6. Sex offenders-Rehabilitation. I. Ward, Tony. II. Laws, D. Richard. III. Hudson, Stephen M.
HQ71 .S398 2003
306.77—dc211
                    2002007105

02 03 04 05 10 9 8 7 6 5 4 3 2 1

Acquiring Editor:	Margaret H. Seawell
Editorial Assistant:	Alicia Carter
Production Editor:	Claudia A. Hoffman
Copy Editor:	Kristin Bergstad
Typesetter:	C&M Digitals (P) Ltd
Indexer:	Molly Hall
Cover Designer:	Janet Foulger

Contents

Introduction: Theoretical Issues in Sexual Deviance   xi
Tony Ward, D. Richard Laws, and Stephen M. Hudson
    Outline of the Book   xiii

PART I. EXPLANATIONS OF SEXUAL DEVIANCE   1

1. Explaining Child Sexual Abuse:
   Integration and Elaboration   3
   Tony Ward and Laura Sorbello
       Finkelhor's Precondition Theory   4
       Hall and Hirschman's Quadripartite Theory   8
       Marshall and Barbaree's Integrated Theory   10
       The Pathways Model of Child Sexual Abuse   14
       Conclusions   18

2. Good Lives and the Rehabilitation of Sexual Offenders   21
   Tony Ward and Claire A. Stewart
       The Good Lives Model of Offender Rehabilitation   25
       Good Lives and the Treatment of Sex Offenders   29
       Conclusions   42

3. Back to the Future? Evolutionary Explanations of Rape   45
   Richard Siegert and Tony Ward
       Selection, Adaptation, and Evolution   46
       What Is Evolutionary Psychology?   47
       An EP Perspective on Human Mating Strategies   49
       Evolutionary Psychology and Theories of Rape   51
       General Discussion   59
       Conclusions   61

4. Behavioral Economic Approaches to the Assessment
   and Treatment of Sexual Deviation   65
   D. Richard Laws

What Is Behavioral Economics? 66

Demand: Assessment 70

Conclusions 79

5. Penile Plethysmography: Will We Ever Get It Right? 82
   D. Richard Laws

   Getting Started 82

   What This Chapter Is Not About 84

   What Is Penile Plethysmography? 84

   What About Construct Validity? 90

   Is PPG a Genuine Test? 92

   Can PPG Scores Predict Reoffense? 93

   Legal Challenges to PPG 94

   Does It Have Any Utility? 97

   Will We Ever Get It Right? 99

6. Cultural Components of Practice: Reflexive
   Responses to Diversity and Difference 103
   Marie Connolly

   Cultural Knowledge Within the Practice Setting 104

   Locations of Cultural Thinking 105

   Cultural Thinking and Its Impact on Practice 108

   The Cultural-Reflective Model 113

   Conclusions 116

7. Developmental Antecedents of Sexual Offending 119
   Thomas Keenan and Tony Ward

   Developmental Psychopathology 120

   Self-Regulation and Sexual Offending 122

   Theory of Mind 124

   Implicit Theories 127

   Conclusions 131

8. Cognitive Distortions, Schemas, and Implicit Theories 135
   Ruth E. Mann and Anthony R. Beech

   The Development of the Concept of
   Cognitive Distortions in Relation
   to Sexual Offending 136

   Models of Cognition and Behavior 138

   Schemas in Sexual Offending:
   A Review of Current Research 141

   A Schema-Based Model of Sexual Assault 145

   Implications for Current Treatment
   Approaches of a Schema-Based Approach 147

   Schema-Focused Treatment With Sexual Offenders 149

   Conclusions 150

9. The Classification of Sex Offenders   154
    Devon L. L. Polaschek
        Psychiatric Diagnosis of Sexual Deviance   155
        General Observations   156
        The Case of Pedophilia   159
        The Exclusion of Rape   160
        Functional Analytic Approaches
            to Offender Classification   161
        Nondiagnostic Classification of Sexual Offenders   164
        Conclusions and Future Directions   167

10. Empathy and Victim Empathy   172
    Devon L. L. Polaschek
        What Is Empathy?   173
        Models of Empathy   173
        Measurement of Empathy   175
        Empathy Research With Sex Offenders   177
        Empathy-Based Interventions   179
        Theory   183
        Directions for the Future   186

PART II. RESPONSES TO SEXUAL DEVIANCE

11. Research and Practice With Adolescent Sexual
    Offenders: Dilemmas and Directions   190
    Robin Jones
        Research Issues   190
        Clinical Issues   198
        Conclusion   204

12. The Promise and the Peril of Sex Offender Risk Assessment   207
    Stephen Hart, D. Richard Laws, and P. Randall Kropp
        Key Terms and Concepts   209
        Approaches to Sexual Violence Risk Assessment   210
        Evaluating Sexual Violence Risk Assessment Procedures   214
        Current Controversies   220
        Conclusion   223

13. Treatment Models for Sex Offenders:
    A Move Toward a Formulation-Based Approach   226
    Christopher R. Drake and Tony Ward
        Formulation- Versus Manual-Based Treatments   228
        Situations Where Formulation-Based
            Approaches Are Useful   231
        Theoretical Advancements and
            Development of Treatment   232
        Conclusions   241

14. Responsivity Factors in Sexual Offender Treatment   244
     Michael J. Proeve
         Motivation   245
         Self-Esteem   247
         Attachment Style   248
         Shame   249
         Relationship Among the Internal Responsivity Factors   251
         Therapist Style   251
         Format of Treatment   253
         Implications for Practice and Research   255

15. Integrating Pharmacological Treatments   262
     William Glaser
         The Ideal Pill   263
         Pharmacological Treatments   265
         Assessment and Management: Integrating
            Pharmacological and Other Approaches   271
         Ethical and Legal Issues   275
         Conclusion   277

16. Harm Reduction and Sexual Offending:
     Is an Intraparadigmatic Shift Possible?   280
     D. Richard Laws
         What Is Harm Reduction?   280
         Where Do We Go From Here?   293
         Conclusion   293

17. Sexual Offending Is a Public Health Problem:
     Are We Doing Enough?   297
     D. Richard Laws
         Levels of Prevention in Public Health   298
         The Public Health Approach to Sexual Violence   300
         Sexual Abuse as a Public Health Issue   307
         STOP IT NOW!: The Campaign to
            Prevent Child Sexual Abuse   309
         Conclusion   313

18. Enhancing Relapse Prevention Through the Effective
     Management of Sex Offenders in the Community   317
     Astrid Birgden, Karen Owen, and Bea Raymond
         External Supervision in Relapse Prevention   319
         Sex Offender Programs in Victorian Corrections   320
         Enhancing Motivation to Change   322
         Staff Attitudes Toward Sexual Offenders   326

	A Model for Training Correctional Staff	327
	Evaluation	331
	Future Directions	333
	Conclusion	333
19.	The Risk-Need Model of Offender Rehabilitation: A Critical Analysis	338
	Tony Ward and Mark Brown	
	The Risk-Need Model	339
	The Concepts of Risk and Need	341
	Critical Comments	343
	Conclusions	353
	Index	355
	About the Editors	367
	About the Contributors	369

Introduction

Why do men rape women? What are the psychological, biological, cultural, and situational factors that predispose some males to sexually assault a woman? What causes an adult to sexually molest a prepubescent child? Why would a man in a stable intimate adult relationship want to have a sexual relationship with a teenage girl? How is it possible for someone to become sexually aroused to a child who is neither physically mature nor sexually motivated? The answers to such questions matter. They are not simply abstract questions with no discernible impact on individuals' everyday lives. Understanding why child molestation occurs, and how it develops and changes over time, is of the utmost importance in helping us to prevent it. Moreover, such understanding helps to design intervention programs to stop men from reoffending (Ward & Siegert, in press).

Theories provide an explanation of certain phenomena. This may involve specifying the nature of hidden mechanisms that generate the phenomena of interest or integrating a diverse set of findings with a relatively small number of assumptions and ideas (Hooker, 1987). Human beings can be studied from a number of quite distinct perspectives (e.g., sociocultural, biological, psychological, and functional). Arguably a comprehensive explanation of human action requires an understanding of each of these distinct levels and the way they interact. For example, a theory of rape that appealed to adversarial attitudes toward women and a range of associated mental states would need to be consistent with current knowledge about the architecture of the mind and the biological factors underpinning its structure and organization (Hudson & Ward, 1997).

Theory generation is not a luxury to be indulged in after the task of detecting basic phenomena and their relationships has taken place. All treatment programs for sex offenders are based on theoretical assumptions concerning the psychological, biological and sociocultural mechanisms that result in sexual abuse. The actual choice of explanatory hypotheses in a case formulation is guided by the theories of psychopathology and research literature within a particular area. This helps the clinician to narrow down the search for plausible causes and to ensure that theories with the most research support are initially considered as possible explanations. This constraint is entirely consistent with one of the core requirements of the scientist-practitioner model—that clinical work be based on existing empirical findings. However, this strategy means that case formulation is a theory-driven enterprise and the content of any particular formulation will reflect the theoretical allegiances of the clinician in question (Ward, Vertue, & Haig, 1999).

In addition, there are always clinical theories underlying the selection of the modules contained in treatment manuals. For example, the inclusion of relapse prevention strategies in most state-of-the-art intervention programs for sexual offenders follows from the theoretical assumption that relapse is a sequential process influenced by different cognitive, affective, and contextual factors (Laws, Hudson, & Ward, 2000).

The etiological and clinical theories used by therapists in their everyday practice assume a particular view of human nature; for example, whether or not our minds share a common architecture. Therapy goals are based on judgments concerning the best possible outcomes for clients, essentially a vision of human flourishing and well-being. Such assumptions have distinct ethical implications and impact on the way clinicians approach their professional practice. From the perspective of an evolutionary or naturalistic model, overlooking the innate need to establish a sense of meaning and value in our lives will diminish the chances of an effective therapy outcome (Tooby & Cosmides, 1992). Or, attempting to foster nonviolent conflict resolution skills in males while ignoring their proclivity to engage in competitive behavior may prove fruitless. This process involves ethical judgments because of the relationship between natural goods and ideal therapy outcomes. The assessment and intervention phases of clinical reasoning are shot through with normative commitments and judgments.

This brief discussion of the way theory impacts upon the assessment and treatment of sexual offenders suggests that it is not possible to remain theoretically disengaged. All clinicians and researchers are committed to a plethora of general assumptions about the nature of sexual offending, offenders, and the treatment process. These assumptions in turn can be unpacked into more fine-grained beliefs concerning the role of psychological processes, cultural factors, and biological systems in generating sexual deviance. In addition, theories concerning the salient phenomena associated with sexual offending have direct clinical implications for therapists.

Though in recent years some texts have contained chapters on etiological theories in the sexual offending area, there has been a remarkable lack of attention paid to ongoing theoretical issues and the relationship between theory and practice. This is unfortunate and in our opinion has resulted in an unsophisticated approach to clinical practice and research. Theories provide maps with which to negotiate our way through the maze of day-to-day clinical problems. If they remain unarticulated, they still exert an effect on the way practice occurs. In our view it is imperative to critically discuss, debate, and review the ideas and values underpinning research and treatment of sex offenders. The agenda for such a debate will need to cover a wide range of ongoing issues and controversies. These include the specific contribution of biological, developmental, cultural, and learning factors in the genesis of sexual deviancy and the values and assumptions underpinning different models of treatment delivery. This book represents an attempt to provide a context for such a debate.

Outline of the Book

The first part of the book contains Chapters 1 through 10 and focuses more on conceptual issues; the second part contains Chapters 11 through 19 and is concerned with therapeutic responses to sexual deviance.

In Chapter 1, Tony Ward and Laura Sorbello consider the role of theory in the assessment and treatment of sexual offenders. They make the point that explanations of child sexual abuse tend to occur in isolation, with theorists typically failing to build on promising ideas put forward by other researchers. They introduce the idea of theory knitting and argue for the importance of a collaborative strategy when constructing theory. This suggestion is illustrated by the exposition and critique of three prominent theories of child sexual abuse and the development of a comprehensive theory, the pathways model, that integrates the strengths of each of these models and also introduces some novel ideas. From a clinical perspective, the pathways model suggests that sexual offenders will have different deficits, depending on the offense pathway traversed. For example, some individuals will need to acquire increased levels of relationship skills whereas others would benefit from learning how to manage their moods more effectively.

In Chapter 2, Tony Ward and Claire Stewart argue that the risk-need model of rehabilitation currently dominant in the correctional area is insufficient to guide the treatment of offenders adequately. Rather, they suggest that the major aim of offender rehabilitation should be to give offenders the necessary capabilities to secure important personal and social goods in acceptable ways rather than primarily the reduction and management of risk. That is, the way to reduce reoffending is arguably to give individuals the necessary conditions to lead *better lives* (i.e., "good" lives) than simply to teach them how to minimize their chances of being incarcerated. Goods underpin goals and as such provide the normative source or justification for intrinsic goals. Programs that focus concretely on securing better lives for offenders are skill and competency based, but also freely acknowledge and seek to develop the values that underpin their therapeutic endeavors. This process involves value judgments because of the relationship between natural goods and ideal therapy outcomes.

In Chapter 3, Richard Siegert and Tony Ward provide a critical introductory review of some of the major attempts to apply evolutionary psychology to understanding why rape occurs. They begin with a brief account of Darwin's principles of selection and adaptation and then describe contemporary evolutionary psychology. Next, they describe in some detail the major conclusions of an evolutionary psychological perspective on human mating strategies and then provide a summary of three recent attempts to incorporate evolutionary psychology principles into theoretical accounts of rape. In each case, they describe the main features of the theory followed by a brief evaluation of its strengths and weaknesses. Finally, they offer some suggestions for how work in this area might best proceed in the future. They stress that at this point in time there are too many unanswered questions concerning the nature of the relevant adaptations and the contribution of sociological and cultural theories to conclude that evolutionary theories are sufficient to explain sexual aggression.

In Chapter 4, Richard Laws discusses behavioral economic approaches to the assessment and treatment of sexual deviation. His aim is to present some limited general theoretical assumptions that place human sexual behavior, in the present case, deviant sexual behavior, within an economic context. This chapter focuses primarily on two major features of behavioral economics and their possible application to sexual deviation: demand and discounting of the delay of reinforcement. He argues that the research on discounting of delay is one of those remarkable instances where a well-understood procedure developed in animal research has found an almost identical application in research with humans. Laws concludes that assessment procedures of deviant sexual behavior will be developed that will ultimately tell us much, not only about choice, but about the underlying schemas that permit some people to engage in deviant sexual behavior while spurning more conventional alternatives. The constructs of economic psychology may well assist in this task.

In Chapter 5, Richard Laws reviews some of the key issues associated with penile plethysmography. He considers the following areas: how he became involved with the technology; PPG as a technology, procedure, and art; standardization problems with the procedure; construct validity; whether or not it is a genuine test; how well it predicts sexual reoffending; legal challenges to the procedure; and whether it has any real utility. He concludes with rather a negative verdict on the utility of PPG and suggests that the changes that have been made (superior electronics in PPG equipment, computer-generated images, data management by computer) are actually differences that really do not make a difference. He predicts that assessment of deviant sexual preferences will very likely move in a number of new directions: the use of visual reaction time procedures, computer-generated images, and noninvasive self-report procedures that deal frankly with deviant sexual interest and behavior.

In Chapter 6, Marie Connolly looks at culture, diversity, and difference broadly, exploring the way in which cultural thinking impacts client outcomes. She states that the developing nature of practice and how cultural components impact on the work have received little attention in the practice literature. Although acknowledging the importance of specific cultural knowledge for practice, she argues that it is our tacit cultural knowledge that creates the most difficulty in cross-cultural communication. She uses a case example to demonstrate the way in which cultural thinking influences the direction of clinical work, and provides a model of self-analysis that can be used to navigate cross-cultural pathways. A major aim of the chapter is to provide clinicians with a model to help them to reflect critically on the cultural assumptions that underpin their work.

In Chapter 7, Thomas Keenan and Tony Ward examine the contribution of a developmental psychopathology approach to sex offenders in three research domains: self-regulation, theory of mind, and implicit theories. The study of developmental psychopathology can be thought of as a marriage between developmental psychology and the study of psychological disorders. Self-regulation consists of both internal and external processes that allow an individual to engage in goal-directed actions over time and across different contexts. The term *theory of mind* refers to a person's understanding that both the person and other people act on the basis of mental states such as *desires, intentions, emotions,* and *beliefs,* and furthermore, that they use these mental states both to predict and to explain behavior. Implicit theories are folk psychological knowledge structures and represent everyday understandings of close relationships, other peoples' actions, the structure of the natural world, and the nature of mental states. Keenan and Ward apply the theories and research findings in these three developmentally oriented domains to the sexual offending area.

In Chapter 8, Ruth Mann and Tony Beech outline a theory for the role of cognition in sexual offending. The cognitive behavioral model assumes that cognitions—thoughts, attitudes, and beliefs—play a key role in determining behavior. In order to attempt a more precise understanding of how cognition affects behavior, they briefly review two popular models: social cognition theory and cognitive therapy theory. These two models are not mutually exclusive but have considerable overlap, and in particular both theories place heavy emphasis on the concept of *schema* as an organizer of thought and the processing of information. Mann and Beech then examine existing research to see what can be concluded about cognitive processing and cognitive structures (schemas) in sexual offenders. Some common themes have started to emerge; these include, for rapists, schemas involving entitlement, control, grievance, and deceitful women beliefs. For child molesters, belief schemas to do with worthlessness and category schemas involving beliefs that children are sexual seem to be indicated. They then describe their own schema-based model of sexual assault based on consideration of social cognition and cognitive therapy theory approaches. Finally, the implications for treatment of using a schema-based approach are discussed, and it is concluded that such an approach may enhance treatment effectiveness.

In Chapter 9, Devon Polaschek considers a number of issues associated with the classification of sex offenders. The classification of sex offenders is a topic that has received sporadic attention, despite its potential importance in the understanding of sexual assaults and their perpetrators, and in the construction of good etiological theory. A reliable and valid classificatory system also informs the assessment of offenders, the design and evaluation of treatment, and prediction of future risk. This chapter first reviews the relevance of psychiatric diagnosis to the assessment and treatment of sexual offending; focusing on the approach taken by the *Diagnostic and Statistical Manual of Mental Disorders,* Fourth Edition (*DSM-IV;* American Psychiatric Association [APA], 1994). Second, the utility of functional analysis is compared with diagnosis. Last, Knight and Prentky's (1990) sexual offender classification models are described and evaluated for their potential to improve our understanding of how sexual offenders are heterogeneous, and what these variations might mean for their management.

In Chapter 10, Devon Polaschek first examines how empathy is defined and modeled, and evaluates instruments that purport to measure this important construct. Then research on empathy in sex offenders is summarized, concentrating on the evidence for the presence or absence of empathy deficits. Third, she outlines typical interventions and reviews the small number of outcome studies purporting to measure clinical changes in empathy. Finally, a section on theory critiques how empathy is related to both predisposition to offend, and the offense process itself. Polaschek argues that the degree to which offenders have empathy deficits, whether specific or general; the degree to which interventions actually target deficits; and our ability to evaluate whether change occurs are all challenged by fundamental difficulties in defining and measuring empathy. Relatedly, theoretical views remain relatively underdeveloped at this point in time.

In Chapter 11, Robin Jones selects some salient dilemmas relevant to research and practice with adolescent sex offenders, and suggests some directions that will help generate relevant knowledge in areas where it is most needed. Two major themes run through this chapter. First is the frequently noted heterogeneity of the adolescent sex offender population, and the enormous implications this has for undertaking meaningful research. Three research areas have been chosen to illustrate and explore these implications: offender classification, etiology, and recidivism studies. The second theme concerns the need to respond effectively to the developmental needs of adolescent sex offenders. Jones concludes that both research and practice with adolescent sex offenders need to be approached with a more systematic and critical eye. The heterogeneity of the identified population, combined with the severe methodological problems in existing research, has put quite a low ceiling on what we can confidently conclude from the literature thus far.

In Chapter 12, Steve Hart, Richard Laws, and Randall Kropp consider a number of important conceptual issues associated with the risk assessment of sexual offenders. They state that risk assessment is a cornerstone of effective offender management in contemporary corrections and add that it is crucial to identify the risks posed by offenders, the factors associated with these risks, and the interventions that could be taken to manage or reduce risk. In this chapter, they discuss both the promise and the peril of sex offender risk assessment—more properly, sexual violence risk assessment. Hart et al. conclude that sexual violence risk assessments can be considered promising insofar as they have the potential to help people make informed and important decisions about sex offenders but also caution that they have not delivered on the promise that they can be used to make precise predictions about future sexual violence. Finally, they suggest that mental health professionals who conduct sexual violence risk assessments must be careful to appreciate and communicate the limits of their knowledge and practice, especially given the harm that may stem from bad decisions.

In Chapter 13, Chris Drake and Tony Ward argue for the utility of a formulation-based approach to the assessment and treatment of sex offenders. In essence, a case formulation is a clinical theory that specifies how an offender's symptoms or problems are generated by psychological mechanisms, for example, dysfunctional core beliefs or behavioral deficits. In contrast to a manual-based approach, formulation-based approaches assume that in order to treat sexual offenders effectively therapists need to develop a comprehensive understanding of offenders' psychological vulnerabilities and problems. In this chapter it is suggested that a formulation-based approach based on more adequate etiological and offense chain theories can overcome most of the difficulties often documented in such approaches. Drake and Ward state that a well-constructed, theory-based formulation can assist in understanding the developmental factors giving rise to psychopathology related to offending, identify the specific steps involved in the process of offending, and clarify how offending has been maintained over time for individuals. It can also provide clinicians with guidance when there is a paucity of treatment options for certain types of offenders or where previous treatment has been unsuccessful.

In Chapter 14, Michael Proeve reviews the literature concerning internal (motivation, self-esteem, attachment style, shame) and external (therapist style, treatment format) responsivity factors in sexual offender treatment. The term *responsivity* refers to the interaction of characteristics of offenders with the style and mode of therapy, and has essentially the same meaning as "process issues" in the general psychotherapy literature. The relationships among the internal responsivity factors and interactions between the internal and external responsivity factors are discussed and recommendations made regarding therapist style. Moreover, the circumstances in which individual therapy might be recommended in addition to group therapy are considered. Proeve concludes that measurement of internal responsivity variables of motivation, self-esteem, shame, and attachment would assist the process of matching therapist style and treatment format to client characteristics and thereby increase treatment effectiveness. In addition, he suggests that the development and investigation of appropriate measures of internal responsivity are urgently needed.

In Chapter 15, William Glaser aims to describe both the advantages and the shortcomings of pharmacological agents against the background of the sometimes unrealistic claims made about them. He then attempts to place them in the context of integrated treatment programs for sex offenders and demonstrate how, in particular, lessons learned from the application of cognitive-behavioral techniques can guide us in introducing these agents, encouraging compliance with them, and monitoring their effects. Finally, ethical and legal issues are discussed, particularly with respect to the growing preoccupation of sex offender treatment programs with the interests of the community, rather than those of the offender.

In Chapter 16, Richard Laws analyzes the possible contribution of a harm reduction perspective to the treatment of sexual offenders. Harm reduction is a public health alternative to the current disease, immoral, or criminal models of sexual deviance. It recognizes abstinence as an ideal goal but accepts alternatives that reduce harm to self and others. It promotes low-threshold access to services to encourage the fearful and reluctant to come forward. It is based on an approach of humanitarian pragmatism and uses whatever works to achieve the best possible outcomes in the individual case. Harm reduction would view sexual deviation as a chronic, entrenched disposition to engage in deviant behavior, a condition that is incurable but one that could be managed, probably imperfectly. Laws concludes that reduction of sexual harm from a public health perspective requires a reframing of the problem, an intraparadigmatic shift of attitude.

In Chapter 17, Richard Laws investigates the utility of viewing sexual offending through the lens of a public health perspective. The major purpose of his chapter is to examine the general public health approach and how it may be applied in the management of sex offenders, and whether it can be effective. The classical public health approach identifies three levels of prevention: (a) primary (prevent deviant behavior from ever starting), (b) secondary (early identification and intervention), and (c) tertiary (treating with chronic offenders). Laws describes these levels of prevention and explores their application to sexual deviance. He concludes that if we are ever to have a major impact on the problem of sexual abuse, we must focus intense effort on primary prevention, stopping the behavior before it ever gets started.

In Chapter 18, Astrid Birgden, Karen Owen, and Bea Raymond address relapse prevention in the context of a service delivery model developed for sex offenders in Victoria, Australia. The assumptions of the model are: (a) relapse prevention is applied after cognitive-behavioral intervention; (b) relapse prevention plans are based on such interventions, which in turn are based on individualized case formulations regarding offense pathways; and (c) motivation to change sex offending behavior does not necessarily exist. A difference from accepted relapse prevention practice is that more emphasis is placed on the external supervision component of the relapse prevention model. This emphasis is enhanced by the application of stages of change readiness, motivational principles, and dramatherapy techniques. A three-dimensional model based on theories and techniques provided by stages of change readiness, motivational interviewing, and masks and personas of offenders is presented. The model takes into account the principles of relapse prevention and addresses (a) the degree of denial and minimization expressed by ex offenders, (b) the skills required of correctional staff, and (c) beliefs and attitudes that impact upon staff responses to sex offenders.

Finally, in Chapter 19, Tony Ward and Mark Brown critically analyze the risk-need model of offender rehabilitation. This model has been developed principally by Andrews and Bonita over the past decade and is among the most highly influential frameworks in correctional psychology. In this chapter they offer a critical assessment of its conceptions of risk and need. They argue that despite widespread adoption of the risk-need model, the two concepts remain overlapping and potentially confusing. In addition, the confusion of different types of risk factors and risk assessment and the failure to clarify the role of criminogenic needs in the offending process are major problems. They propose an alternative conceptualization of need that emphasizes categorical needs and basic human goods in the promotion of human well-being. This model of need is linked to risk analysis through a broader conception of risk and an acknowledgment of the limitations of extant empirically grounded theoretical constructions.

References

American Psychiatric Association. (1994). *Diagnostic and statistical manual of mental disorders* (4th ed.). Washington, DC: Author.

Hooker, C. A. (1987). *A realistic theory of science.* Albany: State University of New York Press.

Hudson, S. M., & Ward, T. (1997). Rape: Psychopathology and theory. In D. R. Laws & W. O'Donohue (Eds.), *Sexual deviance: Theory, assessment, and treatment* (pp. 332-353). New York: Guilford.

Knight, R. A., & Prentky, R. A. (1990). Classifying sexual offenders: The development and corroboration of taxonomic models. In W. L. Marshall, D. R. Laws, & H. E. Barbaree (Eds.), *Handbook of sexual assault: Issues, theories, and treatment of the offender* (pp. 23-52). New York: Plenum.

Laws, D. R., Hudson, S. M., & Ward, T. (Eds.). (2000). *Remaking relapse prevention with sex offenders: A sourcebook.* Thousand Oaks, CA: Sage.

Tooby, J., & Cosmides, L. (1992). The psychological foundations of culture. In J. H. Barkow, L. Cosmides, & J. Tooby (Eds.), *The adapted mind: Evolutionary psychology and the generation of culture.* (pp. 19-136). New York: Oxford University Press.

Ward, T., & Siegert, R. J. (in press). Toward a comprehensive theory of child sexual abuse: A theory knitting perspective. *Psychology, Crime, & Law.*

Ward, T., Vertue, F. M., & Haig, B. D. (1999). Abductive method and clinical assessment in practice. *Behaviour Change, 16,* 49-63.

PART I

Explanations of Sexual Deviance

1

Explaining Child Sexual Abuse:

Integration and Elaboration

Tony Ward

Laura Sorbello
University of Melbourne

The consensus in the literature is that a phenomenon as complex as child sexual abuse is unlikely to be explained by single-factor theories (Marshall, 1996; Ward & Hudson, 1998). A number of multifactorial theories have therefore been developed that attempt to highlight the social-cultural, biological, psychological, and functional perspectives of child molestation. The most influential include Finkelhor's (1984) precondition model, Hall and Hirschman's (1992) quadripartite model, and Marshall and Barbaree's integrated theory (1990). Although these important theories have numerous strengths, each has weaknesses that limit its ability to provide a satisfactory explanation of child sexual abuse. Of some concern is the fact that their explanatory adequacies have never been conceptually critiqued or empirically evaluated within the literature. It is necessary to value ideas, but not to be captured by them. We show our colleagues enormous respect by taking their theories and research seriously enough to criticize them, and also by then attempting to extend their work in new directions.

In order to advance the process of theory construction in the sexual offending domain, we have recently proposed a meta-theoretical framework for classifying existing theories. This framework explores theory according to level of generality of focus and the extent to which the relevant factors within a theory are anchored in either developmental or contemporary experiences and processes—the distal/proximal distinction (for more detail see Ward & Hudson, 1998). Specifically, we distinguished between Level I (multifactorial), Level II (single-factor), and Level III (micro-level or offense process models) theories (Ward & Hudson, 1998). In terms of the distal/proximal distinction, *distal factors* constitute predispositional or vulnerability causal factors (i.e., psychological mechanisms) that emerge from both developmental experiences and genetic inheritance. *Proximal factors* are triggering processes or events (i.e., state or contextual variables) that emerge from the functioning of underlying vulnerabilities.

Finally, this meta-theoretical framework advances one step farther, suggesting that theory development not only involves *structure* (i.e., levels of focus, distal/proximal distinction), but also *process*, or the dynamics of constructing theory. In this sense, process refers to how all three levels of theory can interact to form a truly integrated and multifactorial etiological theory of child molestation. This is based on Kalmar and Sternberg's (1988) notion of "theory knitting." This strategy stipulates that researchers ought to knit together the best aspects of competing theories with their own ideas about a specific phenomenon to construct new theoretical frameworks.

In the area of child molestation, the current chapter illustrates a recent example of this theory-knitting process, the *pathways model*. This model integrates the best elements of the theories proposed by Finkelhor, Hall and Hirschman, and Marshall and Barbaree, with some unique ideas, into a comprehensive etiological theory. In this chapter we summarize each of the three multifactorial theories and outline their major strengths and weaknesses (for more detail see Ward, 2001, in press; Ward & Hudson, 2001), and then consider the pathways model (for more detail see Ward & Siegert, in press).

Finkelhor's Precondition Theory

Finkelhor (1984) suggests that four underlying factors have typically been used to explain the occurrence of child sexual abuse, usually in the form of single-factor or Level II theories. These theories are built around the following claims: Sex with children is emotionally satisfying to the offender (emotional congruence); men who offend are sexually aroused by a child (sexual arousal); men have sex with children because they are unable to meet their sexual needs in socially appropriate ways (blockage); and finally, these men become disinhibited and behave in ways contrary to their normal behavior (disinhibition).

He suggests that the first three factors explain why some individuals develop sexual interest in children and the fourth why this interest manifests as sexual deviance.

In Finkelhor's theory, these four factors are grouped into four preconditions that must be satisfied before the sexual abuse of a child occurs. The first precondition suggests that the offender must be motivated to sexually abuse a child, and encompasses three of the four factors (i.e., emotional congruence, sexual arousal, and blockage). The second precondition involves overcoming internal inhibitions (e.g., alcohol, impulse disorder, senility, psychosis, severe stress, socially entrenched patriarchal attitudes, or social tolerance of sexual interest in children), and is related to the disinhibition factor. The third precondition involves overcoming external inhibitions, or conditions that increase the possibility of offending (e.g., maternal absence or illness, lack of maternal closeness, social isolation of family, lack of parental supervision, unusual sleeping conditions, or paternal domination or abuse of the mother). The final precondition suggests that the offender must overcome a child's resistance to the abuse (e.g., giving gifts, desensitizing a child to sex, establishing emotional dependence, using threats or violence). These two remaining preconditions are associated with the how of the offense process and do not relate to the four causal factors. Finkelhor hypothesizes that these preconditions occur in a temporal sequence with each being necessary for the next to occur.

CRITICAL COMMENTS

The preconditions model was one of the first comprehensive theories of the sexual abuse of children and represents an impressive achievement.

Finkelhor persuasively argues that child molestation is a multifaceted phenomenon incorporating both psychological and sociological variables. Finkelhor also highlights the important contribution of sexual motivation to the occurrence of child abuse, but is also careful to point out that emotional congruence, one of the three motivational factors, can still be expressed in more socially benign ways, such as teaching or coaching children's sport. He also suggests that different combinations of needs may motivate different offenders, proposing that the model provides a typology of child molesters. Furthermore, he diligently suggests that individual psychopathology, related to history of abuse, explains only some forms of child sexual abuse, emphasizing the importance of pervasive socialization patterns, cultural norms and values, and biological factors in bringing about offending behavior.

The model, therefore, has provided a clear framework for the study of men who sexually abuse children, and has led to clear treatment goals and clinical innovations. For example, targeting deviant sexual arousal, strengthening emotional regulation skills, working on intimacy issues, focusing on sociocultural factors, and teaching offenders how to identify and manage high-risk situations. These undoubted strengths are offset, however, by conceptual difficulties that point to a need to reformulate the model in light of current theory and empirical research (for more detail see Ward & Hudson, 2001).

First, its utilization of psychological theories and constructs from markedly different traditions, for example, psychoanalytic, attributional, and learning theories (Howells, 1994), creates inconsistency and incoherency. To speak of castration anxiety alongside skill deficits and classical conditioning is to engage very different theories and competing causal mechanisms.

Second, Finkelhor emphasizes that an adequate theory should demonstrate why psychological and social factors result in sexual offenses rather than some other type of behavior. In this way, he proposes that psychological motives such as a need for intimacy or emotional congruence, in combination with social factors, such as external disinhibition, drive sexual offenses against children. However, he also states that each of the three motivational factors may operate independently or in combination. If they can function as independent factors, then it is hard to see why these motives result in a *sexual* offense. It is, therefore, unclear why in some circumstances nonsexual needs such as emotional congruence or blockage are expressed sexually.

Third, there is a lack of attention to developmental factors and a tendency to focus on proximal causes of sexual offending. For example, although the motives for sexual offending are outlined in precondition I, there is no clear sense as to their developmental trajectory or how early events impact on cognitive, behavioral, and affective factors to create the vulnerability to commit a sexual offense. The precondition model is strongest in the way it links motives and the process of offending with environmental conditions; however, this is at the cost of failing to be explicit concerning the importance of distal causal factors.

Fourth, as mentioned above, Finkelhor hypothesizes that any one of emotional congruence, blockage, or sexual arousal can motivate an individual to sexually abuse a child. Essentially, he seems to be arguing that some sexual offenses are caused by a single (psychological) factor, contradicting his earlier claim that this problem is typically caused by diverse interacting factors. Therefore, there appear to be multiple causal models embedded in the one theory. Apart from making it difficult to test, this weakness points to the model's lack of conceptual clarity, questioning whether or not it is a genuine multifactorial theory of child sexual abuse.

A fifth difficulty with Finkelhor's model is that the psychological vulnerabilities outlined in precondition I are all *motives* of various kinds. There is virtually no attention paid to the role of cognitive factors such as implicit theories, beliefs, or attitudes. For example, emotional congruence depends on beliefs concerning children's abilities to satisfy an offender's emotional needs, whereas both sexual arousal and blockage are influenced by beliefs concerning the nature and desires of children. It is clear that Finkelhor tacitly assumes that cognitive factors do causally interact with drives, needs, and emotions; however, he does not identify them or clarify their role sufficiently.

A sixth criticism is that the distinctions between many of the key constructs are unsustainable. For example, there appears to be some overlap in meaning between developmental blockage and emotional congruence. Both occur in precondition I and are postulated to motivate individuals to commit a sexual offense against a child; however, both refer to developmental conflicts and vulnerabilities. For example, the disruption of early attachment relationships may result in an individual's fearing rejection from adults. He may subsequently seek to establish emotional contacts with children perceived as trustworthy (Marshall, 1996)—emotional congruence—thereby failing to meet his sexual and emotional needs in prosocial ways—blockage. It is difficult, therefore, to understand exactly how each makes separate contributions to the Finkelhor theory, with many examples of blockage able to be described as instances of emotional congruence.

Seven, a glance at Finkelhor's list of internal disinhibitions indicates that some of these may be temporary, or state factors (e.g., alcohol), while others may be more enduring, or trait factors (e.g., distorted beliefs). Although the role of alcohol or stress in overcoming internal inhibitions is relatively straightforward, values or beliefs (via goals) may be related to the control of behavior in a number of ways (Baumeister & Heatherton, 1996; Ward & Hudson, 2000). First, in the presence of negative emotional states, individuals can fail to control their behavior or emotions, and behave in a disinhibited manner, that is, they lose control. Second, the use of ineffective strategies to achieve goals can backfire and ultimately result in a loss of control: a misregulation pattern. The third pattern involves effective self-regulation, where the setting, planning, and implementation of goals may be impeccable and are usually associated with positive emotional states; however, the difficulty resides in the choice of inappropriate goals and associated values and beliefs. These latter two misregulation and self-regulation patterns represent enduring cognitive factors, thus it is misleading to refer to these as examples of disinhibition. The model, therefore, fails to consider the possibility that offenders may have different types of self-regulatory problems.

Finally, different types of offenders presumably use correspondingly distinct strategies to create sexual access to a child and to overcome his or her resistance. These individual differences are not, however, spelled out in the preconditions model, and their relationships to distinct motives, or combinations of motives, are unclear. Related to this problem of individual differences, Finkelhor suggests that his model provides a useful classification system for child molestation. Yet there remains a confusion of levels, ranging from a surface description of offender behavior to putative mechanisms derived from psychodynamic theory. Thus not only is a functional typology absent, one is unlikely to result from the model as it stands.

Hall and Hirschman's Quadripartite Theory

Hall and Hirschman's (1992) quadripartite model of child molestation is based on four components: physiological sexual arousal, inaccurate cognitions that justify sexual aggression, affective dyscontrol, and personality problems. The first three factors are considered primarily state and situation dependent (state factors), whereas personality problems represent enduring vulnerability factors (trait factors). This implies that personality deficits are the source of vulnerabilities to sexually abuse children, which are activated in certain contexts and opportunities, resulting in deviant arousal, affective disturbance, and/or distorted thinking.

A key idea in the Hall and Hirschman model is that although each of the above factors serves as a motivational precursor that increases the probability of offending, usually one factor is prominent for each child molester and constitutes his primary motive. The activation of this primary motivational precursor functions to increase the intensity of the others. This synergistic interaction may in turn propel an individual above the *critical threshold* for performing a sexually deviant act.

Furthermore, various combinations of the above factors are hypothesized to characterize a particular type of child molester with distinct treatment needs. The first subtype has deviant sexual arousal and strong sexual preferences for children (i.e., the classic preferential offender), and tends to commit offenses against large numbers of children. Treatment would revolve around the reduction of deviant sexual arousal using a range of conditioning strategies, for example, directed masturbation. Offenders who are characterized by cognitive motivation typically misinterpret children's behavior as revealing sexual intent and also possess good self-regulatory and planning skills (e.g., incest offenders). Therapy may involve the challenging of their sense of entitlement and the modification of other dysfunctional cognitions. The third group of offenders is defined by its susceptibility to negative affective states, and frequently behaves in an impulsive and unplanned manner (i.e., situational offenders). Treatment would center on learning how to control and regulate negative emotions. The final subgroup of offenders is those who have developmentally related personality problems and experience difficulties establishing intimate adult relationships and functioning effectively in the world (i.e., preferential offenders). Treatment would be prolonged and intensive, requiring the modification of entrenched and maladaptive interpersonal strategies and beliefs about themselves and other people.

CRITICAL COMMENTS

Hall and Hirschman's model represents an important contribution to the literature. The focus on multiple factors is a major strength as is the suggestion that sexual offending may be the product of converging causal pathways. The explicit attention given to both state and trait factors is useful and functions to explain how psychological deficits can be translated into offending behavior. Moreover, the introduction of the idea of a critical threshold is unique and helps to explain how enduring vulnerability factors interact with situational variables to produce sexual offending. Another positive feature is the attention to individual differences and the associated suggestion that an offender typology can be constructed on the basis of the primary motivational precursors. Finally, the concept of motivational precursors is novel, providing the motivational underpinning of the theory and aims to explain how the different factors interact.

Alongside these strengths the model has a number of significant weaknesses (for more detail see Ward, 2001). First, according to Hall and Hirschman it is possible that each factor may account for different types of child sexual offenders in the absence of the other three factors. Similar to the criticism of Finkelhor's model, it seems then that this theory essentially consists of a cluster of quite distinct submodels embedded in an overall four-factor framework. This seems unduly simplistic and unlikely given the complexity of sexual offending and the fact that each of these primary causes are likely to have an adverse impact in the other domains. It, therefore, does not represent a true multifactorial theory and lacks conceptual clarity, making it difficult to test its overall adequacy.

A second criticism is that the theory lacks specificity in a number of areas. It does not unpack each of the core constructs in enough detail. For example, cognition distortions may be *positive* and explicitly permit sexually abusive actions, or *negative,* where a person denies and minimizes his sexually abusive behavior (Ward, Hudson, Johnston, & Marshall, 1997). Affective dyscontrol is also multifaceted, involving either *misregulation,* where a person possesses good self-regulatory abilities but simply chooses an ineffective strategy, or *disinhibition,* where he might be unable to manage strong negative emotions and turns to deviant sex as a way of coping (Ward & Hudson, 2000). In addition, the theory also fails to identify the core phenomena and explicate the underlying causal mechanisms associated with each of the phenomena. For example, it is unclear exactly how cognitive distortions or affective dyscontrol may generate sexual offending. Relatedly, the four factors are not conceptually distinct and overlap to some degree—the quadripartite model fails to explore these inter-relationships adequately. For example, deviant sexual arousal is underpinned by enduring sexual preferences and therefore contains cognitive elements. This relationship is not easily accounted for within the model. Therefore, in a sense Hall and Hirschman's model constitutes a *framework* theory rather than a fully developed explanation of child sexual abuse.

Third, the distinction between state and trait factors causes further problems for this theory of child molestation. For example, there are different kinds of cognitive variables such as cognitive structures (e.g., schemata or implicit theories), operations (e.g., information processing), and products (e.g., self-statements, beliefs, and attributions). Cognitive structures are hypothesized to emerge from an offender's early developmental experiences (i.e., trait factors), whereas cognitive products are state factors generated by combining environ-mental events and longstanding cognitive structures (Ward, 2000; Ward et al., 1997). Therefore, it is a mistake to consider cognition as purely a state factor. Arguably, it is the underlying cognitive structures, the trait factors, that are the major cause of offenders' distorted thoughts concerning children. Similar problems are also evident with the so-called state factors, physiological sexual arousal and affective dyscontrol, with both having state and trait forms, and both forms playing a critical role in child molestation.

Finally, the notion of "primary motivational precursors" intensifying the remaining causal factors and pushing an individual over the offense threshold appears somewhat vague. It is not clear why each causal factor exerts a power-ful effect on the others. It is even less obvious why a primary motivational pre-cursor should intensify each of the other factors. Perhaps it makes more sense to view a threshold as representing the transition point between a vulnerability factor and its subsequent mental state. For example, deviant sexual preferences (a trait factor) will elicit sexual arousal (a state factor) under certain conditions, such as sexual deprivation or presence of erotic stimuli. The point at which the state of sexual arousal emerges constitutes the critical threshold. Therefore, to establish conceptual clarity, the construct of threshold requires reformulation.

Marshall and Barbaree's Integrated Theory

Marshall and Barbaree's integrated theory (1990) proposes that the sexual abuse of children occurs as a consequence of a number of interacting distal and proximal factors. Specifically, this theory suggests that individuals experiencing developmentally adverse events (e.g., poor parenting, inconsistent and harsh discipline, physical and sexual abuse) are likely to exhibit distorted internal working models of relationships, particularly with respect to sex and aggression, resulting in poor social and self-regulation skills from an early age.

For these individuals, the transition into adolescence is a particularly critical period. It is at this stage that individuals are most receptive to acquiring enduring sexual scripts, preferences, interests, and attitudes. Further, the massive increase of sex hormones during this period increases the salience and potency of these sexual cues. According to Marshall and Barbaree, sex and aggression originate from the same neural substrates (e.g., hypothalamus, amygdala, septum, etc.) and are thought to cause qualitatively similar experiences. If an individual comes from an adverse background and, therefore, is already predisposed to behaving in an antisocial manner, the pubertal release of hormones may serve to fuse sex and aggression and to consolidate or enhance already acquired sexually abusive tendencies.

For young adults, the lack of effective social and self-regulation skills makes it more probable that relationships, or attempted relationships, with women will be met by rejection and result in lowered self-esteem, anger, and negative attitudes toward females. These powerful negative emotions may fuel the intensity of sexual desires and the development of deviant sexual fantasies. Masturbation to these fantasies will increase their strength and also function as mental rehearsals in which future sexual offenses are planned. Young children may be viewed as more inherently trustworthy and as constituting a "safe haven" for the individual. The individual may, therefore, see deviant sex or fantasies as meeting a multitude of needs, including releasing sexual tension, and increasing personal effectiveness and control, interpersonal closeness, self-esteem, and masculinity.

According to the integrated theory, the above vulnerability factors interact with more transient situational elements such as stress, intoxication, strong negative affect, sexual stimuli, and the presence of a potential victim to impair an individual's ability to control his behaviors, resulting in a sexual offense. The reinforcing effects of deviant sexual activity and the development of cognitive distortions maintain offending. This reinforcement may be positive (e.g., sexual arousal, sense of power) or negative (e.g., reduction of low mood) in nature.

CRITICAL COMMENTS

Marshall and Barbaree's integrated theory of sexual offending represents a considerable achievement. It is a dynamic model and portrays sexual abuse as the outcome of interacting biological, psychological, social, cultural, and situational factors. In addition, the explicit focus on resilience and psychological vulnerability constitutes a real advance over its competitors and clarifies how developmental adversity contributes to sexual offending. It has also led to important treatment innovations and focused researchers on a number of important domains. For example, Marshall (1999) has explored intimacy deficits from a developmental perspective, which has resulted in the development of therapeutic strategies to enhance intimacy skills in offenders. A particularly impressive aspect of the theory is its postulation of causal mechanisms (e.g., attachment style, self-regulatory deficits, and maladaptive beliefs) thought to generate phenomena associated with child molestation. In addition, the impact of these mechanisms on each other is explicitly considered, giving the theory its dynamic flavor. This degree of specificity is absent in its competitors.

Alongside its many strengths, the integrated theory contains a number of conceptual weaknesses (for more detail see Ward, in press). First, different types of sexual offenders have some specific symptoms and problems in common that set them apart from other offenders. A concern is that because Marshall and Barbaree's theory is so general, it fails to adequately address the issues associated with different sexual crimes. Similarly, there are subgroups of sexual offenders within an overall category, each with different characteristics and problems. For example, a useful distinction has been drawn between situational and preferential child molesters based on their offending history, deviant sexual preferences, and general social competence (Ward, 1999). Although the integrated theory is able to explain early onset offenders (i.e., preferential offenders), it is unclear how it would account for those individuals who have negotiated the transition from adolescence to adulthood reasonably effectively, but start offending as adults (i.e., situational offenders).

Second, according to Marshall and Barbaree, sexual offenses tend to occur because individuals fail to inhibit deviant desires and impulses, which stem from an offenders' developmentally adverse history. Recent empirical research and theoretical work, however, indicates that only a small number of sex offenders appear to have significant problems with self-regulation (Hudson, Ward, & McCormack, 1999). Some individuals may fail to control their behavior or emotions and behave in a disinhibited manner, while others appear quite capable of setting goals and selecting appropriate strategies to achieve them, the major problem being their choice of goals. The theory, therefore, needs to be broadened to allow for the possibility that for some individuals offending is associated with positive emotions, and explicit and immaculate planning rather than disinhibition.

Third, although the previous two theories of child molestation both address the issue of typology, the integrated theory is somewhat silent on this issue.

However, a closer examination reveals that there are distinct offense pathways embedded in the model that are not explicitly identified by Marshall and Barbaree. First, some offenders acquire negative attitudes toward women as a result of being exposed to inappropriate models during their childhood. These attitudes result in adversarial behavior toward women, with children being regarded as appropriate sexual partners. Second, some offenders may become distrustful and suspicious of females because of their unsuccessful attempts to establish adolescent relationships. This may result in resentment toward women, with children being viewed as trustworthy and capable of providing affection and intimacy. A third group uses masturbation to regulate low mood and, therefore, fails to learn how to solve problems in a more adaptive manner. During times of stress such individuals may become sexually aroused and sexually disinhibited. A fourth group engages in either violent (e.g., "I will get even") or nonviolent (e.g., "I will be loved") deviant sexual fantasies as a way of enhancing their self-esteem and expressing their frustration with the world, with both possibly leading to a sexual offense. A fifth group fails to learn to discriminate between aggressive and sexual motives and is therefore inclined to behave in an antisocial manner in sexual contexts. Each of these represents a distinct offense trajectory and needs to be considered separately rather than simply examined under the general rubric of developmental and biological factors. Furthermore, it is unclear just why individuals who are associated with some of these pathways commit a sexual offense rather than some other offense type. Simply referring in a general way to hormonal increases at puberty does not really clarify the matter, as all adolescents experience this phenomenon. The theory, therefore, needs to specify further mechanisms directly invoking sexual needs and predilections and their interaction with distorted attitudes.

Fourth, Marshall and Barbaree mistakenly focus on the way individuals learn to control aggression in the context of sexuality. They justify this by suggesting that aggression and sexuality originate from the same neural substrates, resulting in a fusion or confusion of these two motivational states. However, while aggressive behavior is a central characteristic of rape, it is less so in child molestation (Knight & Prentky, 1990). In addition, it is not sufficient simply to state that sex and aggression are mediated by the same neural substrates; such structures subsume a wide range of quite distinct drives and responses (Kolb & Whisaw, 1995). Relatedly, just because physical structures are close together does not mean that they are functionally similar or likely to cause qualitatively similar experiences. Sex and aggression are each associated with different meanings and response tendencies (Lazarus, 1994). Given this, the notion that sex and aggression can be "fused" is ambiguous, and may suggest that (a) both are associated with a common factor, for example, physiological arousal; (b) when one is experienced the other is likely to be activated; (c) offenders are not able to discriminate reliably between sexual and aggressive *mental* states, mistakenly inferring sexual motivation when in fact they may be angry, subsequently seeking sexual satisfaction in the wrong context; and (d) an offender may interpret all sexual cues as aggressive ones and be unable to reliably identify sexual states at all. These different interpretations point to separate etiological pathways, thus "fusion" needs to be explicitly clarified.

A final difficulty is that the integrated theory views low self-esteem as a core component of offenders' predisposition to sexually abuse a child. There are good theoretical and empirical reasons, however, for viewing sex offenders as suffering from a variety of self-esteem disturbances (Baumeister, Smart, & Boden, 1996; Hudson & Ward, 1997; Ward, Hudson, & Marshall, 1996). These disturbances are likely to be associated with different offense styles and psychological problems.

The Pathways Model of Child Sexual Abuse

It is clear, then, that all three major theories of child sexual abuse have limitations (for more details see Ward, 2001, in press; Ward & Hudson, 2001). An unresolved issue concerns the direction any future theoretical development should take. In our view, it is worth building on the virtues of each of the three major theories in order to construct a more comprehensive explanation of child sexual abuse. Briefly, Finkelhor's theory neatly links offenders' psychological vulnerabilities with the offense process, Hall and Hirschman comprehensively address the issue of typology, and Marshall and Barbaree convincingly describe the way developmental adversity can result in vulnerability to sexually abuse a child. It would be a waste of intellectual resources to simply dismiss these theories as inadequate and start from scratch. Ideally, a comprehensive theory of child sexual abuse should incorporate the strengths of each of the above three theories—this is what Ward and Siegert (in press) have attempted to do in the pathways model (see the paper for more details).

Briefly, the pathways model suggests that there are multiple pathways *leading* to the sexual abuse of a child; it does not attempt to explain why child molestation may *continue*. Each pathway involves a core set of dysfunctional psychological mechanisms. In this sense, mechanisms are psychological processes that cause specific outcomes, effects, or clinical phenomena. These mechanisms constitute vulnerability factors and are influenced by distal and proximal factors, including learning events and biological, cultural, and environmental factors.

In line with the previous three theories, the pathways model suggests that the clinical phenomena evident among child molesters are generated by four distinct and interacting psychological mechanisms: intimacy and social skill deficits; distorted sexual scripts; emotional dysregulation; and cognitive distortions. Each mechanism depicts a specific offense pathway with different psychological and behavioral profiles, and separate etiologies and underlying deficits. The number and type of etiologies will vary depending on a pathway's particular developmental trajectory.

Although each pathway is hypothesized to be associated with a unique set of primary mechanisms and cluster of symptoms or problems, the mechanisms always interact to cause a sexual crime. That is, *every* sexual offense involves emotional, intimacy, cognitive, and arousal components; however, each distinct pathway will have at its center a set of primary dysfunctional mechanisms that impact on the others. The primary causal mechanisms involve other types of mechanisms in order to generate the range of symptoms typically seen in child molesters. But these additional causal mechanisms may be functioning normally and exert a dysfunctional effect only because of the driving force of the primary set of mechanisms. This is similar to Hall and Hirschman's thesis that one of four factors may be a primary motivational precursor that activates the other elements. However, these authors suggest that each factor can also operate on its own to cause sexual deviance. The pathways model, in contrast, argues that *every* sexual offense involves all four sets of mechanisms.

Specifically, the first etiological pathway, *intimacy deficits*, contains individuals who are hypothesized to possess normal sexual scripts and offend only at specific times, for example, if a preferred partner is unavailable or during periods of rejection or sustained emotional loneliness. Therefore, the primary cause of the sexual abuse resides in intimacy deficits, with loneliness leading to a need to engage in a sexual relationship with a vulnerable child (Marshall, 1996). The primary causal mechanism underlying this pathway is insecure attachment and subsequent problems establishing satisfactory relationships with adults (Ward et al., 1996). The substitution of children for adult sexual partners will also be accompanied by cognitive distortions concerning the rights or entitlement of the offender to have sex with whom he pleases. This will result in sexual arousal in the context of a sexual encounter with a child, possibly intimate and "loving" emotions, and often an attempt to create an adult-like relationship with the child. The onset of sexual offending is expected to be in adulthood, with self-esteem being low or high depending on the domain in question and the psychological makeup of the individual concerned.

The second etiological pathway, *deviant sexual scripts*, contains individuals whose core causal mechanism involves subtle distortions in their sexual scripts, which interact with dysfunctional relationship schemas (where relationships are represented in purely sexual terms). These individuals may have experienced sexual abuse as children and as a consequence become prematurely sexualized. However, unlike the fifth group, there is hypothesized to be no major distortions resulting in the development of sexual preferences for children and/or sexually abusive behaviors. The major script flaw is that sex is equated with intimacy: It is the context in which sex is stipulated to occur, rather than the choice of partners or activities, that is the problem (Marshall, Anderson, & Fernandez, 2000). Interpersonal closeness is, therefore, achieved only via sexual contact. This, coupled with a fear of rejection by others, is likely to lead to unsatisfying adult sexual encounters and enduring relationship problems, resulting in unhappiness and frustration. Sexual offenses against children perceived as more trustworthy and accepting may occur following periods of rejection by adults, disappointment, or extreme loneliness, with the offense largely a question of opportunity and sexual and/or emotional need. Postoffense, cognitive distortions may emerge in an attempt to justify or excuse the sexual abuse. Finally, the onset of sexual offending is expected typically to start in adulthood, with self-esteem anticipated to be low, reflecting this group's sensitivity to rejection and craving for love and approval.

The third etiological pathway, *emotional dysregulation,* contains individuals who are hypothesized to possess normal sexual scripts but have dysfunctional mechanisms associated with their emotional regulation system (Thompson, 1994). This may be a problem identifying emotions, modulating negative emotions, or an inability to utilize social supports in times of emotional distress (Ward, Hudson, & Keenan, 1998). This inability to manage mood states effectively may result in a loss of control that, in conjunction with sexual desire, might lead an individual either to become disinhibited or else opportunistically use sex with a child as a soothing strategy to meet emotional and sexual needs. These individuals are likely to prefer sex with age-appropriate partners but will engage in the sexual abuse of a child when emotionally stressed. Exposure to sexual activities such as compulsive masturbation during early adolescence, and the absence of alternative means of increasing self-esteem or mood, will create a profound link between sex and emotional well-being (Cortini & Marshall, 2000). Sexual fantasies will typically accompany sexual behaviors (e.g., masturbation, sex with a child); however, given the possession of normal sexual scripts, these fantasies function to increase the offenders' sense of well-being, rather than reflect entrenched deviant sexual preferences. It is anticipated that these child molesters may offend at any time during adolescence and adulthood, and when not under stress are likely to exhibit normal sexual interests and behaviors, although their base level of masturbation may be high and typically occur in response to periods of emotional dysphoria. Self-esteem may also vary depending on the domain in question and an individual's psychological makeup.

The fourth etiological pathway, *antisocial cognitions,* contains individuals who have no distortions in their sexual scripts but possess general procriminal attitudes and beliefs, and whose offending reflects this general antisocial tendency. Research supports the existence of child molesters who have extensive criminal histories in addition to their sexual offenses, for example, substance abuse problems and impulsivity (Andrews & Bonta, 1998; Smallbone & Wortley, 2000). Offending may also be further facilitated by the existence of patriarchal attitudes toward children and offenders' sense of their own *superiority,* with this group likely to be diagnosed with Conduct Disorder as children and adolescents (American Psychiatric Association, 1994). Their antisocial attitudes and beliefs, in conjunction with sexual desire and opportunity, will therefore result in sexual molestation. Such individuals are likely to experience positive emotional states when abusing a child because of the pleasure experienced and the fact that they are meeting their need for self-gratification in a personally acceptable manner.

The fifth etiological pathway, *multiple dysfunctional mechanisms,* will contain individuals who have developed deviant sexual scripts, which will activate deviant fantasies and usually reflect a history of sexual abuse or exposure to sexual material or activity at a young age. Coinciding with this will be pronounced flaws in all the other primary psychological mechanisms. They will therefore have dysfunctional implicit theories about children's sexuality and their ability to make informed decisions about sex, inappropriate emotional regulation, intimacy deficits, and impaired relationship and attachment mechanisms (Ward et al., 1997; Ward et al., 1998). Thus this group is likely to exhibit a multitude of offense-related deficits and constitute "pure" pedophiles. The predisposition to sexually abuse children is hypothesized to translate into offending behavior only under certain circumstances, including the presence of a victim (i.e., opportunity to offend) and the absence of any conflicting goals. The ultimate aim of deviant behavior is to achieve pleasure or other primary or secondary goals (e.g., a sense of control). Finally, self-esteem will often be high because of this group's entrenched preferences for children as sexual partners and their accompanying beliefs that these interests are legitimate and healthy.

In addition to the five etiological pathways, this model attempts to explain why the majority of sexual or physical abuse victims do not subsequently victimize others. The model suggests that this is moderated by factors such as the response of others to their own abuse, the severity and nature of their abuse, its length of duration, and so on (Davis & Petretic-Jackson, 2000). This is mediated by the degree of distortion of their sexual scripts, and/or degree of disruptions to other socioemotional mechanisms (e.g., emotional regulation). Second, the role of culture is clear in the pathways model. Cultures that sexualize children or have distorted attitudes and beliefs about relationships and the relative status and value of women and children are more likely to have high levels of sexual crimes. Third, the model suggests that biological variables exert differential effects depending on the particular pathway under consideration, and at different points in the offense process. Comments are made regarding the effects of puberty, physiological changes in arousal as the sexual offense unfolds, and males' greater sexual drive and predilection to engage in impersonal sex. Finally, the model suggests that most child sexual offenses are committed by males, given the frequency of the pathways deficits in males and the different representations of male and female sexuality in society (for a more detailed discussion of these issues see Ward & Siegert, in press).

Conclusions

Although the pathways model is only a provisional framework that needs further refining, it effectively addresses the weaknesses and knits together the strengths of theories by Finkelhor, Hall and Hirschman, and Marshall and Barbaree. Additionally, in contrast to these theories, it meets *all* the required features of a comprehensive theory of child sexual abuse (for a more detailed evaluation see Ward & Siegert, in press). For example, it meets the requirement that an adequate theory should contain multiple offense pathways or trajectories and allow for different types of child molesters.

From a clinical perspective, the pathways model suggests that sexual offenders will have different deficits, depending on the offense pathway traversed. For example, some individuals will need to acquire increased levels of relationship skills while others would benefit from learning how to manage their moods more effectively. Additionally, individuals with distorted sexual scripts will need intensive reconditioning interventions to modify the entrenched deviant sexual preferences and beliefs generated from the underlying dysfunctional sexual scripts.

References

American Psychiatric Association. (1994). *Diagnostic and statistical manual of mental disorders* (4th ed.). Washington, DC: Author.

Andrews, D. A., & Bonta, J. (1998). *The psychology of criminal conduct* (2nd ed.). Cincinnati, OH: Anderson.

Baumeister, R. F., & Heatherton, T. F. (1996). Self-regulation failure: An overview. *Psychological Inquiry, 7*, 1-15.

Baumeister, R. F., Smart, L., & Boden, J. M. (1996). Relationship of threatened egotism to violence and aggression: The dark side of high self-esteem. *Psychological Review, 103*, 5-33.

Cortini, F., & Marshall, W. L. (2000). Sex a coping mechanism in sex offenders. *Sexual Abuse: A Journal of Research and Treatment, 12.*

Davis, J. L., & Petretic-Jackson, P. A. (2000). The impact of child sexual abuse on adult interpersonal functioning: A review and synthesis of the empirical literature. *Aggression and Violent Behavior, 5,* 291-328.

Finkelhor, D. (1984). *Child sexual abuse: New theory and research.* New York: Free Press.

Hall, G. C. N., & Hirschman, R. (1992). Sexual aggression against children: A conceptual perspective of etiology. *Criminal Justice and Behavior, 19,* 8-23.

Howells, K. (1994). Child sexual abuse: Finkelhor's precondition model revisited. *Psychology, Crime, & Law, 1,* 201-214.

Hudson, M. S., & Ward, T. (1997). Intimacy, loneliness, and attachment styles in sexual offenders. *Journal of Interpersonal Violence, 12,* 323-339.

Hudson, S. M., Ward, T., & McCormack, J. (1999). Offence pathways in sexual offenders. *Journal of Interpersonal Violence, 14,* 779-798.

Kalmar, D. A., & Sternberg, R. J. (1988). Theory knitting: An integrative approach to theory development. *Philosophical Psychology, 1,* 153-170.

Knight, R. A., & Prentky, R. A. (1990). Classifying sexual offenders: The development and corroboration of taxonomic models. In W. L. Marshall, D. R. Laws, & H. E. Barbaree (Eds.), *Handbook of sexual assault: Issues, theories, and treatment of the offender* (pp. 23-52). New York: Plenum.

Kolb, B., & Whisaw, I. Q. (1995). *Fundamentals of human neuropsychology* (4th ed.). New York: Oxford University Press.

Lazarus, R. S. (1994). *Emotion and adaptation.* New York: Oxford University Press.

Marshall, W. L. (1996). Assessment, treatment, and theorizing about sex offenders: Developments over the past 20 years and future directions. *Criminal Justice and Behavior, 23,* 162-199.

Marshall, W. L. (1999). Current status of North American assessment and treatment programs for sexual offenders. *Journal of Interpersonal Violence, 14,* 221-239.

Marshall, W. L., Anderson, D., & Fernandez, Y. M. (2000). *Cognitive behavioural treatment of sexual offenders.* Chichester, UK: Wiley.

Marshall, W. L., & Barbaree, H. E. (1990). An integrated theory of the etiology of sexual offending. In W. L. Marshall, D. R. Laws, & H. E. Barbaree (Eds.), *Handbook of sexual assault: Issues, theories, and treatment of the offender* (pp. 257-275). New York: Plenum.

Smallbone, S., & Wortley, R. (2000). *Child sexual abuse in Queensland: Offender characteristics and modus operandi.* Brisbane, QSLD: Queensland Crime Commission.

Thompson, R. A. (1994). Emotional regulation: A theme in search of definition. In N. A. Fox (Ed.), The development of emotion regulation: Biological and behavioral considerations (pp. 25-52*). Monographs of the Society for Research in Child Development, Vol. 59,* Serial No. 240.

Ward, T. (1999). Competency and deficit models in the understanding and treatment of sexual offenders. *Journal of Sex Research, 36,* 298-305.

Ward, T. (2000). Sexual offenders' cognitive distortions as implicit theories. *Aggression and Violent Behavior, 5,* 491-507.

Ward, T. (2001). Hall and Hirschman's quadripartite model of child sexual abuse: A critique. *Psychology, Crime, and Law, 7,* 291-307.

Ward, T. (in press). Marshall and Barbaree's integrated theory of child sexual abuse: A critique. *Psychology, Crime, and Law.*

Ward, T., & Hudson, S. M. (1998). The construction and development of theory in the sexual offending area: A meta-theoretical framework. *Sexual Abuse: A Journal of Research and Treatment, 10,* 47-63.

Ward, T., & Hudson, S. M. (2000). A self-regulation model of relapse prevention. In D. R. Laws, S. M. Hudson, & T. Ward. (Eds.), *Remaking relapse prevention with sex offenders: A sourcebook.* Thousand Oaks, CA: Sage.

Ward, T., & Hudson, S. M. (2001). A critique of Finkelhor's precondition model of child sexual abuse. *Psychology, Crime, & Law, 7,* 333-350.

Ward, T., Hudson, S. M., Johnston, L., & Marshall, W. L. (1997). Cognitive distortions in sex offenders: An integrative review. *Clinical Psychology Review, 17,* 479-507.

Ward, T., Hudson, S. M., & Keenan, T. (1998). A self-regulation model of the sexual offense process. *Sexual Abuse: A Journal of Research and Treatment, 10,* 141-157.

Ward, T., Hudson, S. M., & Marshall, W. L. (1996). Attachment style in sex offenders: A preliminary study. *Journal of Sex Research, 33,* 17-26.

Ward, T., & Siegert, R. J. (in press). Toward a comprehensive theory of child sexual abuse: A theory knitting perspective. *Psychology, Crime, & Law.*

2

Good Lives and the Rehabilitation of Sexual Offenders

Tony Ward
University of Melbourne

Claire A. Stewart
Deakin University

The model of offender rehabilitation currently dominant in the correctional domain is concerned with *risk management,* where the primary aim of rehabilitating offenders is to avoid harm to the community rather than to improve offenders' quality of life; the model is known as the risk-need approach to offender rehabilitation (Andrews & Bonta, 1998; Garland, 2001; Hannah-Moffat, 1999; McGuire, 2000; Ward & Brown, in press). According to this perspective, although the enhancement of offenders' functioning may be viewed as desirable, it should not be the primary objective of program developers and policymakers. Rather, the relationship between offenders' levels of functioning and recidivism rates is an instrumental one: It is a means to the end of reduced risk to the community. Even when the focus has been on offenders' needs, policymakers have tended to be concerned with reducing further crimes or the incidence of disruptive behavior within prisons rather than with a broader enhancement of offenders' well-being and capabilities. For example, Ashford, Sales, and Reid (2001) have distinguished between the subjective needs of the offender and the objective needs of the justice and correctional system, and society at large. They make the point that offender needs not linked to reduced recidivism are considered comparatively unimportant. They also argue that such decisions are at least partly normative and reflect the overarching values of the institutions in question.

The tendency to focus on risk management has resulted in the conceptualization of offender needs as dynamic risk factors, or criminogenic needs, while simultaneously downplaying the importance of psychological needs that, if met, would increase an individual's well-being or welfare. This view effectively links and restricts the notion of need to that of risk and suggests that by treating or managing offenders' characteristics that are statistically associated with offending, reoffending will be reduced and the needs of the offender will be met (Hannah-Moffat, 1999). Thus, according to Hannah-Moffat (1999), "unsatisfied needs are seen as both risk factors and mental health concerns" (p. 85).

The risk-need model makes a number of basic claims. First, risk assessment should drive need assessment and the treatment process. That is, offenders' level of risk should determine the required intensity and duration of treatment. Second, allocating offenders to rehabilitation streams based on their assessed level of risk results in better outcomes, that is, lower rates of recidivism (Andrews & Bonta, 1998). Conversely, giving low-risk offenders high levels of treatment may actually *increase* their chances of reoffending (Andrews & Bonta, 1998). Third, focusing rehabilitation on criminogenic needs, dynamic risk factors, will result in better outcomes by reducing or controlling risk factors and thereby reducing their influence on vulnerable individuals. Fourth, an offender's level of risk increases with the presence of each additional risk factor.

Underlying these claims are a number of basic assumptions that give the model its theoretical coherency, but that are not necessarily clearly articulated. First, the severity of risk (i.e., whether low, medium, or high) is assumed to covary with the number of criminogenic needs, and in addition, the severity or strength of each need. That is, low-risk offenders will have few, if any, criminogenic needs whereas high-risk offenders will display a significant range of such needs. Second, risk factors are viewed as discrete, quantifiable characteristics of offenders and their environment that can be identified and measured. Third, the only important treatment targets are those offender characteristics that extant research associates with potentially reduced recidivism rates. Everything else is at best of marginal relevance and at worst, potentially obstructive and harmful. Fourth, the identification of risk factors and/or criminogenic needs is an empirical and therefore value-free process. Fifth, the primary aim of offender rehabilitation should be to reduce the risk to society rather than enhance the well-being of offenders. In fact, risk management is the only legitimate goal of treatment and any other aim is misguided and empirically unwarranted.

We have extensively criticized the risk-need model in a number of recent publications and will not repeat our arguments in detail here (Ward & Brown, in press; Ward & Stewart, in press). Briefly, we argue that risk assessment should not drive the rehabilitation of offenders. Once the critical ambiguity in the terms *risk factors* and *needs* is exposed, it is apparent that the primary focus of treatment should be the modification of the dispositional factors underlying an individual's criminal actions. These dispositional factors are best understood by referring to the way they obstruct or frustrate the meeting of offenders' basic needs and access to human goods. The assessment of risk (i.e., risk estimates) is of secondary importance. In addition, therapists should be wary of basing treatment on level of risk and assuming that need and risk are reliably linked. The clinical reality is likely to be more complex than this and therefore needs or dispositions should be the major focus and their relationships to contextual and proximal causes described.

Finally, it is arguable that the primary aim of offender rehabilitation should be to give offenders the necessary capabilities to secure important personal and social goods in acceptable ways rather than simply the reduction and management of risk. Goods underpin goals and as such provide the normative source or justification for intrinsic goals. Negative goals such as the reduction of risk do not provide constructive guidance for therapists and also run the danger of ignoring an important feature of human functioning: Human beings are goal-directed organisms and are naturally inclined to seek a range of distinct goods (Emmons, 1999; Mann, Webster, & Schofield, 2002). We suggest that the way to reduce reoffending is to give individuals the necessary conditions to lead *better lives* (i.e., "good" lives) rather than simply to teach them how to minimize their chances of being incarcerated. However, it must be noted that the good lives approach is not simply about giving offenders better quality of life: The primary aim is to reduce offending, and it is argued that this is best achieved by taking a more constructive and holistic approach to rehabilitation. Programs that focus concretely on securing better lives for offenders are skill and competency based, but also freely acknowledge and seek to develop the values that underpin their therapeutic endeavors.

In this chapter we present the good lives model of offender rehabilitation recently developed by Ward (Ward, in press; Ward & Stewart, in press) as an alternative to the risk-need model and outline its utility in the assessment and treatment of individuals who have sexually abused children. We would like to note that recent work in the sexual offending area has taken a more holistic perspective and is based on the idea that the concept of wellness should drive rehabilitation efforts rather than that of risk management (e.g., Ellerby,

Bedard, & Chartrand, 2000; Freeman-Longo, 2001). These models stress the importance of helping offenders to function in more balanced and integrated ways and to work toward establishing a constructive and positive view of how their lives could be different. In support of these models, a recent study by Mann et al. (2002) found that an approach-goal–oriented intervention with sex offenders performed as well in improving relapse knowledge as a typical avoidance-oriented (based on risk management) intervention.

In addition, Haaven and Coleman (2000) have developed a model for the treatment of developmentally disabled sex offenders based on the construction of personal identity. In this model, treatment is based around the distinction between a "new me" and an "old me." The "old me" constitutes the individual who committed sexual offenses and encompasses values, goals, beliefs, and ways of living that directly generate offending behavior. The construction of a "new me" involves the endorsement of a new set of goals that specify a "good" life for an individual, that is, a life in which important primary goods are achieved in ways that are socially acceptable and personally fulfilling.

Although these approaches are innovative and a step in the right direction, they do not concern themselves with supporting the above practical suggestions with theoretical arguments and empirical evidence. In this chapter we pay more attention to the underlying theoretical basis of wellness (i.e., well-being) and personal identity, and also directly address the contextual nature of human functioning. We also clarify the relationship between risk management and the realization of good lives conceptualizations. In our view, risk factors are simply obstacles to the achievement of human goods and point to the need for individuals to possess the internal and external conditions necessary to lead more fulfilling lives. In other words, the other side of the coin to risk is the possession of skills, beliefs, and values that reduce the chances of relapse occurring *because* they help individuals to obtain valued outcomes (i.e., human goods).

The good lives model of offender rehabilitation, therefore, differs from a standard relapse prevention treatment program in a number of ways. In a sense, we are making explicit what clinicians may have always suspected and implicitly endorsed: It is fruitless to base treatment on problems alone, a positive vision is needed. However, we argue that there is no theoretically and empirically grounded conceptual framework currently existing that can guide therapists in the implementation of more constructive therapy with sex offenders.

We briefly outline the key features of our approach. First, the ultimate grounding of human strivings or goals resides in primary goods: valued states of affairs, states of mind, characteristics, activities, or experiences that are sought for their own sake and that are derived from substantive facts about human nature. Rehabilitation is a value-laden process and this involves prudential values (what is in the best interests of the offenders), ethical values (what is in the best interests of the community), and epistemic or knowledge-related values (what are our best practice models and methods). Second, there is an important focus on personal identity and the concept of good lives. Our day-to-day activities are ultimately directed at the achievement of basic human goods and in seeking to realize these goods in specific ways of living, we construct personal identities. The relationship between a good lives conceptualization, lifestyle, and a sense of meaning is a powerful one.

This is well captured by Archer (2000) who states,

> In short, we are who we are because of what we care about: In delineating our ultimate concerns and accommodating our subordinate ones, we also define ourselves. We give a shape to our lives, which constitutes our internal personal integrity. (p. 10)

Third, the major construct driving rehabilitation should be that of human well-being (i.e., good lives), not risk management or relapse prevention. A conception of human well-being will specify the various goods (e.g., intimacy, health, autonomy, creativity, knowledge, etc.) naturally sought by human beings, the circumstances and conditions necessary to secure these goods, and the possible embodiment of such goods in concrete lives. Fourth, the good lives model assumes that human beings are contextually dependent organisms and as such a rehabilitation plan should always take into account the match between the characteristics of the offender and the likely environments he is to be released into. Thus, we argue that the notion of adaptive or coping skills should always be linked to the contexts in which offenders are embedded.

Fifth, a treatment plan should be *explicitly* constructed in the form of a good lives conceptualization that, taking into account offenders' strengths, primary goods, and relevant environments, specifies exactly what competencies and resources are required to achieve these goods. It is not enough to tinker with standard treatment plans or goals: The process should be explicit, specific, individualized, and based around the constructs of personal identity, primary goods, and ways of living.

The Good Lives Model of Offender Rehabilitation

Primary goods are actions, states of affairs, characteristics, experiences, and states of mind that are viewed as intrinsically beneficial to human beings and are therefore sought for their own sake rather than as means to some more fundamental ends (Deci & Ryan, 2000; Emmons, 1996, 1999; Schmuck & Sheldon,

2001). Primary goods are viewed as objective and tied to certain ways of living that if pursued involve the actualization of potentialities that are distinctively human. Individuals can, therefore, be mistaken about what is really of value and what is in their best interests; human goods are not simply individual preferences or desires. Primary goods emerge out of basic needs whereas instrumental or secondary goods provide concrete ways of securing these goods, for example, certain types of work, relationships, or language ability. A good life becomes possible when an individual possesses the necessary conditions for achieving primary goods, has access to primary goods, and lives a life characterized by the instantiation of these goods.

There are three classes of primary goods derived from the facts of the body, self, and social life, and the basic human needs associated with such facts (this discussion draws from the excellent work of Kekes, 1989). The primary goods of the *body* include basic physiological needs for sex, food, warmth, water, sleep, and the healthy functioning of the body as a whole. The primary goods of the *self* are derived from the basic needs of autonomy, relatedness, and competence (Deci & Ryan, 2000). Each of these needs is associated with a cluster of related primary goods. For example, relatedness can be further broken down into goods of intimacy, understanding, empathy, support, sexual pleasure, and sharing. The primary goods of *social life* include social support, family life, meaningful work opportunities, and access to recreational activities. A conception of good lives should be based on these three classes of primary goods and specify the forms they will take in each individual's life plan.

Basic or primary goods have been repeatedly identified in psychological research on human well-being and self-regulation, indicating that human beings are by nature organisms that strive to achieve certain ends (Deci & Ryan, 2000; Emmons, 1996, 1999; Schmuck & Sheldon, 2001). For example, in his research on personal strivings, Emmons has detected a number of higher-level goals that bear a remarkable resemblance to the primary goods outlined above. These include achievement, affiliation, intimacy, power, personal growth and health, self-presentation, independence, emotionality (emotional regulation), generativity, and spirituality goals (Emmons, 1999). The notion of primary goods also overlaps to some extent with the domains of life satisfaction identified by Cummins (1996), that is, material well-being, health, productivity, intimacy, safety, community, and emotional well-being. In addition, theorists such as Nussbaum (2000) and Arnhart (1998) argue that social and political systems should take into account the fact that human beings are naturally disposed to seek certain goods or valued outcomes, and suggest that "human ethics is natural insofar as it satisfies natural human desires" (Arnhart, 1998, p. 29). As stated above, in a fundamental sense primary goods provide the rationale or justification for the goals and ends sought by individuals

(Austin & Vancouver, 1996). That is, goals are the psychological representations of desired states that are ultimately derived from primary goods; goods justify or underpin goals from a conceptual point of view.

The term *good lives* is preferred to the singular "good life" as we accept the view that there is no one ideal or preferred lifestyle for any given individual (Kekes, 1989; Rasmussen, 1999). A general plan or conception can be unpacked into related, but diverse, specific kinds of lives. The possibility of constructing and translating such conceptions of good lives into actions and concrete ways of living depends crucially on the possession of internal and external conditions (capabilities). The specific form that a conception will take depends on the actual abilities, interests, and opportunities of each individual and the weightings he or she gives to specific primary goods. The weightings or priority allocated to specific primary goods is constitutive of an offender's *personal identity* and spells out the kind of life sought, and relatedly, the kind of person he or she would like to be. However, because human beings naturally seek a range of primary goods or desired states, it is important that all the classes of primary goods are addressed in a conception of good lives; they should be ordered and *coherently* related to each other. For example, if an offender decides to pursue a life characterized by service to the community, a core aspect of his identity will revolve around the primary goods of relatedness and social life. The offender's sense of mastery, self-esteem, perception of autonomy, and control will all reflect this overarching good and its associated sub clusters of goods (e.g., intimacy, caring, honesty). They should be organized in ways that ensure each primary good has a role to play and can be secured or experienced by the individual concerned. A conception that is fragmented and lacks coherency is likely to lead to frustration and harm to the individual concerned, as well as a life lacking an overall sense of purpose and meaning. In addition, a conception of good lives is always *context dependent;* there is no such thing as the right kind of life for an individual across every conceivable setting.

In a sense, when offenders agree to enter a rehabilitation program, they are implicitly asking therapists, "How can I live my life differently?" and "How can I be a different kind of person?" This requires clinicians to offer concrete possibilities for living good or worthwhile lives that take into account each individual's abilities, circumstances, interests, and opportunities. Of course, we cannot choose or live offenders' lives for them, but we should be clear about what are reasonable possibilities and help them acquire the requisite skills and capabilities to increase their chances of living such lives. An enhancement model, not a harm-avoidance one, should drive the rehabilitation of offenders.

By the term good lives we are referring to ways of living that are beneficial and fulfilling for individuals. The primary goods comprising good lives are outcomes sought by individuals for their own sake and typically reflect propensities evident in basic human needs. The conception of a possible good life for an offender should also include a concrete understanding of the possible ways of living that are realistic for him. It should take note of each offender's capabilities, temperament, interests, skills, deep commitments (i.e., basic value system and preferred ways of living in the world, for example, as a teacher or provider), and support networks. These goods include friendship, enjoyable work, loving relationships, creative pursuits, sexual satisfaction, positive self-regard, and an intellectually challenging environment. The presence of internal and external obstacles results in impaired social and psychological functioning and therefore a less fulfilling life. Rehabilitation should focus on identifying the various obstacles preventing offenders from living a balanced and fulfilling life and then equip them with the skills, beliefs, values, and supports needed to counteract their pernicious influence.

COMPONENTS OF A GOOD LIVES CONCEPTUALIZATION

Taking into account the above discussion, a good lives conception for a given offender in a rehabilitation program should be based on the following information:

- A case formulation derived from the detection of the clinical phenomena or problems associated with an individual's offending
- A list of primary goods (based on the three classes outlined earlier); this should include goods associated with relationships, competency, autonomy, physical health and functioning, social roles and community links
- The selection of a primary good or value around which the other goods are oriented (i.e., spelling out a way of living that relates to the establishment of personal identity)
- The selection of secondary goods or values that specify how the primary goods will be translated into ways of living and functioning (e.g., specifying what kinds of relationships would be beneficial to the person concerned, taking into account his preferences and strengths plus what is considered ideal or appropriate)
- Identification of the contexts or environments the person is likely to be living in once he completes the program. This will require information concerning opportunities for work, social supports, culture of the likely community and neighborhood(s), and possible living arrangements.
- Taking into account the primary goods and the central good(s), ways of living that embody these primary goods (secondary values), and the kinds of contexts or environments the person is likely to be living in or that will at least minimally support lifestyles incorporating the primary goods, the necessary internal and external conditions for implementing the good lives conceptualization are noted. Internal conditions refers to skills, beliefs, attitudes, and so on, and external

conditions refers to the contextual variables outlined above. A program is then developed that effectively links the good lives conception with treatment interventions.

We now outline in detail how such a good lives approach could work, detailing the different assessment and intervention tasks required to implement such a model. In order to make the discussion a little more concrete, we refer to a state-of-the-art cognitive behavioral program for sex offenders as we go along. For the sake of convenience we base our discussion on child molesters rather than sex offenders in general, although the points apply to all sex offenders. It must be noted that the good lives approach bites most deeply in the assessment and program orientation phases of treatment. It is here that information concerning offenders' risk factors is integrated with a constructive model of how such individuals can live different kinds of lives, and in doing so, construct more meaningful and prosocial identities.

Good Lives and the Treatment of Sex Offenders

PROGRAM ORIENTATION

The treatment framework of programs for men who sexually abuse children is typically that of relapse prevention (Laws, Hudson, & Ward, 2000). The aim is to teach offenders ways of managing high-risk situations through the utilization of adaptive coping responses. The overarching value evident in this type of treatment is that of risk or harm reduction rather than the enhancement of capabilities to enable offenders' to live better lives. Treatment programs based on risk management are essentially focused on avoidance goals, and as such are not likely to result in high levels of well-being and functioning for the individuals concerned (Emmons, 1999; Mann et al., 2002). It is possible that an individual may have his risk factors reduced but end up living an impoverished life without friends, lacking access to meaningful employment and recreational activities, and grappling with a reduced sense of agency and personal identity. A difficulty with simply addressing risk factors is that it is not clear what exactly is the overall aim of treatment: the reduction of risk or the development of a prosocial and fulfilling life for an offender.

A related issue is that therapists must ensure that in the rush to reduce offenders' level of risk they do not inadvertently extinguish the qualities that make human lives worth living (Harris, 1997). The qualities that make up a worthwhile human life (based on our natural proclivities) make us vulnerable to breakdown under certain circumstances. However, this does not entail that therapists should seek to boost the "strength" of offenders to the point where these qualities are eradicated or weakened. Engaging in new activities, being open to the unexpected, seeking novel events and challenges, starting new relationships, and falling in love contain within them the possibility of disappointment, rejection, and emotional pain. In other words, growth opportunities, aspects of human well-being or flourishing, are also opportunities for loss and failure: You simply cannot have one without the other. But a life denuded of these goods would be barely human, and may in fact lead back to an offending lifestyle.

In traditional RP (relapse prevention) programs, any discussion or utilization of the concept of human goods (if present at all) is often at too general a level to be useful for rehabilitation planning. The concept of good lives is a *contextual* one where the basic human goods sought by all individuals are translated into different forms (i.e., concrete realizations). Such distinct forms reflect the weighting individuals give to different values and their capacities, social supports, and opportunities. A conceptualization of good lives is tied together by personal identity, a way of characterizing the direction and meaning of each person's life. To offer offenders overly general or "prepackaged lives" (even if only tacitly) is a mistake. Such abstract conceptions lack applicability to individuals and therefore suffer from irrelevance and meaninglessness.

The reliance on manual-based interventions in the treatment of offenders can add to this problem. Because therapists tend to follow standardized procedures, they may fail to consider the appropriate form of life for a given individual. Instead, they may uncritically accept the *generic* conception of good lives implicit in the treatment manual. For example, with sex offenders it is often assumed that all offenders should be able to establish personally satisfying, intimate relationships with other adults. Therefore, therapy may emphasize the value of personal disclosure, learning how to be mutually supportive, and acquiring the ability to listen to another person's feelings and opinions. However, the valuing of relationships to this degree may not be appropriate for certain individuals and may even be unrealistic and harmful. They may place more significance on developing vocational skills or consorting with friends rather than intimates. While it may be true that most individuals need some degree of human contact, there are certainly individual differences in the type and intensity of relations preferred (and needed). In addition, some offenders may be so damaged by a history of abusive relationships that it is unrealistic to expect them ever to be able to establish and maintain deeply intimate relationships. The point is that conceptions of good lives require a consideration of the offender's particular profile of capacities, preferences, commitments, and the possible opportunities available in the world. It is a question of trying to ensure that a full range of human goods (from all three sources) are accessible but accepting that they can (and should) be realized in varying ways for different offenders.

ASSESSMENT

We argue that clinicians ought to explicitly construct a conception of good lives to guide the rehabilitation of each offender. The identification of individuals' psychological dispositions or vulnerability factors causally related to their offending is an important step in the assessment process. This provides information on the internal and external obstacles that are frustrating the meeting of basic human needs and, therefore, preventing the achievement of primary human goods. Once this is done, it is necessary to construct a conception of good lives that is tailored to each offender's overarching good and to inquire about the necessary conditions required to live a different kind of life. As stated above, a conception of human well-being should outline the primary goods to be installed in good lives and the range of specific forms they can take. The ordering or relationship between the various goods should also be described and the internal and external conditions necessary for their attainment noted. This process is spelled out in more detail in the next section.

Effective treatment of child molesters requires a dedicated and systematic assessment period targeting a number of domains and utilizing a number of methods to collect clinical information (Marshall, 1999; Ward, Hudson, & Keenan, 2000). These methods include a clinical interview, the administration of psychological scales, and phallometric testing. It is important to use multiple methods to gather clinically relevant data; relying on just one source of data, for example self-report, is risky (Ward & Haig, 1997). The assessment process should culminate in a clinical formulation (Ward & Haig, 1997) that serves to guide the customization of the program content to the individual. A comprehensive clinical formulation of sexually aggressive behavior needs to consider an individual's background, psychological vulnerabilities, current stresses, and the problem behavior itself. The result of this process is a conceptual model representing the client's various problems, the hypothesized underlying mechanisms, and their interrelationships. In essence, this clinical theory specifies how the symptoms or problems are generated by psychological mechanisms, for example, dysfunctional core beliefs or behavioral deficits.

The problem with the usual assessment of sex offenders is that what the therapist is left with is a depiction of an individual's psychological vulnerability factors and problems; in essence, the identification of offense related and offense specific needs or clinical targets (Marshall, 1999). What is missing is the integration of this knowledge with concrete ways of living, that is, a good lives formulation. The detection of clinical phenomena and their underlying causes is certainly of crucial importance; in our language they represent obstacles that frustrate the achievement of primary goods. What they point to is the need for the offender to acquire the skills and competencies necessary to achieve important (and prosocial) goods in ways that are more fulfilling and satisfying. A necessary step in the construction of such a good lives conceptualization is the explicit linking of primary and secondary goods, personal identity, and internal and external conditions with specific contexts and social circumstances.

Steps in the Good Lives Assessment Process

We return to the major features outlined earlier and relate these to the assessment of sex offenders in more detail.

First, the construction of a case formulation based on the detection of the clinical phenomena or problems associated with an individual's offending. The case formulation is essentially a causal narrative that ties together the various problems, psychological mechanisms, and the activating events and situations. This task also involves the standard risk assessment and identification of criminogenic needs.

Next is a consideration of the primary goods (based on the three classes outlined earlier) necessary for leading a fulfilling, human life. This should include goods associated with relationships, competency, autonomy, physical health and functioning, social roles, and community links. It must be noted that good lives conceptualizations are usually implicit, and the offender will often be unaware of what his goals are and how they relate to underlying goods and ways of living that are thought to embody these goods. They may be embedded in social scripts or lifestyles that are simply unquestioned. The therapist should examine the assessment data and ascertain whether the offender has pursued the full range of primary goods in his life and note down any problems in the way they have been pursued. There are three major types of problems typically evident in offenders' lives: inappropriate means (or secondary goods), lack of scope, and lack of coherence or integration between the goods constituting a good lives conceptualization.

We now consider the problem of pursuing human goods through inappropriate means. Recall that secondary goods represent means or ways of realizing primary goods: they are activities, characteristics, states of mind, or states of affairs that an individual believes will secure primary goods. In this instance, an individual seeks a primary good such as intimacy or competency through activities or the cultivation of personal characteristics that are harmful to him or to someone else. For example, an attempt to establish an intimate relationship may be compromised by a tendency to remain emotionally aloof or perhaps to become physically abusive in certain circumstances.

The problem of restricted scope occurs when an offender neglects some primary goods because of his pursuit of other goods. The research literature on human needs and evolutionary psychology indicates that individuals are naturally inclined to seek certain ends (Deci & Ryan, 2000; Emmons, 1999; Kekes, 1989). The fulfillment of all fundamental needs, and the goods that are partially derived from these needs, is a necessary prerequisite for living a deeply satisfying and fulfilling life. In addition, the exercise of basic needs is constitutive of human nature and, in part, defines who we are; they are not means to some other, more fundamental end. Categorical needs, and their related primary goods, in effect are *constitutive* of what it means to be a (optimally functioning or fulfilled) human being, and their value rests entirely on the intrinsic value of human beings. Thus loving, acting autonomously, and mastering the world not only enable human beings to develop into their best possible form, they actually make us what we essentially are. The failure to meet the basic needs for autonomy, relatedness, and competence will inevitably cause psychological distress and result in the acquisition of maladaptive defenses (Deci & Ryan, 2000). In other words, thwarted basic needs result in stunted lives, psychological problems, and social maladjustment. For example, if an individual is preoccupied with the need to exert power and control over his partners and acquaintances, it is likely that there will be less attention given to the development and maintenance of satisfying, intimate relationships. His life will become fragmented and unbalanced and, given the psychological necessity of meeting needs such as intimacy, it is likely he will experience periods of unhappiness and possibly resentment. This may cause him to become sexually aggressive or turn to sex with children as a substitute for adult relatedness.

The final problem typically seen in offenders' good lives conceptualizations is that of incoherence or fragmentation. The failure to explicitly acknowledge the construct of good lives can result in a lack of coherence in treatment planning and in the life plans offenders construct during this process. Psychological research suggests that a lack of coherency (i.e., conflict) among goals is associated with lower levels of subjective well-being and less life satisfaction (Emmons, 1996, 1999; Schmuck & Sheldon, 2001).

There are two types of coherence relevant to this problem, horizontal and vertical coherence (Kekes, 1989). Horizontal coherence refers to the degree to which goods (and their psychological embodiment in goals) are explicitly related to each other in the sense that they are mutually consistent and enabling. For example, an individual might secure the primary good of intimacy in an exclusive sexual relationship with an adult partner and yet in his leisure time socialize with peers who devalue notions of exclusive relationships and endorse sexual promiscuity. There is conflict between the two goods, which is likely to cause emotional distress. Emmons (1999) states that "empirical evidence is continually accruing in support of the notion that conflict is stressful and is associated with both psychological and physical ill-being" (p. 77).

The second form of coherence, vertical coherence, concerns the degree to which lower-level or secondary goods are derived from primary goods or ultimate concerns. The requirement for vertical coherence is that there is a clear, hierarchical relationship between the myriad activities of everyday life and primary goods or values. Higher-level goods yield meaning and identity but need to be linked to concrete action via lower-level ones in order to transfer that meaning into peoples' everyday lives (Emmons, 1999). A lack of vertical coherence will result in a sense of meaninglessness, an aimless, fragmented existence where individuals orient themselves toward immediate gratification rather than seeking to achieve longer-term plans or life projects (Maruna, 2001). Emmons (1999) captures the relationship between vertical coherence and personal identity and meaning nicely when he states, "A meaningful life is one that is characterized by a deep sense of purpose, a sense of inner conviction, and assurance that in spite of one's current plight, life has significance" (p. 138). For example, an individual might be in a reasonable job, enjoy friendships and hobbies, but be left with no overall sense of where his life is going: He lacks an overall sense of direction and purpose (i.e., meaning). Sex with children might be the result of an attempt to establish an emotional connectedness to children, perhaps because they are available or are perceived as more optimistic and less threatening. Another possibility is that the meaning or personal identity vacuum will be filled by affiliation with antisocial peers, perhaps in the form of gang identification or with other such groups.

Third, the process of selection of a primary good or value around which the other goods are oriented (i.e., spelling out a way of living that relates to the establishment of personal identity) may be impaired in some way. A necessary step in desisting from a criminal career appears to be the construal of the self as someone who does not need to offend and who is able to secure important goods in socially acceptable and personally rewarding ways (Maruna, 2001). The process of reconstructing a personal identity depends crucially on fashioning a conception of good lives. Such a conception specifies what is most important to offenders and indicates how they can live their lives in different and more meaningful ways. Personal identity is pivotal in cementing together a conception of good lives and is based on values and their associated human goods.

In his excellent book on ultimate concerns and human fulfillment, Emmons (1999) states that, "It is clear from goal research that in order to optimize long-term well-being, people should strive for outcomes that are consistent with the type of person they envision becoming" (p. 116). That is, primary goods should be embedded in ways of living that confer a sense of personal identity and meaning on a person. The concrete ways of living in different domains (work, personal relationships, leisure, etc.) are secondary goods or values, believed to result in the realization of primary goods. For example, working as a mechanic might be a means to secure the primary good of competence and its related goods of skilled performance, positive self-esteem, and pride.

In formulating this aspect of a rehabilitation plan, a therapist should consider the strengths or aspirations and talents of an offender (see Rapp, 1998). What kind of person would he like to be? What kind of life (i.e., way of living) would this require? What is he good at, what does he obtain pleasure from, and from what activities does he derive a sense of purpose and dignity? The aim is to identify a core primary good and translate it into a cluster of goods embedded in particular ways of life. For example, an offender might want to train as a drug counselor in order to help other individuals recover from their addiction. Therefore, the primary goods associated with relatedness (e.g., serving, helping, healing) would be selected as the core or superordinate good and used to construct the other aspects of an individual's rehabilitation plan. It is important to note that the other primary goods should be incorporated into any such plan, but the way they are expressed will vary depending on the overarching good selected. In a sense, the choice of the primary good dictates the blueprint for the construction of an individual's personal identity, linked to ways of living.

Fourth, the next step is to select the secondary goods or values that specify how the above core primary good, and the others, will be translated into ways of living and functioning (e.g., specifying what kinds of relationships would be beneficial to the person concerned, taking into account his preferences plus what is considered ideal or appropriate). As stated above, this is a matter of considering what secondary goods are necessary and also how they will be organized with respect to each other. For example, an offender might be a practical person and enjoy repairing machines. The overarching value would be that of competence and its associated goods, such as doing a good job, solving problems, and knowing how things work. The secondary goods required to install the core value could involve working as a volunteer at a garage, taking courses in mechanical engineering, joining a club, making friends with like-minded people, or planning to train as a motorcycle mechanic. Note that other primary goods, such as those of friendship, independence, or taking on new challenges, are embedded in a good lives plan centered around the good of competency and its unpacking in terms of mechanical interests and opportunities.

Fifth, it is necessary to identify the contexts or environments the person is likely to be living in once he completes a treatment program. A conception of good lives stipulates or recommends certain kinds of living for individuals, and in its application to individual lives provides a plan for living well that takes into account the skills, temperament, opportunities, and social context of each person. The concept is a *contextual* one where the basic human goods sought by all individuals are translated into different forms (i.e., concrete realizations). Such distinct forms reflect the weighting individuals give to different values as well as their capacities, social supports, and opportunities. In our view, it is a mistake to seek to equip offenders with generic skills that will enable them to flourish, or live in a fulfilling manner, in any number of environments within a particular society. Rather, it is necessary to consider carefully the contexts a given individual is likely to be released into, keeping in mind short-, medium-, and long-term possibilities. This will require information concerning opportunities for work, social supports, the culture of the likely community and neighborhood(s), possible living arrangements, and so on. For example, a sex offender who was a teacher is likely to want to work in an environment where he can help others, or at least use his intellect, rather than engaging in manual work. He might also want to have access to bookshops, theaters, cafes, and a good library. For another individual, living in a particular ethnic neighborhood near sports facilities or certain religious support groups might be viewed as more important.

Sixth, taking into account the results from the above steps, the necessary internal and external conditions for implementing the good lives conceptualization are noted. The key question is: Taking into account the kind of life that would be more fulfilling and meaningful to this individual (i.e., primary goods, secondary goods, and their relationship to ways of living and possible environments), what capabilities or competencies does he require to have a reasonable chance of putting his plan into gear? The rehabilitation process is crucially dependent on identifying the internal and external *obstacles* that have been thwarting an individual's ability to meet his fundamental needs and to secure primary goods. These may be defensive strategies, personal and vocational skill deficits, maladaptive attitudes and beliefs, and lack of social support and integration. Internal conditions refer to psychological characteristics such as skills, beliefs, attitudes, and values and reflect the constructive competencies individuals require once their criminogenic and clinical needs are noted. For example, the existence of empathy deficits in an individual means that he would benefit from the acquisition of perspective-taking skills and an awareness of the way sexual abuse affects the development of children. Likewise, the presence of intimacy deficits points to the need for the development of more adaptive attachment models and greater levels of interpersonal trust, disclosure, and conflict resolution skills. Finally, a personal identity to be constructed around the core good of competency and repairing machinery could require the opportunity to work as a volunteer in a garage and also the acquisition of specific mechanical skills. The detection of problems is only of value, from our perspective, if it directly suggests the shape and form of psychological (and vocational) competencies that will help the individual to lead a more satisfying and fulfilling life. This would mean that he would be less likely to meet his needs (or secure human goods) through deviant sexual behavior or other types of antisocial behavior.

External conditions refer to social, cultural, and interpersonal factors that facilitate the development of the above psychological characteristics and include effective parenting, education, vocational training, social supports, and the opportunity to pursue goods. Because human beings are viewed as always functioning within certain contexts, it is necessary to ensure that offenders' social and physical circumstances contain the resources (secondary goods) and opportunities necessary for them to live "good lives" (Rapp, 1998). This means that the psychological, vocational, and social aspects of rehabilitation should be integrated within a coherent multifaceted treatment plan, rather than be considered separately (see the mechanic example above).

In summary, the assessment phase of rehabilitation should follow the dictates of the good lives model and ensure that criminogenic and clinical needs or problems are always related to a constructive or positive view of how an offender could live a different kind of life. The offender is directly involved in the treatment process, particularly in the selection of the core goods and the operationalization of personal identity in terms of daily activities and personal goals (derived ultimately from primary goods).

TREATMENT

In the treatment phase of rehabilitation, the plan developed above is used to select and tailor interventions for offenders in order to increase their chances of living a more fulfilling life. Basically, the aim is to ensure that the internal (i.e., psychological skills, etc.) and external (i.e., supports, opportunities) conditions necessary to implement the good lives conceptualization are in place. We now consider the different treatment modules typically seen in a cognitive behavioral treatment program for sex offenders in order to illustrate how this tailoring process works (Ward et al., 2000). In the process, the role of human goods in implicitly shaping the kind of interventions that take place in a therapy program will become apparent. We use technical language in order to make the links to the notion good lives easier for the reader to follow, but clearly when working with offenders it is necessary to follow the responsivity principle and use language they understand (Andrews & Bonta, 1998).

Module 1: Norm Building

The primary aim for this module is to establish the rules of conduct that are essential if the group is to function effectively, and to provide an overview of the treatment philosophy, that is, the "the big picture." In a typical CBT program, at the first session, the underlying social learning model of human behavior change is described. The men are told that the therapists do not intend to cure them of their problems, but rather to teach them to control their behavior by helping them break dysfunctional habits and learn prosocial ways of satisfying their needs. From the good lives perspective, the notion of living a different kind of life would be made a central feature of this session. The focus would be on linking their offending with unhelpful ways of pursuing valued outcomes or human goods, and it would be stressed that the aim of treatment is to acquire the skills and opportunities (as allowed by legal constraints) to live more fulfilling lives. In addition, it would be stressed that the offenders will have a significant say in choosing the core primary good(s) and designing different ways of living—essentially constructing the outlines of a new personal identity (i.e., a "new me"). The focus will be on activities, characteristics, and states of mind that matter to individual group members and that reflect what is most valuable and meaningful to them.

In this module, the acceptance of personal responsibility and respect for other individuals as persons are stressed. In addition, there is an attempt to link offending behavior with the meeting of offenders' needs at the expense of those of the victim. Moreover, issues pertaining to personal identity are raised when it is pointed out that the offender is someone who has committed a sexual offense rather than being essentially a sexual offender. The notion of activity goals would be stressed: Where the intrinsic benefits of some human goods are derived from the exercise of certain capacities, they are not a means to some further ends. For example, the goods associated with intimate relationships (e.g., sharing activities, expressing feelings, discussing problems, and making love) are created through engaging in certain actions (talking, loving, caring, etc.). The primary goods of the self and social life are obliquely referred to in this module and are thought to motivate the offender to acquire a new understanding of his abusive behavior.

Module 2: Understanding Offending (Cognitive Restructuring)

Sexually aggressive behavior is often facilitated and justified by distorted thinking. In this module, the distorted views offenders frequently have of their offenses are challenged and more accurate and constructive alternative ways of thinking about these issues developed. This process is partially facilitated by encouraging the man to understand his offense cycle fully. Using a collaborative approach, with help from group members, the man is expected to develop an understanding of how background factors—such as low mood, lifestyle imbalances, sexual difficulties, intimacy difficulties—set the scene for offending.

From a good lives perspective, a major focus is on the values that are associated with knowledge generation, for example, evaluating each offender's account of his sexually abusive actions by comparing it to alternative explanations in terms of its explanatory depth, accuracy, interpretation of "evidence," simplicity, depth, and consistency. Self-esteem and identity issues are raised by the management of challenges, and the therapist is careful to reinforce honest and thoughtful responses on the behalf of the offender. The aim here is to help the offender disengage his core self from his sexually abusive actions and also to learn to honestly appraise his behavior.

In addition, the offender is encouraged to ask questions such as, "What kind of person do I want to be?" alongside, "What kind of life do I want to live?" This makes the link between the process of identity construction and intentional actions explicit; character is formed as a result of repeated actions in specific contexts (Harris, 1997). These types of questions also function to reduce conflict among the components of a good lives conception (i.e., different types of goods); the offender strives to create coherence or consistency between his goods and the actions that reflect them.

Module 3: Arousal Reconditioning

Inappropriate or deviant sexual arousal to children is hypothesized to be an important factor causing and maintaining sexual offending (Ward et al., 2000), and indeed is described as an important part of the problem behavior process. In terms of the procedures used in this module, there is a limited amount of evidence suggesting that reconditioning strategies can reduce inappropriate sexual arousal in some categories of child molesters (Marshall, 1999). There are usually three components to this intervention: covert sensitization, directed masturbation, and satiation training.

From a good lives perspective, the focus would be on achieving the goods of sexual satisfaction, intimacy, and emotional regulation, or self-soothing. Sex would be linked to a multitude of personal goods and be disentangled from the destructive goals of power and control. In addition, the relationship between the goods associated with sex would be clearly integrated with the other domains of functioning and their associated goods, for example, relationships: vertical and horizontal coherence would be sought. Sexual preference for, and arousal to, consenting adult sex are simply the necessary psychological conditions for realizing a different kind of life. The core goods and their associated secondary goods (e.g., types of employment, hobbies, relationships) embodied in a good lives conceptualization help to tailor this module to different individuals. A final aim would be to clarify that sexual gratification can occur through a number of legally acceptable avenues and is not confined to intercourse between adults. This is an important consideration for those offenders whose chances of establishing intimate adult relationships are minimal, perhaps due to the profound nature of their psychological problems and dysfunction. In this situation, using prostitutes or masturbating to nondeviant erotic material might be viewed as appropriate sexual outlets, taking into account the individual's overall conception of good lives. In this respect, the good lives approach is entirely compatible with the harm reduction perspective (see Laws, Chapter 16 in this volume).

Module 4: Victim Impact and Empathy

Typically, a general or specific deficiency in the capacity to be empathic is seen as facilitating offending, where things that are manifestly harmful are done to others. The victim impact material may serve to reinstate individuals' capacity to empathize with potential victims and reduce the future risk of reoffending. The primary goods evident in this module concern the need to take the well-being and perspectives of other people into account when interacting with them. The putative mental states and needs of the victim become a focus and remind the offender to value equally the well-being of others alongside his own. In fact, in view of the substantive view of human nature (basic needs and propensities to seek certain goods) inherent in the good lives model, the offender should begin to understand that what constitutes a good life for him, in broad terms also applies to others. If all human beings obtain deep satisfaction from creative challenges, mastery experiences, and close friendships, then the distinction between the offender's needs and best interests and those of others is weakened (Kekes, 1989). In addition, the fact that human beings are usefully construed as social or interdependent beings means that it is possible to flourish or to achieve significant degrees of well-being only if others also have the opportunity to do so. The value basis of empathy is made very clear, in both its prudential and ethical forms.

There is a focus on the nature of harms (related to deprivation of goods such as self-autonomy and choice) that can be inflicted on victims of sexual offenses. The skills, beliefs, and values underlying empathic responses are viewed as internal conditions necessary for the achievement of the goods of relatedness, self-respect, and intimacy. In addition, the kind of relationship that an offender is realistically likely to be engaged in when released from prison would guide specific aims of this cluster of interventions. If an individual is extremely damaged and therefore unlikely to enter into intimate, loving sexual relationships, the focus might be to give him the empathy skills needed to form more basic or superficial kinds of friendships. The good lives formulation functions as a regulatory ideal: The aim is to try to get as close to it as realistically possible, but also to ensure that such a plan is practically feasible for any given individual.

Module 5: Mood Management

Negative mood states are a frequent precipitating stimulus for the offense chain, usually depression or feelings of rejection, or more rarely anger (Ward et al., 2000). Deficiencies in affect regulation are therefore a critical part in the management of risk. However, it is important to keep in mind that positive mood states can also be associated with sexual offending for some individuals. From a good lives perspective, emotional regulation would be introduced within the context of personal goal theory, and the relationship between goal progress (and coherence) and emotional states emphasized (Emmons, 1999). In addition, the core competencies required to function in an autonomous manner and to achieve the human goods associated with this overarching need (e.g., self-control, planning, problem solving, or intimacy) involve the ability to identify and manage emotional states in appropriate ways. The good lives models or plans of each offender will be used to fine-tune and tailor this set of interventions, as it is anticipated that the degree to which offenders suffer from self-regulation deficits will vary according to their particular offense pathways (Ward & Hudson, 1998; Ward & Siegert, in press).

Module 6: Relationship Skills

In this module the focus is typically on intimate relationships, first establishing their benefits and then examining ways in which they can be enhanced. The goods associated with different types of relationships are canvassed with the focus being on establishing a link between each individual's need for safety and his habitual interpersonal strategies. The initial aim is to provide offenders with the capacity to form deeply satisfying intimate and supportive relationships and thus to cease using deviant sex as a substitute for such relationships. However, the types of relationships individuals are likely to be involved in when they are released will determine the scope and depth of intimacy interventions and social skill training. For some offenders, this might mean learning how to relate to individuals in the context of certain hobby groups, while for others the concern might be to help them develop truly fulfilling and satisfying close relationships. The actual nature of the interventions will depend on each offender's deficits and, therefore, the psychological and social conditions necessary to live the best type of life possible in the environment or contexts the offender is likely to be released into.

Module 7: Relapse Prevention

The relapse prevention module is typically designed to help the offender to identify the external and internal factors that put him at risk for further sexually abusive behavior, and to ameliorate these by utilizing appropriate coping responses (Laws et al., 2000). The use of the good lives model means that these risk factors are viewed as obstacles that might erode an offender's capacity to live a more fulfilling, that is a good, life. Thus the therapeutic focus is on implementing the offender's good lives conceptualization rather than simply managing risk, although risk is not neglected. This issue is dealt with in more detail in a paper (Ward, 2002).

A recent study illustrates how this part of treatment can be implemented in a more constructive manner, consistent with a good lives perspective. Mann et al. (2002) have developed a way of teaching relapse prevention concepts and knowledge based on approach goals, rather than using the risk management approach seen in the majority of programs. Offenders were taught to distinguish between approach and avoidance goals and to set subgoals that would enable them to establish a "new me" (i.e., a more adaptive personal identity). For example, the kind of approach goals formulated included developing better adult relationships, considering other peoples' points of view before acting prematurely, and showing more respect for the rights of others. They also learned to identify factors that may prevent them from achieving approach goals and to deal with these by focusing on constructive goals and life plans.

Conclusions

In this chapter we have outlined the good lives model of offender rehabilitation, and after stating its major theoretical assumptions, briefly discussed its application to the assessment and treatment of sex offenders. The consideration of the application of the model has been necessarily brief, given the space constraints of this chapter. However, it is clear that the adoption of a good lives approach will result in a number of different treatment practices. First, a major task of assessment will be to integrate information concerning offenders criminogenic and treatment needs with that describing the necessary conditions for living more personally fulfilling (and prosocial) lives. Second, treatment will be tightly focused on instilling the psychological skills and competencies necessary to institute each offender's good lives model rather than simply concentrating on the reduction of risk factors. The latter is a necessary condition of successful rehabilitation, but is not sufficient. Third, the type, intensity, and range of interventions given to offenders will depend crucially on the kinds of contexts or environments they are likely to be living in once released from prison (or parole or probation conditions). We suggest that the idea of equipping individuals for a generic or ideal life is misconstrued and neglects the fact that human beings are contextually dependent organisms. Fourth, rehabilitation is a value-laden process, and it is a mistake to ignore or play down this aspect of the behavior change process because of a misguided belief that acknowledging the important role of human goods or values seriously compromises the integrity of treatment. Finally, it is crucially important to ensure that treatment goals are coherently organized and related to a core set of values (primary and secondary goods—ways of living, relationships, characteristics) that yield a sense of personal identity and meaningfulness. A life without meaning and purpose is not a real life at all.

References

Andrews, D. A., & Bonta, J. (1998). *The psychology of criminal conduct* (2nd ed.) Cincinnati, OH: Anderson.

Archer, M. S. (2000). *Being human: The problem of agency*. Cambridge, UK: Cambridge University Press.

Arnhart, L. (1998). *Darwinian natural right: The biological ethics of human nature*. Albany: State University of New York Press.

Ashford, J. B., Sales, B. D., & Reid, W. H. (2001). Political, legal, and professional challenges to treating offenders with special needs. In J. B. Ashford, B. D. Sales, & W. H. Reid (Eds.), *Treating adult and juvenile offenders with special needs* (pp. 31-49). Washington, DC: American Psychological Association.

Austin, J. T., & Vancouver, J. B. (1996). Goal constructs in psychology: Structure, process, and content. *Psychological Bulletin, 120*, 338-375.

Cummins, R. A. (1996). The domains of life satisfaction: An attempt to order chaos. *Social Indicators Research, 38*, 303-328.

Deci, E. L., & Ryan, R. M. (2000). The "what" and "why" of goal pursuits: Human needs and the self-determination of behavior. *Psychological Inquiry, 11*, 227-268.

Ellerby, L., Bedard, J., & Chartrand, S. (2000). Holism, wellness, and spirituality: Moving from relapse prevention to healing. In D. R. Laws, S. M. Hudson, & T. Ward (Eds.), *Remaking relapse prevention with sex offenders: A sourcebook* (pp. 427-452). Thousand Oaks, CA: Sage.

Emmons, R. A. (1996). Striving and feeling: Personal goals and subjective well-being. In P. M. Gollwitzer & J. A. Bargh (Eds.), *The psychology of action: Linking cognition and motivation to behavior* (pp. 313-337). New York: Guilford.

Emmons, R. A. (1999). *The psychology of ultimate concerns*. New York: Guilford.

Freeman-Longo, R. E. (2001). *Paths to wellness: A holistic approach and guide for personal recovery*. Holyoke, MA: NEARI Press.

Garland, D. (2001). *The culture of control: Crime and social order in contemporary society*. Chicago: University of Chicago Press.

Harris, G. W. (1997). *Dignity and vulnerability: Strength and quality of character*. Los Angeles: University of California Press.

Haaven, J. L., & Coleman, E. M. (2000). Treatment of the developmentally disabled sex offender. In D. R. Laws, S. M. Hudson, & T. Ward (Eds.), *Remaking relapse prevention with sex offenders: A sourcebook* (pp. 369-388). Thousand Oaks, CA: Sage.

Hannah-Moffat, K. (1999). Moral agent or actuarial subject: Risk and women's imprisonment. *Theoretical Criminology*, 3, 71-49.

Kekes, J. (1989). *Moral tradition and individuality*. Princeton, NJ: Princeton University Press.

Laws, D. R., Hudson, S. M., & Ward, T. (Eds.). (2000). *Remaking relapse prevention with sex offenders: A sourcebook*. Thousand Oaks, CA: Sage.

McGuire, J. (2000). Explanations of criminal behavior. In J. McGuire, T. Mason, & A. O'Kane (Eds.), *Behavior, crime and legal processes: A guide for legal practitioners* (pp. 135-159). Chichester, UK: Wiley.

Marshall, W. L. (1999). Current status of North American assessment and treatment programs for sexual offenders. *Journal of Interpersonal Violence*, 14, 221-239.

Mann, R., Webster, S., & Schofield, C. (2002). Approach versus avoidance goals in relapse prevention with sex offenders. Manuscript under review.

Maruna, S. (2001). *Making good: How ex-convicts reform and rebuild their lives*. Washington, DC: American Psychological Association.

Nussbaum, M. C. (2000). *Women and human development: The capabilities approach*. New York: Cambridge University Press.

Rapp, C. A. (1998). *The strengths model: Case management with people suffering from severe and persistent mental illness*. New York: Oxford University Press.

Rasmussen, D. B. (1999). Human flourishing and the appeal to human nature. In E. F. Paul, F. D. Miller, & J. Paul (Eds.), Human flourishing (pp. 1-43). New York: Cambridge University Press.

Schmuck, P., & Sheldon, K. M. (Eds.). (2001). *Life goals and well-being*. Toronto, Ontario: Hogrefe & Huber.

Ward, T. (in press). Good lives and the rehabilitation of offenders: Promises and problems. *Aggression and Violent Behavior*.

Ward T., & Haig, B. (1997). Abductive reasoning and clinical assessment. *Australian Psychologist*, 32, 93-100.

Ward, T., & Hudson, S. M. (1998). A model of the relapse process in sex offenders. *Journal of Interpersonal Violence*, 13, 700-725.

Ward, T., Hudson, S. M., & Keenan, T. (2000). The assessment and treatment of sexual offenders against children. In C. R. Hollin (Ed.), *Handbook of offender assessment and treatment* (pp. 359-361). London: Wiley.

Ward, T., & Siegert, R. J. (in press). Toward a comprehensive theory of child sexual abuse: A theory knitting perspective. *Psychology, Crime, & Law*.

Ward, T., & Stewart, C. A. (in press). Criminogenic needs or human needs: A theoretical critique. *Psychological, Crime, & Law*.

3

Back to the Future?

Evolutionary Explanations of Rape

Richard Siegert
University of Otago

Tony Ward
University of Melbourne

In recent years psychology has witnessed growing interest in the relevance of evolutionary theory for understanding human behavior (e.g., Barkow, Cosmides, & Tooby, 1992; Caporael, 2001; Pinker, 1997; Richards, 1987). This renaissance of Darwinian thinking in psychology has been given the name Evolutionary Psychology (Buss, 1999; Plotkin, 1997).[1] Evolutionary psychologists have argued for the value of this new approach in understanding such diverse aspects of human behavior as language (Pinker, 1997; Pinker & Bloom, 1992); sexuality and mating strategies (Buss & Schmidt, 1993; Miller, 2001; Symons, 1979); child abuse, male violence, and homicide (Daly & Wilson, 1985, 1988); cooperation and social exchange (Tooby & Cosmides, 1992); and psychopathology (Siegert & Ward, in press; Stevens & Price, 2000). However, the most controversial application of evolutionary psychology has almost certainly been the attempt to explain rape, and more generally sexual coercion, from an evolutionary perspective (e.g., Thornhill & Palmer, 2000). The debate over the utility and validity of an evolutionary perspective on why men rape women has attracted considerable publicity and generated a heated controversy, not only among academics but also in the popular press (e.g., Fischman, 2000; Goode, 2000; Ochert, 2000).

The aim of the present chapter is to provide a critical introductory review of some of the major attempts to apply evolutionary psychology (EP) to the area of rape. To do this we begin with a brief account of Darwin's principles of selection and adaptation and then describe contemporary evolutionary psychology. Next, we describe in some detail the major conclusions of an EP perspective on human mating strategies, as this is essential for understanding EP theories about rape and sexual coercion. Then we provide a summary of three recent attempts to incorporate evolutionary psychology principles into theoretical accounts of rape.[2] The three theories we consider are those of Ellis (1989), Malamuth (1998), and Thornhill and Palmer (2000).[3] In each case we attempt a fairly neutral description of the main features of the theory followed by a brief evaluation of the strengths and weaknesses of each one. Lastly, we offer some suggestions as to how work in this area might best proceed in the future.

Selection, Adaptation, and Evolution

In 1859 Charles Darwin published *The Origin Of Species* (1859/1998). In this text he marshaled a vast array of observations and facts about plant and animal life forms into a coherent and integrated theory that provided a plausible scientific explanation for the great diversity of species on the Earth and also explained the fossil evidence of extinct life forms. Most important, Darwin identified the process by which the evolution of species occurred—a process known as natural selection.

There are three essential elements in Darwin's ideas about natural selection. First, individual members of a species (be it plant or animal) all *vary*. Thus no two elephants, aphids, starlings, or oak trees, when examined closely, are ever completely identical. Second, some individual members of a species will demonstrate variations that make them better able to survive or adapt to changing environmental conditions. For example, the faster antelope is more likely to escape predatory lions. Third, those individuals better equipped to survive will be more likely to breed and in doing so will pass on these characteristics to their progeny. Consequently, these inherited characteristics will become more common within that species.

In addition to natural selection, Darwin also discerned one other important process in evolution—sexual selection. This is the idea that male and female members of a particular species will demonstrate distinct preferences in their choice of mates based upon the physical or behavioral characteristics of such organisms. Consequently, individuals with characteristics or traits that are highly preferred in mates will leave behind more offspring and these characteristics will become more frequent in the population. For example, in certain species of birds (e.g., peacocks), the females demonstrate a preference for mates with extravagant, brightly colored plumage.

What Is Evolutionary Psychology?

Evolutionary psychologists argue that millions of years of evolution provided specific environmental challenges, which have resulted in specific cognitive mechanisms to meet those challenges, through the processes of natural selection and sexual selection. As a consequence, the newborn human brain is anything but a general learning device that is programmed by culture. Rather, the mind is believed to be a set of domain-specific mental modules (Fodor, 1983; Hirschfeld & Gelman, 1994) that operate independently but in a coordinated fashion (Tooby & Cosmides, 1992). Such modules are considered to be independent, self-contained information processors that function quickly and automatically and mostly outside of conscious awareness. Tooby and Cosmides (1992, p. 90) posit modules for mate selection, language acquisition, family relationships, and cooperation, as well as a "belief-desire folk psychology—a so-called theory of mind."

Each of these modules represents an adaptation that has evolved to solve a specific problem facing our ancestors, such as avoiding predators, forming friendships and alliances, selecting mates, and communicating with others. Failure to solve these problems satisfactorily would have lessened an individual's chances of surviving and passing on his or her genes to future generations. Modules are psychological structures or information-processing mechanisms that operate according to specific rules in certain domains, and only when exposed to quite specific information. For example, a predator-avoidance module would function to detect designated predators and instruct individuals to adopt certain strategies to avoid or escape from them. Or a mate selection module would help males and females to maximize their chances of finding a suitable mate and producing offspring that survived. Adaptations are not easily identified, and evolutionary psychologists use a number of methodological rules to help them to do so in a reliable and valid way (Tooby & Cosmides, 1992). These include demonstrating (a) that the trait in question has design features that appear to solve an adaptive problem, (b) that these features are unlikely to have arisen by chance alone, and (c) that they are plausibly the product of a module, rather than being the by-product of another module designed to solve a different adaptive problem. In addition, the module or mechanism in question should develop reliably and efficiently in all human beings unless linked to a subgroup, for example, gender-related adaptations. Thus, according to evolutionary psychologists, it is these modules or information processing mechanisms that are selected for, rather than specific behaviors. It is also important to note that these inherited mechanisms are not necessarily operating at birth. In fact, they may come "on line" at different developmental stages. So for example, mate selection modules only really start to exert a profound influence during adolescence. In addition, modules are only activated once the relevant environmental conditions obtain and specific information is available as input to the mechanism. The nature of these inputs may also channel individuals down one of several possible developmental pathways by virtue of their effect on the relevant mechanism. For example, the absence of a father during childhood may result in a male adopting short-term mating strategies and not investing in a permanent relationship (Malamuth & Heilman, 1998). Or, being exposed to different levels of "mind talk" may cause individuals to develop different theories of mind (Ward, Keenan, & Hudson, 2000). In a sense, environmental events serve to activate a mechanism and to calibrate it, thereby setting its threshold of activation and the particular form it takes.

As stated above, not all human capacities are the result of adaptations (Buss, 1999). Some traits have been selected for their capacity to solve problems faced by our ancestors, thereby increasing their chances of reproductive success and survival, but others are probably by-products of selected mechanisms or simply represent "noise" or random effects created by mutations or environmental changes. For example, though the ability to develop and speak a language may be an adaptation, our capacity to write is likely to be a by-product of the mechanisms generating speech. An example of a physical characteristic produced by noise is the particular shape of a person's belly button (Buss, 1999).

There are two major forms of evolutionary explanations of human traits, ultimate and proximate. Ultimate explanations attempt to identify the function of a given trait or mechanism by determining its role in solving a particular adaptive problem, whereas a proximate explanation focuses on the nature of the causal mechanisms that underpin its functional role (Buss, 1999). An important strength of evolutionary psychology is that it explains behavior in terms of both *ultimate* and *proximate causes*. In the language of EP, *ultimate* means all the evolutionary factors that contribute to the development of a psychological mechanism or pattern of behavior. By contrast, *proximate* refers to the more recent factors involved. Thus ultimate causes will include such things as the ancestral environment, sexual selection, and natural selection. Proximate causes will include such variables as the person's genes, his or her developmental history, learning, and environmental stimuli. Symons (1979) comments that ultimate causes explain *why* an animal exhibits a specific behavior pattern—in ancestral environments that behavior pattern promoted the reproductive success of the individuals displaying it. Proximate causes, says Symons, explain *how* animals eventually develop and display specific behavior patterns. Thus given a certain genetic endowment, the right developmental circumstances, and appropriate contingencies of reinforcement, the pattern of behavior will emerge. Moreover, any comprehensive explanation of a pattern of behavior should invoke both ultimate and proximate causes and suggest how proximate causes might activate the relevant mental mechanisms involved. Consequently, evolutionary psychologists argue that only evolutionary psychology, through its consideration of both ultimate and proximate causes, can provide a comprehensive explanation of patterns of human behavior, including rape.

An EP Perspective on Human Mating Strategies

A common theme in all of the evolutionary theories of rape that is considered below is the notion that males and females have evolved different mating strategies. This argument rests upon the observation that sexual reproduction has very different biological consequences for men and women. A male can pass on 50% of his genes to the next generation simply through a few minutes of pleasurable physical exertion. Moreover, given an unlimited supply of willing partners it is theoretically possible for one male to impregnate several thousand women in his lifetime. By contrast, a woman who conceives has to bear the child in utero for 9 months and also survive the hazards of childbirth. Assuming she chooses to raise the child, she is then committed to several years of time-consuming and energy-intensive parenthood. Gaulin and McBurney (2000) note in this regard that for most of human evolution children were probably breastfed for the first 4 or 5 years of life. In addition, unlike her male counterpart, a woman's fertility ends at menopause. Consequently, it is physically impossible for even the most fertile and sexually active of women to produce more than a few dozen offspring in a lifetime. Thus evolutionary theory suggests that men and women must have evolved quite different strategies for choosing the best mate with whom to copulate.

For a woman living in the uncertain and often dangerous environment that characterized most of our evolutionary past, choosing a good mate was a decision of enormous consequence. She needed a mate who was both fertile and free of disease and parasites. She also needed a mate who was reliable, one who would stick around and help with the rearing of any children, in particular the gathering of food.[4] Consequently, the defining characteristic of female mating strategies is "choosiness." Women are thought to prefer men who have high status or are rich in resources. By contrast, men are seen as having evolved a much less discriminating and competitive mating strategy, one in which youth and beauty are seen as prime attributes in a prospective mate because these are indicators of (reproductive) fitness. These are general strategies, however, not absolutes. There will certainly be considerable variation among males and females in how discriminating individuals are. They are also conditional strategies that will vary depending upon the context. For example, in times of food shortage a male might invest a great deal of time and energy in ensuring the survival of a small number of children, thus ensuring that some of his genes survive and can replicate. Or a younger female with an older mate of declining health and virility may choose to copulate with a younger male to increase her chances of conceiving.

Moreover, most of human evolution was probably characterized not by monogamy and state-sanctioned marriage—but rather by what Miller (2001) calls "serial monogamy." It is difficult to say exactly what social structures and mating patterns would have been like in prehistoric times. Our best guesses are based upon observations of other primates' social behavior, existing hunter-gatherer societies, and the limited paleontological and archaeological evidence available. Miller suggests that early humans probably became sexually active soon after puberty and went through a series of monogamous relationships that lasted anywhere from a few days to several years. He suggests that relationships that lasted more than a few years will have been the ones that resulted in children. A few high-status males in each group probably enjoyed several mates at any one time, and the sorts of sexual jealousy and brief affairs that are the stuff of contemporary television soap operas were probably common.

Against this background we can begin to see how evolutionary psychology might have relevance for explaining why rape is so commonplace in contemporary society. It is a sine qua non of evolutionary psychology that the psychology of human mating is best understood in terms of the different strategies that evolved for males and females over millions of years in the ancestral environment. Moreover, although cultural evolution has occurred very rapidly in the past few centuries, biological evolution by comparison is very slow and incremental. This means that our modern minds function, in terms of sex and relationships, in much the same way as did the mind of any one of our ancestors who lived a million years ago. As Cosmides and Tooby (2000) put it, "Our modern skulls house stone age minds" (p. 13). Indeed, much of the empirical work of evolutionary psychologists has been directed toward confirming the existence of such "Stone Age" mating strategies in the behavior of modern-day men and women. To this end evolutionary psychologists have collected a wealth of data demonstrating that men prefer mates who are younger than they are (e.g., Buss, 1989, 1994), physically attractive (Buss, 1989, 1999), and sexually faithful (Buss, 1994, 1999). Similarly, studies support the notion that women prefer mates who have resources, power, and status (Buss, 1999; Ellis, 1992). Buss (1999) also notes that both sexes express a preference for partners who are "intelligent, kind, understanding and healthy" (p. 134).

Evolutionary Psychology and Theories of Rape

ELLIS'S (1989) SYNTHESIZED THEORY

Ellis (1989) reviewed three of the major contemporary approaches to explaining rape that he called the feminist theory, the social-learning theory, and the evolutionary theory, and then proposed his own "synthesized theory." Ellis claimed that each of the three theories had its advantages in terms of explaining some of the data on rape, with none of them clearly superior overall. He then proposed a synthesis of all three theories with the addition of some of his own ideas concerning the role of sex hormones in influencing brain function. The resulting synthesized theory can be summarized in terms of Ellis's four propositions plus his additional notion of a "forced copulation threshold."

Ellis's first proposition states that rape is motivated by two innate and powerful drives, one the sex drive, the other a drive to exert power and control over others. This second drive, the "drive to possess and control," is said to be mostly unlearned and "as compelling for most animals as the sex and hunger drives, and may even be more difficult to satiate" (Ellis, 1989, p. 57). The second proposition underpinning the synthesized theory is that the actual behaviors involved in the act of rape, what Ellis refers to as "raping techniques" (p. 65), are learned experientially through operant conditioning. Ellis suggests that this process begins with "ideational learning," which can occur through exposure to "depictions, attitudes and beliefs favorable to rape" (p. 65). For example, he suggests that exposure to pornography may encourage such beliefs and attitudes through its portrayal of sexual scenarios where attractive women typically consent to have sex with total strangers, which quickly proceeds to intercourse with little or no foreplay. However, such ideational learning is of relatively minor importance in the synthesized theory. Of primary importance is experiential learning that Ellis believes comes about only through a man attempting rape (or some sexually coercive behavior) and then being reinforced by the satisfaction of either or both of the two motivating drives—the sexual drive and/or the drive to dominate and control other people. On this point Ellis is clear that "most rapes, are largely tactical (or instrumental) manifestations of the drive to possess and control sexual property" (Ellis, 1989, p. 66).

Ellis's third proposition is that natural selection has resulted in men having a stronger sex drive than women and a preference for multiple sex partners. It also asserts that women have been favored by natural selection to resist sex with partners who have not demonstrated commitment. The fourth proposition in Ellis's theory concerns the role of androgens upon the developing brain and the possible effect this may have upon two brain structures—the hypothalamic limbic system and the reticular activating system. Ellis argues that exposure to high levels of androgens (particularly testosterone) during critical periods influences the development of these two systems in the brain such that the individual concerned is more likely to rape in adolescence or adulthood. The hypothalamic limbic system so affected "will be permanently organized to display hypersexuality and extreme possessiveness toward multiple sexual partners" (Ellis, 1989, p. 76) and the reticular activating system is effectively desensitized to the aversive consequences of an individual's actions (such as the pain and distress of a rape victim or societal disapproval).

The final element essential to an understanding of Ellis's theory, although not one of his four fundamental propositions, is his notion of a "forced copulation threshold" (p. 81). This is an attempt to explain why some but not all males commit rape. Ellis presents the forced copulation threshold in the form of a graph showing the supposed distribution of the two brain functioning patterns arising from the neurohormonal factors highlighted in his fourth proposition. Individuals who were exposed to high levels of androgens at critical developmental periods will demonstrate changes in both the hypothalamic limbic system and the reticular activating system such that they are highly likely to commit rape given the opportunity. As Ellis notes, "on average, the brains of rapists must function differently than the brains of non rapists, at least in the proximity of the opposite sex" (p. 88).

Comments on Ellis's (1989) Synthesized Theory

Ellis presents the synthesized theory in a detailed and scholarly monograph of around a hundred pages that it is difficult to do full justice to given the broad scope, but limited space, of the present chapter. Moreover, certain aspects of his thesis are highly controversial, such as his hypothesis that "rape will be more prevalent in some racial groups than in others" (Ellis, 1989, p. 92). Such controversial speculation can be seriously considered only in an article devoted to that question. Consequently, our present observations on the strengths and weaknesses of Ellis's model are necessarily limited.

Undoubtedly, a major strength of Ellis's theory is its pioneering attempt to integrate data and theory from sociological, social-learning, and biological perspectives. The subject of rape and its causes is highly controversial, and it is frequently characterized by fierce and emotive debate among academics. This heated atmosphere has tended to mean that scholars of different persuasions operate largely within their own school of thought, where their own assumptions and conclusions are rarely challenged. Such a situation is hardly conducive to rigorous scholarship, and it does not foster the development of complex, multidisciplinary approaches to theory building. However, a phenomenon such as rape is probably not going to be explained by a simple, one-dimensional theory. In this context, Ellis's theory has made a major contribution.

At the same time, the synthesized theory seems somewhat arbitrary in deciding which variables are the important ones to include in an etiological account of rape, and which variables can be ignored. For example, the social-learning component of the theory rests chiefly upon the idea that acts of sexual aggression are reinforced by satisfying two "innate drives" (one sexual and the other to exert power and to control other people). Most contemporary psychological explanations of rape have viewed "social learning" in much broader and more sophisticated terms. For example, Marshall and Serran (2000, p. 87) suggest the following factors may be important in the learning history of a man who rapes: insecure childhood attachments, self-confidence and social skill deficits, negative attitudes toward women and anxiety concerning adult relationships, deviant masturbatory fantasies, and media images that denigrate women and glorify male power. In all fairness, this may reflect the rapid developments in both theory and empirical work on sexual offending since Ellis published his monograph in 1989. Nonetheless, to our knowledge, Ellis has not since then proposed a more sophisticated or complex account of what "social learning" might involve in the development of a man who rapes.

A further problem with the synthesized theory, in our view, is the tenuous nature of the physiological component, which is such a major feature of this approach. Certainly there are anatomical differences between the male and the female brain, and there is growing evidence for the influence of androgens upon the developing brain in utero during so-called critical periods. However, to argue that exposure to high levels of testosterone in utero influences brain development such that the individual is more likely to rape later on in adult life seems to us at best unproven, and at worst wildly speculative. Certainly, in consulting two popular undergraduate texts on brain and behavior we found no mention of such a notion (Banich, 1997; Pinel, 1997). This aspect of the synthesized theory demands further empirical support.

An additional problem with this theory is that the notion of a copulation threshold is essentially question begging and is itself in need of explanation.

A critical question is why would those individuals with a higher threshold be more likely to rape than individuals with a lower one? The real problem is that the nature of the mechanisms associated with the "forced copulation threshold" is somewhat mysterious and its relationship to the four postulates a bit unclear.

There are other aspects of Ellis's theory that also cry out for a stronger empirical basis (although we cannot deal with them all fully here). For example, the existence of a powerful, innate drive to exert power and control over other people might come as news to many psychologists. The notion of such powerful innate drives as causal mechanisms of behavior and their scientific and explanatory value has been a contentious one since the days of Freud.

In summary, Ellis's synthesized theory represents the first serious attempt at integrating evolutionary ideas with theory and data from biological, sociological, and social-learning approaches to understanding and explaining rape. As such it is commendable in its attempt to integrate and synthesize data and concepts from a diverse range of disciplines. At the same time it seems to draw upon a very narrow range of ideas from the social-learning arena while placing undue emphasis upon a number of biological variables that seem hypothetical at best.

MALAMUTH'S (1998) EVOLUTIONARY-BASED MODEL

Malamuth (1998) has recently proposed an "evolutionary-based model integrating research on the characteristics of sexually coercive men" (p. 151) known as the confluence model. Malamuth argues that sexually coercive behavior is best understood "within the larger context of reproductive strategies" and the "varied tactics used to implement such strategies" (p. 159). According to this theory, the actual psychological mechanisms involved are calibrated by a combination of genetic and environmental factors. Malamuth is primarily concerned with the environmental factors and suggests that three are of primary importance. It is the confluence of these three factors within the one individual that is believed to put him at a high risk of perpetrating rape.

The three factors, or in Malamuth's words, "constellations of characteristics," that combine in the development of sexually coercive behaviors include: (a) a dominance versus nurturance personality dimension—males whose personalities demonstrate a strong need to dominate and control other people combined with minimal need (or ability) to nurture others, are considered to be more likely to be sexually coercive; (b) the second constellation of characteristics is derived directly from the literature on evolved mating strategies and is a short-term mating strategy, whereby the man develops a preference for many sexual partners and brief, uncommitted, and impersonal sexual encounters.

Malamuth calls this dimension "impersonal vs. personal sexuality" (p. 161); (c) the third constellation of characteristics includes a range of negative and hostile beliefs and attitudes regarding men, women, relationships, and the acceptability of violence to achieve goals. Malamuth calls this constellation "hostile masculinity." An important feature of the confluence model is that an individual's early environment is hypothesized to be of primary importance during development in the calibration of those psychological mechanisms that determine adult mating strategies. This is summarized concisely in the following passage: "early experiences may 'lock' a person into one reproductive strategy to the exclusion of others ... it is suggested that in harsh early environments in which exploitation occurs frequently, mechanisms may be calibrated in line with divergent strategies, including a general self-centered personality, a short-term mating strategy, and hostile masculinity" (Malamuth, 1998, p. 162). The model allows for a number of permutations by which different environmental antecedents can act together in the calibration of the various mechanisms that combine to produce different male mating tactics (i.e., manipulative, sexually coercive, or cooperative).

Comments on Malamuth's (1998) Evolutionary-Based Model

There are a number of very positive features to Malamuth's model, but arguably the strongest is his serious attempt to combine ultimate and proximate explanations of behavior into a well-integrated and plausible theoretical structure. The theory is, as Malamuth states, firmly based in evolutionary theory, and in particular the literature on human mating strategies. In this regard it places rape back in the domain of sex, courtship, and heterosexual relationships in general. Malamuth (1998) comments that "the use of sexually coercive tactics can be understood within the larger context of reproductive strategies and varied tactics used to implement these tactics" (p. 159). As Quinsey and Lalumiere (1995) noted, "One of the most puzzling aspects of the literature on sexual offending is that, although it deals with reproductive behavior, it is almost completely divorced from the literature on reproduction" (p. 301). Thus Malamuth's approach attempts to include ultimate explanations for rape—that is, to explain *why* rape exists in the first place. In so doing it provides an important balance for those influential feminist theorists who have argued that rape is exclusively about power and not about sex (e.g., Brownmiller, 1975). Moreover, it allows for differences in male and female mating strategies and for individual differences thereof.

At the same time, much of the value of Malamuth's model stems from its careful attempts to specify the proximate mechanisms that act in the lifetime of an individual to determine which men are most likely to commit rape and which men are likely to form equal, cooperative, longer-term relationships.

Although acknowledging the evolutionary basis of human mating patterns, the model therefore places great weight upon environmental and developmental variables. A critic might indeed wonder whether the evolutionary basis for this model is required at all. For example, Malamuth's concept of hostile masculinity could fit quite neatly into most sociocultural or social-learning accounts of rape. There is arguably little heuristic value to be added here by considering life on the African savanna two million years ago. In reply it could be argued that such a criticism misses the point, for it is the concept of mating strategies that unites all the disparate strands of the confluence model. Moreover, the evolutionary basis of this model has considerable heuristic value, and Malamuth presents a number of testable hypotheses that arise from the model.

A final point concerns Malamuth's failure to refer to, and build upon, the work of the other rape theorists. The failure to take into account competing theories has a number of unfortunate consequences. First, it is inefficient and wasteful. Interesting ideas are often not developed to their full extent, and other theorists may, inadvertently, duplicate them. Second, it results in a fragmented and uncoordinated theoretical landscape. Third, theorists and empirical researchers are frequently unaware of where the explanatory gaps exist and may ignore fruitful avenues of inquiry.

For example, Marshall and Barbaree's (1990) integrated theory of sexual offending is a dynamic model and portrays sexual abuse as the outcome of multiple, interacting, factors. These include biological, psychological, social, cultural, and situational factors. The explicit focus on resilience and psychological vulnerability constitutes a real advance on its competitors and clarifies how developmental adversity contributes to sexual offending. Marshall and Barbaree have explained the relationship among attachment style, intimacy deficits, and cognitive distortions in some depth and as such could clarify the nature of the mechanisms generating hostile masculinity and its associated variables. Basically, Malamuth's work needs fleshing out and would benefit from engaging with some of the promising social learning theories currently in the literature.

THORNHILL AND PALMER'S EVOLUTIONARY THEORY OF RAPE

Thornhill and Palmer appear to accept the basic assumptions of evolutionary psychology outlined earlier, for example, a view of the mind as radically modular. They emphasize the biological nature of the mind and are extremely critical of social science explanations of rape, which they believe depend on erroneous assumptions about the mind's architecture and functioning. Thornhill and Palmer argue for an evolutionary theory of rape on the grounds that human beings are essentially animals and part of the natural world. They are therefore dismissive of rape theories that emphasize the role of culture and learning in the acquisition of rape-prone traits, arguing that culture is possible only because individuals have evolved capacities that enable them to learn.

Thornhill and Palmer (2000) view rape as a consequence of the mating strategies that evolution must have favored among men and women. Finding a mate was an intensely competitive process with high-quality males likely to dominate the sexual arena and secure exclusive sexual access to females. Therefore, males with the highest status and the most resources were more likely to obtain sexual access to females, thereby increasing the chances that their genes would be passed on and their offspring survive. Males evolved to prefer females who were fertile and therefore more likely to conceive. Because fertility is not directly observable, they developed preferences for females with features associated with reproductive success, for example, a youthful appearance. In addition, Thornhill and Palmer argue that males would have most likely evolved to possess intense sexual desires that increased their motivation for sexual experiences and activities. The tendency to seek multiple sexual partners was also facilitated by the fact that because fertilization in females occurs internally, males could never be certain of their paternity. By attempting to have sex with as many women as possible males thereby increased their chances of reproductive success.

Thornhill and Palmer assert that rape is either an adaptation *directly* selected for because it resulted in a reproductive advantage for males or it is the *by-product* of other psychological adaptations that were selected for because of their ability to solve adaptive problems. An example of such a mechanism is males' relatively strong interest in low commitment sex. The two authors disagree concerning which of these two ultimate explanations of rape is likely to be true but agree that rape should be viewed as a *sexual* crime rather than occurring as a consequence of nonsexual motives such as needs for power and control.

Thornhill and Palmer also assert that rape is likely to be a conditional strategy employed only when circumstances are judged to be favorable. They suggest that from this perspective rape represents one of three condition-dependent strategies, along with honest courtship and deceptive courtship. An individual is hypothesized to use rape to secure sexual access to a female only if he believes that the advantages outweigh any disadvantages relative to the other possible strategies. Therefore, rape as an adaptation will not occur under every possible circumstance; rather only when the circumstances are considered to favor it as a sexual strategy. Several factors are hypothesized to increase the chances of males utilizing rape under conducive conditions, including a lack of physical and psychological resources, social alienation, limited sexual access to females, and unsatisfying romantic relationships. Thornhill and

Palmer argue that such circumstances may function as developmental switches that shift males into relying primarily on a rape strategy. Therefore, the combination of inheriting a propensity to engage in sexual aggression, in conjunction with specific environmental conditions, may result in the development (proximate mechanisms) of rape supportive attitudes and strategies.

If this argument is to be supported, it is necessary to establish that any suggested mechanisms are designed for rape and therefore solve an adaptation problem, and develop reliably, efficiently, and economically (Tooby & Cosmides, 1992). Thornhill and Palmer review a number of possible proximate mechanisms that could conceivably represent adaptations to rape in human males. These include psychological mechanisms that help males detect potential rape victims; motivate men who lack resources and/or sexual access to rape females; cause males to sexually prefer victims who exhibit certain characteristics such as a younger age; and patterns of sexual arousal that facilitate rape such as sexual arousal to violence. They conclude after examining the relevant evidence that none of these candidates are unequivocally supported and that the research data could either be equally well explained by other mechanisms (by-products) or is of insufficient quality to warrant any substantive conclusions. For example, the fact that high-status men sometimes rape females suggests that vulnerability evaluations may be due to a cost-benefit–evaluation mechanism that is not specific to rape. Therefore, they concede that at this point there is little evidence to support the strongest form of the evolutionary theory of rape. However, they still view it as a promising theoretical possibility.

Thornhill and Palmer next consider the hypothesis that rape may occur as a by-product of adaptations that evolved to establish sexual access to a consenting partner. They consider only Symons's (1979) suggestion that the primary adaptations causing rape are males' greater sexual drive and their predilection to engage in impersonal sex (i.e., be less sexually discriminating). This is nicely captured by the following quote: "the typical male is at least slightly sexually attracted to most females, whereas the typical female is not sexually attracted to most males" (Symons, 1979, p. 267). According to Symons, rape is a side effect of the adaptations producing this situation, but is not an adaptation itself because none of the evolved mechanisms involved were specifically selected for rape. Thornhill and Palmer assert that although rape may be a by-product of other adaptations, only adaptations associated with sexual behavior are likely to be involved.

Comments on Thornhill and Palmer's Evolutionary Theory of Rape

We make just two critical points here regarding Thornhill and Palmer's theory and refer the reader to Ward and Siegert (in press) for an extensive consideration of their theory. The first point relates to the explanatory scope of the theory. In our view, Thornhill and Palmer do not develop a systematic theory of rape. There is no attempt to specify systematically a set of mechanisms that reliably generate rape and its associated phenomena. Although the idea that rape is an adaptation is considered, all the possible candidates are rejected or judgment concerning their possible validity deferred. The second possibility, that rape is a by-product of adaptations relating to male sexuality, is also not systematically explored or a theory explicitly constructed. Thornhill and Palmer simply present a case for the plausibility of an evolutionary explanation of rape. Their style of argument is tentative and general. A *theory* of rape needs to specify the nature of the causal mechanisms in more detail and demonstrate how biological, psychological, social/cultural, and contextual factors interact to result in sexual aggression.

Our second point concerns the extent to which Thornhill and Palmer devote extensive sections of their book to attacking the "standard social science model" (SSSM) of rape. This is a theme throughout their book and forms the subject of an entire chapter. The assumption here seems to be that if this model is proven inadequate, then somehow this substantiates their own theory. This is a "straw man" argument at best. In fact, the SSSM they critique so fiercely borders upon a caricature—and reflects just one influential dimension of modern theories of rape (i.e., the feminist/political approach, which argues that rape is about power not sex). They largely ignore any other "social science" accounts of rape, particularly those models that include a broad range of causal variables or allow for biological influences (e.g., Marshall & Barbaree, 1990).

General Discussion

In the present chapter we have considered some of the specific advantages and disadvantages of three of the leading evolutionary theories of rape. In this section we intend to provide a summary of these, to address the issue of "reductionism," and to make some suggestions as to how work in this field might best advance.

Perhaps the major strength of a theory of rape that is evolutionary based, or one that allows for the relevance of evolutionary theory, is its unifying power and heuristic potential. An evolutionary theory of rape is naturalistic, it assumes that we are biological beings, that we are evolved animals. Consequently, it demands that a sound theory of rape is both a scientific one and one that is consistent with the rest of human biology. In this regard it provides a timely counterbalance to some of the excesses of social constructionist approaches that have denied the relevance of biology for the topic. It also provides a framework within which theoretical ideas and empirical work can develop.

One value of this evolutionary framework is its heuristic value for generating new hypotheses that can then be tested empirically. At the same time it also provides practical constraints upon such theory building, as any hypotheses must be consistent with the known facts and principles of human evolution. To take just one example, Thornhill and Palmer (2000) have suggested that Freud's concept of the Oedipus complex might not have been so influential in clinical psychology if some fundamental evolutionary principles had been considered. Put simply, how long would we have survived as a species if all human males had developed this deep, unconscious urge to have sexual intercourse with their mother? In summary, evolutionary theory can offer theorists of rape a valuable heuristic framework that is naturalistic and allows the study of rape to be more integrated with the study of sex, mating, and human relationships.

A central issue in this regard is the repeated criticism that an evolutionary theory of rape is "reductionist" (Rose, 1998; Rose & Rose, 2000). According to such critics, evolutionary psychology explains the rich tapestry of human behavior in terms of a collection of modular mental mechanisms that arose as adaptations during our hunter-gatherer past, are genetically hardwired, and act automatically and largely outside conscious awareness. How fair are such accusations?

Where the accusations of reductionism ring true, in our opinion, is in the tendency of some evolutionary psychologists to pay lip service to the important role of proximate mechanisms without ever really specifying their form or how they relate to ultimate causes. In order to explain rape scientifically it is necessary to construct a theory that specifies the nature of the causal mechanisms generating the relevant phenomena and to ensure the concepts used in this process are consistent and coherently related (Hooker, 1987). A comprehensive explanation of any human phenomenon is likely to be multifactorial in nature and involve a variety of different causal mechanisms. These may include factors associated with our early evolutionary history as well as cultural, developmental, physiological, and psychological causal mechanisms. Adversarial attitudes to women, poor conflict resolution skills, lack of intimacy skills, insecure attachment, mood regulation deficits, and deviant sexual fantasies are all examples of causal mechanisms that have been linked to rape (Polaschek, Ward, & Hudson, 1997). The mechanisms (proximate) in each of these distinct domains exert their own causal influence and should not be ignored or minimized. Of the three theories we have reviewed only Malamuth's clearly and explicitly identifies the proximate mechanisms by which rape is believed to occur. Consequently, we view the major issue for the development and refinement of an evolutionary approach to rape to be the need for a closer integration with the existing theoretical and empirical work on proximate mechanisms. This is neatly exemplified by a discussion we had recently with a clinical colleague who works most days in a treatment program for sex offenders. During our discussion of the present chapter with this colleague he responded along the following lines: "But even if I accept all this evolutionary stuff, it has no real relevance for my work with offenders—we can only ever deal with proximate mechanisms in therapy." We found it difficult to argue with such a pragmatic approach. However, when evolutionary theories of rape have achieved a better integration of ultimate and proximate mechanisms of rape, we believe that we will have found the answer to our colleague's dismissal of evolutionary theories of rape.

Conclusions

The EP perspectives outlined above have attempted to explain rape by appealing to evolutionary theory and hypothesize that rape is either directly or indirectly associated with inherited traits that increased our ancestors' reproductive success. We do not believe that any of the above theorists have established that evolutionary theories of rape are better theories than social science explanations. At best their arguments present a powerful case for the important, but not exclusive, role of biological factors in the etiology of rape and gender relationships. Evolved psychological mechanisms may predispose males to behave in sexually inappropriate ways, but they may represent only constraining influences.

   At this point in time there are too many unanswered questions concerning the nature of the relevant adaptations and the contribution of sociological and cultural theories to conclude that evolutionary theories are sufficient to explain sexual aggression. We suggest that an explanation of human actions cannot be reduced to purely biological causes, although such factors may shape individuals' capacities and constrain their choices and actions. Because human beings are naturally social animals, any kind of flourishing or meaningful life can be achieved only in a social context. In other words, individuals are mutually interdependent and can achieve personal goods only if others provide them with the necessary social, physical, and psychological nourishment. Crimes such as rape may well be the result of a failure to provide such support and/or the entrenchment of inappropriate norms, beliefs, and attitudes. In other words, any explanation of rape will necessarily be a combination of biological and cultural factors: We are just that kind of animal.

Notes

1. Caporael (2001) notes that evolutionary theory has influenced many areas of psychology at several different levels of analysis. She argues that there is not one, but rather several different "evolutionary psychologies." However, it is the approach represented by the works of Buss (1999), Thornhill and Palmer (2000), and Tooby and Cosmides (1992) to which we refer in the present article—because it is this line of work that has been influential in evolutionary-based theories of sexual offending. At the same time we readily acknowledge the important contributions of the other "evolutionary psychologies" as exemplified in the works of Corballis (1991), Deacon (1997), Jerison (1973), Tomasello (1997), and numerous other scholars.

2. For a concise and readable introduction to the topic of "Evolutionary Perspectives on Sexual Offending" we recommend Quinsey and Lalumiere's (1995) article of that title.

3. Readers may also wish to consult the recent paper by Figueredo, Sales, Russell, Becker, and Kaplan (2000), which offers an evolutionary theory of adolescent sex offending.

4. Trivers (1972) coined the term "*parental investment*" to describe the amount of effort (in energy, time, etc.) that an adult is willing to invest in the raising of a child. Although male parental investment is somewhat greater among humans than in many other species, it is nonetheless always much greater for female humans than for males.

References

Banich, M. T. (1997). *Neuropsychology: The neural bases of mental function*. Boston, MA: Houghton Mifflin.

Barkow, J. H., Cosmides, L., & Tooby, J. (Eds.). (1992). *The adapted mind: Evolutionary psychology and the generation of culture*. New York: Oxford University Press.

Brownmiller, S. (1975). *Against our will: Men, women and rape*. Harmondsworth, Middlesex, England: Penguin.

Buss, D. M. (1989). Sex differences in human mate preferences. *Behavioral and Brain Sciences, 12,* 1-49.

Buss, D. M. (1994). *The evolution of desire: Strategies of human mating*. New York: Basic Books.

Buss, D. M. (1999). *Evolutionary psychology: The new science of the mind*. Boston: Allyn & Bacon.

Buss, D. M., & Schmidt, D. P. (1993). Sexual strategies theory: An evolutionary perspective on human mating. *Psychological Review, 100,* 204-232.

Caporael, L. R. (2001). Evolutionary psychology: Toward a unifying theory and a hybrid science. *Annual Review of Psychology, 52,* 607-628.

Corballis, M. C. (1991). *The lopsided ape*. Oxford, UK: Oxford University Press.

Cosmides, L., & Tooby, J. (2000). Evolutionary psychology: A primer. Retrieved June 14, 2002, from University of California, Santa Barbara, Center for Evolutionary Psychology Web site: http://cogweb.english.ucsb.edu/EP/EP-primer.html

Daly, M., & Wilson, M. (1985). Child abuse and other risks of not living with both parents. *Ethology and Sociobiology, 6,* 197-210.

Daly, M., & Wilson, M. (1988). Evolutionary psychology and family homicide. *Science, 242,* 519-524.

Darwin, C. (1998). *The origin of species*. Hertfordshire: Wordsworth Editions Ltd. (Original work published 1859)

Deacon, T. (1997). *The symbolic species: The co-evolution of language and the human brain*. London: Penguin.

Ellis, B. J. (1992). The evolution of sexual attraction: Evaluative mechanisms in women. In J. H. Barkow, L. Cosmides, & J. Tooby (Eds.), *The adapted mind: Evolutionary psychology and the generation of culture* (pp. 267-288). New York: Oxford University Press.

Ellis, L. (1989). *Theories of rape: Inquiries into the causes of sexual aggression.* New York: Hemisphere.

Figueredo, A. J., Sales, B. D., Russell, K. P., Becker, J. V., & Kaplan, M. (2000). A Brunswikian evolutionary-developmental theory of adolescent sexual offending. *Behavioral Sciences and the Law, 18,* 309-329.

Fischman, J. (2000, February 7). A fight over the evolution of rape. *U.S. News and World Report, 128,* p. 48.

Fodor, J. A. (1983). *The modularity of mind.* Cambridge: MIT Press.

Gaulin, S. J. C., & McBurney, D. (2000). *Psychology: An evolutionary approach.* Upper Saddle River, NJ: Prentice Hall.

Goode, E. (2000, March 14). Human nature: Born or made? *The New York Times,* p. F1.

Hirschfeld, L. A., & Gelman, S. A. (Eds.). (1994). *Mapping the mind: Domain specificity in cognition and culture.* Cambridge, UK: Cambridge University Press.

Hooker, C. A. (1987). *A realistic theory of science.* Albany: State University of New York Press.

Jerison, H. J. (1973). *Evolution of the brain and intelligence.* New York: Academic Press.

Malamuth, N. M. (1998). An evolutionary-based model integrating research on the characteristics of sexually coercive men. In J. G. Adair & D. Belanger (Eds.), *Advances in psychological science: Vol.1. Social, personal and cultural aspects* (pp. 151-184). Hove, England: Psychology Press/Erlbaum.

Malamuth, N. M., & Heilman, M. F. (1998). Evolutionary psychology and sexual aggression. In C. B. Crawford & D. L. Krebs (Eds.), *Handbook of evolutionary psychology: Ideas, issues and applications* (pp. 515-542). Mahwah, NJ: Lawrence Erlbaum.

Marshall, W. L., & Barbaree, H. E. (1990). An integrated theory of the etiology of sexual offending. In W. L. Marshall, D. R. Laws, & H. E. Barbaree (Eds.), *Handbook of sexual assault: Issues, theories, and treatment of the offender* (pp. 257-275). New York: Plenum.

Marshall, W. L., & Serran, G. A. (2000). Current issues in the assessment and treatment of sexual offenders. *Clinical Psychology and Psychotherapy, 7,* 85-96.

Miller, G. (2001). *The mating mind.* London: Random House.

Ochert, A. (2000, February 4). *The Times Higher Educational Supplement,* p. 17.

Pinel, J. P. J. (1997). *Biopsychology* (3rd ed.). Boston: Allyn & Bacon.

Pinker, S. (1997). *How the mind works.* New York: Norton.

Pinker, S., & Bloom, P. (1992). Natural language and natural selection. In J. H. Barkow, L. Cosmides, & J. Tooby (Eds.), *The adapted mind: Evolutionary psychology and the generation of culture* (pp. 451-494). New York: Oxford University Press.

Plotkin, H. (1997). *Evolution in mind: An introduction to evolutionary psychology.* London: Penguin.

Polaschek, D., Ward, T., & Hudson, S. M. (1997). Rape and rapists: Theory and treatment. *Clinical Psychology Review, 17,* 117-144.

Quinsey, V. L., & Lalumiere, M. L. (1995). Evolutionary perspectives on sexual offending. *Sexual Abuse: A Journal of Research and Treatment, 7,* 301-315.

Richards, R. J. (1987). *Darwin and the emergence of evolutionary theories of mind and behavior.* Chicago: University of Chicago Press.

Rose, H., & Rose, S. (2000). *Alas poor Darwin: Arguments against evolutionary psychology.* London: Johnathon Cape.

Rose, M. R. (1998). *Darwin's spectre: Evolutionary biology in the modern world.* Princeton, NJ: Princeton University Press.

Siegert, R. J., & Ward, T. (in press). Evolutionary psychology and clinical psychology: Towards a dialogue. *Review of General Psychology.*

Stevens, A., & Price, J. (2000). *Evolutionary psychiatry: A new beginning* (2nd ed.). London: Routledge.

Symons, D. (1979). *The evolution of human sexuality.* New York: Oxford University Press.

Thornhill, R., & Palmer, C. T. (2000). *A natural history of rape: Biological bases of sexual coercion.* Cambridge: MIT Press.

Tomasello, M. (2001). *The cultural origins of human cognition.* Cambridge, MA: Harvard University Press.

Tooby, J., & Cosmides, L. (1992). The psychological foundations of culture. In J. H. Barkow, L. Cosmides, & J. Tooby (Eds.), *The adapted mind: Evolutionary psychology and the generation of culture.* (pp. 19-136). New York: Oxford University Press.

Trivers, R. L. (1972). Parental investment and sexual selection. In B. Campbell (Ed.), *Sexual selection and the descent of man* (pp. 139-179). Chicago: Aldine.

Ward, T., Keenan, T., & Hudson, S. (2000). Understanding cognitive, affective, and intimacy deficits in sexual offenders: A developmental perspective. *Aggression and Violent Behavior, 5,* 41-62.

Ward, T., & Siegert, R. J. (in press). Rape and evolutionary psychology: A critique of Thornhill and Palmer's theory. *Aggression and Violent Behavior.*

4

Behavioral Economic Approaches to the Assessment and Treatment of Sexual Deviation

D. Richard Laws

The goal of this chapter is to present some limited general theoretical assumptions that place human sexual behavior, in the present case, deviant sexual behavior, within an economic context. There is no attempt here to provide a comprehensive account but rather to present some of the central concepts of behavioral economics as they might apply to human sexual behavior. Behavioral economics is a vast literature that has been primarily focused upon animal behavior. Only in recent years has there been a focus upon human behavior. This research has centered on addictive behaviors. Although many behavioral economic concepts are clearly applicable, there has been no attempt to apply them to human sexual behavior. I am aware of only a single publication in this area (O'Donohue, Penix, & Oksol, 2000). Historically as well as contemporaneously, human sexual behavior and its deviant variations have been viewed from a variety of perspectives, many of which are in conflict with one another. What behavioral economics offers us is a unifying perspective, a set of operations that apply in any situation and that do not require selecting explanations from many theoretical orientations to account for its effects. What follows, then, is offered as a context for discussion and research, a different way of viewing the troublesome phenomena we call deviant sexual behavior.

What Is Behavioral Economics?

Our approach to the understanding and treatment of sexual deviation, whether by dynamic psychotherapy or, currently, the more popular cognitive-behavior therapy called relapse prevention (Laws, Hudson, & Ward, 2000), relies upon internal mediational constructs (e.g., self-efficacy, cognitive deconstructionism, abstinence violation effect) to account for behavioral change. Marlatt, Tucker, Donovan, and Vuchinich (1997), in their work on substance abuse, have noted that "contextual environmental forces outside the psychotherapy situation have powerful effects on addictive behavior . . . and it is difficult to characterize these contextual variables by incorporating them into internal mediational constructs" (p. 69). Because of this problem, which is equally applicable to the treatment of sex offenders, Marlatt et al. (1997) suggest that behavioral economics offers a new conceptual avenue for understanding the effects of therapeutic and extratherapeutic variables.

Bickel, Madden, and Petry (1998) define behavioral economics as "the study of the allocation of behavior . . . (i.e., choice) . . . within a system of constraint . . . and examines conditions that influence the consumption of commodities" (p. 546). Scarcity is a fundamental fact of life (O'Donohue et al., 2000), and behavioral economics is fundamentally the study of how people make choices to distribute scarce resources (time, money, work, leisure, sex, socializing, etc.) in order to maximize reinforcing consequences.

The roots of behavioral economics lie in the odd coupling of the experimental analysis of behavior (operant psychology) and demand theory in microeconomics. Two major ancestors of this marriage are the writings of Premack (1959, 1962, 1965) and Herrnstein (1961, 1970). Green and Freed (1998, p. 276) have described the importance of this early theorizing and its relation to behavioral economics. They noted that Premack's (1965) prepotent response or *relativity theory of reinforcement* changed how reinforcement is viewed. Premack dismissed the idea that reinforcers inherently have some positive, negative, or neutral quality. Instead, he said that "of any two responses, the more probable response will reinforce the less probable one" (Premack, 1965, p. 132). This is popularly known as the Premack Principle. The reinforcement relation was reversible. "If the probability of occurrence of two responses can be reversed in order, so can the reinforcement relation between the two responses" (pp. 132-133). So, a stimulus or event that in one situation was a positive reinforcer could become a punisher if the probability of its occurrence changed. Green and Freed (1998, p. 276) also noted that, historically, the main focus had been on how individual reinforcers strengthened individual responses, with no regard for whatever else was going on in the situation. Context was ignored. They state that Herrnstein's (1961, 1970) *matching law* changed that by highlighting the importance of the context within which reinforcement occurred. Green and Freed (1998) state:

> The matching law predicts that a given response is influenced not only by the reinforcers contingent upon it but also by other reinforcers within the situation. Thus ... [an organism] ... is always choosing between reinforcement alternatives, and a given reinforcer's effect depends upon the context of the other reinforcers in the situation. Consequently, the strengthening value of a reinforcer will depend on its value relative to other reinforcers in the current situation. (p. 276)

The importance of these earlier observations to behavioral economics is fairly obvious. Premack (1959, 1965) stated that a behavior of high probability could be used to reinforce a behavior of lower probability by making access to the former contingent upon performance of the latter. This is sometimes referred to as Grandma's Rule ("Eat your spinach and you can go out to play"). Herrnstein (1961, 1970) stated that you cannot ignore the context within which a reinforcing event occurs. Both animals and humans are constantly shifting back and forth between various schedules of reinforcement at varying times in order to maximize reinforcement. The application to behavioral economics is nicely summarized by Green and Freed (1998):

> Economics, after all, is the study of how consumers choose among scarce and different resources (respond under constraint), and explicitly acknowledges that commodities (reinforcers) interact in multiple ways. . . . The value of such concepts is that they provide a broad understanding of reinforcer interactions, thereby extending our ability to predict choice in . . . realistic situations. (p. 277)

Vuchinich (1999) termed the work of Premack (1965) and Herrnstein (1970) "a revolutionary change in studying choice": "Instead of focusing upon individual responses, this work showed that behavioral allocation is critically affected by the more general context of environmental conditions that surround individual responses" (p. 192).

To date, most of the work in behavioral economics has been done with animals, primarily by investigators within operant psychology. Hursh (1980) has provided a rather comprehensive review of the basic findings of this work. It has been only in recent years that these concepts have begun to be applied to human behavior and choice, notably in the field of substance abuse (Bickel et al., 1998; Marlatt et al., 1997; Vuchinich, 1999) and, more recently, deviant sexual behavior (O'Donohue et al., 2000).

Substance abuse could be characterized as a disorder of impulse control (Laws, 1995), and some of its characteristics have been noted to bear striking similarities to deviant sexual behavior. Like substance abusers, sexual deviants also exhibit two of the major behaviors studied by behavioral economics: (a) they spend inordinate amounts of time, effort, and money to obtain access to their preferred sexual reinforcers, often to the exclusion of other potential reinforcers; and (b) they exhibit impulsivity, irrationality, loss of control, and an unwillingness to follow through on pledges to curtail or stop sexual abuse. This chapter examines a behavioral economic approach to these two dimensions of deviant sexual behavior: (a) demand and (b) impulsivity or loss of control.

DEMAND

The basic Law of Demand states that consumption is inversely related to price, that is, as price increases consumption decreases. Behavioral economics has demonstrated that the first problem stated above, obsessive seeking and consumption, can be decreased by (a) increasing constraints on access (price) to the preferred reinforcer (sex), and (b) by making other substitutable reinforcers available. In management of sexual deviation this might refer to adjusting the balance between behavioral constraints (confinement, probation orders, fines) and possible alternative reinforcers (treatment or desired skill training). The latter is far more difficult to effect than the former (Marlatt et al., 1997). The second problem described above, loss of control, is less easy to manage. This could be characterized as a preference for *smaller-sooner* reinforcers (having sex right now) rather than *larger-later* reinforcers (working for a living, being with one's family, living a straight life). This is referred to as temporal discounting of the value of delayed reinforcers. Marlatt et al. (1997) have suggested several ways to overcome this problem in the substance abuse area. Some of these methods could apply equally as well to sexual deviation (see below).

Vuchinich (1999) has said that there are two central issues for an application of behavioral economics to substance abuse, and these would apply equally well to engaging in deviant sexual behavior (p. 193): (a) whether abused substances obey the Law of Demand, and (b) whether the quantitative properties of the demand curve aid in the description and analysis of substance consumption. Vuchinich says that in both animal and human experiments the participants have to emit a specified number of responses in order to receive a specified amount of the substance. Therefore, number of responses = price. In these experiments, he says, using a wide range of potentially abusable substances, the demand curves showed *mixed elasticity*, with demand being *inelastic* (staying the same) at low prices and *elastic* (decreasing) at high prices. This broad generality of effect in demand for drugs, says Vuchinich, is a clear

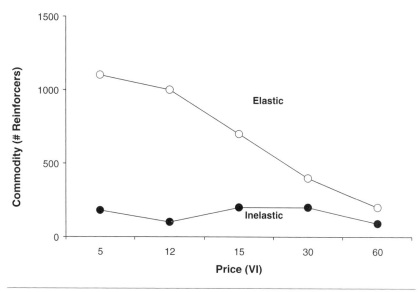

Figure 4.1   Elastic and Inelastic Demand

Demand curves for consumption of two different commodities. Demand is elastic when it changes with increases or decreases in price (variable-interval schedule); demand is inelastic when it shows no change as price changes.

example of what Bickel et al. (1998, p. 181) called a "ubiquitous behavioral process," indicating that "drugs are not a special class of commodities that requires unique concepts for analysis" (Vuchinich, 1999, p. 194). Thus, these researchers reason, behavioral economics has broad explanatory value.

Figures 4.1 and 4.2 are typical examples that illustrate these concepts. Figure 4.1 shows the demand curve of an organism responding for access to two different reinforcers (commodities) across five different variable-interval (VI) schedules of reinforcement (price). In a VI schedule, reinforcement will occur on average around a specified time interval (e.g., in Figure 4.1, 5 sec, 10 sec, 15 sec, etc.). The lower curve (filled circles) shows inelastic demand in that demand for the reinforcer does not change with increases in price. The upper curve (open circles) shows highly elastic demand; as price increases, demand dramatically decreases. Figure 4.2 shows a hypothetical curve of mixed elasticity. Consumption is plotted against increasing values of a fixed-ratio schedule (FR) of reinforcement. An FR schedule requires that a specified number of responses must occur before reinforcement will be available. Here, up to FR-10, demand is inelastic. From that point onward, as the FR increases, demand drops dramatically.

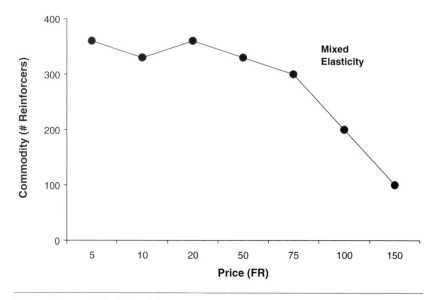

Figure 4.2   Mixed Elasticity

At low values of price (fixed-ratio schedule), demand is inelastic. As price increases, demand becomes elastic.

Demand: Assessment

Let us now apply these principles to the hypothetical study of deviant sexual preference and behavior. In order to demonstrate this, I attempt to mimic the substance abuse research paradigms. Consider first the assessment of sexual interest using a simple approach. Assume that we have an array of 40 slide transparencies of males and females across five age categories (e.g., Laws, Gulayets, & Frenzel, 1995). There are four slides per category. All of the sub-jects are nude. The participant faces a projection screen. In his hand he holds a pushbutton. The slides are randomly distributed in a slide projector tray. The projector lamp is on, the lens is fully retracted and is out of focus. By pressing the pushbutton, the participant can extend the lens and focus the slide, then respond at a much slower rate and keep the slide in focus for as long as he wishes to view it. Thus we have a relatively long fixed-ratio (FR) schedule to bring the slide into focus, chained to a second fixed-ratio schedule (essentially an FR-1), in which a single button press keeps the slide in focus. The slides are randomly distributed so he must complete or nearly complete the initial FR to determine what kind of slide is available for viewing. Let us further assume that this participant has a long history of deviant sexual behavior and little or no

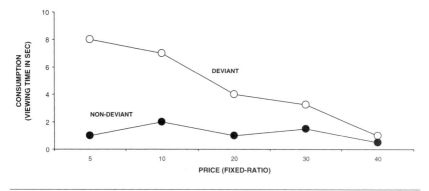

Figure 4.3   Assessment

Client performs a fixed-ratio schedule of increasing value to view deviant and nondeviant sexual images. As price increases, viewing time for deviant images decreases (becomes elastic). Viewing time for nondeviant images does not change (is inelastic).

experience of nondeviant behavior. The empirical question is: How much will this participant pay (how many responses will he make) to view a preferred erotic stimulus?

Figure 4.3 suggests an answer to this question. Imagine that the described assessment procedure was presented to a client with suspected deviant sexual interests. In Figure 4.3 the open circles show the participant's average viewing time in seconds for deviant stimuli, and the filled circles show his viewing time for nondeviant stimuli. Clearly the demand for nondeviant stimulus viewing is inelastic; the participant hardly looks at all. On the other hand, his viewing of deviant stimuli is elastic. At the lowest values of FR-5 and FR-10 he looks longest. From FR-20 through FR-40 his "interest" declines substantially. From an assessment perspective one could conclude the following from this example. As expected, this participant should not show much interest in non-deviant stimuli, and he shows none. More important, we could conclude that he does not actually show very much interest in erotic images. He shows high interest only at low fixed-ratio values; as soon as the price markedly increases, interest falls off. It should also be noted that this is a gross example of deviant and nondeviant interest. In the figure, "deviant" refers to infant, prepubescent, pubescent, and postpubescent males and females, while "nondeviant" refers only to male and female adults. If this were broken down into finer age and gender categories, the elasticity picture might change. It should also be noted that the described procedure is extremely easy to implement, takes very little time, is not personally offensive, and is not physically intrusive. It could be an alternative to penile plethysmography.

DEMAND: TREATMENT

It is possible to apply similar principles to the control of deviant sexual behavior. It was mentioned above that excessive demand (seeking deviant behavior contacts) might be controlled by increasing constraints on access to the behavior (increasing price). Let us say that we wish to control the community behavior of a pedophile with a long history of cruising and making the acquaintance of potential young victims. If cruising and victim seeking obey the Law of Demand, then imposing various sets of conditions should make contact with these behaviors. Figure 4.4 shows some possibilities. If we examine the top panel of Figure 4.4, we see that, if the price (total number of conditions) is excessive, this will have the effect of reducing consumption (deviant behavior seeking) to near zero. It may also have the undesirable effect of demotivating the client to such an extent that nothing else can be done with him. Therefore, a more promising alternative would be the selection of a smaller but more sensitive number of conditions. The center and lower panels of Figure 4.4 show the hypothetical effects of two types of conditions: mild and stringent. Table 4.1 shows a list of these conditions. *Mild* conditions include: no contact with previous victims or families, attend and complete counseling, no-go zones, and so on. These are easy to comply with, easy to evade, easy to fake one's way through. *Stringent* conditions, which are assumed to be enforceable, include: breathalyzers, urinalysis, curfews, no pornography, unannounced residence inspection, and so on. While not perfect, these are much harder conditions to evade. Referring again to Figure 4.4 we can see the hypothetical effects of the imposition of these two types of conditions. In the center panel (mild conditions) we see that easy-to-evade conditions have little effect on deviant behavior seeking (inelastic demand), and in the lower panel (stringent conditions) we see that tougher conditions produce a reduction in deviant behavior seeking (elastic demand).

It could be argued that this is not an example of treatment but rather of externally imposed control. Let us therefore consider a typical behavior ther-

Table 4.1   Examples of Mild and Stringent Conditions of Probation

Mild	*Stringent*
No contact with victims or families	Reside where directed
No contact with underage children	Residence may be inspected at any time
Attend and complete counseling	Respect curfews
No-go zones (red zones)	No pornography
Stay away from home/school/work of victim(s)	Urinalysis on demand
Stay away from parks, playgrounds, or other risky situations	Breathalyzer on demand

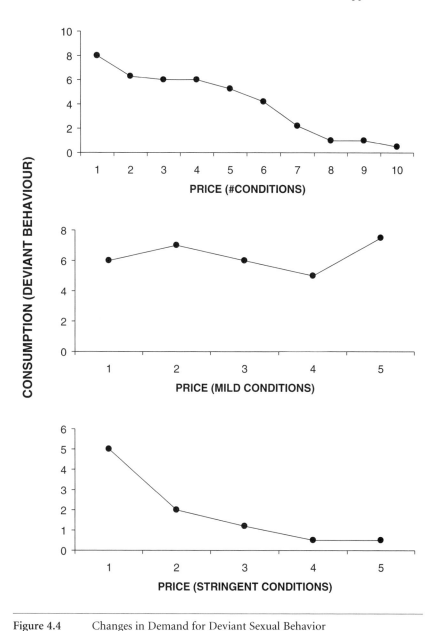

Figure 4.4   Changes in Demand for Deviant Sexual Behavior

As a function of three different sets of probation conditions (total number of conditions, mild conditions, and stringent conditions). As total number of conditions or stringency of conditions increases, demand decreases. Mild conditions produce no effect.

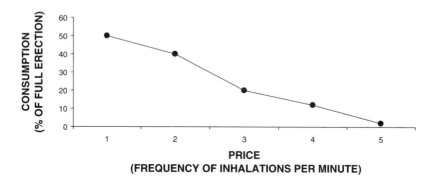

Figure 4.5   Odor Aversion Treatment

Amount of penile erection to deviant images decreases as price (number of inhalations of noxious agent per unit of time) increases.

apy treatment to control deviant sexual arousal in behavioral economic terms. In odor aversion (Laws, 2001b; Laws, Meyer, & Holmen, 1978; Laws & Osborn, 1983) the client is required to view either attractive deviant stimuli, emit deviant sexual fantasies, or listen to a recording of deviant sexual fantasies. The requirement is that the stimulus must be one that is known to produce deviant sexual arousal. In a typical procedure, after stimulus onset the client is required to periodically and noncontingently inhale the fumes of spirits of ammonia. Obviously, the intensity of the stimulus cannot be altered. In behavioral economic terms, then, consumption (production of deviant arousal) should be reduced as price (frequency of inhalation) increases. Figure 4.5 shows the hypothetical effect of this contingency. As predicted, the more frequently the client smells the ammonia fumes, the greater the decrease in deviant sexual arousal.

The preceding descriptions of behavior control represent two common approaches to the management of sex offenders in the community. It is clear that both of these approaches can be adequately described in behavioral economic terms.

LOSS OF CONTROL, IMPULSIVITY

This phenomenon is considerably more complex than the inverse relationship between demand and price. Bickel et al. (1998) describe the problem in drug dependency terms:

Drug-dependent individuals may state a preference for larger, more-delayed rewards, yet nonetheless later choose smaller, more-immediate rewards, thus demonstrating a reversal in preference. . . . Loss of control may be a phenomenon that derives from an important aspect of behavior; that is, the effect on behavior of reinforcer amount is modulated by the delay to the delivery of that reinforcer. . . . Said another way, the value of a delayed reward is discounted (reduced in value or considered to be worth less) compared to the value of an immediate reward. (pp. 557-558)

Since anyone would rather have $9.75 right now rather than $10.00 a week from now, the discounting of delay is a phenomenon familiar to all of us. However, it becomes quite important when we consider how this functions in drug dependence and the pursuit of deviant sexual activities. Vuchinich (1999) has noted that,

in the natural environment, the abused substance and the activities with which it competes typically are available at different times; that is, individuals choose between substance use, which typically is readily available with little delay, and engaging in behavior that will produce access to more valuable activities (e.g., vocational or academic success, satisfying intimate and social relations) that usu- ally are available only after delays that sometimes might be considerable. (p. 196)

Vuchinich refers to this as *intertemporal choice,* the choice between smaller- sooner rewards (SSR) and larger-later rewards (LLR).

Figure 4.6 illustrates the so-called loss of control or impulsivity pheno- menon. In behavioral economic terms, the relationship shown in Figure 4.6 is called a *hyperbolic discounting function* (Bickel et al., 1998, pp. 558-559; Vuchinich, 1999, p. 197). The smaller-sooner reward is available at Time 2 and, at a later time, a reward double in value is available. The value of each reward is described by the hyperbolic function extending from the vertical axis of the figure to each of the reward values. The curves are hyperbolic rather than expo- nential to show that the value of each reward increases the closer one comes to the reward itself. To make this clear, let us describe this in sexual deviance terms. When both rewards are distant in time, Bickel et al. say, choice behavior is "self-controlled" and "rational." Note that at Time 1, according to the hyper- bolic function, the value of the larger-later reward (LLR) is greater. The indi- vidual is likely to say to himself, "I want to go to school, work hard, be with my family, and not molest children any more" (LLR). However, as the smaller- sooner reward (SSR) becomes available, the hyperbolic function for the SSR crosses over the LLR function so that, at Time 2, the curve is higher in relation to the SSR. The SSR is chosen and preference is reversed. The individual may now say to himself, "How do I know that any of that will happen? I'd like to

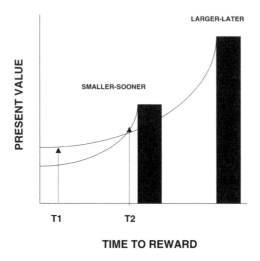

Figure 4.6   Hyperbolic Discounting Function

Preference reversal for a small reward obtained sooner compared to a much larger reward available later. Subject "discounts" the probability of obtaining the larger reward and takes the smaller.

SOURCE: Redrawn from Vuchinich (1999) with permission of Guilford Publications, Inc.

have sex with a child now." Thus he *discounts* the probabilistic value of the more desirable LLR. Bickel et al. describe this process as "impulsive" and "irrational" and inconsistent with the objective facts of the situation. They conclude that the hyperbolic discounting function seems to account for both loss of control and impulsive behavior. This has become the major paradigm in contemporary behavioral economic research in this area (Green, Fry, & Myerson, 1994; Green, Myerson, Lichtman, Rosen, & Fry, 1996; Madden, Bickel, & Jacobs, 1999; Petry, 2001). Most recently, researchers have begun examining the relationship between delay discounting and probability discounting (i.e., estimates of the likelihood that the LLR will even occur; Green, Myerson, & Ostaszewski, 1999).

There are similar analyses in the cognitive behavioral literature regarding why sex offenders tend to discount non-offending alternatives. A number of psychological mechanisms are described to account for apparently impulsive behavior and loss of control. These include disinhibition (Finkelhor, 1984), primary motivational precursors (Hall & Hirschman, 1992), vulnerability to stressors (Marshall & Barbaree, 1990), autoerotic influences (Laws & Marshall, 1990), abstinence violation effect (Marlatt, 1985; Pithers, 1990), failure of self-regulation (Ward & Hudson, 2000), or distorted sexual scripts and cognitive distortions (Ward & Siegert, in press), to name only a few. All of these, in combination with other variables, are said to contribute to the phenomenon of loss of control, the discounting of alternative, prosocial behaviors, and the precipitation of sex offending. Cognitive behavioral theories tend to be rather complex (e.g., Ward & Hudson, 2000; Ward & Siegert, in press) and require the integration of a wide range of psychological mechanisms to account for behavioral effects. Behavioral economics theory, on the other hand, is elegant, straightforward, and requires many fewer explanatory constructs to account for behavior change.

HYPERBOLIC DISCOUNTING: RESEARCH AND TREATMENT IMPLICATIONS

Bickel et al. (1998, pp. 560-561) state that investigation of delay discounting and impulsivity may have a variety of implications for studying deviant social behavior. Once again, they are discussing drug dependence but the issues apply to sexual deviation as well.

1. The delay discounting function shown in Figure 4.6 is already considered a major experimental model for the impulsivity phenomenon (preference reversal). It is currently used as a paradigm for examining control of impulsivity by behavioral (Green et al., 1999) and pharmacological interventions (Madden et al., 1999; Richards et al., 1999).

2. Such research could reveal novel treatment approaches by application of procedures previously demonstrated to engender shifts toward self-controlled choice (e.g., precommitment, motivational interviewing, teaching tolerance of delay, or cost-benefit reasoning).

3. The delay discounting function is almost certainly the behavioral mechanism by which certain precursors lead to impulsive sexual behaviors.

4. The examination of preference for small gains can provide empirical insight into the wide array of life problems experienced by socially deviant people.

5. Discounting of delayed rewards may go far toward improving our understanding of vulnerability to participation in deviant sexual behavior.

HYPERBOLIC DISCOUNTING: HELP-SEEKING IMPLICATIONS

Marlatt et al. (1997) have examined the relation of discounting to help seeking in drug abusers. Their observations apply almost equally as well to sex offenders. As these authors see it, the basic problem posed by discounting is that entry into treatment places the drug abuser or sexual deviant in a position of having to give up a certain, readily available, and highly valued commodity (drugs or deviant sex) in order to obtain a vague, probabilistic, and surely delayed outcome (benefit of treatment). Due to discounting of delay and negatively estimating probabilities, it is hardly surprising that these clients do not actively seek treatment. Marlatt et al. (1997) suggest that abusers discount delayed outcomes more than nonabusers:

> It is possible that alcohol and drug abusers engage in excessive consumption partly as a result of heavily discounting delayed and probabilistic outcomes. If so, then such populations present a doubly difficult problem: They are substance abusers because they heavily discount the future, and because they heavily discount the future, they are unlikely to enter treatment. (p. 70)

That statement applies equally well to sex offenders.

Marlatt et al. (1997) suggest three methods for potentially increasing help seeking and retention in treatment.

First, they suggest that help seeking might increase if total abstinence from drugs was somewhat relaxed. Obviously, permitting sex offenders to continue offending but at a lower rate would not be acceptable. However, Laws (1996, 1999, 2001a) has suggested that harm reduction is very likely what we are really accomplishing in treating sex offenders and that many clients accepted into treatment are continuing to offend with some frequency.

Second, "Benefits from current treatment are far from certain, but if they were better defined, more probable, and occurred sooner, their value would be discounted less and treatment would be engaged in more" (Marlatt et al., 1997, p. 71). The author has long believed that the best way to retain clients is to show results on the front end. This can be accomplished, for example, by producing penile plethysmographic data that clearly demonstrate deviant sexual interest, and/or engaging the client immediately in some form of behavior therapy so that he can see early on that behavior is malleable and changeable, or presenting information to the client in a motivational interviewing format and allowing him to assess the logic of entering treatment.

Third, treatment should swiftly move to place clients in direct contact with desired activities other than substance abuse or deviant sexual behavior. Marlatt et al. (1997) say that

> individuals seek treatment more because of the life problems caused by their addictive consumption than because of the addictive consumption itself. Thus, if treatments focused on these life problems as much or more than they focus on consumption ... then treatment-seeking and retention might be increased. (p. 71)

This failure is clearly evident in much of sex offender treatment. Problems other than sexual deviation are either ignored or they are put off as something to deal with *after* the *important* treatment has been completed. The harm reduction literature (Marlatt, 1998) is replete with examples of lowering barriers to treatment and a holistic approach that treats the life problems of the client, only one of which may be alcoholism, substance abuse, or sexual deviation.

The observations of Marlatt et al. (1997) apply equally to retaining sex offenders in treatment. Unfortunately, much of sex offender treatment is structured around what Ward and Hudson (2000; Hudson & Ward, 2000) have labeled "avoidance goals." Indeed, Mann (1998) titled a paper, "Relapse Prevention: Is That the Bit Where They Told Me All the Things I Couldn't Do Anymore?" I refer here to the fact that most contemporary treatment programs frame the alternatives to sexual offending in negative terms: eliminate or reduce deviant fantasizing, eliminate or reduce deviant sexual arousal, control impulses, manage emotions, avoid risky situations, and so on. Therefore it becomes quite easy for the client to discount treatment goals that are not formulated in positive terms that clearly indicate what is to be gained rather than what is to be avoided. Ward and Stewart (in press) have noted that "every therapeutic intervention is buttressed by assumptions about what constitutes a desirable outcome, and therefore points to a vision of human well being and fulfillment" (p. 37). This cannot be achieved by avoidance alone.

Conclusions

This chapter has focused primarily upon two major features of behavioral economics and their possible application to sexual deviation: demand and discounting of the delay of reinforcement. The focus upon demand illuminates some of the clear advantages of the behavioral economic approach to social deviation. A set of simple, easily understood, and easily implemented operations can help us to understand complex phenomena without resorting to overly complex procedures. The research on discounting of delay is, in my judgment, one of those remarkable instances where a well-understood procedure developed in animal research has found an almost identical application in research with humans. The addition of probability discounting will expand this area enormously. The operations are simple and straightforward and tell us much about the conscious choice behavior of human beings without resorting to clinical terms loaded with surplus meaning. With regard to deviant sexual behavior, I would expect that assessment procedures will be developed that will ultimately tell us much, not only about choice, but about the underlying schemas that permit some people to engage in deviant sexual behavior while spurning more conventional alternatives.

References

Bickel, W. K., Madden, G. J., & Petry, N. M. (1998). The price of change: The behavioral economics of drug dependence. *Behavior Therapy, 29,* 545-565.

Finkelhor, D. (1984). *Child sexual abuse: New theory and research.* New York: Free Press.

Green, L., & Freed, D. E. (1998). Behavioral economics. In W. O'Donohue (Ed.), *Learning and behavior therapy* (pp. 274-300). New York: Allyn & Bacon.

Green, L., Fry, A. F., & Myerson, J. (1994). Discounting of delayed rewards: A life-span comparison. *Psychological Science, 5,* 33-36.

Green, L., Myerson, J., Lichtman, D., Rosen, S., & Fry, A. (1996). Temporal discounting in choice between delayed rewards: The role of age and income. *Psychology and Aging, 11,* 79-84.

Green, L., Myerson, J., & Ostaszewski, P. (1999). Amount of reward has opposite effects on the discounting of delayed and probabilistic outcomes. *Journal of Experimental Psychology: Learning, Memory, and Cognition, 25,* 418-427.

Hall, G. C. N., & Hirschman, R. (1992). Sexual aggression against children: A conceptual perspective of etiology. *Criminal Justice and Behavior, 19,* 8-23.

Herrnstein, R. J. (1961). Relative and absolute strength of response as a function of frequency of reinforcement. *Journal of the Experimental Analysis of Behavior, 4,* 267-272.

Herrnstein, R. J. (1970). On the law of effect. *Journal of the Experimental Analysis of Behavior, 13,* 243-266.

Hudson, S. M., & Ward, T. (2000). Relapse prevention: Assessment and treatment implications. In D. R. Laws, S. M. Hudson, & T. Ward (Eds.), *Remaking relapse prevention with sex offenders: A sourcebook* (pp. 102-122). Thousand Oaks, CA: Sage.

Hursh, S. R. (1980). Economic concepts for the analysis of behavior. *Journal of the Experimental Analysis of Behavior, 34,* 219-238.

Laws, D. R. (1995). A theory of relapse prevention. In W. O'Donohue & L. Krasner (Eds.), *Theories of behavior therapy* (pp. 445-473). Washington, DC: American Psychological Association.

Laws, D. R. (1996). Relapse prevention or harm reduction? *Sexual Abuse: A Journal of Research and Treatment, 8,* 243-247.

Laws, D. R. (1999). Harm reduction or harm facilitation? A reply to Maletzky. *Sexual Abuse: A Journal of Research and Treatment, 11,* 233-240.

Laws, D. R. (2001a, November). *Harm reduction: A public health approach to sexual deviance.* Plenary presented at the meeting of the Association for the Treatment of Sexual Abusers, San Antonio, Texas.

Laws, D. R. (2001b). Olfactory aversion: Notes on procedure, with speculations on its mechanism of effect. *Sexual Abuse: A Journal of Research and Treatment, 13,* 275-287.

Laws, D. R., Hudson, S. H., & Ward, T. (Eds.). (2000). *Remaking relapse prevention with sex offenders: A sourcebook.* Thousand Oaks, CA: Sage.

Laws, D. R., Gulayets, M. J., & Frenzel, R. R. (1995). Assessment of sex offenders using standardized slide stimuli and procedures: A multisite study. *Sexual Abuse: A Journal of Research and Treatment, 7,* 155-166.

Laws, D. R., & Marshall, W. L. (1990). A conditioning theory of the etiology and maintenance of deviant sexual preferences and behavior. In W. L. Marshall, D. R. Laws, & H. E. Barbaree (Eds.), *Handbook of sexual assault* (pp. 209-229). New York: Plenum.

Laws, D. R., Meyer, J., & Holmen, M. L. (1978). Reduction of sadistic sexual arousal by olfactory aversion: A case study. *Behaviour Research and Therapy, 16,* 281-285.

Laws, D. R., & Osborn, C. A. (1983). How to build and operate a behavioral laboratory to evaluate and treat sexual deviance. In J. G. Greer & I. Stuart (Eds.), *The sexual aggressor* (pp. 293-335). New York: Van Nostrand Reinhold.

Madden, G. J., Bickel, W. K., Jacobs, E. A. (1999). Discounting of delayed rewards in opioid-dependent outpatients: Exponential or hyperbolic discounting functions? *Experimental Clinical Psychopharmacology, 7,* 284-293.

Mann, R. E. (1998, November). *Relapse prevention?: Is that the bit where they told me all the things I couldn't do anymore?* Paper presented at the annual meeting of the Association for the Treatment of Sexual Abusers, Vancouver, British Columbia.

Marlatt, G. A. (1985). Relapse prevention: Theoretical rationale and overview of the model. In G. A. Marlatt & J. R. Gordon (Eds.), *Relapse prevention* (pp. 3-70). New York: Guilford.

Marlatt, G. A. (Ed.). (1998). *Harm reduction: Pragmatic strategies for managing high-risk behaviors.* New York: Guilford.

Marlatt, G. A., Tucker, J. A., Donovan, D. M., & Vuchinich, R. E. (1997). Help-seeking by substance abusers: The role of harm reduction and behavioral economic approaches to facilitate treatment entry and retention. In L. S. Onken, J. D. Blaine, & J. J. Boren (Eds.), *Beyond the therapeutic alliance: Keeping the drug-dependent individual in treatment* (National Institute on Drug Abuse Research Monograph Number 165, pp. 44-84). Rockville, MD: U.S. Department of Health and Human Services, Public Health Service, National Institutes of Health.

Marshall, W. L., & Barbaree, H. E. (1990). An integrated theory of the etiology of sexual offending. In W. L. Marshall, D. R. Laws, & H. E. Barbaree (Eds.), *Handbook of sexual assault* (pp. 257-275). New York: Plenum.

O'Donohue, W., Penix, T., & Oksol, E. (2000). Behavioral economics: Understanding sexual behavior, preference, and self-control. In D. R. Laws, S. H. Hudson, & T. Ward (Eds.), *Remaking relapse prevention with sex offenders: A sourcebook* (pp. 123-139). Thousand Oaks, CA: Sage.

Petry, N. M. (2001). *Delay discounting of money and alcohol in actively using alcoholics, currently abstinent alcoholics, and controls* (Abstract) [on-line]. Retrieved July 30, 2001, from http://link.springer.de/link/service/jour . . . contents/00/00638/s002130000638ch002.html

Pithers, W. D. (1990). Relapse prevention with sexual aggressors: A method for maintaining therapeutic gains and enhancing external supervision. In W. L. Marshall, D. R. Laws, & H. E. Barbaree (Eds.), *Handbook of sexual assault* (pp. 343-362). New York: Plenum.

Premack, D. (1959). Toward empirical behavior laws: I. Positive reinforcement. *Psychological Review, 66,* 219-233.

Premack, D. (1962). Reversibility of the reinforcement relation. *Science, 136,* 235-237.

Premack, D. (1965). Reinforcement theory. In D. Levine (Ed.), *Nebraska Symposium on Motivation* (pp. 123-180). Lincoln: University of Nebraska Press.

Richards, J. B., Zhang, L., Mitchell, S. H., & de Wit, H. (1999). Delay or probability discounting in a model of impulsive behavior: Effect of alcohol. *Journal of the Experimental Analysis of Behavior, 71,* 121-143 (Abstract) [On-line]. Retrieved July 30, 2001, from http://www.envmed.rochester.edu/wwwrap/behavior/jeab_htm/71/_71-121.htm

Vuchinich, R. E. (1999). Behavioral economics as a framework for organizing the expanded range of substance abuse interventions. In J. A. Tucker, D. M. Donovan, & G. A. Marlatt (Eds.), *Changing addictive behavior* (pp. 191-218). New York: Guilford.

Ward, T., & Hudson, S. M. (2000). A self-regulation model of relapse prevention. In D. R. Laws, S. M. Hudson, & T. Ward (Eds.), *Remaking relapse prevention with sex offenders* (pp. 79-101). Thousand Oaks, CA: Sage.

Ward, T., & Siegert, R. J. (in press). Toward a comprehensive theory of child sexual abuse: A theory knitting perspective. *Psychology, Crime, & Law.*

Ward, T., & Stewart, C. (in press). Criminogenic needs and human needs?: A theoretical model. *Psychology, Crime, & Law.*

5

Penile Plethysmography

Will We Ever Get It Right?

D. Richard Laws
South Island Consulting
Victoria, British Columbia, Canada

This is a wide-ranging chapter that is intended to review many of the problems that beset the use of penile plethysmography. In the chapter I consider the following areas: how I became involved with the technology; PPG as a technology, procedure, and art; standardization problems with the procedure; construct validity; whether or not it is a genuine test; how well it predicts sexual reoffending; legal challenges to the procedure; and whether it has any real utility. What follows, then, is what my clinical experience and an emerging literature have taught me over the past 35 years. I am a former true believer who has become an apostate.

Getting Started

In the spring of 1967 I was looking for a research project for my doctoral dissertation. At this time I had been working part-time in an operant conditioning laboratory for more than a year. My supervisor was an experimental psychologist on my faculty who was investigating the sexual behavior of rabbits. My dissertation required human subjects, and I began searching for a topic. Because my doctoral study program centered on behavior analysis (although it had not yet acquired that name), I began searching the behavior therapy literature. I found an article by Bancroft, Jones, and Pullan (1966) that described the use of a device called the penile plethysmograph. This was my initial exposure to the circumferential strain gauge. The Bancroft et al. (1966) article proposed that this device could accurately measure and quantify penile erection responses and might be useful for assessment of sexual interest and possibly in behavior therapy treatment. I proposed to my supervisor that I use this device in my dissertation research. He agreed but said that we should find a different way to measure the response. For months we labored trying one procedure after another; all of them failed to measure penile circumference change accurately. Finally I told him that I was going to use the Bancroft et al. (1966) approach but redesign the sensing unit. We were ultimately able to produce a workable and reliable penile transducer that appeared to have linear characteristics. There was a soundproof human test chamber in the laboratory and we set up shop there. We bought some pornographic films on the underground market and set to work. It was immediately apparent that the device worked and was reliable from test to test.

The problem now was to find a paradigm in which to use it. One day I was talking with a fellow graduate student who also worked in the laboratory. He asked me how the research was going, and I told him that I could now accurately measure the response but did not know what to do with it. He laughed and said, "Why don't you bring it under stimulus control?" Although this was intended as a joke, I realized that he had identified a researchable problem. I recruited several normal subjects and presented the pornographic films to them in several variations of an ABA reversal design. In the A condition I instructed them to allow themselves to become sexually aroused; in the B condition I instructed them to attempt to inhibit their arousal by mental means. In brief, the results showed that instructional control was effective irrespective of the order in which the stimulus films were presented. I had no idea at the time what a striking result this was. This investigation (Laws & Rubin, 1969) and the one that followed (Henson & Rubin, 1971) formed the basis for (a) teaching self-control of sexual arousal in behavior therapy, and (b) evaluating the ability of a client to suppress sexual arousal in penile plethysmography assessments by manipulating mental images. This suppression effect would later become important in investigations of faking the sexual response (Laws & Holmen, 1978).

A year later I set about building a career in sex research. I was not alone, although there were very few investigators in this area in the early 1970s. I began to work with sex offenders in a maximum security hospital and built a laboratory such as the one in which I had trained. Assisted by clinical psychology interns, by 1975 I was convinced that we could successfully evaluate sexual response in sexually deviant males.

I have been doing this sort of work, as well as training and supervising others doing it, off and on for more than 30 years. From the late 1970s until the late 1980s I was a major evangelist for this procedure in the United States. I spread the good news far and wide and attracted many adherents to the technology. Many of those people believe in the technology as fervently today as they did then. I am now rather sorry that I assumed that evangelical role. I believe now that, in promoting a technology and procedures that have never been adequately proven to be what they were purported to be, I did more harm than good. There are, to be sure, some good things to be said about penile plethysmography (PPG), and I will state what I think they are. However, this chapter is more about what I think is wrong with the technology.

What This Chapter Is Not About

This will not be one more review of studies comparing one kind of offender with another or with normals, comparing one type of stimulus modality with another, or the psychometric characteristics of the procedure. The interested reader is referred to the rather exhaustive reviews by O'Donohue and Letourneau (1992), Murphy and Barbaree (1994), and Marshall, Anderson, and Fernandez (1999) to obtain the flavor of this research. Earlier work by Simon and Shouten (1991) and Barker and Howell (1992) and more recent reviews by Marshall and Fernandez (2000, 2001, in press) are briefer and focus primarily on what the procedure fails to do.

My focus is somewhat different. I propose that the procedure is inherently faulted by the idiosyncratic fashion in which it is conducted. There are major problems with PPG that I believe are irremediable. At this writing there is a move to include PPG data as a variable in assessment of risk for sexual offending (e.g., Hanson & Bussiere, 1998; Quinsey, Harris, Rice, & Cormier, 1998). This means that PPG data could have a role in legal decision making. Since it is my belief that PPG fails to meet the standard for admissibility in court in support of expert testimony, this is a serious matter indeed.

What Is Penile Plethysmography?

PPG is a technology, a procedure, and an art.

PPG AS A TECHNOLOGY

Dorlund's Illustrated Medical Dictionary (1994) defines *plethysmography* as "the recording of the changes in the size of a [body] part as modified by the circulation of the blood in it" (p. 1306). This is done by measuring electrical *impedance,* "a technique for detecting blood volume changes in a part by measuring changes in electrical resistance." Impedance changes are detected by a *strain gauge,* "a technique for detecting blood volume changes in . . . circumference employing a rubber tube filled with a conductive liquid; as the tube expands and contracts, the resistance in the fluid changes in proportion to the circumference." A *plethysmograph* is "an instrument for determining and registering variations in the volume of an organ" (p. 1306).

In medicine, plethysmography is primarily used for "measuring changes in body volume, used especially in measuring pulmonary ventilation" as well as for "measuring change in blood volume taking place in a single finger." This description shows that it is a small step from measuring blood volume in a single finger to measuring circumferential change in a penis. This impressive definition lends an aura of respectability to penile plethysmography, cloaking it in the mantle of science.

There are two general methods for measuring changes in penis size. The first, called the *volumetric method,* was developed by Freund in Czechoslovakia. This method encloses the penis in a glass tube and measures changes in air volume in the tube as the penis expands or contracts (Freund, Sedlacek, & Knob, 1965). Although this approach is highly sensitive and favored by a small coterie of researchers, it has never seen wide use due to its expense and cumbersome nature.

The second approach, called the *circumferential method,* is virtually identical to the medical definition given above. A loop of silicone rubber tubing is filled with mercury or indium-gallium and plugged with electrodes attached to electronic circuitry that passes a weak current through the mercury (Bancroft et al., 1966). This is called "the mercury gauge." The transducer loop is fitted over the penis. In a state of flaccidity the resistance in the circuit is zeroed. Any expansion of the penis will thin out the column of mercury and increase the resistance. These changes are read out most typically as a tracing of the response. An alternative device (the "Barlow gauge") was developed by Barlow, Becker, Leitenberg, and Agras (1970). This method employs a mechanical strain gauge (the Barlow gauge) attached to the top of a thin band of surgical steel shaped like a ring and open at one end. The strain gauge is attached to a flat portion at the top of the ring. It is placed on the penile shaft in the same way as the mercury transducer. When the penis expands, the strain gauge is slightly bent, which increases the resistance. The function of the two gauges is quite similar (Laws, 1977).

These are obviously very scientific methods. If used properly, they should produce reliable and valid data. The manufacturers of penile plethysmographs such as Behavioral Technology or Medical Monitoring Systems in the United States provide extensive instructions and protocols for the use of their equipment. However, it is widely recognized by researchers in the field that PPG equipment and procedures are used highly idiosyncratically, very likely without continued reference to the user manuals. Nonetheless, there resides an enormous confidence in the technology. "Machines don't lie," one of my assistants once said. Since we know that PPG evaluations can differ widely from site to site (Howes, 1995) it matters little whether machines lie or not.

PPG AS A PROCEDURE

Although PPG has the potential to be creatively used in a variety of ways, there are two typical procedures that have developed over the years.

Age and Gender Assessment

In this procedure, visual depictions of males and females of various ages are presented to the client. There are typically five or six age categories with two to four exemplars per category. The pictures are presented for a predetermined period of time, usually 2 minutes. The client is instructed to allow himself to become sexually aroused if he finds the picture sexually attractive. The resulting erection response values are scored as millimeters off baseline, percentage of full erection, or transformed to ipsative z-scores. Means are computed for each category, and the resulting scores per category are used to determine sexual interest by age and gender. This procedure has proven most useful with extra-familial child molesters.

Sexual Activity Assessment

In this procedure, audiotaped scenarios are constructed that describe various forms of consenting and nonconsenting sexual activities. These can be constructed by the client but most often are prepared in a standard set by the researcher/clinician. The scenarios are usually 2 to 3 minutes in length. As with the age/gender assessment, the client is instructed to allow himself to become sexually aroused if he finds the taped description sexually attractive. This procedure is typically used with both child molesters and rapists. The scripts contain different content to reflect the supposed sexual interests of these two groups.

The two procedures are directed primarily at child molesters and rapists because they make up the majority of clients assessed. Incest offenders are frequently exposed to the age/gender assessment but tend to respond like non-offenders. Specially prepared assessments using audiotapes are sometimes prepared to evaluate clients such as exhibitionists, voyeurs, or frotteurs.

PPG AS AN ART

I refer to PPG as an art because there are no agreed-upon standards for performing the procedure. Howes (1995) conducted a survey of 48 plethysmographic assessment centers in 25 U.S. states and 6 of the 10 Canadian provinces. He was concerned that

> although the technical adequacy of plethysmographic assessment is the subject of some disagreement, and validity studies are not entirely convincing, plethysmography had nonetheless been accepted as both a reasonably precise quantification of sexual arousal . . . and a diagnostic instrument about which there is every reason to be optimistic. . . . Perhaps the most substantial criticism of this procedure . . . is its apparent lack of standardization. (p. 14)

The agencies responding to Howes's questionnaire reported being in the plethysmographic testing business for an average of 5.5 years ($R = 6$ mo-25 yr). Technicians performing the assessments reported an average of 3.4 years of experience ($R = 6$ mo-25 yr). Forty-two percent of the technicians had been doing the assessments for 2 years or less. Formal training in the procedure was 1 week or less for 76% of the technicians, and 18% had received no training at all. Admittedly, the extent to which Howes's sample of 48 is representative of North American practice is unknown. However, the data he reported are truly appalling. My 25 years of experience with the procedure and with a variety of assessment centers suggest to me that he is right.

O'Donohue and Letourneau (1992) also noted that "there does not appear to be a standardized penile tumescence assessment, but rather there is a family of procedures which share some common aims and features" (p. 126). They listed the following potential sources of procedural variation (in the assessment of child molesters):

1. Type of gauge used (mechanical, mercury) and transducer placement

2. Type of stimuli used (audiotapes, slides, videotapes)

3. Content of stimuli used (differences in models)

4. Duration of stimulus presentation (2 sec to > 4 min)

5. Length of interstimulus (detumescence) intervals (fixed time vs. return to baseline)

6. Nature of stimulus categories sampled (Tanner scale vs. age scales)

7. Number of categories and of stimuli used for each category

8. Instructions to subjects (imagine sexual behavior with target vs. no instructions)

9. Whether a warm-up was used and number of assessment sessions

10. Type of recording instrumentation used (computer-generated graphs vs. strip chart recorder)

11. Whether calibration was used to correct for any nonlinear characteristics of recording

12. Data sampling rate (every 5 sec vs. every min)

13. Whether methods were used to attempt to assess for faking

14. Gender and other characteristics of the evaluator

15. Type of data transformation (z-score vs. a deviance index)

16. Characteristics of the laboratory (degree of privacy)

17. Type of sample and setting (outpatient, prison)

These appear to be a formidable set of requirements but actually they are not. They are exactly the problems that one encounters every day in performing this assessment. Over the years, I have visited many assessment centers and spoken to the persons in charge of assessment. I have stressed the absolute necessity of standardization to them. I have routinely received responses such as, "We've always done it this way," or "We do what works for us," or "We've tested hundreds of people using this method. Why should we change?" For 8 years, I served first as President and then as a member of the Executive Board of the Association for the Treatment of Sexual Abusers (ATSA), the largest umbrella organization in the world for workers in this field. I repeatedly stressed the need for proper training in assessment. It appeared that this organization did not wish to become involved in certifying that individuals possessed particular skills.

However, ATSA made an effort, which I feel was insufficient. In their *Practice Standards and Guidelines for Members of the Association for the Treatment of Sexual Abusers* (ATSA; 1997), they included an appendix (pp. 40-43) dealing with the plethysmographic examination. It should be emphasized that this appendix is *not* intended as a training manual. It is simply a set of recommendations and guidelines. It includes, in part, (a) requirements for training, (b) appropriate client groups, (c) screening of clients, (d) informed consent, (e) appropriate stimulus sets, (f) legislation regarding use of erotic stimuli, (g) stimulus material, visual and audio, (h) documentation of assessment data, and (i) data scoring and interpretation. This set of very general guidelines meets some but not all of the issues raised by O'Donohue and Letourneau (1992). To my knowledge, no effort has ever been made to determine the extent to which practitioners followed earlier versions of these guidelines, if at all. The latest revision of this manual is even more non-specific (ATSA, 2001).

A single major attempt has been made to standardize the age and gender assessment for child molesters. In 1987 a group of senior researchers in penile plethysmography met at the National Institute of Mental Health in Rockville, Maryland. The purpose of the meeting was to define a standard protocol for stimulus type and procedure in the age and gender assessment (Abel et al., 1989). This was to be called the Multisite Assessment Study and was to be carried out at five sites in the United States and three in Canada. Only one Canadian site (Laws, Gulayets, & Frenzel, 1995) actually completed the study. The protocol (see Laws et al., 1995, pp. 48-52) specified: (a) characteristics of the research participant, (b) characteristics of the individual stimulus slides, (c) characteristics of the slide set, (d) calibration of equipment, (e) details of the assessment procedure, (f) informed consent, (g) data reduction, and (h) statistical analysis of data. This protocol addressed most of the concerns raised by O'Donohue and Letourneau (1992). Given my low expectations for inter-site cooperation in this field, the fact that only one of eight sites actually reported data does not surprise me. The Laws et al. (1995) study reported on only 30 participants. Had the other sites reported only that many subjects, we would have had the beginnings of an international, norm-referenced database. No further attempt has been made to complete this project.

Murphy and Barbaree (1994) observed that most of the published studies in the literature have originated in the laboratories of a small number of senior investigators. Students and colleagues of these researchers continue to publish their findings. At least for this small coterie of investigators one may reasonably surmise that there is a rough consistency in their procedures and manner of reporting data. But what of the vast majority of clinicians/researchers who were not part of this elite group, who learned to do PPG by listening to conference presentations or reading the publications of this group? Therein, I think, lies the major continuing problem in standardization.

Marshall, Fernandez, Marshall, and Mann (2001) have proposed a multisite study that addresses many of the outstanding problems cited above. This will be an investigation conducted over a period of 2 years at 19 sites, 9 in Canada and 10 in the United Kingdom. The study will compare responses of extra-familial child molesters, incest offenders, rapists, and normals. They estimate that the final data set will exceed 1,000 participants. The stimulus sets will be audiotaped descriptions of sexual activity between adult males and children and of sexual violence against adult women. These sets will be updated versions of stimuli previously tested and reported by Quinsey and his colleagues (Quinsey & Chaplin, 1988a; Quinsey, Chaplin, & Varney, 1981). The project will proceed in four phases: standardization, data collection, psychometric analyses, and establishment of normative data. All sites will use the same assessment protocol, the same PPG equipment, the same stimulus sets, and the same data-reporting format. Three studies will be conducted. The first will focus upon internal consistency, the second on test-retest reliability, and the third on criterion validity, examining differences between the four groups. The distribution of scores for the normal groups will be determined. Percentile scores for those distributions will be established in order to compare the offenders' responses to them. The researchers involved in this investigation are highly experienced and come from the Correctional Service of Canada, Ontario Provincial Corrections, the Centre for Mental Health and Addictions, Forensic Branch (Toronto), an outpatient clinic in Kingston, Ontario, and H. M. Prison Service in the United Kingdom. In my judgment, this is a breakthrough study that has been too long in arriving. It will undoubtedly solve many of the existing problems that have plagued PPG over the years. We may reasonably ask: Will this information be accepted beyond the proposed study sites? If it is simply reported in the psychological literature, the answer is probably: no. On the other hand, if the researchers package the protocols, the stimulus sets, and the normative data, sell it or even give it away, then there is an excellent chance that this model could be adopted. We must hope that that will be the result.

What About Construct Validity?

Vogt (1993) defines a "construct" as "something that exists theoretically but is not directly observable. . . . A theoretical (not operational) definition in which concepts are defined in terms of other concepts" (p. 44). "Deviant sexual arousal" is such a construct. Construct validity, says Vogt, refers to, "The extent to which variables accurately measure the constructs of interest. . . . Do the operations really get at the things you are trying to measure?" (p. 44). In terms of present concerns, is the phenomenon that PPG measures—penile erection—a valid measure of deviant sexual arousal (i.e., deviant sexual interest and preference)? Opinion has been divided on this issue for more than 40 years. Many clinicians and researchers believe that PPG is, in fact, a valid measure of deviant sexual interest.

This point of view has not gone unchallenged. For example, O'Donohue and Letourneau (1992) note,

> Penile measurement is often used to gather information so that inferences can be
> made concerning naturalistic behavior (e.g., Does this individual prefer children

over adults as sexual partners?). However, this type of measurement as currently practiced uses neither naturalistic stimuli nor naturalistic responses. . . . Penile tumescence measurement is more directly an assessment of penile response to erotica than a measure of actual sexual behavior in naturalistic situations.

As with any analogue assessment, the nature of this methodology may miss many critical elements that are relevant to sexual behavior and sexual offending (e.g., affection, fear, tactile and olfactory clues). Moreover, the only sexual behavior measured is penile responding, and other relevant behavior such as verbalizations, approach behavior, touching, cognitions, etc. are usually ignored. . . . Thus, penile measurement techniques do not involve a direct sampling of the domain of interest, but, rather, involve an indirect, analogue approach. More bluntly, pen deflection is not directly sexual preference and viewing a slide is not a naturalistic potential sexual interaction. (pp. 162-163)

An opposing position was advanced by Barlow in 1977:

The function of behavioral assessment in an ideal world would be the direct and continuous measurement of the . . . behavioral problem in the setting where the behavior presents a problem. . . . In some cases the behavior cannot be conveniently produced even in contrived situations. When this happens, as in the case of sexual behavior, clinicians move back down the behavioral chain and measure sexual arousal, presumably an earlier component in the chain of sexual behavior. (cited in Laws & Osborn, 1983, p. 294)

Laws and Osborn (1983, p. 295) acknowledge that the problem of ecological validity is an important one but agree with Barlow that the erection response is measured because it is the one behavior in the chain that *can* be (more or less) objectively measured.

Murphy and Barbaree (1994) reported that early research in construct validity centered on comparing subjects' reports of their level of sexual arousal with the measured values. Some researchers (e.g., Abel, Blanchard, Murphy, Becker, & Denjeredjian, 1981; Wincze, Wenditti, Barlow, & Mavissakalian, 1980) found high correlations among these variables. Murphy and Barbaree (1994) noted that competing stimuli and demand characteristics of the situation can dramatically affect self-report of arousal. For example, they cite (p. 65) Farkas, Sine, and Evans (1979) who examined the effects of film explicitness (high or low), distraction (counting tones), and demand characteristics (informing subjects that others have found the stimuli arousing or not arousing, and have responded or not responded to them). In this situation, correlations between measured and self-report of arousal were quite low.

In recent years there has been a movement toward investigating construct validity in terms of convergent validity. This more straightforward approach compares PPG measures with other measures of deviant and nondeviant sexual interest. For example, Day, Miner, Sturgeon, and Murphy (1989) reported a classification study in which they compared PPG responses to slides, audiotapes, and videotapes with a self-report measure that was constructed from the item pool of the Multiphasic Sex Inventory (MSI; Nichols & Molinder, 1984). The PPG measures correctly classified 82% of the offenders by sex of victim and 74% by both victim gender and use of force. The MSI measures correctly classified 86% by sex of victim and 85% by use of violence. The combination of PPG and self-report was not tested.

Laws, Hanson, Osborn, and Greenbaum (2000) reported a similar study. Child molesters completed a self-report card-sort measure of sexual interest, and PPG responses were obtained from slides and audiotapes. All three measures of pedophilic interest significantly differentiated boy-object child molesters from girl-object offenders. The card-sort measure showed the greatest classification accuracy and was the only measure to improve accuracy, once the other two modalities were considered. Consideration of all three modalities provided classification accuracy (91.7%) greater than any single measure.

The Day et al. (1989) and Laws et al. (2000) studies pose a rather obvious question. If simple (albeit imperfect) self-report measures can perform so well, and if classification by sexual interest and preference is the diagnostic question (which it most often is), then is it necessary to subject individuals to the highly intrusive and cumbersome routine of PPG? It seems unlikely that this is a question that will be answered any time soon.

Is PPG a Genuine Test?

O'Donohue and Letourneau (1992) have noted that the PPG procedure is not equivalent to typical standardized psychological tests such as the WAIS-R, which uses an invariant administration protocol. They ask whether PPG is a *norm-referenced* test where a client's scores can be compared to established norms to determine if his score is "deviant," or whether it is a *criterion-referenced* test, where the purpose is to indicate whether the subject responds to some established treatment criterion such as a "normal" as opposed to a "deviant" sexual response. Clearly, as indicated above, PPG is so cluttered with procedural inconsistencies and the failure to establish a standard protocol that it could not, in its present state, come close to being termed a norm-referenced test. I am aware of only one attempt to produce normative PPG data. Howes (2001) collected data on 724 subjects from nine sites. He was able to establish norms for the interpretation of low arousal scores in cases where full erection could not be obtained. In treatment, but to my mind only in behavior therapy,

PPG becomes a criterion-referenced test. In this application the aim of the treatment is to decrease deviant sexual arousal and increase nondeviant arousal. Another possibility, say O'Donohue and Letourneau (1992), is that PPG is not really a test in the typical meaning of that term but is rather a *direct observation* of behavior. This is a staunchly behaviorist point of view that would argue that sexual response is an entity worth studying in its own right. Examples of this approach can be seen in work by Abel (1979), Abel, Blanchard, Barlow, and Mavissakalian (1975), and Laws (1984). In these investigations, differing levels of ongoing erection responding were compared to the content of concurrently presented audiotaped scripts.

Can PPG Scores Predict Reoffense?

Opinion and empirical research are divided on this issue. There have been reports over the past 20 years that suggest that PPG scores are (usually weakly) related to sexual recidivism (e.g., Barbaree & Marshall, 1988; Quinsey, Chaplin, & Carrigan, 1980; Rice, Quinsey, & Harris, 1991). In the early 1990s PPG use lay somewhat dormant due to concerns about stimuli depicting nude children or violent and degrading sexual acts. In 1998 Hanson and Bussiere (1998) published a large meta-analysis that demonstrated that a "pedophile index" (deviant responses divided by nondeviant responses) was a robust predictor of recidivism. Historically this was important. The publication coincided with a continuing intense interest in meta-analysis and a new surge of confidence regarding the use of actuarial assessment to predict sexual recidivism. PPG was respectable again. An example of this use may be seen in Quinsey et al. (1998, pp. 241-243), the *Sex Offender Risk Appraisal Guide* (SORAG). The SORAG is a 14-item algorithm based solely upon static risk factors. Item 13 is *Phallometric test results.* There are only two choices under this item:

All indicate nondeviant sexual preferences = −1

Any test indicates deviant sexual preferences = +1

Note the words *any test.* This indicates to me that *any* erection response to a deviant stimulus considered "significant" by the evaluator adds one point to the total score. Because we do not know what a clinically significant response is, it seems to me that this nullifies this item. There is another issue here. When I was employed in a forensic outpatient clinic, I considered using the SORAG in presentence reports. We had PPG capability in that clinic but it was offered on a voluntary basis and we had few takers. I telephoned Grant Harris in Quinsey's laboratory and asked how to score this item if PPG data were unavailable. He recommended scoring it 0. This does not argue for the strength of this item. I am unconvinced that PPG scores add very much to actuarial prediction.

Legal Challenges to PPG

Lawyers for the defense often persuasively argue that their clients are being abused by legal, psychiatric, or psychological procedures when PPG testing is proposed. They may argue that the procedure is humiliating to their client, that he is being forced to participate in what is clearly a degradation ritual. It is true that the procedure is highly invasive of personal privacy. It is equally true that the majority of technicians go to considerable lengths to ensure the comfort and well-being of their testees. Further, sex offenders are not attractive plaintiffs, and this argument is usually given little weight.

Much more important are the growing legal challenges to PPG based on civil law. Consider the following hypothetical (adapted from Rulo, 1999, p. 1):

John Smith is a defendant who has just pleaded guilty to several counts of child molestation. John is awaiting his sentencing hearing when he is told that the court has ordered him to take a test. John is told that in the administration of this test a device will be attached . . . to his penis, to monitor his responses to various graphic images to which he will be exposed. The results of this test, John is told, will be used as evidence in his sentencing hearing to establish his current status as a sexual deviant and later as a condition of his release, to make predictions about his future as a sexual deviant and monitor his rehabilitative progress.

The prosecution will argue that PPG is a well-established procedure for evaluating sexual deviants that has been in constant use for over 30 years and is supported by hundreds of publications in the professional literature. John's lawyer may counter-argue that existing precedents in civil law have determined that PPG is an unreliable and invalid procedure, totally lacking in standardization both for administration and interpretation and therefore is inadmissible as evidence in court (see Smith, 1998, for examples of recent decisions regarding PPG inadmissibility). John's lawyer is highly likely to win this point.

From 1923 to 1993, the standard for admissibility of scientific evidence in court was the Frye test. The Frye standard is that a scientific finding or practice be generally accepted in the scientific community from which it comes. Frye states,

> Just when a scientific principle or discovery crosses the line between the experimental and demonstrable stages is difficult to define. Somewhere in this twilight zone the evidential force of the principle must be recognized, and while courts will go a long way in admitting expert testimony deduced from a well-recognized scientific principle or discovery, the thing from which the deduction is made *must be sufficiently established to have gained general acceptance in the field in which it belongs* [italics added]. (Frye v. United States, 293 F. 1013 [D.C. Cir. 1923])

It is obvious that plethysmographic evaluation of sex offenders is a very small portion of behavioral science inquiry. Even within that narrow band of interest, PPG has never been fully accepted for the reasons enumerated in previous sections of this chapter. In my judgment, PPG has never met the stipulation of the Frye test.

A new, more comprehensive standard of admissibility was set in 1993 (Daubert v. Merrell Dow Pharmaceuticals, 509 U.S. 579, 113 S. Ct. 2786, 1125 L.Ed.2d 469 [1993]). Smith (1998) noted that

> *Frye* mandated that scientific evidence was admissible only if "generally accepted" by the scientific community. . . . In 1993 the United States Supreme Court adopted a somewhat more flexible, factor-based approach to the admission of scientific evidence in *Daubert v. Merrell Dow Pharmaceuticals.* . . . Where the *Frye* test rigidly adhered to a rule requiring "general acceptance" . . . the *Daubert* standard focuses on the "reliability" and "fit" (relevance) of the evidence. (pp. 2-3)

Smith (1998) reviews much of the legal literature surrounding the admissibility of PPG evidence in court, an account too lengthy to summarize here. The main factors that emerged from *Daubert* are the following:

1. Has the technique been tested?

2. Has the technique been subject to peer review and publication?

3. What is the known or potential rate of error?

4. Do standards exist for the control of the technique's operation?

5. Has the technique been generally accepted within the relevant scientific community?

PPG appears to meet the standard for points 1 and 2 to some extent. The technique has been tested thousands of times, but with highly variable results depending upon what "rules" the examiner is following. It has been peer reviewed and published hundreds of times. My own work has been reviewed, and I have participated in these reviews as well. Opinions of reviewers vary widely and are rarely unanimous. However, it is with the remaining points that PPG encounters severe difficulty.

The absolute rate of error is unknown (point 3). The potential for error is enormous. Smith (1998) states, "Penile plethysmography cannot meet Daubert's standard of validity or relevance tests because the test results are not generally accepted, are not sufficiently accurate, the test is subject to faking and voluntary control by test subjects" (pp. 5-6).

To obtain a flavor of the error rate in the procedure one need only consult primarily favorable reviews by Murphy and Barbaree (1994) and O'Donohue and Letourneau (1992) and the more negative ones by Marshall and Fernandez (2000, 2001, in press). Taken as a whole we would have to conclude that the error rate is substantial.

The fourth point in *Daubert* asks if standards exist for control of the technique's operation. Adequate standards do not exist for administration of the procedure (Barker & Howell, 1992; Howes, 1995; Simon & Shouten, 1991). There are no centers where technicians may be trained. ATSA (2001, pp. 40-43) listed some guidelines for proper use of the procedure. No survey has been conducted to determine if anyone adhered to earlier versions of them. The major formal attempt at standardization, the Multisite Assessment Study (Laws et al., 1995), was never completed.

The final point in *Daubert* is a reiteration of *Frye:* Is PPG generally accepted in the relevant scientific community? PPG should not be accepted for the following reasons:

1. O'Donohue and Letourneau (1992, p. 126) listed potential sources of variation in the procedure. Some of these are present in all testing centers.

2. Marshall and Fernandez (2000, p. 813) state that the PPG procedure appears to show reasonable but not terribly impressive internal consistency. However, test-retest reliability has not been adequately established.

3. Marshall and Fernandez (in press) argue that there is no strong evidence for the criterion validity of the PPG test. This refers to the ability of the test to differentiate sex offenders from one another as well as from non-offender males. The authors state, "the agreement across phallometric studies of child molesters is much greater than is evident with rapists" (p. 8). And later, "If most rapists and exhibitionists appear normal at phallometric assessment and only those nonfamilial child molesters who admit to being deviant display

deviant arousal . . . then we might be tempted to suggest that these assessments have quite limited value" (p. 9).

4.   Laws and Rubin (1969) demonstrated that it was quite easy for males to suppress their erection responses. Laws and Holmen (1978) later demonstrated that, depending upon the type of instruction provided to a single client, the client could produce a credible response or suppress the response at will, even while speaking a fantasy unrelated to the stimulus displayed. Attempts have been made to control for faking during assessment (Quinsey & Chaplin, 1988b) using a fairly intricate procedure. Though it may be difficult to produce a response in the presence of a nonpreferred stimulus, a profile of no responding is uninterpretable.

5.   In recent years there have been an increasing number of legal challenges to the admission of PPG data in court. Smith (1998, pp. 1-6) cites numerous civil law cases that have challenged PPG based on the *Daubert* criteria. Smith concludes that PPG is not reliable, not valid, is poorly administered, is subject to faking, and does not fit the relevance standard of *Daubert*.

6.   The Safer Society Foundation, Inc., Brandon, Vermont, periodically conducts surveys of sex offender treatment programs in North America that offer services to adults and juveniles. The most recent survey (T. Kennedy, personal communication, June 21, 2001) provided the following results. Of 461 adult programs reporting, 71 (15%) used PPG. Of 291 juvenile programs reporting, 17 (6%) used PPG. While these programs are obviously not all of the programs operating in North America, this is likely a representative sample. The Safer Society Foundation survey shows very clearly that there is a minimal endorsement of this technology.

Within the "relevant scientific community" that routinely uses PPG, none of the preceding will, of course, have any impact. PPG will live on. What PPG will probably not be doing is going to court very often.

Does It Have Any Utility?

In the conclusion of their monograph, Murphy and Barbaree (1994, pp. 84-85) consider the appropriate and inappropriate uses of PPG:

APPROPRIATE USES

1. Examining the impact of variations of stimulus content on sexual arousal measures

2. Research or clinical studies that classify subjects into groups based on sexual responding to various stimuli or differential responding to various types of stimuli

3. Use of erection responses to indicate the need to target deviant sexual arousal for treatment and to monitor the effectiveness of that treatment

4. Use of erection responses to confront subjects who deny having deviant arousal

INAPPROPRIATE USES

1. Use of erection responses to determine or make statements about whether someone has committed a specific sexual offense or whether someone "fits the profile" of a sex offender.

2. Use of erection responses as a sole criterion to decide someone's release from custody or from a treatment program

3. Use of erection responses to screen general populations in search of potential sex offenders

Under appropriate uses, points 1 and 2 will mean more of the same if they refer to the seemingly endless progression of studies providing ambiguous data. If the points refer to performing front-end PPG assessments to partially corroborate collateral information, then these are appropriate uses (e.g., Laws et al., 1995; Laws & Osborn, 1983). Lacking normative data, however, one must view such results skeptically. Points 3 and 4 refer to identifying the need for behavior therapy to reduce deviant sexual arousal, and these are appropriate uses. Erection responses are frequently used as a baseline against which to track the success or failure of these treatments (e.g., Laws, 1980, 1989, 1995, in press; Laws, Meyer, & Holmen, 1978; Laws & O'Neil, 1981; VanDeventer & Laws, 1978). Norm-referenced data are not at issue here. Point 4 seems to me to be a "gotcha!" strategy that is probably unnecessary. However, Abel, Cunningham-Rathner, Becker, and McHugh (1983) report its effectiveness in prompting admitting of offenses.

Murphy and Barbaree (1994, p. 85) make two additional points that are worth mentioning:

First, erection measures should always be used with other data, including police and victim statements as well as other psychometric instruments. They should never be used as the only means of assessing sex offenders.

Second, failure to respond in PPG evaluations may occur for a variety of reasons, only one of which is faking. Such data ("flatlines") should simply be viewed as uninterpretable.

Will We Ever Get It Right?

I have written here a rather negative account of a procedure that I once warmly embraced and vigorously sold to my colleagues and students. That faith has simply been seriously eroded as I have witnessed things going on and on for 30 years and never changing substantively. The changes that have been made (superior electronics in PPG equipment, computer-generated images, data management by computer) are actually differences that really do not make a difference. They are artifacts of technological change. The basic procedure is what it has always been and is still subject to all of the same shortcomings. It is boring for both client and evaluator, it is highly labor intensive, and it takes up considerable periods of valuable clinical time. And, at the end of this, the actual yield of new information in the data is typically quite small. PPG oftentimes tells us what we already know.

Is the sun setting on PPG? If so, what of the future? Marshall's report (personal communication, August, 2001) of the new multisite assessment protocol is certainly a good sign. It could result in the resolution of some of the standardization problems that I have described. It could as likely result in more of the same. It is my belief that sex offender assessment will very likely move in two new directions. Viewing time procedures (e.g., Abel, Huffman, Warberg, & Holland, 1998), in which the time a stimulus is viewed becomes the dependent variable, are a promising development. The Abel et al. (1998) procedure uses nonerotic slides of real people. A similar, but simpler, procedure has been reported by Zabarauckas and Laws (2000) that used computer-generated images. My belief is that the latter type of stimulus will come to be used more frequently. Another promising development is the use of noninvasive self-report procedures that deal frankly with deviant sexual interest and behavior. The studies by Day et al. (1989) and Laws et al. (2000) are examples of the movement in this area.

Time will tell if my optimism is ill founded. Of one thing we can be certain. Whether empirical evidence supports its continued use or not, whether its inherent procedural faults are remedied or not, I am certain that PPG will survive. We have wasted a great deal of time on a procedure that has given us very little in return.

Things could always have been different, and they still could be different. The effort to make them different, however, would require a degree of procedural cooperation among clinicians and researchers that has never been a trademark of this field. Will we ever get it right? History would strongly suggest that we will not.

References

Abel, G. G. (1979). *Assessment and treatment of child molesters.* Grant proposal submitted to the National Institute of Mental Health, No. MH33678, Rockville, MD.

Abel, G. G., Becker, J. V., Card, R. D., Cunningham-Rathner, J., Farrall, W. R., Jensen, S. H., Laws, D. R., Murphy, W. D., Osborn, C. A., Quinsey, V. L., & Wormith, J. S. (1989, May). *The stimulus standardization study of the Multisite Assessment Group.* Paper presented at the First International conference on the Treatment of Sex Offenders, University of Minnesota, Minneapolis.

Abel, G. G., Blanchard, E. B., Barlow, D. H., & Mavissakalian, M. (1975). Identifying specific erotic cues in sexual deviation by audiotaped descriptions. *Journal of Applied Behavior Analysis, 8,* 247-260.

Abel, G. G., Blanchard, E. B., Murphy, W. D., Becker, J. V., & Djenderedjian, A. (1981). Two methods of measuring penile response. *Behavior Therapy, 12,* 320-328.

Abel, G. G., Cunningham-Rathner, J., Becker, J. V., & McHugh, J. (1983, December). *Motivating sex offenders for treatment with feedback of their psychophysical assessment.* Paper presented at the World Congress of Behavior Therapy, Washington, D.C.

Abel, G. G., Huffman, J., Warberg, B., & Holland, C. L. (1998). Visual reaction time and plethysmography as measures of sexual interest in child molesters. *Sexual Abuse: A Journal of Research and Treatment, 10,* 81-95.

Association for the Treatment of Sexual Abusers (ATSA). (1997). *Ethical standards and principles for the management of sexual abusers: Appendix B. Plethysmograph examination* (pp. 44-51). Beaverton, OR: Author.

Association for the Treatment of Sexual Abusers (ATSA). (2001). *Practice standards and guidelines for members of the Association for the Treatment of Sexual Abusers: Appendix A. Phallometry* (pp. 40-43). Beaverton, OR: Author.

Bancroft, J. H. J., Jones, H. C., & Pullan, B. P. (1966). A simple transducer for measuring penile erections with comments on its use in the treatment of sexual disorders. *Behaviour Research and Therapy, 4,* 239-241.

Barbaree, H. E., & Marshall, W. L. (1988). Deviant sexual arousal, demographic and offense history variables as predictors of reoffense among child molesters and incest offenders. *Behavioral Sciences & the Law, 6,* 267-280.

Barlow, D. H. (1977). Assessment of sexual behavior. In A. R. Ciminero, K. S. Calhoun, & H. E. Adams (Eds.), *Handbook of behavioral assessment* (pp. 461-508). New York: John Wiley.

Barlow, D. H., Becker, R., Leitenberg, H., & Agras, W. S. (1970). A mechanical strain gauge for recording penile circumference change. *Journal of Applied Behavior Analysis, 3,* 72.

Barker, J. G., & Howell, R. J. (1992). The plethysmograph: A review of the literature. *Bulletin of the American Academy of Psychiatry and Law, 20,* 13-25.

Day, D. M., Miner, M. H., Sturgeon, V. H., & Murphy, J. (1989). Assessment of sexual arousal by means of physiological and self-report measures. In D. R. Laws (Ed.), *Relapse prevention with sex offenders* (pp. 115-123). New York: Guilford.

Daubert v. Merrell Dow Pharmaceuticals, 509 U.S. 579, 113 S. Ct. 2786, 125 L.Ed.2d 469 (1993).

Dorland's Illustrated Medical Dictionary. (1994). (28th ed). Philadelphia: W. B. Saunders.

Farkas, G. M., Sine, L. F., & Evans, I. M. (1979). The effects of distraction, performance demand, stimulus explicitness, and personality on objective and subjective measures of male sexual arousal. *Behaviour Research and Therapy, 17,* 26-32.

Freund, K., Sedlacek, F., & Knob, K. (1965). A simple transducer for mechanical plethysmography of the male genital. *Journal of the Experimental Analysis of Behavior, 8,* 169-170.

Frye v. US, 293 F. 1013 (D.C. Cir. 1923).

Hanson, R. K., & Bussiere, M. T. (1998). Predicting relapse: A meta-analysis of sexual offender recidivism studies. *Journal of Consulting and Clinical Psychology, 66,* 348-362.

Henson, D. E., & Rubin, H. B. (1971). Voluntary control of eroticism. *Journal of Applied Behavior Analysis, 4,* 38-44.

Howes, R. J. (1995). A survey of plethysmographic assessment in North America. *Sexual Abuse: A Journal of Research and Treatment, 7,* 9-24.

Howes, R. J. (2001). *Interpretation of low arousal in plethysmographic assessment: An empirical basis.* Unpublished manuscript, Stony Mountain Institution, Winnipeg, Manitoba, Canada.

Laws, D. R. (1977). A comparison of the measurement characteristics of two circumferential penile transducers. *Archives of Sexual Behavior, 6,* 45-51.

Laws, D. R. (1980). Treatment of bisexual pedophilia by a biofeedback-assisted self-control procedure. *Behaviour Research and Therapy, 18,* 207-211.

Laws, D. R. (1984). The assessment of dangerous sexual behavior in males. *Medicine and Law, 3,* 127-140.

Laws, D. R. (1989). Direct monitoring by penile plethysmography. In D. R. Laws (Ed.), *Relapse prevention with sex offenders* (pp. 105-114). New York: Guilford.

Laws, D. R. (1995). Verbal satiation: Notes on procedure, with speculation on its mechanism of effect. *Sexual Abuse: A Journal of Research and Treatment, 7,* 155-166.

Laws, D. R. (2001). Olfactory aversion: Notes on procedure with speculation on its mechanism of effect. *Sexual Abuse: A Journal of Research and Treatment, 13,* 275-287.

Laws, D. R., Gulayets, M. J., & Frenzel, R. R. (1995). Assessment of sex offenders using standardized slide stimuli and procedures: A multisite study. *Sexual Abuse: A Journal of Research and Treatment, 7,* 155-166.

Laws, D. R., Hanson, R. K., Osborn, C. A., & Greenbaum, P. E. (2000). Classification of child molesters by plethysmographic assessment of sexual arousal and a self-report measure of sexual preference. *Journal of Interpersonal Violence, 15,* 1297-1312.

Laws, D. R., & Holmen, M. L. (1978). Sexual response faking by pedophiles. *Criminal Justice and Behavior, 5,* 343-356.

Laws, D. R., Meyer, J., & Holmen, M. L. (1978). Reduction of sadistic sexual arousal by olfactory aversion: A case study. *Behaviour Research and Therapy, 16,* 281-285.

Laws, D. R., & O'Neil, J. A. (1981). Variations on masturbatory conditioning. *Behavioural Psychotherapy, 9,* 111-136.

Laws, D. R., & Osborn, C. A. (1983). How to build and operate a behavioral laboratory to evaluate and treat sexual deviance. In J. D. Greer & I. Stuart (Eds.), *The sexual aggressor* (pp. 293-335). New York: Van Nostrand Reinhold.

Laws, D. R., & Rubin, H. B. (1969). Instructional control of an autonomic sexual response. *Journal of Applied Behavior Analysis, 12,* 93-99.

Marshall, W. L., Anderson, D., & Fernandez, Y. (1999). *Cognitive behavioural treatment of sexual offenders.* Chichester, UK: Wiley.

Marshall, W. L., & Fernandez, Y. M. (2000). Phallometric testing with sexual offenders: Limits to its value. *Clinical Psychology Review, 20,* 807-822.

Marshall, W. L., & Fernandez, Y. M. (2001). Phallometry in forensic practice. *Journal of Forensic Psychology Practice, 1,* 77-87.

Marshall, W. L., & Fernandez, Y. M. (in press). Sexual preferences: Are they useful in the assessment and treatment of sexual offenders? *Aggression and Violent Behavior: A Review Journal.*

Marshall, W. L., Fernandez, Y. M., Marshall, L. E., & Mann, R. E. (2001). *A proposal to conduct a multi-site standardization study of phallometric assessments.* Unpublished document, Rockwood Psychological Services, Kingston, Ontario.

Murphy, W. D., & Barbaree, H. E. (1994). *Assessments of sex offenders by measures of erectile response: Psychometric properties and decision making.* Brandon, VT: Safer Society Press.

Nichols, H. R., & Molinder, L. (1984). *The Multiphasic Sex Inventory manual.* (Available from Nichols and Molinder, 437 Bowes Drive, Tacoma, WA, 98466)

O'Donohue, W., & Letourneau, E. (1992). The psychometric properties of the penile tumescence assessment of child molesters. *Journal of Psychopathology and Behavioral Assessment, 14,* 123-174.

Quinsey, V. L., & Chaplin, T. C. (1988a). Penile responses of child molesters and normals to descriptions of encounters with children involving sex and violence. *Journal of Interpersonal Violence, 3,* 259-274.

Quinsey, V. L., & Chaplin, T. C. (1988b). Preventing faking in phallometric assessments of sexual preference. In R. A. Prentky & V. L. Quinsey (Eds.), *Annals of the New York Academy of Sciences: Human sexual aggression: Current perspectives* (pp. 49-58). *Annals of the New York Academy of Sciences, 528.* New York: New York Academy of Sciences.

Quinsey, V. L., Chaplin, T. C., & Carrigan, W. F. (1980). Biofeedback and signaled punishment in the modification of inappropriate age preferences. *Behavior Therapy, 11,* 567-576.

Quinsey, V. L., Chaplin, T. C., & Varney, G. (1981). A comparison of rapists' and non-sex offenders' sexual preferences for mutually consenting sex, rape, and physical abuse of women. *Behavioral Assessment, 3,* 127-135.

Quinsey, V. L., Harris, G. T., Rice, M. E., & Cormier, C. A. (1998). *Violent offenders: Appraising and managing risk.* Washington, DC: American Psychological Association.

Rice, M. E., Quinsey, V. L., & Harris, G. T. (1991). Predicting sexual recidivism among treated and untreated child molesters released from a maximum security psychiatric institution. *Journal of Consulting and Clinical Psychology, 59,* 381-386.

Rulo, D. H. (1999). Can we identify the sexual predator by use of penile plethysmography? Retrieved June 16, 2001, from the World Wide Web: www.forensic-evidence.com/site/Behv_Evid/BeE00005_2.html.

Simon, W. T., & Shouten, P. G. W. (1991). Plethysmography in the assessment and treatment of sexual deviance: An overview. *Archives of Sexual Behavior, 20,* 75-91.

Smith, S. K. (1998). Evidence of penile plethysmography, psychological profiles, inventories and other "Not a pedophile" character and opinion evidence offered on behalf of a defendant in a child sexual abuse case is inadmissible under *Daubert v. Merrell Dow Pharmaceutical.* Retrieved June 14, 2001, from the World Wide Web: *http://www.smith-lawfirm.com/Scientific_Evidence.Brief.html*

VanDeventer, A. D., & Laws, D. R. (1978). Orgasmic reconditioning to redirect sexual arousal in pedophiles. *Behavior Therapy, 9,* 748-765.

Vogt, W. P. (1993). *Dictionary of statistics and methodology: A nontechnical guide for the social sciences.* Newbury Park, CA: Sage.

Wincze, J. P., Wenditti, E., Barlow, D., & Mavissakalian, M. (1980). The effects of a subjective monitoring task in the physiological measure of genital response to erotic stimulation. *Archives of Sexual Behavior, 9,* 533-545.

Zabarauckas, C. L., & Laws, D. R. (2000, November). *Innovations in sex offender assessment using computer-generated stimuli: An assessment package of physiological and self-report measures.* Poster presented at the meeting of the Association for the Treatment of Sexual Abusers, San Diego, CA.

6

Cultural Components of Practice

Reflexive Responses to Diversity and Difference

Marie Connolly
University of Canterbury

Feelings tell us where we are and what is happening to us. They are also the traces of where we have been and of what has happened to us there. If we advance gropingly we do so with the aid of our feelings. Whether we are moving through the worlds of perception or through the infinitely rich symbolic worlds of meaning collectively created by ourselves— ourcultures—we must have systems of navigation in place if we are not to lose our way and become disoriented or lost.

—Ciarràn Benson,
The Cultural Psychology of Self (2001, p. 103)

Practice is inevitably enriched by the cultural diversity of those taking part. Pasts are culturally saturated, and it is easy to lose one's way when navigating the cultural landscape of another. Indeed, one's own cultural landscape is often so complexly embedded that its impact on our beliefs and understandings can sometimes be underestimated. Being so familiar, our own way of thinking and our own way of life can so easily seem "simply human" to us: "it is other people who are ethnic, idiosyncratic, culturally peculiar. In a similar way, one's own views are reasonable, while other people are extremist" (Eagleton, 2000, pp. 26-27).

This chapter is essentially concerned with the way in which cultural thinking impacts and contributes to the practice context. Whether a worker is working with men who sexually offend, young people who act abusively, or with children who have been abused, an examination of the cultural self as an integral and active agent with this complex matrix can help us to navigate through the inevitable meaning barriers that exist when working cross culturally. Meaning barriers exist between all people, and when there are cultural differences, meaning barriers can be even more acute. What happens between the worker and the client, and between the client, client system, and worker can be, of course, a most dynamic force for change. The way in which the worker system and the client system intersect and engage in a process of reciprocal exchanges will, by necessity, influence client outcomes. Because of the familiarity of cultural thinking, we may underestimate just how much impact it has on client outcomes. Nevertheless, it is inevitably a component within the worker-client relationship and it is therefore important to understand how cultural contexts influence the direction of the work and the process of change.

This chapter explores the way in which professional and personal cultural experience contributes to our interpretation, understanding, and power to influence the direction of the work within the clinical setting. It looks broadly at cultural diversity, explores the nature of explicit and tacit cultural knowledge, and uses an interview with a man in treatment for abusing children to demonstrate a process of cultural reflexivity in practice. Illustrating the way in which professional cultural thinking influences the pathway of a client-worker process, the interview highlights the importance of understanding cultural thinking within the reflexive process as a central component of practice within the abuse field. The chapter then offers a model of self-awareness that is designed to help workers navigate their way through their own, and the client's, cultural thinking.

Cultural Knowledge Within the Practice Setting

There is a tendency when thinking about culture to assume that if a worker learns about a client's culture—what Spradley (1994) refers to as explicit cultural knowledge—then there will be some kind of template for working within that culture. Explicit cultural knowledge includes the specifics around what to do when you enter the cultural world of another—cultural protocols, customs, rituals, and the like. However, as Berlin (2002) quite rightly notes, classifying people on the basis of group membership only gives us the illusion that we are being culturally sensitive, when, in fact, we are failing to look beyond easy characterizations for the particular and specific ways that *this* person is understanding, feeling, and acting. (p. 144)

Although it is clearly important to avoid cultural transgression by becoming familiar with cultural aspects of the populations we work with, it is perhaps even more important to understand the nature of tacit cultural knowledge:

Tacit cultural knowledge . . . is often outside our awareness. . . . How we respond within a situation will depend on the complex transmission of cultural signs and symbols. Our responses to these are often automatic and deeply embedded. The values underpinning our cultural views also reflect ways of thinking that may have been handed down over generations. Such cultural views influence our behaviour. (Connolly, 2001, p. 24)

It is often our tacit cultural understandings that get us into trouble cross-culturally. Because tacit cultural knowledge is frequently outside our awareness, we neglect to see its impact and the way in which it influences the process of the work. According to Giddens (1984), "the knowledgeability of human actors is always bounded on the one hand by the unconscious and on the other by unacknowledged conditions/unintended consequences of action" (p. 282). Having explicit cultural knowledge does not necessarily protect a worker from being influenced by tacit cultural assumptions. Indeed, as noted earlier, such knowledge can give the illusion of cultural sensitivity while cross-cultural misunderstandings remain camouflaged. Being aware of the potential impact of one's own cultural thinking helps to avoid unintended consequences that may emerge from client/worker misunderstandings. Hence, cultural self-knowledge can be seen as the first step toward understanding the components of cultural practice.

Locations of Cultural Thinking

Culturally reflexive reactions can be identified in a number of locations. The *personal self* provides one location for reflexive reactions. Using Bourdieu's (1990) notion of personal identity and its impact on the construction of the object, the personal self can be seen to be critically influenced by a range of differing factors: the person's gender, class, nationality, race, education, family background, experience, and so forth. The scope for cultural reflexivity is broad. As Nussbaum (2001) notes, "culture only exists in the histories of individuals, . . . individuals vary greatly, and . . . the existence of diverse personal patterns creates spaces for diversity in the culture itself" (p. 171). Individuals may be members of overlapping subgroups. Though we often associate issues of culture with ethnicity, we have, in fact, a proliferation of cultural contexts—from gang culture to deaf culture, from gay culture to youth culture, from gray culture to cultures of offending. According to Eagleton (2000), "culture is just everything which is not genetically transmissible" (p. 34). This has important implications for understanding culture within the clinical setting. Within this broad analysis, *theoretical cultures* will also generate culturally reflexive responses. Some will be helpful, while others not so.

Theoretical cultures are important when exploring the second location for reflexive reactions, the sphere of the *professional self*. Again adapting Bourdieu's work and his notion of the "intellectual field" (Wacquant, 1998), the professional self, infused with explanatory theories and professional attitudes, can also create a reflexive response to client/worker situations. Bourdieu suggests that workers have the capacity to develop "disciplinary and institutional attachments" (Wacquant, 1998, p. 226). For example, if a worker has an integrated knowledge of abuse etiology that reinforces a single common explanation, then this knowledge may unwittingly restrict the worker's exploratory investigation. Because clinical practice in the abuse area is infused with strong emotions, values, and beliefs around what constitutes abuse and how society should respond, the degree to which cultural reflexivity influences professional judgment and conduct within the clinical setting is important. The need for vigilance regarding the impact of theoretical cultures and the "censorship exercised by disciplinary and institutional attachments" (Wacquant, 1998, p. 226) therefore gains significance, together with the need to recognize, work with, and critique cultural reflexivity within both the personal self and the professional self.

A lack of appreciation of the power of personal and professional reflexivity can create the potential for theory and practice to be built upon reflexive responses that have more to do with the theorist, clinician, or researcher than the subject being studied. Writing from a sociological perspective, Bourdieu cautions against such theorizing:

> In my view, one of the chief sources of error in the social sciences resides in an uncontrolled relation to the object which results in the projection of this relation onto the object. What distresses me when I read some works by sociologists is that people whose profession it is to objectivize the social world prove so rarely able to objectivize themselves, and fail so often to realize that what their apparently scientific discourse talks about is not the object but their relation to the object. (Bourdieu & Wacquant, 1992, pp. 68-69)

It could be argued that one of the more dramatic examples of this dulled awareness of cultural reflexivity is to be found in the psychological work of Sigmund Freud. In 1897, when Freud was in the midst of a personal crisis—and 10 years before he published his theory of the Oedipus complex—he wrote to an intimate confidant:

> Being totally honest with oneself is a good exercise. A single idea of general value dawned on me. I have found, in my case . . . the phenomenon of being in love with my mother and jealous of my father, and I now consider it a universal event in early childhood . . . (the Greek legend seizes upon a compulsion which everyone recognizes because he senses its existence within himself). Everyone in the audience was once a budding Oedipus in fantasy and each recoils in horror from the dream fulfillment here transplanted into reality, with the full quantity of repression which separates his infantile state from his present one. (Toews, 1998, p. 65)

Essentially, we may be looking here at an entirely egocentric discovery that later became the basis from which Freud convinced the scientific community of a universal process. Despite having no clinical evidence to the contrary, he quickly and completely abandoned his earlier seduction theory in favour of this new idea that was so potently reinforced within his own experience. Later he was to claim "the beginning of religion, morals, society and art all converge on the Oedipus complex" (Toews, 1998, p. 66).

The obscuration of professional judgment by early belief systems can also be found closer to the adult sexual offending area. For example, Kinsey's (Kinsey, Pomeroy, & Martin, 1948) record of sexual activity in young boys is clearly describing children being sexually tortured and abused by pedophiles whose behavior Kinsey seemingly condoned, and arguably encouraged. Kinsey's crusade to rid society of sexual repression and hypocrisy, having experienced it negatively himself (Jones, 1997), can be seen to have clouded his professional judgment. As noted by Jones (1997), "Kinsey's fascination with Mr. X transcended the thrill of discovery. It was as much personal as professional" (p. 513). That Kinsey's early findings are still being used to support evidence of "normal" sexuality in children (e.g., see Mayer-Bahlburg, 1993) points to the continuing influence of the work and the need to scrutinize such findings and their basis critically.

Few have had the power to influence the world's thinking in the way of Freud or Kinsey, and clearly these are extreme examples of how the personal self can have the capacity to influence outcomes. Nevertheless, reflexivity functions as an unavoidable but normal process and will inevitably influence how we operate as researchers, clinicians, workers, and theorists, for good or ill.

Cultural Thinking and Its Impact on Practice

A research interview with a man undergoing group treatment for molesting children is now used to illustrate how cultural thinking can function to inhibit or enhance a worker's capacity to see clearly the impact of the self within an interactive process. By a careful analysis of this process between the two people in the interview, an argument is made supporting the importance of the need to better understand the power of cultural thinking and its significance within a critically reflective approach to practice. Sections of the text of the interview are used, followed by a reflective discussion on the interactive process. The first area discusses the interactive process during the interview within which cultural thinking does not seem to prevent the exploration of areas even when ethnic cultural values differ. Thus the transparent side of reflexivity is discussed. This is followed by an illustration of the potential "cloudy side" of reflexivity when the cultural thinking of the worker unwittingly dominates the direction of the work, and the outcome is more consistent with the researcher's thinking than the client's.

TRANSPARENT REFLEXIVITY:
THE CLEAR SIDE OF CULTURAL THINKING

During the interview the man, whom we will call Joe, began to share how he felt about his offending and how this had impacted upon the way he felt about his relationship with his *whanau, hapu,* and wider *iwi.*[1] Joe had a supportive early family experience that was characterized by a large extended family, placing a strong emphasis on the importance of Maori culture and the values embodied within it. Joe begins by telling the researcher about his early experience of being taught important values by his grandfather:

Joe:　What was really important was honor and respect. My grandfather taught me that. Most importantly, I think, he taught me about my genealogy. About Maori protocol.

Int:　What lessons about Maori protocol did he give you?

Joe:　Oh, plenty. It's tied in with honor and respect really. It's always important to, you know, show elders respect. To, . . . to honor them. But not just elders, everyone. But elders were particularly important.

Int:　How were they honored?

Joe:　It's interesting thinking back about that. It wasn't so much that they were, you know, put up high or anything. But it had to do with them being respected for the knowledge they had. It was important to listen. You wanted to though. It wasn't a chore to listen. I loved my grandfather. He taught me everything.

Int: When you say your grandfather taught you about genealogy, what does that mean to you?

Joe: It gives me a place. It gives me a place in the world. It connects me with people who are important to me. And I guess, I'm important to them.

REFLECTION ON PROCESS

Here the interview proceeds in an exploratory way, teasing out Joe's meaning in terms of the cultural learning he received from his grandfather. Although the interviewer is not Maori, the interviewer's cultural assumptions are kept to a minimum by probing questions that explore the precise meaning of terms and concepts. Following up on cultural themes (e.g., genealogy in this extract) and following the direction of interviewee also reduces the potential for interviewers to use their own interpretation of concepts and for the interview to follow a pathway directed by the interviewee.

Later Joe talked about his offending and its impact on his position within his *whanau* (family):

Joe: Being here [in treatment] has really changed things. It's, . . . it's well, . . . it's. Aw.

Int: It's changed things for you and your *whanau?*

Joe: Yeah, yeah. They've been supportive alright. Aw, but I've brought all this on them. It's hard to go back.

Int: In what way have they been supportive?

Joe: Well, you know, they've been in touch. But I feel badly about that.

Int: So people in your family want to keep in touch, but you feel it's hard to respond, to go back?

Joe: Yeah. I'm ashamed to go back. What I've done makes me ashamed to go back.

Int: What would going back be like for you?

Joe: Well, you know, I've disgraced everyone. They may not think that, but I do. I've broken all those rules about honor and respect.

Int: The lessons your grandfather gave you?

Joe: Yeah, yeah, exactly.

Int: What advice do you think he would give you now?

Joe: Aw, I dunno. I guess he'd say there are lots of ways to make amends. This is wrong. Yeah, it's wrong alright. But I'm still part of the *whanau* I guess.

REFLECTION ON PROCESS

Again, the interview follows the direction set by the interviewee. The interviewer's response, following the theme of shame, honor, and respect, helps Joe to explore his thoughts about his situation and his differentiation between how he feels about his offending and how he thinks his *whanau* (family) feels. The additional probe relating to his grandfather's advice encourages Joe to expand on this differentiation as he explores the connection between his perception of his position (in disgrace) and the possible reaction of his *whanau* about his position, which is reflected in his grandfather's advice (remains connected). Similar to the earlier extract, the process can be seen to have helped the interviewer maintain a sense of distance from her own perceptions and assumptions about how Joe or his *whanau* may be responding to his offending.

In this part of the interview, the interviewer is tracking and following the cues of the interviewee, and in so doing is minimizing the potential for her cultural thinking to be the directing factor. In the next set of extracts, the interviewer's theoretical culture (or institutional attachment) can be seen to influence the process more strongly as the direction of the interview becomes less responsive to the interviewee's interest.

NONTRANSPARENT REFLEXIVITY: THE CLOUDY SIDE OF CULTURAL THINKING

Within the interview, Joe spent some time describing the steps toward his sexual offending. Joe had abused two little girls. As a trusted adult, he was in a position of power with respect to the children. The following extract describes the grooming process he undertook before the first act of significant abuse:

Joe: A thing that happened in that classroom, you know, sort of jolted me. Um, a couple of girls that were playing with one another. It was only just a fluke I spotted them. And they were sitting in the back of the class. Just caught a glimpse. I thought, no, it couldn't be. But then I um, I moved around so I could actually see without them knowing that I was watching, . . . them playing with one another. And I, yeah, it did, it reminded me, you know, sort of jolted my memory back when I was that age. It was like I was there. It was a real jolt.

Int: How old were the girls?

Joe: Um eight. Yeah, and um, you know, so I, . . . I sort of smiled to meself you know. And, well, there you go, this wasn't only me, wasn't only us, you know.

Int: You were able to maneuver yourself so you could see them.

Joe: Yeah.

Int: How did you do that?

Joe: Well, I could get the kids to sit near me. I could arrange it. But I can't get over what a jolt it was at first.

Int: How long did that go on for?

Joe: Aw, for a few weeks I suppose.

REFLECTION ON PROCESS

Here the interviewer, while following Joe's cues to some extent, chose not to pursue the clear direction offered by Joe to explore further the nature of the "jolt" he felt by seeing the two little girls playing with each other. He mentioned it four times in this short passage, which might have indicated an important area to explore. However, here the interviewer is focused on Joe maneuvering the girls so that he could watch them. Hence, the grooming process was more important to the interviewer than the way Joe felt about the experience. In the next extract, which follows the above, the researcher's assumptions about what motivates this grooming of the girls becomes increasingly apparent.

Int: And during this time you arranged it so that you could watch the girls?

Joe: Yeah, that's right.

Int: What happened then?

Joe: Well, you know. And, ah, and I started to use those two girls. I made them pets, they're my pets, you know, any old thing to get them to be with me. Be in my sight where I could see them, ah, playing with each other. And like I was getting so bad that I wanted to touch them too, soon.

Int: You had the power to get them to do what you wanted?

Joe: Yeah, I suppose. But you see it was them playing with each other. I started to fantasize about that.

Int: What kind of things helped you to get them to do what you wanted?

Joe: Praising them in front of the class even though their grades were way down, sort of thing. . . . I remember when I first touched, . . . the first time. I got so aroused by them playing with each other you see. I'd been fantasizing about that.

Int: And the fantasy led to touching the girls?

Joe: I got so aroused by it. That's when the fantasizing sort of went beyond my control. No, that would be wrong because it was under my control, I'm learning that here. But you know it felt out of control.

Int: How did you move from fantasizing about the girls to touching them?

REFLECTION ON PROCESS

Following on from the earlier extract, the interviewer here is pursuing the notion of Joe "arranging" the activities of the girls in order to increase his access and ultimately enable him to abuse them. When Joe says that the urge to touch them became so great, the interviewer continues exploring his control over them. Joe, while not disagreeing with the interviewer, consistently provides alternative possibilities. The language he uses to describe his feelings and behavior is much more related to issues of arousal, fantasy, and his lack of control of his feelings. By comparison, the interviewer is the first to introduce *power*—Joe's power over the girls—into the conversation. Words related to the notion of "power" had been introduced earlier, significantly, the interviewer's use of *maneuver* to describe Joe's activities. Even though Joe reiterates the importance of his response to the girl's behavior, his fantasy, and the strong sexual urges he experienced, the interviewer again clearly prefers an exploration of power and control issues and how they relate to Joe's offending. This is despite Joe's persistent efforts to alert her to alternative possibilities. As a consequence, potentially rich areas of discussion relating to Joe's motivation for abusing the girls, and the way in which his urges impact on his sense of control, are neglected, creating an interactive pathway that is more clearly directed by the interests of the interviewer.

While one explanation for this could obviously be related to the interviewing skill of the researcher and the lack of appropriate probing and follow-up questions, this deficit was not apparent in the earlier examination of the interviewing process. When looking critically at the interview text, it is also important to note that in practice with offenders it is considered important that an environment of responsibility is created since denial is a common characteristic of offenders. Nevertheless, the purpose of the interview was to investigate aspects of the offender's early experience and in that sense it was set up to be exploratory in nature. A plausible alternative explanation may be found in the analysis of professional cultural thinking. As noted earlier, the power of personal and professional cultural thinking can create the potential for theory and practice to be built upon reflexive responses that have more to do with the theorist, clinician, or researcher, than the subject being studied. Here, a detailed examination of the interview extracts above suggests that the interviewer, either consciously or unconsciously, may well have been more persuaded by power and control as an etiological factor in sex offending than other explanations, for example, sexual motivation, impulsivity, and sexual need.

The Cultural-Reflective Model

In general, the literature discussing professional attitudes and how they impact on the delivery of services has been macro-focused, reinforcing the significance of etiological explanations and their impact on the nature and extent of services provided. By contrast, theoretical cultures in the micro sense, along with personal cultural thinking, have received scant attention in the literature. The analysis of this interview suggests that it may well be productive to investigate further how personal and professional cultures influence the practice setting. How these impact upon the direction and pathway of an interview is likely to affect practice outcomes. It would seem important, therefore, to develop strategies that may help the worker not only better appreciate the significance of cultural thinking, but also how it might be identified and worked with as a conscious process.

Three phases in a reflective process are offered in the following conceptual model of self-analysis (Figure 6.1). Within this model the worker can identify culturally driven reactions, critically reflect upon them, and explore the potential for developing reflective practice outcomes. By this delineation, the model reinforces the possibility of reflexivity being a conscious process and therefore able to be confronted and worked with as a micro practice issue.

The phases in Figure 6.1 include cultural thinking responses, critical reflection, and reflective practice outcomes. Each of these phases is explored in detail.

CULTURAL THINKING RESPONSES

As noted earlier, tacit cultural knowledge can have the potential to influence behavior as automatic and often unconscious responses to interactions within the environment. Whenever we confront a situation our reactions influence our response to that situation, and the situation changes as a result. The model identifies two spheres within which cultural thinking is relevant and may impact on the way in which the situation changes: the personal sphere and the professional sphere. Within the personal sphere, the family provides a powerful socializing effect with respect to the developing individual. The way we view a situation or phenomenon can be critically shaped by values and beliefs developed during our formative years. Although family values and attitudes are inevitably filtered by other experiences within the environment, they can also be reinforced by societal values and beliefs, creating an even more compelling influence. Because offending work specifically, and work in the child protection area more generally, is infused with strong emotions, values, and beliefs around what constitutes abuse and how society should protect children, the

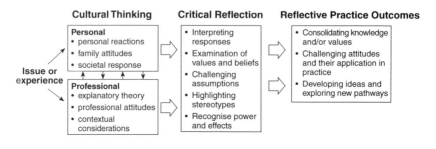

Figure 6.1   Phases in the Cultural-Reflective Model

degree to which cultural thinking influences professional judgment and conduct is important.

The professional sphere also provides a rich repository for cultural thinking. The professional self, infused with explanatory theories and professional attitudes within context, can also create culturally based responses to client-worker situations. For example, as illustrated with the interview above, if a worker has integrated knowledge about abuse etiology that reinforces a single common explanation, then this knowledge may unwittingly restrict the worker's exploratory investigation. Because of this, the need to recognize, work with, and critique cultural thinking in the spheres of the personal and professional self becomes important. This encourages "critical dissection of the concepts, methods, and problematics (the worker) inherits as well as for vigilance toward the censorship exercised by disciplinary and institutional attachments" (Wacquant, 1998, p. 226).

Because cultural thinking responses are often automatic and outside our control, it is not possible for us not to have them. Indeed, our cultural responses—whether they relate to how we approach the work, the pace, or directions we take—become the cultural components of our practice. These, and other cultural components within a practice repertoire, if left on their own, are likely to remain constant regardless of cross-cultural differences in practice. Unchallenged, they have the potential to interfere with the clinical process. However, critically reflecting on these cultural components that emerge from an analysis of the personal and professional self offers an opportunity to achieve more reflective practice outcomes by identifying and responding to cross-cultural misunderstandings when they occur.

CRITICAL REFLECTION

Reflection as a strategy within practice has been part of practice discourse for a number of years (Gould & Taylor, 1996; Schon, 1983, 1987). More recently, the notion of critical reflection has taken hold (Pease & Fook, 1999). Fook (1999) draws a distinction between reflection and critical reflection in practice. Rather than merely reflecting upon or thinking about practice, a critical reflective response can be seen to significantly challenge the values and attitudes associated with professional conduct and provide a more productive means by which practice can be critiqued. Returning to the three-phase framework outlined in Figure 6.1, undertaking a critical reflective process follows the cultural thinking response phase.

Within the critical reflection phase, a process of *interpretation* is explored. Interpreting responses initially requires an identification of cultural thinking reactions. Carefully listening to language used within the practice relationship can help to identify these reactions. The interview used earlier in this chapter was taped and transcribed to allow full analysis of the details of the interaction. Transcribing interviews into text can be helpful in tracking reactions, and similar processes can be used in practice (Rossiter, 1995). Carefully analyzing interviews provides a rich source of material that can reveal much in terms of a worker's ability to follow cues, develop exploratory pathways, and identify what interactive processes influence direction. While it is clearly unrealistic to reflect critically upon every practice encounter, doing it from time to time, with different practice relationships, can have the effect of sensitizing a worker to cultural thinking responses. Here we are talking about critical reflection in retrospect, and generally it is discussed in this way (Fook, 1999). However, workers could also practice critical reflection *during* practice encounters. Being able to think about and respond to reflexive reactions during a session (and thereby understanding the driving forces within the interview) would seem to be preferable to fixing it up later. However, the "fixing up" is a strong reinforcer of vigilance as the worker becomes increasingly aware of, and attuned to, cultural dominance within a practice encounter.

In addition to identifying reflexive reactions, a reflective process can encourage an examination of the *values and beliefs* underpinning these reactions. Because reactions are often buried in tacit cultural knowledge, it is likely that they will also be connected to a set of cultural values and beliefs that are reinforced within the personal and professional process of socialization. Examining the origins and the implications of these values and beliefs is an important aspect of a critical reflective process. Concomitant with this, two associated processes are identified: the *challenging of assumptions* and the *highlighting of stereotypes*. Any critical examination of beliefs and values will also include an interrogation of the underpinning assumptions that are supportive of them. The earlier example of the researcher being informed by professional stereotyping of sex offender motivation illustrates this point. Because the researcher was persuaded by a power and control analysis of sex offending, areas of discussion relating to sexual motivation and impulsivity were not vigorously pursued, despite cues offered by the interviewee. Professional expertise can be powerful in the development of theoretically reinforced cultures. While professional expertise can, of course, enhance understanding, it can also have the potential to inhibit exploratory enquiry. A process of critical reflection can be used to identify, better understand, and reconstruct unhelpful assumptions and stereotypes based within the social and the professional sphere.

Recognizing *power and its effects* can also be helpful in a critically reflective process. Critically exploring power and how it operates within the clinical setting is promoted here as an important feature of critically reflective practice. It requires an understanding of the potential use of personal and professional power (Connolly, 1999) and how this may influence the direction of practice. Power, or influence, changes a course of interaction, whether exerted by the worker or the client. Using one's power to influence a process, or the behavior of another, may be viewed negatively and can have negative effects. If a power response is an unconscious reaction to a culturally driven thinking process, the worker may not be aware of its genesis and may respond unhelpfully to the client. Notwithstanding this, power is inevitably used by both workers and clients as part of the usual process of interaction and, if understood, can have the effect of positively influencing processes. Recognizing and understanding power and how it operates within systems of interaction is an important component of reflective practice.

Conclusions

In general, practice literature within the offending area has been largely contextual and dominated by research into offending causation and behavior. Although this is clearly important practice-building knowledge that contributes to a more in-depth understanding of the complex matrix surrounding people who sexually offend, there has been little theorizing and research into practice *process* in the abuse field. The developing nature of practice, and how cultural components impact on the work, has received less attention in the practice literature. Given practice in this area is so strongly influenced by individual, professional, and societal values and beliefs around abuse and offending, the need to explore clinical praxeology—the nature of professional conduct within the practice area—becomes increasingly important. Understanding the nature of the evolving clinical process, identifying the ways in which this is influenced by the personal and professional self, and reflecting upon the cultural components of practice to explore creative outcomes becomes a necessary part of practice evaluation and development.

Note

1. *Whanau, hapu,* and *iwi* form the organizational structure of Maori society and relate approximately to family, extended family, and tribal network, respectively. Maori are the indigenous people of Aotearoa, New Zealand.

References

Benson, C. (2001). *The cultural psychology of self: Place, morality and art in human worlds.* London: Routledge.

Berlin, S. B. (2002). *Clinical social work practice: A cognitive-integrative perspective.* New York: Oxford University Press.

Bourdieu, P. (1990). *Language and symbolic power.* Cambridge, UK: Polity Press.

Bourdieu, P., & Wacquant, L. (1992). *An invitation to reflexive sociology.* Chicago: University of Chicago Press.

Connolly, M. (1999). *Effective participatory practice: Family group conferencing in child protection.* New York: Aldine de Gruyter.

Connolly, M. (2001). The art and science of social work. In M. Connolly (Ed.), *New Zealand social work: Contexts and practice.* Auckland: Oxford University Press.

Eagleton, T. (2000). *The idea of culture.* Oxford, UK: Blackwell.

Fook, J. (1999). Critical reflectivity in education and practice. In B. Pease & J. Fook (Eds.), *Transforming social work practice: Postmodern critical perspectives.* St. Leonards, NSW: Allen & Unwin.

Giddens, A. (1984). *The constitution of society: Outline of the theory of structuration.* Los Angeles: University of California Press.

Gould, N., & Taylor, I. (Eds.). (1996). *Reflective learning for social work research, theory and practice.* Brookfield, VT: Ashgate.

Jones, J. H. (1997). *Alfred C. Kinsey: A public/private life.* New York: Norton.

Kinsey, A. C., Pomeroy, W. B., & Martin, C. E. (1948). *Sexual behavior in the human male.* Philadelphia: W. B. Saunders.

Mayer-Bahlburg, H. F. L. (1993). Sexuality in early adolescence. In B. Wolman & J. Money (Eds.), *Handbook of human sexuality.* Northvale, NJ: Jason Aronson.

Nussbaum, M. C. (2001). *Upheavals of thought: The intelligence of emotions.* Cambridge, UK: Cambridge University Press.

Pease, B., & Fook, J. (1999). Postmodern critical theory and emancipatory social work practice. In B. Pease & J. Fook (Eds.), *Transforming social work practice: Postmodern critical perspectives.* St. Leonards, NSW: Allen & Unwin.

Rossiter, A. (1995). Teaching social work skills from a critical perspective. *Canadian Social Work Review, 9,* 627-643.

Schon, D. (1983). *The reflective practitioner.* London: Temple Smith.

Schon, D. (1987). *Educating the reflective practitioner: Towards a new design for teaching and learning in the professions.* San Francisco: Jossey-Bass.

Spradley, J. (1994). Ethnography and culture. In J. Spradley & D. McCurdy (Eds.), *Conformity and conflict: Readings in cultural anthropology* (8th ed.). New York: HarperCollins College.

Toews, J. E. (1998). Having and being: The evolution of Freud's Oedipus theory as a moral fable. In M. S. Roth (Ed.), *Freud: Conflict and culture.* New York: Knopf.

Wacquant, L. (1998). Pierre Bourdieu. In R. Stones (Ed.), *Key sociological thinkers.* New York: New York University Press.

7

Developmental Antecedents of Sexual Offending

Thomas Keenan
University of Canterbury

Tony Ward
University of Melbourne

G iven the ever-increasing awareness of children's rights; the growing realization that the effects of sexual assault on children are numerous, long-lasting, and many times severe (e.g., Rutter, Giller, & Hagell, 1998); and the importance of understanding the developmental origins of sexual offending (e.g., Marshall, 1989), there is a compelling need to better understand the causes of sexual offending against children. Theoretical and empirical research has identified a number of important factors that are associated with the etiology and maintenance of sexual offending, including biological predispositions such as difficult temperament (Barbaree, Marshall, & McCormick, 1998) and hyperactivity and inattention (Loeber, 1990); insecure attachment (Marshall, 1989); low self-esteem (Finkelhor, 1984); cognitive distortions (Ward, 2000); the delayed or deviant acquisition of theory of mind (Keenan & Ward, 2000); and self-regulation (Ward, Hudson, & Keenan, 1998). Though far from complete, this list represents many of the factors that have been identified as important in cutting-edge research on sexual abuse.

In this chapter we examine the contribution of a developmental approach to sex offenders in three research domains: self-regulation, theory of mind, and implicit theories. First, we outline the basic assumptions of developmental psychopathology and consider its ability to shed light on offender characteristics. Second, we apply the theories and research findings in these three developmentally oriented areas and discuss their implications for sexual offending. Finally, we briefly conclude with some comments on the clinical and research implications of these ideas.

Developmental Psychopathology

One way in which psychopathology has been conceptualized is as the study of normal development gone askew (Wenar & Kerig, 2000). This conceptualization has led directly to a distinctly developmental approach to the study of psychopathology, an area of inquiry known as *developmental psychopathology*. The study of developmental psychopathology can be thought of as a marriage between developmental psychology and the study of psychological disorders. This framework stresses the importance of examining a wide range of human functioning to understand fully the development of psychopathology, including ontogenetic, biochemical, genetic, physiological, cognitive, social-cognitive, socioemotional, and environmental influences (Cicchetti, 1993).

The adoption of a developmental psychopathology approach to the question of mental disorders generally assumes a continuum of behavior, with normal behavior at one end of the scale and abnormal behavior at the other end. Under this model, developmental principles are important to the understanding of both normal and psychopathological behavior, as the same life-course principles are hypothesized to apply along the continuum (Cicchetti, 1993). Thus, the same mechanisms that lead to healthy development can also be involved in poor functioning, at the other end of the spectrum. Therefore, an understanding of normal development is important for the development of knowledge about psychopathology, and understanding psychopathology may lead to further knowledge about normal functioning. Cicchetti (1993) has further pointed out that to understand normal development is to be as interested in the children who are at risk of developing a disorder, rather than simply those who do actually develop a disorder.

Rutter and Garmezy (1983) have suggested that the discipline of developmental psychopathology is based on a number of tenets arising from a dual consideration of developmental issues and the study of child psychiatric disorders. First, the child's developmental level, or age, is of central importance to understanding the onset, significance, and course of psychopathology. The age at which a behavior becomes manifest is an important consideration. For example, a behavior such as enuresis takes on very different meanings depending on whether the individual is 2, 10, or 20 years of age. A related point is that susceptibility to stress or risk of psychopathology is linked to the child's age, such that individuals are more vulnerable at different times in their lives. The second major tenet is that the development of a disorder such as depression is often based on experiences at an earlier point in development, which calls for a life-span approach. Third, developmental psychopathologists are interested in individual differences, examining the many different paths that can lead to the development of psychopathology in general, as well as to specific disorders. There are many different ways that children come to manifest disturbed behavior (Keenan, 2002), a concept known as *equifinality* (Cicchetti & Rogosch, 1996). A related concept is *multifinality,* meaning that particular risk factors can lead to a variety of different developmental outcomes depending on the characteristics of the individual, the individual's previous experiences, and the environmental context. The fourth tenet of a developmental psychopathology approach is a focus on the continuity and discontinuity of behavior. The presence of a problem in childhood is often associated with continued vulnerability in adulthood; in many cases, however, early problem behaviors do not continue on into later life. Antisocial behavior is a good example of a problem behavior that shows both continuity and discontinuity. Thus, a significant issue in the study of developmental psychopathology is discovering which factors promote or prevent a childhood disorder from continuing or reoccurring.

The developmental psychopathology approach provides a rich source of ideas for clarifying the developmental antecedents of sexual aggression. In recent years there have been a number of attempts to construct explanatory theories of sexual offending that incorporate developmental variables. For example, Ward and Siegert (in press) argue that there are multiple pathways leading to the sexual abuse of a child, each involving developmental influences of one type or another, a core set of dysfunctional mechanisms, and an opportunity to commit the offense. Whether or not adverse learning events result in the establishment of dysfunctional mechanisms depends on the existence of moderators, such as family support. The causal mechanisms include those associated with emotional regulation, attachment style, cognition, and sexual preferences and arousal. These vulnerability factors are also likely to play a role in maintaining offending behavior.

Again, Marshall and Barbaree's (1990) integrated theory proposes that the sexual abuse of children occurs as a consequence of a number of interacting distal and proximal factors. From the perspective of the integrated theory, it is the transition to adolescence that is particularly challenging for a vulnerable individual. Negative childhood experiences leave offenders without the necessary social competence to develop and maintain heterosexual relationships. It is at this stage that individuals are most receptive to acquiring sexual preferences and associated behaviors. In a sense, the onset of puberty represents a critical period for the acquisition of enduring sexual scripts, interests, and attitudes.

These two examples illustrate the developmental turn now occurring in the sexual offending domain. We would like to take this one step further by examining the three single factors currently the focus of research and theoretical interest: self-regulation, theory of mind, and implicit theories.

Self-Regulation and Sexual Offending

In the discussion that follows, we use the term *self-regulation* to refer to self-initiated and self-directed activity and to the dynamic processes involved in organizing and implementing goal-directed behavior across time (Kanfer & Scheft, 1988). Self-regulation involves the *monitoring, evaluation, selection,* and *modification* of behavior to accomplish personal goals in an optimal or satisfactory manner (e.g., Thompson, 1994). Moreover, self-regulation consists of both internal and external processes that allow an individual to engage in goal-directed actions over time and across different contexts (Heatherton, 1996; Karoly, 1993). Finally, self-regulation is not concerned solely with the inhibition or suppression of behavior, but can include the enhancement, maintenance, or elicitation of behavior as well. On some occasions, the enhancement of emotional states (e.g., steeling oneself to tackle a challenging rock climb or generating angry feelings to face down a bully) leading to the precipitation of responses is a legitimate goal for one's self-regulatory efforts. An important issue in regard to self-regulation concerns the possible *targets* of a person's self-regulatory efforts. The varieties of processes and behaviors that can be regulated are too numerous to specify in their entirety; however, it is clear that specific behaviors, emotions, attentional processes, cognitions, and physiological arousal are all possible targets of self-regulatory processes (Thompson, 1994).

The self-regulation of behavior can be disrupted in a number of ways. Sometimes plans are unsuccessful, and sometimes people simply become fatigued, losing the desire to monitor, evaluate, and modify their attempts to achieve specific goals. A person might formulate an inappropriate or poorly thought-out plan that has little chance of allowing the person to successfully meet his or her goals. All of these possibilities could play a role in the choice to sexually offend. For example, child molesters might decide that there is nothing wrong with the plan to take up residency near a school or day care center. A lack of metacognitive knowledge about the offense process or a failure to fully consider and think through the possible consequences of their actions could lead to reoffending.

Dysfunctions in any of the component processes of self-regulation can result in maladaptive behavior. Therefore, the pursuit of inappropriate or self-defeating goals; impaired self-monitoring or self-evaluation; or difficulty in monitoring feedback regarding one's efforts and implementing corrective action can all be associated with the failure of self-regulation. The distorting effects of strong preferences or motives can result in a defensive reappraisal of goal relevant knowledge. In addition, problematic behavior can often result from lower-level control and subsequent lack of higher-level evaluation. Such responses are frequently automatic, stereotyped, and performed without much awareness (Kanfer & Scheft, 1988).

In addition, in order to be able to effectively self-regulate their behavior, individuals require certain capacities and knowledge. These include intact attentional and memory processes; declarative knowledge about the world and the self; and the ability to self-reflect, use symbols, learn vicariously, evaluate options, and anticipate the likely outcomes of the actions of oneself and others. Additional constraints include cultural norms and beliefs that dictate expectations, ecological factors such as emotional climate in the home, presence of violence or poor modeling, and developmental trauma that might compromise an individual's capacity to develop effective self-regulation of mood and behavior. For example, the experience of sexual abuse as a child can impact adversely on an individual's identity as well as his or her emotional and behavioral regulation (Cole & Putnam, 1992).

There are a number of patterns of dysfunctional self-regulation (Baumeister & Heatherton, 1996). First, individuals can underregulate their behavior or emotions, usually due to deficient standards, inadequate monitoring, or a lack of the cognitive resources necessary to achieve desired goals. In this situation, a return of problematic emotions or behaviors is evident, for example, excessive drinking or eating. Individuals become disinhibited and lose control over their behavior, thoughts, or emotions. The attempt to manage behavior might be undermined by stress, negative mood, fatigue, physiological pressures, or social pressure (Baumeister & Heatherton, 1996). This type of self-regulatory failure can be associated with either positive or negative emotions.

The second pattern is misregulation, where ineffective or counterproductive strategies are used to achieve certain goals. For example, the use of alcohol or sexual fantasies to modulate negative mood states, or thought suppression to eradicate intrusive thoughts. The paradox is that the faulty use of strategies to achieve certain goals can backfire and lead to the emergence, or reemergence, of problematic behaviors and emotions. Misregulation often occurs because of false assumptions about the relevant contingencies influencing behavior, or inadequate attempts to modify behavior. For example, due to its pharmacological action the use of alcohol to regulate mood can lead to further periods of dysphoria. This type of self-regulation failure is usually associated with negative emotional states.

The third pathway paradoxically involves effective self-regulation. The individual concerned is typically unperturbed by his situation, and it is often external agencies or other people who express dismay at his behavior. The major problem resides in the choice of goals rather than in a breakdown in the components of self-regulation. The reference value or goals around which behavior is regulated may be false, self-serving, and distorted in some way (Ward, Hudson, Johnston, & Marshall, 1997). For example, although the setting of goals and their subsequent planning and implementation by a preferential child molester or predatory rapist may be perfectly adequate, there may be problems in the choice of goals and their associated values and beliefs (see section on implicit theories, below). For example, a rapist may believe that all women enjoy forced sex despite the fact that the rest of society simply does not agree. The emotional state associated with this type of problematic self-regulation is likely to be positive: The person is achieving his goals and does not regard his lifestyle as particularly problematic. This pathway reflects appetitive processes rather than inhibitory ones.

The above types of self-regulation failure arguable have their origins in distinct developmental problems and are associated with distinct offending and relapse patterns (for more detail see Ward et al., 1998). An important goal for research on the role of self-regulation in the development of sexual offending is to examine how self-regulatory processes interact with other processes in the onset of deviant sexual preferences and behaviors.

Theory of Mind

Recently, a framework has emerged within the literature on the etiology of sexual offending that suggests that at least three strands of research demonstrating deficits or problems in the cognitive and emotional processing of sex offenders can be unified and thought of as the result of a single deficit (Ward, Keenan, & Hudson, 2000). A growing body of evidence suggests that sex offenders have cognitive distortions with respect to their victims, thinking about their victims (and potential victims) in distorted ways (e.g., Ward et al., 1997; Ward et al., 1998). There is also empirical support within the literature demonstrating the existence of empathic deficits in sexual offenders (e.g., Marshall, Hudson, Jones, & Fernandez, 1995). Finally, there is clear evidence that sexual offenders have serious difficulty establishing satisfactory intimate relationships with adults and, moreover, that they often lack the skills necessary to manage ongoing interpersonal relationships and relationship problems (e.g., Marshall, 1989). Clearly, the problems that underlie the deviant behavior of sexual offenders are many. However, it is interesting to note that there may be a common thread linking the presence of cognitive distortions, empathic deficits, and intimacy problems in populations of sexual offenders.

In our view, these three classes of psychological problems are all potentially explained by an inability to accurately attribute mental states to other people (Ward et al., 2000). The ability to infer psychological states to other people has been referred to variously as a *theory of mind* (Astington, 1994) or *mind-reading*. Each term invokes a slightly different connotation. Following the literature, we use the term *theory of mind* to refer to a person's understanding that both he and other people have a mind, that is, they act on the basis of mental states such as *desires*, *intentions*, *emotions*, and *beliefs* and, furthermore, that they use these mental states to both predict and explain behavior—their own behavior as well as that of other people. In short, theory of mind denotes the *understanding* of the basic concepts that make up the theory, for example, the understanding that one could act on the basis of a false belief or that different people may interpret the same stimulus differently.

In contrast, we use the term *mindreading* to refer to the deployment of theory of mind in the service of the prediction or understanding of one's self or another. Mindreading takes into account more than simply the nature of the concepts that the person holds. It refers to how the holder utilizes her theory of mind in the service of some goal (such as predicting another's actions), regardless of the level of understanding she may have reached. In other words, both 3-year-old children and adults engage in mindreading, the difference being in the nature of the concepts the two will have formed. In essence, mind-reading is a theory of mind in *action*, as it is being used by the holder.

The notion that sexual offenders might have a deficit in their theory of mind or mentalizing ability is a compelling suggestion. First, it appeals on intuitive grounds, helping to explain the seemingly inexplicable, that is, the question of how someone who could forcibly impose sex on another adult or coerce a child into a sexual relationship could be said to have a reasonable grasp of another's perspective. Second, many of the deficits revealed in the functioning of sex offenders seem to fall clearly within the explanatory realm of the theory-of-mind hypothesis. That is, the deficits in empathy, the presence of cognitive distortions, and problems with intimate relationships are all relevant to theory of mind in that they involve either an inability or a deficiency in the ability to mindread accurately. Thus, the theory-of-mind perspective offers a unifying explanation for these seemingly disparate dysfunctions. Third, the theory-of-mind hypothesis offers a unique perspective and leads to new insights into the disorders shown by sexual offenders. Furthermore, the theory-of-mind perspective opens the area to further empirical inquiries that could shed more light on the etiology and the maintenance of sexual offending. Examining the nature of possible deficits in the theory of mind of sexual offenders leads the researcher to ask questions about the nature of their deficits that might otherwise go unasked.

Ultimately, it seems that global deficits in sex offenders' theories of mind are improbable, and even if they do exist in some individuals are unlikely to lead directly to sexual offending. As Blair (2001) has highlighted, autistic children (children who have a global deficit in their understanding of mental states) are no more likely than children with intact theories of mind to act in aggressive or violent ways. Moreover, previous research by Blair and colleagues with psychopathic individuals has shown that this group is not significantly impaired in its ability to make mental state attributions (Blair, 2001). Thus, the mere presence of a deficit in the ability to grasp concepts such as the interpretative nature of theory of mind (Carpendale & Chandler, 1996) is unlikely to lead to sexual offending in any simple or direct fashion. What seems more probable is the possibility that deficits in the conceptual development of a theory of mind, or lags in the acquisition of a theory of mind, might lead to a developmental cascade of negative effects. This could include adverse effects on attachment bonds, the formation of intimate relationships in adolescence and beyond (e.g., Marshall, 1989), the formation of cognitive distortions about victims and potential victims, and the construction of implicit theories that underlie the reasoning processes of child molesters and other sexual offenders (see below).

Earlier experiences, such as the fact of early sexual abuse that seems to characterize the backgrounds of a large number of offenders (Marshall & Barbaree, 1990), may be related to acquisition of deficits in one's theory of mind and/or ability to mindread. However, under the theory-of-mind framework outlined here and in Keenan and Ward (2000), these earlier experiences are best thought of as distal causes of offending behavior, whereas theory-of-mind deficits are a more proximal cause of offenders' behavior.

It is important to note that theory-of-mind development is increasingly recognized as a process that goes well beyond early childhood. Developing an understanding of second-order mental states, the interpretative nature of mind, and speech acts such as sarcasm and irony that are premised on a sophisticated understanding of mental states are all aspects of theory of mind that are acquired later in development (Keenan, 2002). Delays in constructing theories of mind may lead children/adolescents to process age-appropriate sorts of experiences in light of a developmentally immature theory. For example, adolescents who are delayed in their understanding of the interpretative nature of mind and are not particularly adept at inferring the intentions behind a speaker's communicative attempts may experience particular difficulties with nonliteral types of speech such as sarcasm and irony. Given that one function of these speech acts is to divide an audience into those who "get it" and those who do not, adolescents with a developmentally delayed theory of mind may find themselves to be less accepted by their peer group. It is possible that these sorts of processes could result in feelings of inadequacy and immaturity and could lead to a tendency to associate or identify with younger children. During puberty, where sexual themes and issues are more salient, the presence of this tendency could increase the likelihood of developmentally inappropriate sexual feelings about children.

We suggest that sexual offenders' behavior is most likely the result of a combination of deviant implicit theories and poor mindreading skills. Many offenders are likely to have inadequate mindreading skills and, consequently, will experience difficulties employing their theory of mind in order to understand another's point of view, predict another's behavior, and so forth. Thus, according to our theory, many offenders will engage in deviant behavior because of inaccurate inferences about another individual's mental states. For example, a date rapist may inaccurately assume that a woman's denials mask real sexual interest and as such, represent sexually provocative behavior. This false attribution could result in a failure to self-regulate his actions and to subsequent sexually aggressive comments and behavior.

The relationship between theory-of-mind deficits and sexual crimes is likely to be complex, and it may be that offenders have difficulty in identifying only some types of mental states. For example, some child molesters are very good at grooming victims, gradually gaining their trust and persuading them to engage in sexual behavior. Such individuals may be able to infer feelings of vulnerability accurately but mistakenly attribute sexual desires and needs to such children. Or they may be able to infer desires accurately but not beliefs. Thus, a child who has been sexually abused might have been reinforced for sexual activity with adults and appear to "want" sex. In reality, however, the child may view the situation as one in which he or she is cared for and noticed, rather than as a reciprocal sexual encounter. In other words, the offender has not fully grasped the child's needs and beliefs about the situation in question. In addition, a sex offender may have a robust and comprehensive theory of mind but fail to employ it in some situations because of the influence of intense emotional states, stressors, or simply the presence of competing motives such as sexual desire (for an in-depth discussion of these issues see Ward et al., 2000).

Implicit Theories

In recent years a number of researchers in developmental (e.g., Wellman, 1990), cognitive (e.g., Kuhn, 1989), and personality (e.g., Dweck, Chiu, & Hong, 1995) psychology have argued that understanding and explanation in their area of interest is underpinned by implicit or lay theories. This research suggests that from an early age knowledge is organized into theories that facilitate understanding of the world. Such theories enable individuals to explain and understand aspects of their social environment, and therefore to make predictions about future events. These predictions typically take the form of expectations and help people to control their lives. Theories also constrain the kind of inferences individuals make about unseen or underlying states. For example, inferring that a partner is angry or upset will be based on knowledge of the relationship between certain mental states, conditions, and behavior. Forgetting a birthday (condition) and noting that a partner refuses to converse (behavior) will typically result in a causal inference that he or she is angry (mental state) about the failure to acknowledge the birthday. Knowledge in the form of implicit theories concerning mental states (i.e., what mental states are, how they are expressed, how they interact, etc.), their relationship to social conditions, and their expression in behavior enable individuals to make inferences about what another person is probably experiencing, and to predict his or her future actions.

Lay or implicit theories have also been called folk psychological knowledge and represent everyday understandings of close relationships, other peoples' actions, the structure of the natural world, and the nature of mental states. A variety of terms have been used to refer to this knowledge, for example, implicit theories, commonsense theories, folk psychological theories, lay theories, and intuitive theories. In this chapter we use the term *implicit theory* to cover all these uses. Such theories are called implicit because they are rarely articulated in a formal sense and may not be easily expressed by an individual.

Thus human knowledge is thought to be theory-like in some respects and to share a number of features with scientific theories. First, many implicit theories contain assumptions that specify an ontology, that is, describe the nature of human beings in terms of core psychological structures and processes. Second, these constructs and their relationships are used to explain human actions in different contexts and, like theoretical terms in a scientific theory, refer to unobservable mechanisms or psychological states. For example, socially avoidant behavior might be explained by reference to fears of rejection or to doubts about the trustworthiness of potential partners. Third, implicit theories are relatively coherent and contain a number of beliefs and concepts that are interconnected.

A final feature in common with scientific theories is that implicit theories produce interpretations of evidence, as opposed to theory-neutral descriptions of evidence: Observations are theory-laden. What counts as evidence or information bearing on a theory's truth or falsity depends on its constructs. For example, an implicit theory of mind that was based on desire-related terms (see Wellman, 1990) would view an appeal to cognitive data to refute it as inadmissible or irrelevant. Similarly, if a person who believes that intelligence is fixed and innate fails a test, he or she is likely to regard evidence concerning a lack of effort as irrelevant (see Dweck et al., 1995). Failure would simply point to a lack of ability rather than a lack of application.

In a recent paper, Ward (2000) argued that sexual offenders' cognitive distortions emerge from underlying causal theories about the nature of themselves, their victims, and the world rather than stemming from unrelated, independent beliefs. These implicit theories function like scientific theories and are used to explain empirical regularities (e.g., other people's actions) and to make predictions about the world. They are relatively coherent and constituted by a number of interlocking ideas. This hypothesis is based on research in developmental psychology that views much of cognitive development, for example, acquiring a theory of mind, as driven by children's acquisition of implicit theories in a given domain (e.g., Wellman, 1990). The child is said to act like a scientist, forming hypotheses, testing them, and discarding those that fail to predict behavior. Therefore, just as science progresses through the development of successively more adequate theories, so does children's understanding of other peoples' mental states. According to this perspective, children develop a succession of increasingly adequate understandings (implicit theories) of the mind. This change occurs as a function of the evidence and the ability of their existing theories to explain and predict the phenomenon in question adequately.

Ward argued that maladaptive implicit theories can be constructed to explain a range of unusual interpersonal events confronting sex offenders during their early development; for example, sexual abuse or exposure to inappropriate sexual behavior. Implicit theories enable such individuals to interpret important interpersonal events meaningfully and to increase their capacity to predict and control the world. However, the content of these implicit theories is likely to be maladaptive and not generalize appropriately to the wider community. An offender's implicit theory about his victim's beliefs, preferences, and desires will directly influence any future inferences he makes about his victim's internal states, and how he predicts his victim will react. The implicit theory will also partially determine his reaction to the victim's responses to the abuse. For example, if an offender thinks a victim wanted and sought out sex with him, he is likely to get angry if he is blamed for any sexual contact. Implicit theories dictate what counts as evidence and how it is to be interpreted. If there is a discrepancy between an offender's implicit theory and evidence, the evidence may be reinterpreted or rejected. Rarely, the implicit theory may be modified. These implicit theories guide the processing of information or "evidence" that is relevant to its truth or falsity. Evidence that does not "fit" the implicit theory's basic assumptions and predictions is rejected or interpreted in light of these core assumptions.

Evidence for this idea is provided by Ward and Keenan (1999), who identified a small number of underlying beliefs that appear to underpin child molesters' cognitive distortions. They examined a variety of scales used to measure distortions as well as several studies describing offenders' cognitive distortions and proposed that the majority of these distorted cognitions can be derived from the following five implicit theories. It is important to note that as the following implicit theories have been developed to explain the full range of cognitive distortions seen across a range of sexual offenders, it is likely that only a subset of the following implicit theories will be present in a given sexual offender.

CHILDREN AS SEXUAL OBJECTS

Those holding this implicit theory are likely to have the core belief that children are sexual beings or that they are motivated primarily by pleasure. Although children have a range of normal pleasure-motivated goals, those holding this implicit theory see these goals as including sexual activity with adults. Children are seen as possessing sexual needs, desires, and preferences and as being able to develop their own plans to achieve these goals. They are thought to be capable of making their own choices about how to seek and achieve sexual experiences.

ENTITLEMENT

Those holding this implicit theory have the core belief that some people are superior to others and have a right to impose their desires upon less important individuals. The source of this superiority may be gender, class, or some other factor. For example, such individuals might believe that men are more powerful than women or children and thus have a right to have their sexual needs met. A related belief is that there are no binding truths for those who are more powerful, and therefore whatever one can get away with constitutes a legitimate action. Offenders may develop the entitlement implicit theory as a result of early experiences of rejection.

DANGEROUS WORLD

Those holding this implicit theory have the core belief that the world is dangerous and that other people are inherently abusive and rejecting. This is likely to lead to a number of related beliefs. Therefore, individuals endorsing this implicit theory believe that they are unable to retaliate against other adults and that children are more likely to understand them. This implicit theory may develop as a result of early and continued physical or emotional abuse where the individual learns that he must take special measures in order to avoid harm or to satisfy his own needs or desires.

UNCONTROLLABLE

Those holding this implicit theory have the core belief that personality and sexual preferences are unchangeable and that they have no control over their expression. This implicit theory could be seen as analogous to having an external locus of control. The uncontrollable implicit theory may develop as a result of repeated experiences of feeling out of control in relation to sexual or emotional drives. Individuals may also use this as a convenient excuse for reducing personal responsibility for their offenses.

NATURE OF HARM

Those holding this implicit theory have the core belief that there are degrees of harm one can inflict upon another person and that sexual activity alone is unlikely to hurt another person. The first aspect of this belief centers on the central idea that harm exists in degrees ranging from minor to extreme. Major damage is thought to occur when the victim is physically assaulted, is conscious throughout the experience, and when the abuser is in a position of trust and responsibility. Consequently, if an offense could have been more harmful, offenders regard themselves as having regard for the victim's well-being. Therefore, they should be judged less harshly than one who inflicted more harm. The second belief centers on the idea that sexual activity is beneficial. Harm is believed to result from additional violence imposed during the abuse, society's reaction to the abuse, or a victim being told that sexual activity with adults is harmful. Ward and Keenan (1999) suggested that this implicit theory is often secondary to and used in conjunction with other implicit theories.

Conclusions

The ideas discussed in this chapter have been derived from the developmental literature and applied to the domain of sexual offending. Self-regulation, theory of mind, and implicit theories provide a related network of ideas with which to approach the investigation of a number of seemingly disparate problems frequently identified in sexual offenders. Arguably, the ability to discern what other people feel, think, and need springs from knowledge that others represent the world in a unique way, and that certain cues are suggestive of their underlying mental states. Difficulty in making these types of mental state attributions is likely to result in a lack of attunement with other people, and therefore creates an interpersonal context in which inappropriate, and possibly abusive, behavior can occur. Failure of self-regulation may further lead to an increased likelihood of the offender's acting on distorted ideas about others' needs and wants or a simple failure to stop and fully consider the victim's point of view.

An important issue for future research in this area is to examine the possibility of equifinality and multifinality in the development of sexual offending. Taking the specific case of child molesters as an example, researchers need to address the question of whether there are diverse developmental pathways to the same end (in this case, deviant sexual behavior involving children). For example, the incidence of early sexual abuse in the history of child molesters may lead to problems with self-regulation and the onset of deviant sexual fantasies that are eventually acted upon. Although early sexual abuse may constitute one pathway that leads to sexual abuse, there are certainly other pathways to the same end state, as Ward and Siegert (in press) have suggested. Researchers clearly need to take seriously the possibility of multiple pathways to sexual offending against children, if not only to understand better the origins of such behavior, because knowing how the individual entered the pathway to offending may have important implications for prevention and treatment. Similarly, developing a better understanding of how particular risk factors lead to diverse outcomes for different individuals, or multifinality, may again have important prevention and treatment implications in addition to the knowledge gained about the origins of sexual offending. Psychological theory in the area of sexual offending has come to recognize the importance of a variety of developmental constructs for understanding the etiology of offending. It is now time to capitalize on the promise of developmental approaches in order that we may learn all we can about deviant sexual behavior and minimize its adverse consequences to the best of our ability.

References

Astington, J. W. (1994). *Childhood discovery of the mind.* London: Fontana.

Barbaree, H. E., Marshall, W. L., & McCormick, J. (1998). The development of deviant sexual behaviour among adolescents and its implications for prevention and treatment. *The Irish Journal of Psychology, 19,* 1-31.

Baumeister, R. F., & Heatherton, T. F. (1996). Self-regulation failure: An overview. *Psychological Inquiry, 7,* 1-15.

Blair, R. J. (2001). Theory of mind and antisocial behaviour. In B. Repacholi & V. Slaughter (Eds.) *Individual differences in theory of mind: Implications for typical and atypical development.* London: Psychology Press.

Carpendale, J. I., & Chandler, M. J. (1996). On the distinction between false belief understanding and subscribing to an interpretative theory of mind. *Child Development, 67,* 1686-1706.

Cicchetti, D. (1993). Developmental psychopathology: Reactions, reflections, projections. *Developmental Review, 13,* 471-502.

Cicchetti, D., & Rogosch, F. (1996). Equifinality and multifinality in developmental psychopathology. *Development and Psychopathology, 8,* 597-600.

Cole, P. M., & Putnam, F. W. (1992). The effect of incest on self and social functioning: A developmental psychopathological perspective. *Journal of Consulting and Clinical Psychology, 60,* 174-184.

Dweck, C. S., Chiu, C., & Hong, Y. (1995). Implicit theories and their role in judgments and reactions: A world from two perspectives. *Psychological Inquiry, 6,* 267-285.

Finkelhor, D. (1984). *Child sexual abuse: New theory and research.* New York: Free Press.

Kanfer, F. H., & Scheft, B. K. (1988). *Guiding the process of therapeutic change.* Champaign, IL: Research Press.

Keenan, T. (2002). *An introduction to child development.* London: Sage.

Keenan, T., & Ward, T. (2000). A theory of mind perspective on cognitive, affective, and intimacy deficits in sex offenders. *Sexual Abuse: A Journal of Research and Treatment, 12,* 49-60.

Kuhn, D. (1989). Children and adults as intuitive scientists. *Psychological Bulletin, 96,* 674-689.

Loeber, R. (1990). Development and risk factors associated with juvenile antisocial behavior and delinquency. *Clinical Psychology Review, 10,* 1-41.

Marshall, W. L. (1989). Invited essay: Intimacy, loneliness and sexual offenders. *Behaviour Research and Therapy, 27,* 491-503.

Marshall, W. L., & Barbaree, H. E. (1990). An integrated theory of the etiology of sexual offending. In W. L. Marshall, D. R. Laws, & H. E. Barbaree (Eds.), *Handbook of sexual assault: Issues, theories, and treatment of the offender* (pp. 257-275). New York: Plenum.

Marshall, W. L., Hudson, S. M., Jones, R., & Fernandez, Y. M. (1995). Empathy in sex offenders. *Clinical Psychology Review, 15,* 99-113.

Rutter, M., & Garmezy, N. (1983). Developmental psychopathology. In P. H. Mussen (Series Ed.) & E. M. Hetherington (Vol. Ed.), *Socialization, personality and social development* (4th ed., pp. 775-911). New York: John Wiley.

Rutter, M., Giller, H., & Hagell, A. (1998). *Antisocial behaviour by young people.* Cambridge, UK: Cambridge University Press.

Thompson, R. A. (1994). Emotional regulation: A theme in search of definition. In N. A. Fox (Ed.), The development of emotion regulation: Biological and behavioral considerations (pp. 25-52). *Monographs of the Society for Research in Child Development,* Vol. 59, Serial No. 240.

Ward, T. (2000). Sexual offenders' cognitive distortions as implicit theories. *Aggression and Violent Behavior, 5,* 491-507.

Ward, T., Hudson, S. M., Johnston, L., & Marshall, W. L. (1997). Cognitive distortions in sex offenders: An integrative review. *Clinical Psychology Review, 17,* 479-507.

Ward, T., Hudson, S. M., & Keenan, T. (1998). A self-regulation model of the offense process. *Sexual Abuse: A Journal of Research and Treatment, 10,* 141-157.

Ward, T., & Keenan, T. (1999). Child molesters' implicit theories. *The Journal of Interpersonal Violence, 14,* 821-838.

Ward, T., Keenan, T., & Hudson, S. M. (2000). Understanding affective, intimacy, and cognitive deficits in sex offenders. A developmental perspective. *Aggression and Violent Behavior, 5*, 41-62.

Ward, T., & Siegert, R. J. (in press). Toward a comprehensive theory of child sexual abuse: A theory knitting perspective. *Psychology, Crime, & Law.*

Wenar, C., & Kerig, P. (2000). *Developmental Psychopathology* (4th ed.). New York: McGraw-Hill.

Wellman, H. M. (1990). *The child's theory of mind.* Cambridge: MIT Press.

8

Cognitive Distortions, Schemas, and Implicit Theories

Ruth E. Mann
H. M. Prison Service, London, England

Anthony R. Beech
University of Birmingham, England

Sexual offender treatment programs are well established in many countries (see Marshall, Hudson, Ward, & Fernandez, 1998), and the most effective treatment approach seems to be cognitive behavioral (Alexander, 1999). The cognitive behavioral model assumes that cognitions—thoughts, attitudes, and beliefs—play a key role in determining behavior. But beyond this, theories of the role of cognition in sexual offending are hard to find. Research has focused almost entirely on the measurement of attitudes and beliefs supporting sexual offending such as rape myths or child abuse supportive attitudes (e.g., Abel et al., 1989; Beech, 1998; Bumby, 1995; Burt, 1980). Despite strong calls for a more theory-driven approach to be adopted, in particular differentiating cognitive structures and processing from cognitive products (Segal & Stermac, 1990; Ward, Hudson,

AUTHORS' NOTE: The authors would like to acknowledge the assistance of Clive R. Hollin (Centre for Applied Psychology, University of Leicester, England) in the preparation of this chapter.

Johnston, & Marshall, 1997), research has not really progressed away from the measurement approach.

The challenge in understanding any criminal event—and the prerequisite for reducing crime—is to recognize the multiple factors that underpin and motivate the criminal act. Multiple influences on a criminal event include fixed psychological characteristics (such as personality traits), fluctuating psychological states (such as mood, motivation, or self-talk), and circumstantial and situational factors. Within such a broad model of crime (e.g., Clarke, 1977) it is important to note that cognition is only one factor to be considered in a multifactorial theory of sexual offending.

The Development of the Concept of Cognitive Distortions in Relation to Sexual Offending

Beck (1963) coined the term *cognitive distortions* to describe "idiosyncratic thought content indicative of distorted or unrealistic conceptualisations" (p. 324) in cognitive therapy. The first author to use the term in sexual offender work was Gene Abel (Abel et al., 1989), who defined the concept as referring to

> An individual's internal processes, including the justifications, perceptions, and judgements used by the sex offender to rationalize his child molestation behavior . . . [that] appear to allow the offender to justify his ongoing sexual abuse of children without the anxiety, guilt and loss of self esteem that would usually result from an individual committing behaviors contrary to the norms of society. (p. 134)

Even though it is a term enshrined in the sexual offender literature (Beech & Mann, 2002), with Neidigh and Krop (1992) describing 38 separate categories of distortion, it is a term that has suffered from unclear or inconsistent usage and problems in definition. For example, even in the original Abel et al. definition, it is not clear whether the term means that offenders consciously employ excuses and justifications in order to reduce the level to which they feel vilified by others, or whether cognitive distortions are unconscious processes adopted to protect the offender from shame or guilt, or both.

Also, there is considerable debate as to the purpose that cognitive distortions serve, with some theorists suggesting that they essentially play a maintenance function in offending, namely, they are used to justify previous behaviors (Abel et al., 1989; Murphy, 1990); while others, such as Finkelhor (1984) and Ward and Siegert (in press), see cognitive distortions arising prior to offending and playing a causative role in the offense process. Finkelhor describes the production of cognitive distortions essentially as a way of overcoming internal inhibitions prior to offending, whereas Ward and Siegert view cognitive distortions as the product of underlying schemas.

Ward (Ward & Keenan, 1999) has been one of the few to provide a rigorous definition of the nature of cognitive distortions. Here he suggests that cognitive distortions arise out of a set of core schemas held by the offender. In effect, these underlying schemas generate the cognitive distortions that are measured at the surface level (Ward et al., 1997). Ward goes on to suggest that these schemas are, in effect, "implicit theories" that the offender has about the world. These theories are similar to scientific theories in that they are used to explain, predict, and interpret interpersonal phenomena. Ward and Keenan (1999) identify five implicit theories that account for the majority of specific distortions identified by Neidigh and Krop (1992) in child abusers. Briefly, these implicit theories (as described by Beech & Mann, 2002) are as follows:

Children as Sexual Beings. Here an offender has an implicit theory that perceives children as being able to and wanting to engage in sexual activity and being able to consent to, and not be harmed by, any sexual contact with adults. Here also the offender has the idea that the existence of sexual desires is "natural, benign and harmless."

Entitlement. The nature of this implicit theory is described as the offender thinking that he is superior and more important than others. Therefore, he sees himself as being entitled to have sex when he wants from those who are less powerful/less important than he is.

Nature of Harm. The main aspect of this theory is that sexual activity does not cause harm and may in fact be beneficial to the child (in terms of teaching the child about sex). The offender will also tell himself that there are degrees of harm and that provided the offender does not inflict any serious physical damage, then little harm is caused.

Dangerous World. Here the content of the implicit theory is that the world is a dangerous place and that others are abusive and rejecting. Therefore the offender will tell himself that it is both important to fight back and achieve control over others and that children are less likely to be abusive and rejecting and hence are more likely to be able to give the offender what he needs (sex and affection).

Uncontrollable. This implicit theory may have its roots in the offender's being abused as a child or being exposed to other traumatic events. Hence, the offender perceives the world as uncontrollable. The types of distortions that arise out of this implicit theory relate to offenses that the offender sees as beyond his control.

Some of these theories could equally legitimately be classed as offense supportive attitudes (e.g., children as sexual objects, and the belief that sex with children is not harmful to them). But the notions of entitlement, dangerous world, and uncontrollable world are more obviously suited to the description of schemas.

Along similar lines, Hanson (1998) proposed that sexual offenders have sex offense schemas containing the following elements: egocentric self-perception, sex overvalued in the pursuit of happiness (including a link between sex and power), and an ability to justify to oneself that some victims are legitimate.

At this point it would seem useful to consider some of the broader theoretical ideas that these notions of schema/implicit theories are embedded in before we come back to talk about schemas in sexual offending in more detail.

Models of Cognition and Behavior

As discussed above, the research on role of cognition in sexual offending has been hampered by imprecise definitions and inconsistent use of terms. In order to attempt a more precise understanding of how cognition affects behavior, we briefly review two popular models: social cognition theory and cognitive therapy theory. These two models are not mutually exclusive but have considerable overlap; in particular, both theories place heavy emphasis on the concept of *schema* as an organizer of thought and the processing of information.

SOCIAL COGNITION THEORY

Social cognition theory grew out of attempts by social psychologists in the 1960s and 1970s to avoid the pitfalls of behaviorism. Social psychologists adopted the information processing approach of cognitive psychology and applied this to social behavior, in particular in the contexts of individual and group interactions (Augoustinos & Walker, 1995). The basic premise of social cognition theory is that human beings interpret social situations using expectations, prior knowledge, and assumptions. However, most people are unaware of these influences on their thinking and thus fail to challenge their own interpretations of events, believing they are seeing the world in a literal way.

In social cognition theory, the structures in memory in which prior knowledge and expectancies are organized are known as schemas. This concept became very popular in the late 1970s, unfortunately resulting in some inconsistent definitions and heated disagreement about the exact meaning of the term *schema* (Fiske & Linville, 1980). A relatively safe definition of schema is that it is a cognitive structure that represents knowledge about a type of stimulus, its attributes, and the relationship between them (Fiske & Taylor, 1991). Schemas are the structures within memory that guide our attention, inform our perceptions, prompt our inferences, and save us energy by providing shortcuts to interpreting social situations. Thus, schemas are structures, but they affect our cognitive processes.

Mostly, social cognition psychologists have studied the effect of schemas on information processing, while largely ignoring the relationship between schemas and behavior. Fiske and Linville (1980) concluded, "The link between the schematic bases of cognition and behavior is an untapped gold mine" (p. 549). More recently, the notion of schema-driven information processing has been applied to understanding pathological behaviors such as marital violence or aggression in children (see below for a brief review of this work). The usefulness of social cognition theory in understanding sexual assault was first identified by Segal and Stermac (1990), who suggested that research into sexual offending move away from measures of cognitive products (i.e., measurement of levels of distorted attitudes) toward information processing experiments. More recently, Ward et al. (1997) comprehensively reviewed cognition-focused research in the sexual offender field and concluded that Segal and Stermac's (1990) recommendations had not been implemented. In their view, understanding of sexual abuse would be greatly enhanced by "a full understanding of the cognitive processes, products and structures, their interactions with affective states, and the variability of all these phenomena over time" (Ward et al., 1997, p. 501).

THEORY UNDERLYING COGNITIVE THERAPY

Cognitive therapy is one of the most widely practiced forms of psychotherapy today. Cognitive therapy theory originated when Beck, a psychoanalyst, began to notice that themes of rejection and self-criticism were characteristic in the verbalizations of depressed patients. Beck concluded that cognition, not affect, was the cardinal feature of depression (Beck, 1963, 1964, 1967). Cognitive therapy theory has since been applied to a variety of pathological conditions, including anxiety (Beck, Emery, & Greenburg, 1985), substance abuse (Beck, Wright, Newman, & Liese, 1993), and violence (Beck, 1999).

The concept of schema is central to cognitive therapy (Beck, 1964, 1967). Beck (1964) defined a schema as a "cognitive structure used for screening, encoding and evaluating impinging stimuli" (p. 562). The idea dates back to Bartlett (1932), who defined a schema as a generic cognitive representation that the mind extracts in the course of exposure to a particular instance of a phenomenon. In cognitive therapy, schemas are seen to direct all cognitive activity, such as ruminations, automatic thoughts, and cognitive processing of external events. Schemas contain attitudes, ideas about the self and the world, specific beliefs, conditional (if . . ., then . . .) assumptions, and core issues (the most central ideas about the self). Schemas are strongly related to personal goals and values, and play a key role in the basis of pathological emotional disorders when they contain faulty content such as overly rigid assumptions or negative self-referential ideas.

Because of the importance of interpersonal relationships in our species, Saffran (1990) stresses the importance of encoding such interactions as self-other relationship schemas. According to Saffran, such interpersonal schemas would act as programs for maintaining relatedness. He goes on to suggest that this notion "also clarifies the fashion in which self-worth contingencies, goals, plans, and strategies can be coded as part of the same schematic structure." Further, and of crucial importance to the argument being made here regarding the notion of schemas underpinning the distorted thinking patterns found in sexual offenders, are (a) that such schemas are acquired on the basis of previous interactions relevant to the maintenance of interpersonal relatedness; and (b) that such interpersonal schemas act as implicit rules for maintaining relatedness.

In terms of schemas related to offending, Huesmann (1988) describes the acquisitions of aggressive cognitive scripts (schemas) that act as blueprints for aggression and whether or not rewards or punishment follow the implementation of such scripts. In the case of domestic violence, Dutton (1998) suggests that rewards would include "winning a power struggle," whereas punishment could include anything from feelings of guilt or shame, the relationship breaking down, to police intervention. Beck (1999) has proposed seven schemas related to (nonsexual) violence:

- Authorities are controlling and punitive
- Spouses are deceitful
- Outsiders are hostile
- Nobody can be trusted
- I need to fight back
- Physical force gets respect
- If you don't get even, people will walk over you

Although Beck described these beliefs as separate schemas, they could also be seen as beliefs contained within a single "hostile world" schema.

We now briefly review the research related to schemas and sexual offending. It should be noted that authors have used different terms. For example, Huesmann (1988) used the term *script* interchangeably with schema, whereas Ward and Keenan (1999) chose to use the term *implicit theory* instead of schema, although noting that the two concepts may be identical.

Schemas in Sexual Offending:
A Review of Current Research

There has been only a very small handful of published studies that have explicitly examined cognitive schemas in sexual offenders. However, some of the attitude research in existence contains clues about the nature of schemas that may be related to sexual assault. The first references to schemas as a relevant notion in criminal behavior arose from information processing models of offending. For instance, Huesmann (1988), as mentioned above, proposed a model of aggressive behavior based on information processing principles that included the presence of cynical, adversarial, and hostile schemas about other people. McFall (1990) applied the same principles to sexually aggressive men, suggesting that schemas concerning heterosexual relationships would be distorted in sexual offenders, encouraging men to focus on ambiguous cues from women and interpret them as "come-ons."

Malamuth and colleagues (e.g., Malamuth & Brown, 1994; Malamuth, Sockloskie, Koss, & Tanaka, 1991) were the first researchers to investigate the ideas empirically. Malamuth et al. described and tested the following theory of sexual aggression between known parties (i.e., acquaintance rape). In this theory, the origins of this type of sexual aggression lie in the early home experiences of the aggressor. Certain childhood environments, such as violence between parents, lead to the development of aggressive adversarial schemas about intimate relationships between men and women. The attitudes involved are reinforced by association with delinquent peers and/or the modern Western sociocultural environment where qualities such as power and toughness are admired. At the same time, prosocial protective skills, such as the ability to manage frustration and to negotiate through conflict, do not develop. The development of such a hostile schema is termed the "hostility path." If, at the same time, a boy learns to place undue emphasis on sexual conquest as a source of identity (the "sexual promiscuity path"), the interaction between the two pathways would lead to sexual aggression. That is, sexual promiscuity alone would not lead to sexual aggression, but if moderated by hostile schemas, then such aggression can occur.

In their testing of this model, Malamuth et al. used three measures as indicators of hostility: Burt's (1980) Adversarial Sexual Beliefs scale where women are seen as inherently deceitful, the Negative Masculinity scale (Spence, Helmreich, & Holahan, 1979), and the Hostility Toward Women scale (Check, 1985). Therefore the combination of these three measures could be said to cover a schema about men and women containing properties such as women are deceitful and men should assert themselves. Malamuth et al. (1991) termed this schema "hostile masculinity." Malamuth et al.'s data supported their model, indicating that sexual aggression (from a man to a known woman) resulted from a combination of high levels of hostile masculinity and sexual promiscuity. Hostile masculinity without sexual promiscuity was related to nonsexual aggression against women. Malamuth et al. emphasized that the findings should not be generalized to men who rape strangers without further testing within that group. So far there have been no studies investigating this model with stranger rapists or convicted rapists.

A further schema relevant to sexual aggression was identified by Malamuth and Brown (1994). This study was designed to explore the findings of Murphy, Coleman, and Haynes (1986) that sexually aggressive men were less able to discriminate between hostility and assertiveness than nonaggressive men. Malamuth and Brown (1994) proposed that there were three possible explanations for this finding, which they termed the overperception hypothesis, the negative blindness hypothesis, and the suspiciousness hypothesis. If a woman was assertively to reject a man's advances, overperception would lead to this being seen as aggression, negative blindness would mean that the rejection was not noticed, and suspiciousness would lead to the behavior being perceived as seductive.

As with all Malamuth's experiments, subjects were not convicted sexual offenders, but university and community non-offending males, some of whom self-reported sexual aggression. Participants were shown a video of scenarios where a woman responded in different ways to a sexual advance made by a man in a bar: friendly, seductive, or assertively rejecting or hostile. Results showed that sexually aggressive men perceived the hostile rejections as being seductive, and the seductive reaction as being negative and hostile. Thus the suspiciousness schema hypothesis was confirmed: Sexually aggressive men seem to believe that women are game-playing, deceptive people who use aggression as a form of seduction and who are deceitful when they behave seductively. The more highly aggressive the man, the greater his level of suspicion. The suspiciousness pattern is termed a schema rather than an attitude because, in this experiment, it was clearly shown to be the cause of faulty information processing. However, studies investigating the belief that women are deceitful could also be carried out as attitude studies, and indeed it can be seen above that Malamuth et al. (1991) include this belief as part of the hostile masculinity schema.

Although they did not conceptualize it as a schema, Hanson, Gizzarelli, and Scott's (1994) notion of sexual entitlement may fit the definition. A questionnaire measuring this construct, among others, was administered to incest offenders and two comparison groups: non-offending males and male batterers. An overall difference on the measure between groups was attributable to a mixture of the incest offenders showing more child-abuse–supportive beliefs and scoring more highly on the sexual entitlement subscale. Items related to sexual entitlement included, "A person should have sex whenever it is needed," and "Women should oblige men's sexual needs." Sexual entitlement could be considered to be a schema (or part of a schema) rather than an attitude because it is specifically concerned with the relationship between the self and others.

Myers (2000) compared "life maps" (autobiographies) of rapists, child molesters, and non-sexually violent offenders in terms of themes to do with their views of themselves and the world. She found very different patterns among the three groups. Rapists showed clear patterns (or schemas) of distrust of women and need for control. The clearest patterns for child molesters, in contrast, were worthlessness and passive victim stance. Violent offenders were similar to rapists in their need for control, but did not show the distrust-of-women schema. Sexual entitlement figured for rapists more than for child molesters and not at all for violent offenders. A schema for violent offenders that did not figure for child molesters or for rapists was to see oneself as a protector of others.

Mann and Hollin (2001) reported some data from two investigations into schemas in sexual offenders. Qualitative rather than quantitative studies were undertaken because of the problems inherent in measuring schema content (often not accessible to consciousness) through self-report. In the first study reported, schema content had been inferred from offenders' reported explanations for their offending. Treatment records of 45 rapists were examined and statements they had made to explain their offending were extracted. This methodology was similar to that employed by Neidigh and Krop (1992) to determine excuses used by sexual offenders. The explanatory statements were then sorted into categories, and the ability to distinguish reliably between categories was then tested using four independent raters. The first study found that it was possible for raters to distinguish reliably between excuses for sexual offending and explanations for offending where distorted information processing was implied. Five categories of schemas were identified:

Grievance. This schema had a flavor of aggressive self-pity. Beliefs related to this schema included, "Women are responsible for hurting me," and, "It was always women's fault when something went wrong." Statements often suggested that revenge or punishment was justifiable when the individual perceived he had been wronged.

Self as Victim. These statements had a flavor of passive self-pity. Whereas the grievance beliefs incorporated an aspect of revenge and punishment, the self-as-victim beliefs contained aspects of hopelessness or helplessness in the face of the world's demands. Beliefs related to this schema included, "I'm the only one to go through pain and loss," and, "Bad things just always happened to me."

Control. Beliefs related to this schema suggested a need to be in a position of power or control over others. Sometimes the offense was described as a competition for control, or a response by the offender to someone trying to control or humiliate him; for example, "She was threatening me, trying to big herself up." Control beliefs differed from grievance beliefs in that control was not being sought for reasons of punishment but for the feelings of success and power it brought to the offender.

Entitlement. These beliefs suggested that the offender saw himself as having a right to do what he wanted, whatever the wishes or rights of others. Other people's wishes were often explicitly disregarded ("I don't care that it's wrong"; "If I have to force her, then I will"). In summary, the main belief of the entitlement schema seemed to be that the offender's needs were paramount, and he did not need to consider any factor other than meeting his needs ("She was my wife; it was my right").

Disrespect for Certain Women. This was more a category schema than a belief schema. Statements were made implying that certain women did not deserve normal standards of respectful behavior. The most common subgroup of women seen in this way was prostitutes.

In the second study, Mann and Hollin (2001) widened their investigation to include child molesters as well as rapists. A similar methodology was employed: the analysis of offenders' replies to motivational questions (Taylor, 1972). A template of reply categories was constructed on an initial sample of 62 offenders, and then applied to a further 100 sexual offenders (35% rapists and 65% child molesters). Two of the 10 reply categories appeared to represent possible schemas: "grievance" and "need for respect/control" (the other categories either referred to other factors associated with sexual assault, such as deviant arousal or desire for intimacy, or referred to excuses/justifications, such as victim blame). The idea of a grievance schema was therefore found in both studies. Furthermore, of the 10 categories of explanation in the second study, rapists referred to grievance most frequently as the cause of offending. The notion of the control schema was also found in both studies, although with slightly different content in the second study. In the second study, schemas were much more noticeably observed in the accounts of rapists than they were in the accounts of child molesters, suggesting that other factors are perhaps more salient for child molesters. This is consistent with the most recent comprehensive theory of sexual offending (Ward & Siegert, in press), where it is proposed that distorted thinking would be a dominant causal mechanism for some sexual offenders but not all.

We now describe a schema-based model of sexual assault based on consideration of social cognition and cognitive therapy theory approaches.

A Schema-Based Model of Sexual Assault

The social cognition approach and cognitive therapy theory show marked similarities in their definitions and descriptions of schemas. Both define schemas as cognitive structures, emphasize that they contain knowledge (including attitudes, beliefs, and stereotypes) derived from past experiences, and are used to guide what we notice and how we respond in any given situation. Both approaches see schemas as being closely linked to affective responses and hint that this is also the case with behavioral responses (although in neither field has research proved anything conclusive with respect to this latter notion). However, social cognition theory has been applied mainly in benign social situations and focused on more simple schemas, such as categories of objects. Cognitive therapy theory has tended to focus more on the nature of self-schemas and other-schemas, and the types of thinking that underlie pathological emotional states. To apply either of these theories to behavior such as sexual assault requires something of an assumptive leap; nevertheless, it is our view that this leap is one at least worthy of further investigation. In our view, cognitive therapy theory has more potential than social cognition theory for assisting our understanding of sexual assault; partly because its research tradition more closely matches the kind of issues found with sexual offenders, and also because it is explicitly linked to a therapeutic approach for rebuilding dysfunctional schemas.

Drawing on both theories, but in particular on recent cognitive therapy models of schemas in depression (e.g., Kwon & Oei, 1994) we therefore propose the following schema-based model of cognition in sexual offending (see Figure 8.1).

In this model, a schema is defined as a structure containing beliefs or attitudes that follow a similar theme or pattern and that have developed as a result of trying to make sense of early life experiences. Schemas contain fundamental assumptions about oneself and one's relationship with others and the world, and have become organizing frameworks for processing new information, particularly social and interpersonal information. Schemas are stable structures that are chronically accessible and are particularly relied on to draw inferences in ambiguous or threatening situations, where they focus attention and interpretation resources upon schema-relevant cues.

In this model (see Figure 8.1), underlying dysfunctional schemas interact with life events to produce hostile cognitive output (thoughts). These thoughts, set in the context of other risk factors related to sexual offending (e.g., lack of intimacy, lifestyle impulsivity, poor self-management, deviant sexual interest), increase the likelihood of sexual assaultative behavior being selected as an appropriate course of action.

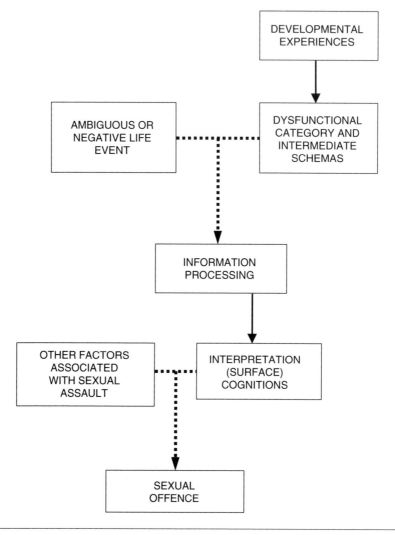

Figure 8.1 A Schema-Based Model of Cognition in Sexual Offending

In particular, two types of schema are hypothesized to be relevant to sexual assault. First, *category schemas* (stereotypes) about women or children may be relevant if they contain abnormal hostile or sexual components, respectively. For example, rapists may carry hostile beliefs about women that involve assumptions that women are deceitful or treacherous. Some child molesters, particularly fixated pedophiles, may carry assumptions that children are sexually interested or sexually knowing. These category schemas would mean that ambiguous information about women or children (such as a woman being peremptory in manner or a female child doing a handstand and displaying her underwear) are interpreted in a biased way consistent with the offender's schema. Here he assumes that rejecting or sexual signals are being sent out. The nature of his biased interpretations increases the likelihood of sexual offending, which in a particular case appears to the offender to be a justified response.

Second, sex offenders are also hypothesized to hold *belief schemas* that contain assumptions about the self and how the world and other people should be. These assumptions are likely to be conditional or compensatory rules. In accordance with Beck's theory, these belief schemas are attached to affective, motivational, physiological, and behavioral stages, the entire structure being viewed as a *mode*. When these schemas are activated by ambiguous or threatening events, information processing becomes biased in favor of the underlying schema. For example, a sexual offender may hold a schema containing the power belief, "I must be in control of others, or they will hurt me." When he feels threatened, perhaps by someone refusing to accede to his attempts to exert control over that person, thoughts intensify around the theme of power. This would trigger the emotional states of anxiety or anger. Then the motivational states of humiliation or domination (Darke, 1990) become engaged. Sexual assault then becomes an appropriate, necessary, or attractive behavioral response for the offender.

It is emphasized that in this model the schema is not seen as the driving force for an offense to take place, but as one component that interacts with other factors related to sexual assault (such as deviant sexual arousal, poor conflict management skills, emotional loneliness) to make sexual assault more likely.

Implications for Current Treatment Approaches of a Schema-Based Approach

Currently in sex offender treatment, approaches to exploring and challenging offense-related cognition are informed by the concept of cognitive distortions outlined above. For instance, in an influential text about the treatment of sexual offenders, Salter (1988) wrote,

> Effective treatment programs . . . pay considerable attention to the issue of cognitive distortions. Identifying and effectively challenging cognitive distortions in a neutral setting, as well as teaching the offender how to identify and challenge distortions while under the influence of deviant urges, is an aspect of treatment that cannot be ignored. . . . Peers may and should challenge rationalizations for such behavior, and their challenges can be facilitated and encouraged by the group leader. (pp. 124-125)

Murphy (1990) and Marshall, Anderson, and Fernandez (1999) detail a similar approach:

> The appropriate way to modify these distorted perceptions and beliefs is to adopt a cognitive restructuring approach. . . . This involves providing clients with: (1) a rationale for the role these cognitions play in maintaining their deviant behavior; (2) corrective information and education; (3) assistance in identifying their specific distortions; and (4) challenges to those distortions. (p. 69)

Bearing in mind the schema-based model of cognition presented in this chapter, it may be that this response is targeting too narrow a conception of relevant cognition. Although many sexual offenders do rationalize, minimize, justify, and excuse their behavior, there is no clear evidence that these processes played a causal role in the offending behavior or that they serve to raise the risk of further offending. Adopting a schema-based model assumes that the thoughts and interpretations produced in any offense chain are situation-specific products of underlying schemas, structures containing enduring beliefs and attitudes about self, the world, and others. If this were the case, challenging situation-specific cognition would not address the underlying problem, which could simply recur in the next threatening or ambiguous situation. To deal with only situation-specific cognition in treatment would be rather like clearing away lava that has flowed from a volcano without any attempt to prevent, prepare for, or manage further eruptions of lava in the future.

Adopting a schema-based model of cognition in sexual offending requires that the treatment response is targeted at the level of intermediate and core beliefs held by the offender. This is, of course, the cognitive therapy approach. One cognitive therapist, Jeffrey Young, has specialized in developing cognitive therapy techniques for working at the schema level in personality-disordered clients (Young, 1999). His recommended approach is much more comprehensive than our usual response to the cognitions of sexual offenders. He proposes four major types of intervention (cognitive, experiential, interpersonal, and behavioral) to enable a client to work toward schema change. Recommended cognitive techniques involve the cornerstone techniques of cognitive therapy: reviewing evidence in support of the schema, critically examining the supporting evidence, reviewing evidence contradicting the schema, illustrating how the schema discounts contradictory evidence, and challenging the schema whenever it is activated during the therapy session. Experiential techniques are drawn from gestalt therapy and involve activities (such as talking to an imaginary parent) that enable clients to see themselves more clearly. Interpersonal techniques include the use of the therapeutic relationship or group process to counteract maladaptive schemas. Behavioral strategies involve supporting the client in changing such schema-driven behaviors as choosing inappropriate partners.

To adopt these strategies into sexual offender treatment would considerably change the focus of many treatment programs. The focus on "ending offending" would be replaced by a more positive focus on enabling the offender to work toward a more functional life (for more information on the "good lives" approach, see Ward & Stewart, Chapter 2 in this volume). Moreover, the focus in many programs on the offense alone as the main issue for disclosure and dissection would change, and underlying and enduring maladaptive themes would become more important topics for analysis.

Schema-Focused Treatment With Sexual Offenders

In 1996, the Prison Service in England and Wales introduced a schema-focused treatment program for high-risk sexual offenders. This program was offered in addition to (not instead of) a more traditional offense-focused program. The additional program (the Extended Program) was developed because evaluation data for the offense-focused program indicated that it was not sufficient to reduce recidivism rates in high-risk offenders (Friendship, Mann, & Beech, 2002). The Extended Program focused on enduring personal characteristics and deficits related to risk of recidivism, such as those listed in dynamic risk procedures (e.g., Beech, Friendship, Erikson, & Hanson, 2002; Thornton, 2002). In this group-work program, offenders were encouraged to identify their habitual patterns of thinking (schemas) by reviewing their life histories and developmental experiences. Schemas identified were then related to other difficulties in their lives, such as relationship difficulties and poor emotional regulation, as well as to their offending behavior.

Schemas were then challenged, using all four methods recommended by Young (1999). First, all group members were taught some basic cognitive therapy techniques and were encouraged to question each others' evidence for their beliefs. Second, group process techniques such as feedback from therapists and peers were used to provide opposing evidence to maladaptive schema-related beliefs. Third, group members participated in role plays of past life situations (such as arguments with partners) to identify how their schemas had affected their information processing in those situations. They then replayed the same situations, using alternative beliefs developed through the earlier cognitive challenging sessions. This enabled group members to see how alternative beliefs can lead to more productive outcomes in interpersonal situations.

Preliminary data on the impact of this program reported by Thornton and Shingler (2001) has found some surprising results. Using a naturalistic design, 58 sexual offenders were tested using various psychometric scales. Thornton combined some scales to create a general offense-related distortions index— these included beliefs that children were sexual and justifications for sexual abuse. He combined other scales to create a schema-related distortions index—this included entitlement thinking and a scale measuring the belief that women are deceitful. Offenders were tested at four points: pre and post the first, offense-focused program and then pre and post the second, schema-focused program. Both programs were of similar length, and usually (but not always) delivered in the same institution.

Offense-related distortions decreased significantly during the offense-focused program, remained stable during the no-treatment phase between programs, and then decreased significantly again during the schema-focused program. Exactly the same pattern was observed for the schema-related distortions, except that in this case, the second decrease (during the schema-focused program) was more noticeable. Further analysis of these data indicated that those offenders who showed only a weak response to conventional treatment showed a larger response during schema focused work. Thornton and Shingler (2001) concluded that adding schema work to offense-focused work leads to further reductions in offense-related distortions and to schema-related beliefs, with this effect being apparent for different types of offender.

Conclusions

Investigation of the schemas of sexual offenders has been hampered by murky definitions, particularly in defining the difference between an attitude and a schema. Some authors have proposed that attitudes about children's sexuality in fact constitute "category" schemas. In other cases, beliefs studied under the umbrella of attitude research (e.g., entitlement) may be appropriately conceived of as schemas. Research in this area to date is little more than exploratory, but some common themes have started to emerge. These include, for rapists, schemas involving entitlement, control, grievance, and deceitful-women beliefs. For child molesters, belief schemas to do with worthlessness and category schemas involving beliefs that children are sexual seem to be indicated.

It is our recommendation that future research move from measurement of attitudes to identification and measurement of schemas. It is particularly important that a variety of assessment methodologies are employed for identification of schemas. Theories of schema such as social cognition theory and cognitive therapy theory indicate that schemas are not usually consciously accessible and therefore may not be uncovered by self-report inventories. Instead, methods such as think-aloud tests, Stroop tests (Stroop, 1938), repertory grids (Kelly, 1955), or even projective tests may be more suitable ways of identifying schemas in sexual offenders.

References

Abel, G. G., Gore, D. K., Holland, C. L., Camp, N., Becker, J. V., & Rathner, B. A. (1989). The measurement of the cognitive distortions of child molesters. *Annals of Sex Research, 2*, 135-153.

Alexander, M. A. (1999). Sexual offender treatment efficacy revisited. *Sexual Abuse: A Journal of Research and Treatment, 11*(2), 101-116.

Augoustinos, M., & Walker, I. (1995). *Social cognition: An integrated introduction.* London: Sage.

Bartlett, F. A. (1932). *A study in experimental and social psychology.* New York: Cambridge University Press.

Beck, A. T. (1963). Thinking and depression: 1. Idiosyncratic content and cognitive distortions. *Archives of General Psychiatry, 9*, 324-333.

Beck, A. T. (1964). Thinking and depression: 2. Theory and therapy. *Archives of General Psychiatry, 9*, 324-333.

Beck, A. T. (1967). *Depression: Causes and treatment.* Philadelphia: University of Pennsylvania Press.

Beck, A. T. (1999). *Prisoners of hate: The cognitive basis of anger, hostility and violence.* New York: HarperCollins.

Beck, A. T., & Emery, G. (with Greenburg, R. L.). (1985). *Anxiety disorders and phobias: A cognitive perspective.* New York: Basic Books.

Beck, A. T., Wright, F. W., Newman, C. F., & Liese, B. (1993). *Cognitive therapy of substance abuse.* New York: Guilford.

Beech, A. R. (1998). A psychometric typology of child abusers. *International Journal of Offender Therapy & Comparative Criminology, 42*, 319-339.

Beech, A. R., Friendship, C., Erikson, M., & Hanson, R. K. (2002). The relationship between static and dynamic risk factors and reconviction in a sample of U.K. child abusers. *Sexual Abuse: A Journal of Research and Treatment, 14*, 155-168.

Beech, A. R., & Mann, R. E. (2002). Recent developments in the treatment of sexual offenders. In J. McGuire (Ed.), *Offender rehabilitation: Effective programs and policies to reduce reoffending.* Chichester, UK: Wiley.

Bumby, K. (1995). Assessing the cognitive distortions of child molesters and rapists. Development and validation of the MOLEST and RAPE scales. *Sexual Abuse: A Journal of Research and Treatment, 8*, 37-54.

Burt, M. R. (1980). Cultural myths and support for rape. *Journal of Personality and Social Psychology, 38*, 217-230.

Clarke, R. V. G. (1977). Psychology and crime. *Bulletin of the British Psychological Society, 30*, 280-283.

Check, J. V. P. (1985). *The Hostility Towards Women scale.* Unpublished doctoral dissertation, University of Manitoba, Winnipeg.

Darke, J. L. (1990). Sexual aggression: Achieving power through humiliation. In W. L. Marshall, D. R. Laws, & H. E. Barbaree (Eds.), *Handbook of sexual assault: Issues, theories, and the treatment of the offender.* New York: Plenum.

Dutton, D. G. (1998). *The abusive personality: Violence and control in intimate relationships.* New York: Guilford.

Finkelhor, D. (1984). *Child sexual abuse: New theory and research.* New York: Free Press.

Fiske, S. T., & Linville, P. W. (1980). What does the schema concept buy us? *Personality and Social Psychology Bulletin, 6*, 543-557.

Fiske, S. T., & Taylor, S. E. (1991). *Social cognition.* Maidenhead, UK: McGraw-Hill International.

Friendship, C., Mann, R. E., & Beech, A. (2002). *Evaluation of a national prison-based treatment programme for sexual offenders in England and Wales.* Manuscript submitted for publication.

Hanson, R. K. (1998, September). *Working with sex offenders.* Keynote address at NOTA Conference, Glasgow.

Hanson R. K., Gizzarelli, R., & Scott, H. (1994). The attitudes of incest offenders: Sexual entitlement and acceptance of sex with children. *Criminal Justice and Behaviour, 21,* 187-202.

Huesmann, L. R. (1988). An information-processing model for the development of aggression. *Aggressive Behavior, 14,* 13-24.

Kelly, G. A. (1955). *The psychology of personal constructs* (Vols. 1 & 2). New York: Norton.

Kwon, S. M., & Oei, T. P. S. (1994). The roles of two levels of cognition in the development, maintenance and treatment of depression. *Clinical Psychology Review, 14,* 331-358.

Malamuth, N. M., & Brown, L. M. (1994). Sexually aggressive men's perceptions of women's communications: Testing three explanations. *Journal of Personality and Social Psychology, 67,* 699-712.

Malamuth, N. M., Sockloskie, R., Koss, M. P., & Tanaka, J. (1991). The characteristics of aggressors against women: Testing a model using a national sample of college students. *Journal of Consulting and Clinical Psychology, 59,* 670-681.

Mann, R. E., & Hollin, C. R. (2001, November). *Schemas: A model for understanding cognition in sexual offending.* Paper presented at the 20th Annual Research & Treatment Conference, Association for the Treatment of Sexual Abusers, San Antonio.

Marshall, W. L., Anderson, D., & Fernandez, Y. M. (1999). *Cognitive behavioural treatment of sexual offenders.* Chichester, UK: Wiley.

Marshall, W. L., Hudson, S. M., Ward, T., & Fernandez, Y. M. (Eds.). (1998). *Sourcebook of treatment programs for sexual offenders.* New York: Plenum.

McFall, R. M. (1990). The enhancement of social skills: An information processing analysis. In W. L. Marshall, D. R. Laws, & H. E. Barbaree (Eds.), *Handbook of sexual assault: Issues, theories, and the treatment of the offender.* New York: Plenum.

Murphy, W. D. (1990). Assessment and modification of cognitive distortions in sex offenders. In W. L. Marshall, D. R. Laws, & H. E. Barbaree (Eds.), *Handbook of sexual assault: Issues, theories, and the treatment of the offender.* New York: Plenum.

Murphy, W. D., Coleman, E. M., & Haynes, M. R. (1986). Factors related to coercive sexual behavior in a nonclinical sample of males. *Violence and Victims, 1,* 255-278.

Myers, R. (2000). *Identifying schemas in child and adult sex offenders, and violent offenders.* Unpublished master's thesis, University of Leicester.

Neidigh, L., & Krop, H. (1992). Cognitive distortions among child sexual offenders. *Journal of Sex Education and Therapy, 18*(3), 208-215.

Saffran, J. D. (1990). Towards a refinement of cognitive therapy in light of interpersonal theory: 1. Theory. *Clinical Psychology Review, 10,* 87-105.

Salter, A. C. (1988). *Treating child sex offenders and their victims: A practical guide.* London: Sage.

Segal, Z. V., & Stermac, L. E. (1990). The role of cognition in sexual assault. In W. L. Marshall, D. R. Laws, & H. E. Barbaree (Eds.), *Handbook of sexual assault: Issues, theories, and the treatment of the offender.* New York: Plenum.

Spence, J. T., Helmreich, R., & Holahan, C. K. (1979). The negative and positive components of psychological masculinity and femininity and their relationships to self reports of neurotic and acting out behaviors. *Journal of Personality and Social Psychology, 37,* 1673-1682.

Stroop, J. R. (1938). Factors affecting speed in serial verbal reactions. *Psychological Monographs, 50,* 38-48.

Taylor, L. (1972). The significance and interpretation of replies to motivational questions: The case of sex offenders. *Sociology, 6,* 23-39.

Thornton, D. (2002). Constructing and testing a framework for dynamic risk assessment. *Sexual Abuse: A Journal of Research and Treatment, 14,* 139-154.

Thornton, D., & Shingler, J. (2001). *Impact of schema level work on sexual offenders' cognitive distortions.* Paper presented at the 20th Annual Research & Treatment Conference, Association for the Treatment of Sexual Abusers, San Antonio.

Ward, T., Hudson, S. M., Johnston, L., & Marshall, W. L. (1997). Cognitive distortions in sex offenders: An integrative review. *Clinical Psychology Review, 17,* 479-507.

Ward, T., & Keenan, T. (1999). Child molesters' implicit theories. *Journal of Interpersonal Violence, 14,* 821-838.

Ward, T., & Siegert, R. J. (in press). Toward a comprehensive theory of child sexual abuse: A theory knitting perspective. *Psychology, Crime, and Law.*

Young, J. E. (1999). *Cognitive therapy for personality disorders: A schema-focused approach.* Sarasota, FL: Professional Resource Press.

9

The Classification of Sex Offenders

Devon L. L. Polaschek

Victoria University
of Wellington, New Zealand

The classification of sexual offenders is a topic that receives only sporadic attention, despite its potential importance in the understanding of sexual assaults and their perpetrators (Grubin & Kennedy, 1991), and in the construction of good etiological theory (Millon, 1991). A reliable and valid classificatory system also informs the assessment of offenders, the design and evaluation of treatment, and prediction of future risk.

At this point in the evolution of sex offender classification systems, two things are clear. First, sexual deviance, even if limited to acts of criminal sexual expression, comprises a diverse range of behaviors, and the people who carry out these behaviors are highly heterogeneous (Bickley & Beech, 2001; Polaschek, Ward, & Hudson, 1997). Second, there are no natural categories that reduce heterogeneity, either of the behavior or the people who carry it out, and so classification schemes for sexual offenders can be evaluated meaningfully only with respect to the intended purpose of such schemes.

This chapter, first, reviews the relevance of psychiatric diagnosis to the assessment and treatment of sexual offending, focusing on the approach taken by the *Diagnostic and Statistical Manual of Mental Disorders*, Fourth Edition (*DSM-IV;* APA, 1994). Second, the utility of functional analysis is compared with diagnosis. Last, Knight and Prentky's (1990) sexual offender classification models are described and evaluated for their potential to improve our understanding of how sexual offenders are heterogeneous, and what these variations might mean for their management.

Sexual deviance can refer to all socially or statistically unusual sexual behavior, and not necessarily to criminally sanctioned behavior. The failure to define the term is one of the pervasive problems in the classification literature, particularly the psychiatric literature. Throughout this chapter, I limit my definition of *sexual deviance* to serious sexual offending, unless it is otherwise noted.

Psychiatric Diagnosis of Sexual Deviance

Psychiatric diagnosis is intended to serve a number of purposes, including the identification of people who share a common cluster of symptoms, reliable and clear communication with other clinicians, effective treatment planning and prognostic estimation, and enhanced understanding of the etiology of the diagnostic category (Scotti, Morris, McNeil, & Hawkins, 1996). The *Penguin Dictionary of Psychology* thus notes that

> a person displaying a particular form of aberrant behavior may be diagnosed as having schizophrenia, or manic-depression or some other specific psychological-psychiatric disorder. Unfortunately, such usage has at times obscured more than it clarified. Such a diagnostic procedure is accurate only to the extent that there in fact exist such specific diseases or syndromes. (Reber, 1985, p. 197)

In both child molestation and rape, it is possible to define a series of characteristics that co-occur often: in other words, a syndrome. The issue then becomes one of whether that syndrome, in and of itself, constitutes a mental disorder or indicates the presence of an underlying mental disorder (Haynes, 1998).

The *DSM III* (APA, 1980) was the first to offer the diagnosis of *paraphilia*. Although the diagnostic criteria have changed over successive editions, the overall category has continued to include a range of sexually unconventional cognitive phenomena (fantasies or urges) or behaviors. For some of the subcategories, the paraphilic behaviors constitute criminal offenses in many jurisdictions. Other subcategories do not. The *DSM-IV* follows a tradition similar to the previous editions: possible diagnoses include pedophilia, sexual sadism, voyeurism, exhibitionism, frotteurism, transvestic fetishism, sexual masochism, and paraphilia NOS. Rape is omitted unless it fits into the diagnostic criteria for sexual sadism.

There are numerous grounds on which to take issue with the *DSM* offerings in respect to sexual deviance. Those presented here are grouped into three categories. I consider general problems, and then present a more detailed critique of pedophilia. Finally, I consider why rape is not included.

General Observations

Any serious consideration of the relationship between sexually offensive behavior and underlying mental disorder must consider the definition of what a mental disorder is. The *DSM-IV* definition of mental disorder is complex and difficult to operationalize. Its basis has come in for considerable criticism, and alternatives have been suggested but not yet adopted (see Wakefield, 1992, for more detail about this issue).

As understandings of both mental disorder and the underpinnings of criminal behavior have become more sophisticated, we have, by and large, ceased to assume that behaving criminally, in and of itself, indicates the presence of mental disorder. In fact, the whole endeavor of psychiatric diagnosis has been encouraged to rely on more than just overt behavior to infer the underlying pathology needed for diagnosis. Of course the basis for this inference is problematic, because with mental disorders, it often relies on patient self-report. Nevertheless, it is conceptually vital that we require other evidence of the presence of a mental disorder in addition to the "symptom" of disordered or socially unacceptable behavior (Haynes, 1998).

There are a number of cases besides the paraphilias where this test is failed; people can meet the behavioral requirements of criteria sets without evidence of any particular underlying disorder. Antisocial Personality Disorder is another example (Lilienfeld, Purcell, & Jones-Alexander, 1997).

However, let us assume for a moment that the current criteria for paraphilias do genuinely distinguish sex offenders with some form of underlying "mental disorder" from others. What do the criteria suggest is the basis of this disorder?

The criteria require the presence of "intense, sexually arousing fantasies, sexual urges or behaviors" (e.g., APA, 1994, p. 526), and these fantasies, urges, or behaviors need to cause distress or impairment. So an immediate source of heterogeneity is the various combinations of features that are possible. For example, a person presents at a mental health clinic because 6 months ago he started wondering what it would be like to look in the window of his neighbor's bedroom while she was undressing. Because of his religious beliefs, he immediately started to feel guilty and distressed about his inappropriate thoughts. However, the more he tried to suppress them, the more he couldn't get the urge to peer at his naked neighbor out of his head. He has no intention of acting on these urges, and hasn't, but he wants help. This presentation may indicate the presence of Obsessive-Compulsive Disorder. Here, however, it also seems to meet the criteria for paraphilia.

A repetitive child sexual offender who currently has a job, is living with a woman in a superficially successful manner, and has no other impairment to "important areas of functioning" (APA, 1994, p. 528) is apparently not a paraphilic. Why not? How does the presence or absence of distress and/or impairment convincingly distinguish between the presence or absence of mental disorder? And how stable is distress or impairment? If it waxes and wanes, as it well may, do these changes indicate genuine changes in the status of the mental disorder?

There are a variety of bases on which a diagnostic category can be of value to the health professionals and researchers who work with the conditions concerned. It can enhance our understanding of etiology, prognosis (or with offensive behavior, risk assessment), and treatment planning, for example. If it doesn't achieve any of these pragmatic aims, then at least it can provide a descriptive basis for grouping like cases together. Really, for sexual offending, the *DSM-IV* fails on all grounds.

There is no evidence that those who meet the criteria for paraphilia are more or less treatable than those who do not, or that they require a similar or a different approach to treatment. There is no evidence that those with the paraphilia are more or less likely to reoffend than those without. What evidence does exist suggests that there are no obvious differences in prognosis or treatment between those offenders who meet criteria and those who do not (Marshall, 1997).

How does the diagnosis inform etiology? Since the *DSM-III*, the *DSM* system has sought to be neutral regarding etiology (APA, 1994). With respect to paraphilias, however, one of the implicit theoretical roots is behavioral; this is discernible both from the use of the term *stimulus* to describe everything from a woman's shoe to the complex social organisms we call children, and in the diagnostic preoccupation with the importance of sexual fantasies and urges. The latter suggests the diagnosis is based on a simple chain model of offending where a person with deviant sexual arousal (toward the relevant specific stimulus) fantasizes about the stimulus and experiences the urge to carry out the fantasies.

Lastly, if it can do nothing else, a diagnostic category can offer a useful way of collecting together co-occurring descriptive features of a syndrome. The *DSM-IV* struggles to do this. The criteria are based predominantly on a small group of factors relevant to sexual offending (e.g., fantasies, urges, distress with symptoms, social and occupational impairment). There is no evidence that these factors have a special status in the etiology or management of sexual offending (Marshall, 1997). There are myriad other variables (e.g., attachment style; patterns of cognitive distortion; affective, intimacy, and self-regulation deficits; see Hanson, 2000) that would be worth considering if we are to develop this psychiatric diagnosis seriously.

Criteria have changed with each edition of the *DSM* since *DSM-II*. In *DSM-III*, paraphilic fantasies or behaviors had to be "insistently and involuntarily repetitive" (APA, 1980, p. 266). This feature appears to overlap with criteria for a disorder of impulse control. By the *DSM-III-R*, "recurrent intense urges and sexually arousing fantasies" were needed, and the person could have acted on these urges or be distressed by them (APA, 1987, p. 279). The involuntary element was gone, but there was still a reliance on self-disclosure of covert events for diagnosis. The *DSM-IV* moved to the requirement of recurrent, intense fantasies, urges, or behaviors that cause distress or impair functioning. The impetus for these changes is unknown.

O'Donohue, Regev, and Hagstrom (2000) suggest that there are difficulties with interrater reliability for specific paraphilias, but it is not clear how these difficulties may have influenced the criteria, since there were evidently no field trials for the *DSM-IV*. Those for the *DSM-III* used a very small number of cases, from the whole category of sexual dysfunctions and paraphilias together, not for the specific subcategories of paraphilia (O'Donohue et al., 2000). Over the 15 years that elapsed in association with these changes, the field of sexual deviance research exploded, especially with respect to pedophilia. By comparison these criteria changes appear trivial, as if their writers were unaware of this research.

Some have argued that paraphilias co-occur in individuals at rates much greater than chance. High comorbidity can suggest, among other things, the presence of a common underlying disorder (Van Velzen & Emmelkamp, 1996). Abel and colleagues (1987) have conducted several studies that support this view. They have reported data on 561 paraphiliacs who disclosed an average of 2.02 paraphilias each (Abel et al., 1987). Despite the popularity of these data, it is clear that they are extremely skewed (e.g., the mean number of paraphilic acts of a pedophiliac with female victims was 23.2, but the median was 1.4), suggesting that a relatively small number of offenders contributed very disproportionately to the data pool. Furthermore, replication has been a problem (Lee, Pattison, Jackson, & Ward, 2001; Marshall & Eccles, 1991). Therefore, there is sparse evidence that offenders typically have multiple paraphilias.

Overall, then, the diagnosis of paraphilia appears to be significantly dated, changes made over the years have not appeared to have either a rational or empirical basis, and changes also appear not to have kept pace with research and practice in this area, especially from those who are treating the majority of sex offenders.

The Case of Pedophilia

DSM-III-R criteria required that the assessor be able to establish that the offender had experienced urges to offend or fantasies about sex with children in the previous 6 months (APA, 1987). However, in the *DSM-IV,* sexually offensive behavior on its own was enough to make the diagnosis as long as the person was distressed by the behavior or the person's social, occupational, or other important areas of functioning were impaired (APA, 1994). This appears to be an important change; the diagnosis appears capable of including more offenders, but still captures the experience of people who are having fantasies they have not acted on.

What is the rationale for such a change? O'Donohue et al. (2000) report that the diagnostic criteria for pedophilia were not identified as problematic during the development of the *DSM-IV.* Yet a cursory examination of both sets of criteria suggests myriad definitional difficulties for the diagnosing clinician. For example, in the *DSM-III-R,* how are "recurrent, intense sexual urges" to be defined (O'Donohue et al., 2000), and how is one to judge that distress has become clinically significant (APA, 1987, p. 285)? In the *DSM-IV* criteria, despite the changes, these same issues remain. Widiger (1997) notes that the *DSM-IV* doesn't define what clinically significant impairment is, even in the section headed "Criteria for Clinical Significance" (APA, 1994, p. 7). In addition, the diagnostician must now work out what constitutes "impairment in social, occupational, or other important areas of functioning" (APA, 1994, p. 528; O'Donohue et al., 2000). The clearest evidence of distress or impairment of functioning is usually seen in the victims of such people, not in the perpetrators themselves. These problems are not unique to this diagnosis, of course; they are similar, for example, to the difficulty in establishing the chronicity and pervasiveness criteria for the maladaptive personality traits implicated in the diagnosis of a personality disorder (Tyrer, 1995). Such concerns directly impact on the potential for reliable diagnosis.

Ironically, current criteria seem over-inclusive, tarring with the same brush individuals whose symptoms are limited to fantasizing about sex with children and being distressed by their fantasies, and individuals who sexually abuse children. Given the putative frequency of fantasies about sex with children in samples of non-offenders, it has been argued that such fantasies cannot be considered deviant, because many people have them and do not act on them. Rather, we should be interested, from a dysfunctional point of view, only when the person crosses the boundary into acting on these thoughts (Leitenberg & Henning, 1995). About 20% of participants from Marshall and colleagues' community-based non-offender control samples are routinely excluded because they admit to at least having fantasized about sex with children

(Marshall, Hamilton, & Fernandez, 2001). The alternative view is that anyone who shows any sexual arousal to children in a plethysmographic assessment will have urges involving children, and these should be diagnosed and treated "before they can act on their attraction" (O'Donohue et al., 2000, p. 104). At present there is a lack of evidence to support the idea that those who only fantasize about sex with children, those who produce arousal to child stimuli on plethysmographic assessment, and those who actually commit sexually offensive acts have the same underlying psychopathology and the same treatment needs. It is unlikely that they represent the same degree of risk to children. However, this is an area that requires further attention (see Marshall, 1997, for discussion of this issue).

At the other end of the spectrum, the category may be under-inclusive. The criterion of distress or impairment in important areas of functioning may fail to capture those whose focus on sexually abusing children is the most concerning to treatment providers in the criminal justice sector. These are men who meet their sexual needs exclusively with young people, are positive about their behavior and its impact on children, and have organized their lives so that they suffer no particular social impairment but are surrounded by like-minded people. Such characteristics taken together might be argued to suggest the most refractory, severe psychopathology (O'Donohue et al., 2000). Currently, the *DSM-IV* excludes these offenders. Why?

Marshall (1997) has also argued persuasively for the arbitrariness of the age criteria. The *DSM-IV* requires that the offender be over 16 and the victim at least 5 years younger, and generally not older than 13 years. He wonders why adolescent offenders have been excluded, and on what basis 13 years was chosen. He further questions the basis for a number of the associated non-diagnostic comments in the manual, including those about the relationships between different offender subgroups' preferred age and gender combinations, and the associated recidivism rates for these subgroups. Such comments appear not to be related to existing research pertinent to these assertions.

The Exclusion of Rape

On the one hand, then, there are arguments for not using the diagnosis of paraphilia in association with criminal sexual behavior. On the other, we have the puzzling omission of any mental disorder associated with contact offending against people over the age of 13 (Marshall, 1997) unless such behavior meets the criteria for sexual sadism. Abel and Rouleau (1990) considered there to be compelling scientific evidence for the inclusion of rape in the *DSM* on the basis of common features of rapists and other paraphiliacs. There was an attempt in 1985 to include a new diagnostic category called *paraphilic rapism* in the *DSM-III-R,* but it was abandoned, apparently because of concern by feminist lobby groups that it would form the basis of a legal defense against criminal responsibility for rape (Kutchins & Kirk, 1997). Of course, this argument applies just as well to the other paraphilias associated with illegal sexual behavior; this is recognized in the introduction to the *DSM-IV,* which contains a cautionary statement about its applicability in legal arenas, particularly for diagnoses such as pedophilia (APA, 1994).

Rape offending, in particular, is less likely to be seen as a "sickness" than paraphilic forms of sexual offending (Bancroft, 1991), and fantasies of forced sex with women are commonly reported in research on the general population (Leitenberg & Henning, 1995). Abel and Rouleau (1990) argued that rape should be a paraphilia because many rapists experience intense urges to offend, but this finding is likely to reflect sampling bias such as overrepresentation of those who self-refer to community clinics. In contrast, only 9% of Grubin and Gunn's (1990) prison sample reported experiencing "difficulty controlling sexual urges or behavior" (p. 30).

Despite its omission from the *DSM,* some researchers have assumed that rape is, nevertheless, a paraphilia (e.g., Abel et al., 1987). Lee et al. (2001), for example, defined a paraphilic rape subgroup in their sample by removing all offenders who also had convictions for violent offending, and by selecting those who met Abel and Osborn's (1992) paraphilic criteria for rapists. The cumulative effect of these selection strategies on a group of offenders who are already harder than others to recruit (Marques, Day, Nelson, & West, 1994) would be to minimize the involvement of men primarily motivated by hostile and aggressive goals, particularly in the absence of a sexual preoccupation with rape (Polaschek, Hudson, Ward, & Siegert, 2001).

Many of the problems identified in diagnosing other paraphilias are perhaps even more pervasive with rape. Rapists are generally acknowledged to be the most heterogeneous of sexual offenders, and at the same time are difficult to distinguish from nonsexual violent offenders on many of the indices that are distinctive in child molesters (Polaschek et al., 1997). Although it is important to understand the reasoning of the *DSM* committees in continuing to omit rape, it would be premature to argue for its inclusion when the diagnoses currently offered are of so little value in the management of sexual deviance.

Functional Analytic Approaches to Offender Classification

Scotti et al. (1996), along with many others, have argued that *DSM-IV* diagnoses are at best essentially structural descriptions of the behaviors of interest. The *DSM*'s insistence on theoretical neutrality conflicts with the necessity for a scientific approach to building theory from repeated observations. For clinicians, this structural focus leaves unspecified the functions of particular behaviors; knowledge that is essential to intervention (Scotti et al., 1996). The debate between functional and structural approaches remains energetic (e.g., Haynes, 1998). However, it is likely that functionally tailored interventions have the potential to be more effective in altering behavior than manualized "one size fits all" interventions (e.g., Linehan, Heard, & Armstrong, 1993).

Functional analysis is a term used in a variety of inconsistent ways (Haynes & O'Brien, 1990), ranging from empirical demonstration of the environmental contingencies that control behaviors (Iwata, Kahng, Wallace, & Lindberg, 2000) to a kind of motivational analysis based on inquiring about what a particular individual intended to achieve from a given behavior (Evans & Paewai, 1999). As the dominance of behavioral theories that focused exclusively on deviant sexual arousal abates, the second usage is more common, particularly with the introduction of a richer, more complex range of theoretical bases (e.g., self-regulation theory, cognitive deconstruction, and attachment theories). A number of existing examples demonstrate the usefulness of applying a functional analytic or case formulation approach to offending behavior. However, in most cases these approaches are used with unusual, complex, or distinctive presentations (e.g., a young fire setter: Clare, Murphy, Cox, & Chaplin, 1992), or with types of offending behavior that have received relatively little attention compared to sexual offending (e.g., stalking: Westrup, 1998).

Case formulation is a related term, referring primarily to a cognitive-behavioral analysis as typified by Persons (1989). Persons distinguished between the observed problems and the mechanisms that underlie them, allocating to cognition a potential causal role. Another important distinction is that functional analysis is concerned with proximal causes, whereas the more inclusive case formulation approach will incorporate the current impact of distal factors as well (Clare et al., 1992; Haynes, 1998). This distinction may allow for elucidation of the relative roles of etiological and maintenance factors in the current presentation.

By comparison with psychiatric diagnosis, case formulation appears to offer much greater utility in classifying sex offenders in useful ways. However, there are problems with functional approaches, too. Where no direct observation and manipulation of the environment is possible, these approaches have been suggested to lack reliability and validity, to require a level of clinical judgment that creates bias and overtaxes cognitive resources of therapists, and to reveal a lack of agreement about the underlying theoretical mechanisms that are reflected in the identified symptoms (Ward, Nathan, Drake, Lee, & Pathè, 2000).

Furthermore, when the main goal of case conceptualization is treatment, Ward et al. (2000) argue that routine individualized assessment for formulation purposes is not an effective use of resources. However, they do suggest that under particular circumstances closer focus is warranted. These circumstances include complex and unusual case presentations, assessments of clients who have recidivated after treatment completion, and when apparently motivated clients show unsatisfactory progress during treatment.

Much of the impetus for applied research on sexual offenders derives from a desire to protect the community through the provision of effective treatment to identified sexual offenders. However, we do not yet agree that we know how to reduce the risk of recidivism in sex offenders (Quinsey, Harris, Rice, & Lalumière, 1993), and at best, gains are modest, often around 10% (e.g., Bakker, Hudson, Wales, & Riley, 1998). Untreated comparison group rates of reconviction often lie between 10% and 20% (e.g., Marques, Nelson, Alarcon, & Day, 2000). It follows from this that half or more of those who would have reoffended anyway, still do so after treatment. That leaves considerable room for improvement in treatment efficacy, even in programs with high therapeutic integrity.

The greater use of a systematic case formulation approach in research associated with treatment, if not in routine treatment delivery, offers one avenue for improving classification and ultimately treatment effectiveness. An example from research on the offense process supports this claim. Descriptive narratives of individuals' offense processes represent a specific class of cognitive-behavioral case formulations. In the early 1990s, analysis of 26 of these narratives using grounded theory (Strauss & Corbin, 1990) resulted in a descriptive model of child sexual offending (Ward, Louden, Hudson, & Marshall, 1995). In turn, this model has assisted in wider recognition of difficulties in the fit between the relapse prevention model and actual offense patterns, particularly positive-affect dominated pathways and the importance of approach goals in sex offending (Ward, Hudson, & Keenan, 1998). Recently, the descriptive model of rape (Polaschek, Hudson et al., 2001) provides more evidence for the multiple functions of sexual assault for rapists, an otherwise overlooked area (Marx, Miranda, & Meyerson, 1999). This body of research has classificatory potential with direct bearing on theory and treatment refinement (Polaschek, Ward, Hudson, & Siegert, 2001).

The collation of case formulations, particularly of unusual or complex presentations, for research purposes might assist us in one of the most important areas of future theory development. Currently the preferred theories of sexual offending are multifactorial, and some include descriptions of how the heterogeneity of sexual offenders can be accommodated using different combinations of putative etiological and maintenance factors (Hall, 1996). However, more often there is no clear indication in such theories of how different factors of interest might cluster together for different types of offenders. For example, it has been asserted that cognitive distortions, victim empathy deficits, and deviant arousal are related to each other. Cognitive distortions and victim empathy deficits have been suggested to be caused by a common process (Fisher, Beech, & Browne, 1999). Anecdotally, treatment of cognitive distortions and victim empathy interventions has been reported to reduce deviant sexual arousal without further intervention (Pithers, 1999). There is evidence of considerable individual variation in scores on measures of these constructs. Putting aside the concerns about the reliability and validity of these measures, it is likely that offenders really do vary on important constructs. What causes this variation, how does it go together with offense features, and what is its relevance for classification and treatment?

Nondiagnostic Classification of Sexual Offenders

Classification of sex offenders using nondiagnostic systems has taken various forms over the past half century. In most enterprises, sexual assaulters of adults ("rapists") generally are seen as a fundamentally distinct group from child molesters (Grubin & Kennedy, 1991), despite the apparent arbitrariness of the legal age criterion that distinguishes child from adult victims, the difficulties in distinguishing reliably penetrative from nonpenetrative assaults, and the heterogeneity that is still evident within each of the resulting subpopulations (Marshall, 1997; Polaschek et al., 1997).

   Like other forms of psychopathology, the absence of natural categories (Millon, 1991) makes the intended function of the system essential to evaluating its validity. Sex offender typologies have been developed to assist disposition (Abel & Rouleau, 1990), assessment and treatment (Beech, Fisher & Beckett, 1999), and risk assessment (Quinsey, Harris, Rice, and Cormier, 1998). Some are syndromes rather than actual taxonomic subtypes (Megargee, 1982). Syndromes of sexual offending may be situation specific (e.g., wartime rape) or mediated events (e.g., psychosis, mental retardation), with each category encapsulating heterogeneous motivations (Prentky, Cohen, & Seghorn, 1985).

   Throughout the field of criminal behavior, many proffered typologies are little more than attempts to sort descriptive features of either the offense or the offender, or some jumble of both, into apparently rationally derived subcategories. In this sense, these are not true classificatory endeavors because no effort is made to specify how particular attributes or variables are empirically connected (Knight, Rosenberg, & Schneider, 1985). Grubin and Kennedy (1991) note that few of them meet minimal criteria for validity. They capture succinctly their common deficiencies in the following evaluation:

On the whole they are like cakes without recipes in which demographic statistics, interview material and offense description are mixed in an intuitive manner to create a dish that tastes strongly of the cook's preconceptions and which, although intellectually satisfying, does not travel well. (p. 124)

Fortunately, there have been some empirical studies that seek to classify general sexual offenders, or offender subgroups into more homogeneous sub-categories. Approaches can be grouped according to whether the categories themselves are formed from (a) demographic variables (e.g., Overholser & Beck, 1986), (b) scores or profiles on psychological or psychometric measures (e.g., Schlank, 1995); (c) broad empirical approaches where a large pool of data from different sources mainly drives the derivation of types (e.g., Knight & Prentky, 1990); and (d) primarily theory-driven systems (e.g., Hall, 1996).

Of these, the most methodologically sophisticated proposal for an offender classification system is contained in the program of research conducted by Knight and Prentky at the Massachusetts Treatment Center.

Knight and Prentky's Rapist Typology: The MTC:R3

The process that led to the third version of the MTC typology for rapists (the MTC:R3) is described by Knight and Prentky (1990; see also Prentky & Knight, 1991), and began with a review of the tradition of clinically intuitive typologies. The Knight et al. (1985) review noted that usually such typologies contain four major components: (a) amount of aggression; at low levels of aggression, (b) antisocial or (c) sexual motives; and at high levels of aggression, (d) whether sadism is present.

The earliest version, the MTC:R1 (Massachusetts Treatment Center: Rape 1), was based on the work of Cohen and colleagues (see Cohen, Garofalo, Boucher, & Seghorn, 1971). Revision and empirical evaluation have led to the latest version, the MTC:R3 (Knight & Prentky, 1990). There are nine subtypes: *opportunistic* (with high or low social competency), *pervasively angry, sadistic* (overt or muted), *sexual nonsadistic* (also with high or low social competency), and *vindictive* (with moderate or low social competency). Opportunistic refers to offending that is impulsive, driven primarily by the presence of an opportunity in the environment, rather than an enduring, internally based offense goal. Pervasively angry offenders evince "global and undifferentiated anger that pervades all areas of the offender's life" (Knight, 1999, p. 312), is directed toward both men and women, and causes significant victim injury. Sexually motivated offenders offend in the context of extensive sexual fantasies that can be sadistic or nonsadistic. For the sadistic subtypes, the actual offense behavior can be overtly sadistic, or nonsadistic but fueled by sadistic fantasies (muted). Lastly, the vindictive offenders are men motivated to harm and humiliate by anger directed at women exclusively (Knight & Prentky, 1990).

This latest version's applicability to broader samples of rapists still requires rigorous testing. Rapists at the Massachusetts Treatment Center may differ in important ways from other samples in that they tend to have been frequent recidivists or to have committed exceptionally violent offenses. Few studies have used the MTC:R3, but those that have suggest that further revision may be necessary to increase generalizability (Barbaree, Seto, Serin, Amos, & Preston, 1994; Polaschek, Hudson, & Siegert, 1996). Knight (1999) indicates that further revisions are expected, but presents an interesting and encouraging range of validity studies from three sources: retrospective interviewing of offenders on developmental antecedents to their offending; the results from the recently developed self-report inventory, the Multidimensional Assessment of Sex and Aggression (MASA; Knight, Prentky, & Cerce, 1994); and a 25-year reconviction study based on 250 offenders who returned to the community from the MTC between 1959 and 1984. Taking these three types of studies together, the strongest validation for the R3's component dimensions was obtained for adult antisocial behavior, followed by juvenile antisocial behavior, pervasive anger, and expressive aggression. Weak or no support from at least two sources was found for sexualization and offense planning (Knight, 1999).

However, whatever the current deficiencies, this is the most highly developed typology of rapists by far, and it would certainly be useful if other researchers continued independent investigations of its validity, particularly since, with nine subtypes, it is not so complex a system as to make it unwieldy to use in research and treatment. One point that would need addressing for wider use is how to deal with coding offense features when an offender has completed more than one known offense and these offenses give different classifications. The stability of offense patterns within offenders may be less than we think.

Knight and Prentky's Child Molester Typology: The MTC:CM3

The strategy for construction was broadly similar to that of the R3: a combination of inductive and deductive strategies with multiple phases. Once again, Knight and colleagues started with a rationally based system by Cohen, Seghorn, and Kalmas (1969). The most significant part of this first revision was the reconceptualization of two core constructs, fixation and regression.

The fixated-regressed dichotomy has the most substantial history of any simple classification system for child molesters. Based on psychodynamic theoretical terms, it has enjoyed intuition-based support from clinicians despite flimsy evidence of its validity. Few studies have attempted to validate it independently. Simon, Sales, Kaszniak, and Kahn (1992), in a study of 136 consecutive convictions, collected data from the MMPI, presentence reports, and police files. They found no evidence of the predicted bimodal distribution.

The problems with the first revision (i.e., the MTC:CM2) were different from those encountered with the rape taxonomy. Knight and Prentky (1990) reported low interrater reliability and high heterogeneity in some subtypes. Furthermore, problems with accommodating some of the cases made it clear that additional restructuring was needed, and this was able to be carried out by examination of cases where raters disagreed.

Interestingly, the degree of fixation was found to be independent of the level of social competence, in contrast to the original psychodynamic theory (Cohen et al., 1979, cited in Knight et al., 1985), and so these two variables were put onto separate axes. Offense-related violence was divided into two variables: physical injury to victim, and sadism.

The resulting MTC:CM3 is visually elegant but complex. There are four types on Axis I and six on Axis II, leading to 24 unique combinations. For the researcher or clinician, there are up to five separate classification decisions to make, compared to between one and three for the rape typology. This level of complexity may explain why, in the dozen years since its first publication, it seems to have attracted little attention from other researchers. Knight, Carter, and Prentky (1989) reported fair to good interrater reliability, but Knight (1989) found 6 of the 24 combinations did not occur, and a further 6 contained three or fewer cases, in a sample of 177. Again, this finding suggests the need for further revision, but replication is also clearly desirable.

Unfortunately, incest offenders (victim related biologically or by marriage; Knight et al., 1989) were omitted from the studies underpinning the development of MTC:CM3 due to low numbers, and this limitation may also affect the utility of the system with other samples in which such offender-victim relationships are common.

Conclusions and Future Directions

Classification by psychiatric diagnosis, evinced in successive *DSM*s, is fraught with problems at present that render it devoid of utility in the management of sexual offenders. Even supposing that the *DSM-IV* showed evidence of a robust connection to scientific research on sexual offending, still the *DSM* purports to be a theoretically neutral, structural, descriptive system. Clearly, then, it is not intended to aid in theory building or understanding of the functions of behavior. Specifically, the *DSM-IV* criteria in the individual categories of paraphilia, appear both under- and over-inclusive; it is unclear what, if any, associated mental disorder exists; and changes to criteria over successive revisions lack a convincing rationale.

Classification based on function offers a more promising approach. However, case formulation strategies are too resource intensive to be used routinely and will have limited use for theory building if they include only proximal factors. Furthermore, it is difficult for clinicians to conduct them with adequate reliability and validity. Despite these reservations, research based on collation and analysis of case formulations will continue to yield fruitful results both in theory generation and, potentially, in the refinement of the match between treatment components and offender need.

From an empirical perspective, the rapist taxonomy of Knight and colleagues (Knight & Prentky, 1990) appears the most promising nondiagnostic classification system for use in research. However, their child molester typology is still very complex. Both of these systems are more than 10 years old, yet few investigators have made use of them other than the original developers themselves (see Langton & Marshall, 2001, and Preston, 1995; these are exceptions).

Currently the highest-level theories of sexual offending are multifactorial (Ward & Hudson, 1998), in order to accommodate sex offender heterogeneity. Many of the relevant etiological factors (e.g., attachment style, intimacy deficits, cognitive distortions) show significant variation within samples of sex offenders. Rather than seeing this as "noise," it may be time to start paying attention to whether such variations are systematically related to other differences among offenders. To make progress in doing this, we need to use a common classification system in our research and theorizing.

References

Abel, G. G., Becker, J. V., Mittelman, M., Cunningham-Rathner, J., Rouleau, J. L., & Murphy, W. D. (1987). Self-reported sex crimes of nonincarcerated paraphilics. *Journal of Interpersonal Violence, 2*, 3-25.

Abel, G. G., & Osborn, C. (1992). The paraphilias: The extent and nature of sexually deviant and criminal behavior. *Psychiatric Clinics of North America, 15*, 675-687.

Abel, G. G., & Rouleau, J.-L. (1990). The nature and extent of sexual assault. In W. L. Marshall, D. R. Laws, & H. E. Barbaree (Eds.), *Handbook of sexual assault: Issues, theories, and treatment of the offender* (pp. 9-21). New York: Plenum.

American Psychiatric Association. (1980). *Diagnostic and statistical manual of mental disorders* (3rd ed.). Washington, DC: Author.

American Psychiatric Association. (1987). *Diagnostic and statistical manual of mental disorders* (3rd ed., rev.). Washington, DC: Author.

American Psychiatric Association. (1994). *Diagnostic and statistical manual of mental disorders* (4th ed.). Washington DC: Author.

Bakker, L., Hudson, S., Wales, D., & Riley, D. (1998). *And there was light: Evaluating the Kia Marama treatment programme for New Zealand sex offenders against children.* Christchurch, NZ: Department of Corrections Psychological Service.

Bancroft, J. (1991). The sexuality of sexual offending: The social dimension. *Criminal Behaviour and Mental Health, 1,* 181-192.

Barbaree, H. E., Seto, M. C., Serin, R. C., Amos, N. L., & Preston, D. L. (1994). Comparisons between sexual and nonsexual rapist subtypes: Sexual arousal to rape, offense precursors, and offense characteristics. *Criminal Justice and Behavior, 21,* 95-114.

Beech, A., Fisher, D., & Beckett, R. (1999). *Step 3: An evaluation of the prison sex offender treatment programme* [UK Home Office Occasional paper]. Available at http://www.homeoffice.gov. uk/rds/adhocpubs1.html

Bickley, J., & Beech, A. (2001). Classifying child abusers: Its relevance to theory and clinical practice. *International Journal of Offender Therapy and Comparative Criminology, 45,* 51-69.

Clare, I. C. H., Murphy, G. H., Cox, D., & Chaplin, E. H. (1992). Assessment and treatment of fire-setting: A single-case investigation using a cognitive-behavioral model. *Criminal Behaviour and Mental Health, 2,* 253-268.

Cohen, M. L., Garofalo, R., Boucher, R., & Seghorn, T. (1971). The psychology of rapists. *Seminars in Psychiatry, 3,* 307-327.

Cohen, M. L., Seghorn, T. K., & Calmas, W. (1969). Sociometric study of sex offenders. *Journal of Abnormal Psychology, 74,* 249-255.

Evans, I. M., & Paewai, M. (1999). Functional analysis in a bicultural context. *Behaviour Change, 16,* 20-36.

Fisher, D., Beech, A., & Browne, K. (1999). Comparison of sex offenders to nonoffenders on selected psychological measures. *International Journal of Offender Therapy and Comparative Criminology, 43,* 473-491.

Grubin, D., & Gunn, J. (1990). *The imprisoned rapist and rape.* London: Institute of Psychiatry.

Grubin, D. H., & Kennedy, H. G. (1991). The classification of sexual offenders. *Criminal Behaviour and Mental Health, 1,* 123-129.

Hall, G. C. N. (1996). *Theory-based assessment, treatment, and prevention of sexual aggression.* New York: Oxford University Press.

Hanson, R. K. (2000). Treatment outcome and evaluation problems (and solutions). In D. R. Laws, S. M. Hudson, & T. Ward (Eds.), *Remaking relapse prevention: A sourcebook* (pp. 485-499). Thousand Oaks, CA: Sage.

Haynes, S. N. (1998). The assessment-treatment relationship and functional analysis in behavior therapy. *European Journal of Psychological Assessment, 14,* 26-35.

Haynes, S. N., & O'Brien, W. H. (1990). Functional analysis in behavior therapy. *Clinical Psychology Review, 10,* 649-668.

Iwata, B. A., Kahng, S. W., Wallace, M. D., & Lindberg, J. S. (2000). The functional analysis model of behavioral assessment. In J. Austin & J. E. Carr (Eds.), *Handbook of applied behavior analysis* (pp. 61-89). Reno, NV: Context Press.

Knight, R. A. (1989). An assessment of the concurrent validity of a child molester typology. *Journal of Interpersonal Violence, 4,* 131-150.

Knight, R. A. (1999). Validation of a typology for rapists. *Journal of Interpersonal Violence, 14,* 303-330.

Knight, R. A., Carter, D. L., & Prentky, R. A. (1989). A system for the classification of child molesters: Reliability and application. *Journal of Interpersonal Violence, 4,* 3-23.

Knight, R. A., & Prentky, R. A. (1990). Classifying sexual offenders: The development and corroboration of taxonomic models. In W. L. Marshall, D. R. Laws, & H. E. Barbaree (Eds.), *Handbook of sexual assault: Issues, theories, and treatment of the offender* (pp. 23-52). New York: Plenum.

Knight, R. A., Prentky, R. A., & Cerce, D. D. (1994). The development, reliability, and validity of an inventory for the multidimensional assessment of sex and aggression. *Criminal Justice and Behavior, 21*, 72-94.

Knight, R. A., Rosenberg, R., & Schneider, B. A. (1985). Classification of sexual offenders: Perspectives, methods, and validation. In A. W. Burgess (Ed.), *Rape and sexual assault: A research handbook* (pp. 222-293). New York: Garland.

Kutchins, H., & Kirk, S. A. (1997). *Making us crazy: DSM: The psychiatric bible and the creation of mental disorders.* New York: Free Press.

Langton, C. M., & Marshall, W. L. (2001). Cognition in rapists: Theoretical patterns by typological breakdown. *Aggression and Violent Behavior, 6*, 499-518.

Lee, J. K. P., Pattison, P., Jackson, H. J., & Ward, T. (2001). The general, common, and specific features of psychopathology for different types of paraphilias. *Criminal Justice and Behavior, 28*, 227-256.

Leitenberg, H., & Henning, K. (1995). Sexual fantasy. *Psychological Bulletin, 117*, 469-496.

Lilienfeld, S., Purcell, C., & Jones-Alexander, J. (1997). Assessment of antisocial behavior. In D. M. Stoff, J. Breiling, & J. D. Maser (Eds.), *Handbook of antisocial behavior* (pp. 60-74). New York: John Wiley.

Linehan, M., Heard, H., & Armstrong, H. (1993). Naturalistic follow-up of a behavioral treatment for chronically parasuicidal borderline patients. *Archives of General Psychiatry, 50*, 971-974.

Marques, J. K., Day, D. M., Nelson, C., & West, M. A. (1994). Effects of cognitive-behavioral treatment on sex offender recidivism: Preliminary results of a longitudinal study. *Criminal Justice and Behavior, 21*, 28-54.

Marques, J. K., Nelson, C., Alarcon, J.-M., & Day, D. M. (2000). Preventing relapse in sex offenders: What we learned from SOTEP's experimental treatment program. In D. R. Laws, S. M. Hudson, & T. Ward (Eds.), *Remaking relapse prevention: A sourcebook* (pp. 321-340). Thousand Oaks, CA: Sage.

Marshall, W. L. (1997). Pedophilia: Psychopathology and theory. In D. R. Laws & W. O'Donohue (Eds.), *Sexual deviance: Theory, assessment, and treatment* (pp. 152-174). New York: Guilford.

Marshall, W. L., & Eccles, A. (1991). Issues in clinical practice with sex offenders. *Journal of Interpersonal Violence, 6*, 68-93.

Marshall, W. L., Hamilton, K., & Fernandez, Y. (2001). Empathy deficits and cognitive distortions in child molesters. *Sexual Abuse: A Journal of Research and Treatment, 13*, 123-130.

Marx, B. P., Miranda, R., & Meyerson, L. A. (1999). Cognitive-behavioral treatment for rapists: Can we do better? *Clinical Psychology Review, 19*, 875-894.

Megargee, E. I. (1982). Psychological determinants and correlates of criminal violence. In M. E. Wolfgang & N. A. Weiner (Eds.), *Criminal violence* (pp. 81-170). Beverly Hills, CA: Sage.

Millon, T. (1991). Classification in psychopathology: Rationale, alternatives, and standards. *Journal of Abnormal Psychology, 100*, 245-261.

O'Donohue, W., Regev, L. G., & Hagstrom, A. (2000). Problems with the *DSM-IV* diagnosis of pedophilia. *Sexual Abuse: A Journal of Research and Treatment, 12*, 95-105.

Overholser, J. C., & Beck, S. (1986). Multimethod assessment of rapists, child molesters, and three control groups on behavioral and psychological measures. *Journal of Consulting and Clinical Psychology, 54*, 682-687.

Persons, J. B. (1989). *Cognitive therapy in practice: A case formulation approach.* New York: Norton.

Pithers, W. D. (1999). Empathy: Definition, enhancement, and relevance to the treatment of sexual abusers. *Journal of Interpersonal Violence, 14*, 257-284.

Polaschek, D. L. L., Hudson, S. M., & Siegert, R. J. (1996, November). New Zealand rapists: An examination of subtypes. Poster paper presented at the 10th annual conference of the Association for the Treatment of Sexual Abusers, Chicago.

Polaschek, D. L. L., Hudson, S. M., Ward, T., & Siegert, R. J. (2001). Rapists' offense processes: A preliminary descriptive model. *Journal of Interpersonal Violence, 16*, 523-544.

Polaschek, D. L. L., Ward, T., & Hudson, S. M. (1997). Rape and rapists: Theory and treatment. *Clinical Psychology Review, 17,* 117-144.

Polaschek, D. L. L., Ward, T., Hudson, S. M., & Siegert, R. J. (2001). Developing a descriptive model of the offense chains of New Zealand rapists: Taxonomic implications. In C. R. Hollin, D. P. Farrington, & M. McMurran (Eds.), *Sex and violence: The psychology of crimes and risk assessment* (pp. 153-174). London: Routledge.

Prentky, R., Cohen, M., & Seghorn, T. (1985). Development of a rational taxonomy for the classification of rapists: The Massachusetts Treatment Center system. *Bulletin of the American Academy of Psychiatry and Law, 13,* 39-70.

Prentky, R. A., & Knight, R. A. (1991). Identifying critical dimensions for discriminating among rapists. *Journal of Consulting and Clinical Psychology, 59,* 643-661.

Preston, D. L. (1995). *Patterns of sexual arousal among rapist subtypes.* Unpublished doctoral dissertation, Queen's University, Kingston, Ontario.

Quinsey, V. L., Harris, G. T., Rice, M. E., & Cormier, C. A. (1998). *Violent offenders: Appraising and managing risk.* Washington, DC: American Psychological Association.

Quinsey, V. L., Harris, G. T., Rice, M. E., & Lalumière, M. L. (1993). Assessing treatment efficacy in outcome studies of sex offenders. *Journal of Interpersonal Violence, 8,* 512-523.

Reber, A. S. (1985). *The Penguin dictionary of psychology.* Hammondsworth, UK: Penguin.

Schlank, A. M. (1995). The utility of the MMPI and the MSI for identifying a sexual offender typology. *Sexual Abuse: A Journal of Research and Treatment, 7,* 185-194.

Scotti, J. R., Morris, T. L., McNeil, C. B., & Hawkins, R. P. (1996). *DSM-IV* and disorders of childhood and adolescence: Can structural criteria be functional? *Journal of Consulting and Clinical Psychology, 64,* 1177-1191.

Simon, L. M. J., Sales, B., Kaszniak, A., & Kahn, M. (1992). Characteristics of child molesters: Implications for the fixed-regressed dichotomy. *Journal of Interpersonal Violence, 7,* 211-225.

Strauss, A., & Corbin, J. (1990). *Basics of qualitative research: Grounded theory procedures and techniques.* Newbury Park, CA: Sage.

Tyrer, P. (1995). Are personality disorders well classified in the *DSM-IV?* In W. J. Livesley (Ed.), *The DSM-IV personality disorders* (pp. 29-42). New York: Guilford.

Van Velzen, C. J. M., & Emmelkamp, P. M. G. (1996). The assessment of personality disorders: Implications for cognitive and behavior therapy. *Behaviour Research & Therapy, 34,* 655-668.

Wakefield, J. C. (1992). The concept of mental disorder: On the boundary between biological facts and social values. *American Psychologist, 47,* 373-388.

Ward, T., & Hudson, S. M. (1998). The construction and development of theory in the sexual offending area: A metatheoretical framework. *Sexual Abuse: A Journal of Research and Treatment, 10,* 47-63.

Ward, T., Hudson, S. M., & Keenan, T. (1998). A self-regulation model of the sexual offense process. *Sexual Abuse: A Journal of Research and Treatment, 10,* 141-157.

Ward, T., Louden, K., Hudson, S. M., & Marshall, W. L. (1995). A descriptive model of the offense chain in child molesters. *Journal of Interpersonal Violence, 10,* 452-472.

Ward, T., Nathan, P., Drake, C. R., Lee, J. K. P., & Pathè, M. (2000). The role of formulation-based treatment for sexual offenders. *Behaviour Change, 17,* 251-264.

Westrup, D. (1998). Applying functional analysis to stalking behavior. In J. R. Meloy (Ed.), *The psychology of stalking: Clinical and forensic perspectives* (pp. 275-294). San Diego, CA: Academic Press.

Widiger, T. A. (1997). Mental disorders as discrete clinical conditions: Dimensional versus categorical classification. In S. M. Turner & M. Hersen (Eds.), *Adult psychopathology and diagnosis.* (3rd ed., pp. 3-23). New York: John Wiley.

10

Empathy and Victim Empathy

Devon L. L. Polaschek
Victoria University of Wellington, New Zealand

Until the last decade, theoretical ideas about the role of empathy in sexual offending differed little in sophistication from common sense or folk theory. Many people think that the only basis on which someone could know-ingly inflict on another human being the harm associated with sexual abuse, would be because the perpetrator was indifferent to the consequences for the victim. So, it is appealing intuitively that sex offenders have empathy deficits, and that these deficits will have a causal role in their offending. This intuition has been widely accepted by treatment providers, with the inclusion of empa-thy-focused interventions in rehabilitation programs. However, advances in research over the past decade suggest that the relationship between empathy and sexual violence is much more interesting and complex than it first appears. This chapter first examines how empathy is defined and modeled, and evalu-ates instruments that purport to measure empathy. Then research on empathy in sex offenders is presented. Third, I outline typical interventions and review the small number of outcome studies. To conclude, a section on theory cri-tiques how empathy is related to both predisposition to offend and the offense process itself. As I will argue, the degree to which offenders have empathy deficits, whether specific or general; the degree to which interventions actually target deficits; and our ability to evaluate whether change occurs are all chal-lenged by fundamental difficulties in defining and measuring empathy. Relatedly, theoretical views remain relatively underdeveloped.

What Is Empathy?

The general construct of empathy is surprisingly difficult to define. The roots of the term *empathy* are said to originate in the German concept *einfühlung*, which translates as "feeling into" (*Oxford English Dictionary*, 2002), and its introduction into psychology at the very end of the 19th century has been credited to Theodore Lipps (Mahrer, Boulet, & Fairweather, 1994). Examination of dictionary definitions immediately suggests confusion about what empathy is. One of the fullest definitions is from the *Merriam-Webster's Collegiate Dictionary* (2002). Here empathy is

> the action of understanding, being aware of, being sensitive to, and vicariously experiencing the feelings, thoughts and experience of another of either the past or present without having the feelings, thoughts and experience fully communicated in an objectively explicit manner, also: the capacity for this.

Evident in this definition is that the process of being empathic is conflated with empathy as a disposition. Furthermore, empathy can be generated in association with both positive and negative experiences. Empathy is often difficult to distinguish from sympathy. For example, sympathy can be distinguished from empathy by its selective application to negative events, in which the sympathetic person feels sorrow, compassion, or pity for the target rather than vicarious emotion. However, it can also refer simply to sharing common feelings with the target, or to being in agreement of opinion or desire (*Oxford English Dictionary*, 2002).

Models of Empathy

When the concept of empathy is imported into the social science arena, the difficulties compound. As Kerem, Fishman, and Josselson (2001) note, empathy has been treated as a trait or a state, as both a process and an outcome. Variations in research definitions are sufficiently significant that different investigators may have been studying different phenomena (Duan & Hill, 1996). Although controversial, a two-component process is most often proposed: perspective taking, and vicarious emotional responding (Kerem et al.; Mahrer et al., 1994; Moore, 1990). Gladstein (1983) labeled the first component "cognitive empathy" and the second "affective empathy" to minimize confusion, but many authors have argued that the dichotomy is artificial; the two are always intertwined (Duan & Hill, 1996).

Research on empathy in psychology has focused historically on its involvement in prosocial activities such as altruistic behavior or the behavior of effective therapists with clients (Gladstein, 1983; Mahrer et al., 1994), and in these contexts these two components may be sufficient, perhaps because those studied are often motivated to appear caring.

Once applied to contexts in which empathy is of interest more for its absence than presence, the two-component model appears incomplete. In criminal psychology, one of its limitations is demonstrated by psychopaths, who reportedly can learn to take others' perspectives and then use such knowledge to better exploit others (Rice, Harris, & Cormier, 1992). These findings imply that in order to feel empathy, one must actually "care" about what is happening to other people.

Recognizing this limitation, Hanson and Scott (1995) added a component called "caring" or "compassion." Whether caring is required for perspective taking and vicarious emotional experience, or just the latter, is not clear. However, in colloquial terms, the element of "caring" may become important in understanding both trait and state empathy deficits. Psychopaths are generally regarded as globally lacking compassion. However, very ordinary people experience empathy deficits when motivated to do so. For example, many people accurately take the perspective and can evaluate the emotions of another when angry. However, the common desire to hurt the target of anger could be argued to result in a state-dependent empathy deficit: Angered individuals feel little or no compassion for their targets and may harm them. When the anger has dissipated, they may "care" again about the impact of their behavior on others, and even regret their actions (Tavris, 1989).

With offenders, this concept of "caring" has sometimes been translated into a requirement to demonstrate compassionate behavior (Geer, Estupinan, & Manguno-Mire, 2000; Marshall, Hudson, Jones, & Fernandez, 1995; Pithers, 1994). This requirement muddies the waters somewhat: The generic ability to be empathic doesn't actually need to include any behavioral element, although it would be easier to measure if it did. Consider the experience of watching a movie about a boy whose pet llama dies. One might feel a strong sense of empathy for the boy, including both perspective taking and mirrored affect. What is the appropriate compassionate behavioral response? And if one makes none, does that mean that there was no empathy? Compassionate behavioral responses to empathic feelings about a negative event may be suppressed for reasons that have nothing to do with whether empathy was experienced. For example, suppose that, instead of watching a movie, one came across the boy as a stranger in some "real-life" context. Then one might make no behavioral response, such as comforting the boy, because of the likelihood of one's behavior being misinterpreted by others.

Marshall and colleagues in a seminal review paper (Marshall et al., 1995) suggested that empathy is a four-stage process. They propose that theirs is a general model of empathy, then outlined how it can apply to sex offenders. The four stages of the model are (a) recognition of the observed person's emotional state (operationalized in their own research as recognition of facial affect; Hudson et al., 1993); (b) perspective taking; (c) emotional replication; and (d) response decision, also called "empathic responding" and referring to "the observer's decision to act or not on the basis of their feelings" (Marshall et al., 1995, p. 102). Like this fourth component, the first component, emotional recognition, is unnecessary, and may even be unhelpful in some cases. For example, most people might feel vicarious positive affect on hearing that a friend has been offered a sought-after job. They do not need to be able to observe or even hear of this experience from the friend concerned, though prior knowledge of the person would increase the accuracy of their responses. On the other hand, on observing a local politician being insulted in a public meeting, one might find the observed facial expression gave no clue as to whether the politician was distressed, and empathic responding might instead require using prior knowledge about the personality of the politician or drawing on how one would respond oneself. These examples include legitimate empathic processes.

Hence there is no consensus at present about the best model for general empathy, and there is a lack of clarity about whether changes need to be made when applying general models to offenders.

Measurement of Empathy

Research on empathy has used a variety of methods of measurement, including scoring free responses to stimuli, self-report questionnaires, and experimental inductions (Miller & Eisenberg, 1988). However, in the sex offender domain, the most common method has been paper-and-pencil questionnaires: either general empathy or specific victim-empathy scales.

GENERAL EMPATHY MEASURES

Three scales are common in research: the Mehrabian-Epstein scale (Mehrabian & Epstein, 1972), the Hogan Empathy scale (Hogan, 1969), and Davis's Interpersonal Reactivity Index (IRI; Davis, 1983). The Mehrabian-Epstein scale is often considered to be a measure of emotional empathy alone, and the Hogan is viewed primarily as a measure of role- and perspective-taking only (Chlopan, McCain, Carbonell, & Hagen, 1985). Marshall et al.'s (1995) review suggested both to be of questionable value.

Davis's IRI is a more comprehensive scale, containing subscales of perspective taking (PT), fantasy (F), personal distress (PD), and empathic concern (EC). However, it essentially asks offenders to evaluate their own abilities, rather than measuring them directly. Given the transparency of the questions, the likelihood that individuals may want to be seen as empathic, and a lack of information about whether people can appraise their empathic abilities accurately, the IRI may also have dubious external validity. The Empat-G is a new 18-item scale that purports to measure general empathy. The scale is unpublished; item examples given by McGrath, Cann, and Konopasky (1998) suggest that it measures cognitive empathy.

VICTIM-SPECIFIC MEASURES

Measures of "victim-specific empathy" are relatively new. They include Hanson and Scott's (1995) Empathy for Women Test (EFWT) and Child Empathy Test (CET), Fernandez and colleagues' Child Molester Empathy Measure (CMEM; Fernandez, Marshall, Lightbody, & O'Sullivan, 1999) and Rapist Empathy Measure (REM; Fernandez & Marshall, in press), the Victim Empathy Distortions Scale (VEDS; see Fisher, Beech, & Browne, 1999), and the Empat-A (McGrath et al., 1998).

Hanson and Scott's two scales use about 15 written vignettes to assess perspective-taking deficits. Some vignettes are clearly sexually abusive, some are clearly not, and some are ambiguous. Respondents report on a single 7-point Likert scale the extent to which the victim is unhappy/upset or happy/good/ cheerful about what has happened in the vignette. Fernandez and colleagues' CMEM (Fernandez et al., 1999) is based on responses to three vignettes: a child who is permanently disfigured after a vehicle accident, a child who has been sexually abused by an unknown assailant, and the respondent's own victim. For each brief vignette, respondents are asked to (a) rate, on a 0-to-10 Likert scale, the degree to which the child is feeling, thinking, or doing each of 30 items (e.g., "self-confident," "problems with school work," "feels sinful"); and (b) on the same scale, rate how much the respondent feels 20 emotions (e.g., guilty, sick, curious). This purported emotional response of the offender is viewed by Fernandez et al. as the affective empathy component. However, it is not possible to distinguish between a vicarious emotional response to the victim versus the offender's own personal distress. It also is not possible to establish the theory about the causes of negative impacts used by the offender in making the responses. Suppose an intrafamilial offender blames the criminal justice system for the impact on the victim (e.g., "if she hadn't told, none of this would have happened"). He could still score highly on A and B. This concern is particularly important when the measure is used pretreatment, when cognitive distortions are presumably still unmodified. The REM (Fernandez & Marshall, in press) is intended to be a parallel version of the CMEM; the protagonists in the vignettes are all adult women.

The final two are non-vignette–based measures and nonspecific with regard to victim age (or gender). Beckett and Fisher's VEDS (1994, cited in Fisher et al., 1999) is a 28-item scale described as measuring understanding of victim impact of sexual abuse, and beliefs about victim emotional responses. So, again it appears primarily to be a cognitive measure. Offenders respond as for their most typical victim, and non-offending controls respond as they imagine a victim would feel. Lastly, the Empat-A (McGrath et al., 1998) is an abuse-specific 34-item questionnaire similar to the Empat-G in format.

So, these measures operationalize empathy in a variety of ways, but all of them appear to contain transparent content. Offenders who are aware that they look more culpable by admitting knowledge of the harm they did may be motivated to fake an empathy deficit at initial assessment, and then answer "more empathically" following an intervention.

Given the lack of clarity about what empathy is, and its essentially covert nature, the development of adequate measures is a formidable challenge. Measurement of victim-specific empathy is very new, however, and to make further progress, we need a clearer theory about the role of empathy in offending, and to consider other ways of measuring it besides static "check-the-box" approaches.

Empathy Research With Sex Offenders

Tables 10.1 and 10.2 summarize the research to date investigating general and specific empathy with sex offender samples. Because of space constraints, the reported findings concern only comparisons of empathy scores between samples, although a number of studies conducted additional analyses and included other variables. Unless otherwise noted, all differences are statistically significant. However, the clinical significance of such differences is often not evaluated by researchers (Marshall et al., 1995).

Overall, on general empathy measures, child sexual abusers rarely have been found to differ from controls or normative non-offender samples. Rapists sometimes score lower than both child molesters and controls (Table 10.1). On victim-specific measures (Table 10.2) the findings are more complex. On the CMEM, child molesters and controls generally do not differ on the accident victim scenario, and molesters endorse less empathy for their own victims than

Table 10.1   General Empathy Studies

Study and Sample	Scale	Results
Fisher et al. (1999) 81 CM prisoners, 59 community treatment CMs, 81 new recruit prison officer Cs	IRI*	CMs scored higher on PD and EC than controls. No differences on PT and F. Extrafamilial CMs did not differ from Cs on EC but had lower PT.
Hayashino et al. (1995) 22 pretreatment incest CM prisoners, 21 pretreatment extrafamilial CM prisoners, 33 R prisoners, 27 non-SO prisoners, 26 community Cs.	IRI (PT, EC only)*	No significant differences.
Langevin, Wright, & Handy (1988) 32 incest CMs, 38 nonfamilial CMs, 21 Rs and 7 exhibitionists (all pretrial)	M-E*	No differences between sex offender types. Only nonfamilial CMs scored lower than original non-offender validation sample. Deniers more empathic than admitters.
Marshall, Jones, Hudson, & McDonald (1993) (1) 92 pretreatment CM prisoners	IRI	No differences cf. Salter's (1988) norms for factory workers and students. No statistical testing.
(2) 20 community CMs, 20 matched Cs	IRI	CMs scored lower on F. Otherwise no differences.
Marshall & Maric (1996) 29 pretreatment CM prisoners 29 community Cs	Hogan M-E	CMs found to be significantly less empathic than controls on both measures.
McGrath et al. (1998) 30 SO prisoners (anonymous), 30 non-SO in community (anonymous), 30 university student Cs (anonymous), 30 SO prisoners (anonymous, fake good), 44 non-anonymous SO prisoners assessed for parole hearing	Empat-G	No differences found between groups.
Pithers (1994) 10 CM prisoners, 10 R prisoners, in CBT program, prior to empathy module	IRI*	CMs obtained higher total score, and higher PT and F subscales than rapists. CM scores similar to Salter (1988) norms.

Study and Sample	Scale	Results
Pithers (1999) (Expt 1) 15 CMs, 15 Rs partway through CBT program, prior to empathy module.	IRI	IRI administered twice to all offenders in (a) typical mood, (b) offense-precursive mood. CMs scored significantly higher than Rs on IRI total and on PT and EC subscales in (a). (b) scores were significantly related to (a) scores. Rs' IRI total scores and EC scores decreased more than CMs' from typical to precursive mood. CM scores for precursive mood similar to typical mood.
Rice, Chaplin, Harris, & Coutts (1994) 14 Rs, 14 non-SO patients in max. security hospital, 11 community Cs	M-E Hogan*	Rs lower on Hogan cf. other two groups. Otherwise no differences.
Tierney & McCabe (2001) 36 CM prisoners, 31 R prisoners, 30 non-SO prisoners, 40 community Cs	M-E Empat-G	Rs scored significantly lower than CM and community Cs on M-E. No significant differences on Empat-G.

NOTES: *also used other, nonempathy scales. CM = child sexual offender; SO = sex offender, R = rapist, C = control; IRI = Davis's Interpersonal Reactivity Index.
Subscales: PT = perspective taking, F = fantasy, PD = personal distress, EC = empathic concern, M-E = Mehrabian-Epstein scale (1972); Empat-G (cited in McGrath et al., 1998).

for other victims. On other measures, there is no consistent pattern of findings. The two REM studies contradict each other, perhaps because one sample of rapists was waitlisted for treatment and the other was not. In both, however, rapists were less empathic toward their own victim than other victim types.

Empathy-Based Interventions

The most widely cited statistic in research on sex offenders is the 94% of North American sex offender treatment programs that already targeted offenders' empathy more than a decade ago (Knopp, Freeman-Longo, & Stevenson, 1992), though not necessarily in a structured way (Pithers, 1999). Curiously,

Table 10.2   Victim Empathy Studies

Study and Sample	Scale	Results
Fernandez et al. (1999) Expt 2: 29 CM prisoners, 29 community Cs	CMEM	Controls and CM scores not different for CAV, Cs scored higher for CSAV. CMs scored lower on OV than other two vignettes.
Fernandez & Marshall (in press) 27 R prisoners, 27 non-SO prisoners	REM*	Rs scored higher than non-SOs on WAV scale. No differences for WRV. Rs were less empathic toward their own victims than WRV.
Fisher et al. (1999) see Table 10.1 for sample	VEDS*	CMs scored higher on victim empathy distortions than Cs.
Hanson & Scott (1995) 21 Rs, 66 CMs, 39 CM+R, 23 deniers (all in prison or treatment), 26 Rs, 14 CMs, 9 CM+R (all in community, admitting offences, never convicted), 84 non-SO prisoners, 84 community Cs, 76 student Cs (EFWT only)	CET EFWT*	No differences between groups on CET scores. SOs currently in treatment made fewer errors on the CET than those not in treatment. Rs (prison and community unconvicted) made more errors than non-offenders combined. Community Rs made more errors than community non-offender Cs on EFWT. No differences between Rs and CMs, or between offenders in and not in treatment.
Marshall, Champagne, Brown, & Miller (1997) 32 CM prisoners, 32 community Cs	CMEM*	As for Fernandez et al. (1999)
Marshall et al. (2001) 34 CM prisoners, 24 non-SO prisoners, 28 community Cs	CMEM*	No differences between groups for CAV (Parts A or B). CMs lower than other two groups on Part A for CSAV. CMs lower on Part A for OV than for other two vignettes. No differences between groups on Part B.

Study and Sample	Scale	Results
Marshall & Moulden (2001) 32 pretreatment R prisoners, 28 violent non-SO prisoners, 31 community Cs	REM*	No differences on WAV between groups. Rapists scored lower for WRV than other two groups. Rapists scored lower on OV than both WRV and WAV.
McGrath et al. (1998) see Table 10.1	Empat-A*	SOs scored lower than university Cs or non-SO group. There were no differences between the SO groups.
Tierney & McCabe (2001) see Table 10.1 for sample	Empat-A	CMs scored lower than other 3 groups on Empat-A. No other intergroup differences.

NOTES: * also used other, nonempathy scales. CM = child sexual offender; SO = sex offender, R = rapist, C = control; CMEM = child molester empathy measure (Fernandez et al., 1999); Part A = child victim's experiences, Part B = how the perpetrator feels about the child's experience. 3 vignettes: CAV = child accident victim, CSAV = victim of child sexual abuse (other perpetrator), OV = own victim; REM = Rapist Empathy (Fernandez & Marshall, in press). 3 vignettes: WAV = woman car accident victim, WRV = woman victim of rape (other perpetrator), OV = own victim; CET = Child empathy test, EFWT = empathy for women test (Hanson & Scott, 1995); VEDS = victim empathy distortions scale, cited in Fisher et al. (1999); Empat-A (child sexual abuse-specific; cited in McGrath et al., 1998).

interventions for empathy have primarily targeted victim-specific empathy during a period when research was still investigating general empathy deficits.

A number of programs describe structured approaches to empathy intervention. Important elements include both the use of the group process, and the order in which intervention components are introduced, to minimize defensiveness and maximize cumulative change. Hildebran and Pithers (1989) provided one of the earliest published accounts. Pithers (1999) summarizes their five stages of intervention: (a) describing the offender's own abusive behavior; (b) reading and summarizing published accounts of abuse survivors' experiences, and describing how their own victims' experiences related to the writers'; (c) viewing, listening to, and discussing audio and videotapes of survivors talking of their abuse and recovery; (d) writing accounts of their victims' experiences from the victim's perspective, then role-playing the account, again from the victim's perspective; (e) role-playing "the victimization" (p. 271), first with the abuser playing himself and another group member playing the victim, and then with the abuser in the victim role. The role play is videotaped and played back to the abuser later.

Some interventions incorporate preliminary training in recognizing, distinguishing, and expressing emotion (Marshall, O'Sullivan, & Fernandez, 1996). Marshall and colleagues, like many others, have the VE component follow on from the challenging of cognitive distortions such as denial and minimization. Offenders' own sexual abuse victimization issues are considered salient by some treatment providers but are overlooked by others, despite the common therapist experience of offenders raising such issues early in any victim impact component. Again, this is an area where more research is needed, but there are at least two main ways that offenders' own victimization may obstruct full involvement in the appreciation of the harmfulness of their behavior. The first is simply that the level of personal distress that can be associated with unresolved victimization can disrupt the capacity to acknowledge others' distress. Second, offenders whose adult view of their own childhood abuse is that it was a positive, nonabusive, even consenting experience are unlikely to pay too much attention to alternative views (Eldridge & Wyre, 1998; Marques, Nelson, Alarcon, & Day, 2000). Those program providers who do address these issues either do so prior to beginning a VE intervention, or perhaps alongside the early stages. However, further investigation into the impact of including or omitting these variations would be helpful for treatment planning.

More recently, offenders' general ability to tolerate negative affect or personal distress has been recognized as a barrier to the effectiveness of these interventions (Eldridge & Wyre, 1998; Schwartz & Canfield, 1998). Offenders who experience intense shame or even guilt in response to recognition of culpability may continue to blame victims and resist victim empathy training despite adequate general empathy (Hanson & Scott, 1995). Bumby (2000) suggests that there are differential consequences of shame and guilt for relapse. Nevertheless, without the ability to tolerate any negative self-referential affect, all negative affect may be avoided. Victim-specific deficits could be specific to sexual matters, or occur in the face of all transgressions the offender commits that have the potential to harm others, whether legal or illegal. Current assessment tools don't allow us to distinguish whether VE-specific deficits are only for sexual abuse. However, a broad difficulty in feeling empathy for those we ourselves have harmed would have a negative impact on intimate adult relationships and so may be worth examining more closely as a treatment issue.

There is very little research evidence on the efficacy (or otherwise) of VE interventions. Important preliminary evaluative issues include whether or not a comprehensive cognitive-behavioral (CBT) program alters victim empathy, and whether VE modules contribute to any changes.

Several published evaluations have looked specifically at empathy scores before and after treatment. Pithers (1994) reported on 10 child molesters and 10 rapists in the Vermont Treatment Program for Sexual Aggressors.

Participants in the VE group had already completed preliminary intervention modules (i.e., on emotional recognition, inappropriate sexual arousal, and own victimization). Measures were taken immediately before and after the VE module, the length of which was not described. Pretreatment IRI total scores for the child molesters were comparable to those of the normative samples cited in Salter (1988). However, rapists' scores appeared to be lower than the norms and were significantly lower than child molesters', both pre- and post-treatment. Both groups demonstrated significant increases on the IRI at post-treatment, along with significant decreases on both the Burt (1980) Rape Myth Acceptance scale and Abel et al.'s (1989) cognitive distortions scale.

Pithers (1999) again evaluated changes in IRI scores and other relevant constructs (e.g., cognitive distortions) before and after a structured empathy intervention. He reported on 15 child sexual offenders and 15 rapists whose pretreatment scores are reported in Table 10.1. Following intervention, analyses indicated that in an offense-precursive mood state there were now no differences on IRI total, EC, or PT compared to pretreatment typical mood scores. This is clearly an important and interesting finding that implies that treatment somehow eroded the priming effects of preoffense mood on general empathy.

Beech, Fisher, and Beckett (1999) reported findings of a general CBT program for 77 child sex offender prisoners. Pre- to posttreatment comparisons showed a statistically significant reduction in both the IRI PD subscale and the VEDS. Treatment was approximately either 80 hours or 160 hours of cognitive behavioral group sessions. However, a specific structured victim empathy component, including writing narratives and role-playing, was included in only the longer program.

Marshall et al. (1996) reported on an earlier version of the CMEM used to evaluate the combined impact of cognitive distortions and VE modules in a comprehensive cognitive-behavioral program for 29 imprisoned nonfamilial child molesters. Overall, statistically significant pre- to posttreatment changes were found in both Part A (identification of impacts on child) and Part B (offender's emotional responses) for the offender's own victim, and on Part B only for the general sexual abuse victim.

Theory

An important distinction in theoretical terms is between explanations focusing on the development of predisposition to offend versus offense process models. This section evaluates each of these and then makes some suggestions about future theoretical development.

The simplest theoretical idea about the role of empathy in offending is that offenders have global, stable empathy deficits. It is unclear whether these deficits motivate offending or simply fail to inhibit motivation when it develops (Araji & Finkelhor, 1985). Marshall and Barbaree's influential 1990 theory of sexual offending proposed that the childhood backgrounds of sex offenders were generally similar to psychopaths. They noted that they "would expect sex offenders to be just as emotionally unresponsive to others as are psychopaths" (p. 263). The typical sex offender's childhood was thought to leave him unable to feel empathy. Clearly, in light of the evidence on general empathy deficits, these theories overpredict and may require revision.

Related theories predict deficits specific to classes of people such as children (Abel et al., 1989; Finkelhor & Lewis, 1988) or women (Barbaree, Marshall, & Lanthier, 1979; Polaschek & Ward, 2002). Again, empirical investigation is unsupportive of this view. Research currently suggests that deficits are for the offender's own victim, and sometimes for those who have experienced similar harm (see Table 10.2).

So, when someone is able to suppress concern for others yet persistently harm them, is this the absence of normal empathy development or some other process in operation? Evidence seems now to suggest the latter. What is that process?

PROCESSES UNDERLYING VICTIM-SPECIFIC EMPATHY

Marshall et al. (1995) proposed the only multiple component model that lays out its components as an unfolding process. They did not specify whether this process is seen as occurring between offenses or during an offense, but it appears capable of application to either situation. From a theoretical point of view, however, there would seem to be a problem with the plausibility of empathy acting as an inhibitor by the time the offender is in the presence of a distressed victim (as required for Stage 1: emotional recognition). The proximity of a powerful reinforcer (positive or negative), perhaps a cognitively deconstructed state (Ward, Hudson, & Marshall, 1995), or the effects of rising arousal are all likely to disrupt the generation of empathy. We would not expect an alcoholic sitting in front of a drink in a bar to be able to feel any concern for the harm that she may do to herself and others if she drinks again, even when she knows and cares about that harm at other times. For empathy to act within an offense process, it would need to be invoked much earlier in the process, when self-control is still possible but victim distress is not yet present.

Alternatively, Marshall et al. (1995) envisioned their model unfolding post-offense, when the offender is presumably no longer aroused but perhaps notices that his victim is distressed. Pithers (1999) assumes that the Marshall et al. model is a theory of empathy unfolding postoffense. He is critical of its utility at that point, too. This is an area of confusion that requires attention if this interesting model is going to be used as more than just an organizing structure for disparate research (Geer et al., 2000; Marshall et al., 1995).

If offenders have specific deficits toward their own victims but do not evince wider deficits, then two possibilities exist: First, they genuinely do not know or accept that sexual abuse of a child is harmful. In this case there is nothing to feel compassionate empathy for, before, during, or after the offense. Second, they may perceive accurately what the victim is experiencing but feel no compassion prior to or during the offense because of a state deficit caused by transient anger, sexual arousal, or a misperception about whether this is offensive sex (in the case of rape). Such offenders may feel empathy when these factors no longer are in operation, especially if they are relatively inexperienced offenders (Polaschek, Hudson, Ward, & Siegert, 2001).

Or perhaps there is a third explanation, that offenders deliberately avoid taking perspective when they could, because to do so is aversive. Developmentally, offenders with unremarkable general empathy may start off suppressing empathy for their own victims in a deliberate way, before, during, and after their offenses. During the offense may be the easiest time to ignore empathic considerations, since strong sexual or affective arousal or cognitive deconstruction causes a narrowing of attentional focus. Before and after the offense, offenders need to be able to continue this "selective empathic inhibition" (Bumby, 2000, p. 149) by finding other ways of exculpating themselves, such as blaming the victim, alcohol, or anger; minimizing the amount of harm done; denying that the behavior was criminal, and so on. This model implies that offenders use cognitive distortions and denial to suppress victim empathy. This process may become so entrenched with repetition that it is automated, and thus produces stable cognitive distortions and lowered empathy toward other victims of sexual abuse.

Back in 1989, Abel et al. suggested that both cognitive distortions and VE-facilitated offending by enabling offenders to avoid negatively evaluating their offense behavior. As Marshall et al. (1995) noted, Abel et al. specifically referred to the avoidance of loss of self-esteem, anxiety, and guilt. Research on self-esteem suggests that people will go to considerable lengths to avoid being forced to revise their self-image in a downward direction (Baumeister, Smart, & Boden, 1996). Bumby (2000) gives more emphasis to the importance of shame, but potentially all negative affect relating to the self might motivate avoidance, particularly if, as Fisher et al. (1999) found, these offenders are particularly prone to personal distress and have a low tolerance for experiencing negative emotions.

If Abel and colleagues were right, then the major cause of the staged failures suggested by Marshall et al. might not be specific stage-skill deficits, but the motivated suppression of empathy in order to avoid negative emotional experiences. Until Marshall and Fernandez's research using the CMEM and REM (e.g., Fernandez et al., 1999; Marshall & Moulden, 2001), it was not possible to distinguish victim-specific deficits from "agent of harm"-specific deficits (i.e., whether offender empathy deficits were generated by the over-looked dimension of the harm having been inflicted by the offender himself). Their research suggests this distinction may be important, although we still can't rule out from their findings that the offender had a preexisting unempathic view of the victim prior to inflicting harm.

Finally, for some offenders, victim empathy suppression may be a skill that is acquired in non-offending contexts and transplanted into the offense process because of its adaptive value. Whenever an individual is motivated to achieve a goal that is incompatible with someone else's needs or may even be harmful to others, then that individual must be able to suppress empathy if he is to carry out the associated actions. Those who work with people must learn these skills if they are to limit their distress at having to dismiss a well-liked employee, tell a student that she has failed an examination, or inform someone that a loved one has been killed.

It is unlikely that a single mechanism will account for all variations in empathy. The evidence is that some offenders do show rather low general empathy, and others, more victim-localized deficits. Still others may evince dynamic deficits that we haven't yet detected in research that still assumes such deficits will be stable.

Directions for the Future

This is a young and challenging area within sexual deviance. One of the frustrating elements of this domain is the degree of confusion. As Marshall, Hamilton, and Fernandez (2001) note, the models of what we are doing are in serious need of clarification. Many important questions remain. For example, are we actually measuring victim empathy with current measures? Do offenders need victim empathy to avoid offending, or would the knowledge of the damage that sexual abuse does, coupled with sympathy, be sufficient? Are we teaching victim empathy or merely making participants more comfortable with articulating the harm they have done?

Theory development needs to keep pace with the research. A fruitful avenue for such development lies in the application of theory of mind and self-regulation theories specifically to empathy. Ward and colleagues have already demonstrated how this body of thinking can accommodate different kinds of deficits, including dynamic suppression (Ward, Keenan, & Hudson, 2000).

There is plenty of future research to conduct, especially in the measurement domain and in treatment evaluation, in diversifying the measurement methodology, and in investigating how reactive empathy is to affective and other state variables.

References

Abel, G. G., Gore, D. K., Holland, C. L., Camp, N., Becker, J., & Rathner, J. (1989). The measurement of the cognitive distortions of child molesters. *Annals of Sex Research, 2*, 135-153.

Araji, S., & Finkelhor, D. (1985). Explanations of pedophilia: Review of empirical research. *Bulletin of the American Academy of Psychiatry & the Law, 13*, 17-37.

Barbaree, H. E., Marshall, W. L., & Lanthier, R. D. (1979). Deviant sexual arousal in rapists. *Behavior Research and Therapy, 17*, 215-222.

Baumeister, R. F., Smart, L., & Boden, J. M. (1996). Relation of threatened egotism to violence and aggression: The dark side of high self-esteem. *Psychological Review, 103*, 5-33.

Beech, A., Fisher, D., & Beckett, R. (1999). *Step 3: An evaluation of the prison sex offender treatment programme.* UK Home Office Occasional paper. Retrieved on July 1, 2002, from http://www.homeoffice.gov.uk/rds/adhocpubs1.html

Bumby, K. M. (2000). Empathy inhibition, intimacy deficits, and attachment difficulties in sex offenders. In D. R. Laws, S. M. Hudson, & T. Ward (Eds.), *Remaking relapse prevention with sex offenders: A sourcebook* (pp. 143-166). Thousand Oaks, CA: Sage.

Burt, M. R. (1980). Cultural myths and supports for rape. *Journal of Personality and Social Psychology, 38*, 217-230.

Chlopan, B. E., McCain, M. L., Carbonell, J. L., & Hagen, R. L. (1985). Empathy: Review of available measures. *Journal of Personality and Social Psychology, 48*, 635-653.

Davis, M. H. (1983). Measuring individual differences in empathy: Evidence for a multidimensional approach. *Journal of Personality and Social Psychology, 44*, 113-126.

Duan, C., & Hill, C. E. (1996). The current state of empathy research. *Journal of Counseling Psychology, 43*, 261-274.

Eldridge, H., & Wyre, R. (1998). The Lucy Faithfull Foundation residential program for sexual offenders. In W. L. Marshall, Y. M. Fernandez, S. M. Hudson, & T. Ward (Eds.), *Sourcebook of treatment programs for sexual offenders* (pp. 79-92). New York: Plenum.

Fernandez, Y. M., & Marshall, W. L. (in press). Victim empathy, social self-esteem and psychopathy in rapists. *Sexual Abuse: A Journal of Research and Treatment.*

Fernandez, Y. M., Marshall, W. L., Lightbody, S., & O'Sullivan, C. (1999). The Child Molester Empathy Measure: Description and examination of its reliability and validity. *Sexual Abuse: A Journal of Research and Treatment, 11*, 17-31.

Finkelhor, D., & Lewis, I. A. (1988). An epidemiologic approach to the study of child molestation. *Annals of the New York Academy of Sciences, 528*, 64-78.

Fisher, D., Beech, A., & Browne, K. (1999). Comparison of sex offenders to nonoffenders on selected psychological measures. *International Journal of Offender Therapy and Comparative Criminology, 43*, 473-491.

Geer, J. H., Estupinan, L. A., & Manguno-Mire, G. M. (2000). Empathy, social skills and other relevant cognitive processes in rapists and child molesters. *Aggression and Violent Behavior, 5*, 99-126.

Gladstein, G. A. (1983). Understanding empathy: Integrating counseling, developmental, and social psychology perspectives. *Journal of Counselling Psychology, 30*, 467-482.

Hanson, R. K., & Scott, H. (1995). Assessing perspective-taking among sexual offenders, nonsexual criminals, and nonoffenders. *Sexual Abuse: A Journal of Research and Treatment, 7*, 259-277.

Hayashino, D. S., Wurtele, S. K., & Klebe, K. J. (1995). Child molesters: An examination of cognitive factors. *Journal of Interpersonal Violence, 10,* 106-116.

Hildebran, D., & Pithers, W. D. (1989). Enhancing offender empathy for sexual-abuse victims. In D. R. Laws (Ed.), *Relapse prevention with sex offenders* (pp. 236-243). New York: Guilford.

Hogan, R. (1969). Development of an empathy scale. *Journal of Consulting and Clinical Psychology, 33,* 307-316.

Hudson, S. M., Marshall, W. L., Wales, D., McDonald, E., Bakker, L. W., & McLean, A. (1993). Emotional recognition skills of sex offenders. *Annals of Sex Research, 6,* 199-211.

Kerem, E., Fishman, N., & Josselson, R. (2001). The experience of empathy in everyday relationships: Cognitive and affective elements. *Journal of Social and Personal Relationships, 18,* 709-729.

Knopp, F. H., Freeman-Longo, R., & Stevenson, W. (1992). *Nationwide survey of juvenile and adult sex-offender treatment programs.* Orwell, VT: Safer Society Press.

Langevin, R., Wright, M. A., & Handy, L. (1988). Empathy, assertiveness, aggressiveness, and defensiveness among sex offenders. *Annals of Sex Research, 1,* 533-547.

Mahrer, A. R., Boulet, D. B., & Fairweather, D. R. (1994). Beyond empathy: Advances in the clinical theory and methods of empathy. *Clinical Psychology Review, 14,* 183-198.

Marques, J. K., Nelson, C., Alarcon, J.-M., & Day, D. M. (2000). Preventing relapse in sex offenders: What we learned from SOTEP's experimental treatment program. In D. R. Laws, S. M. Hudson, & T. Ward (Eds.), *Remaking relapse prevention with sex offenders: A sourcebook* (pp. 321-340). Thousand Oaks, CA: Sage.

Marshall, W. L., & Barbaree, H. E. (1990). An integrated theory of the etiology of sexual offending. In W. L. Marshall, D. R. Laws, & H. E. Barbaree (Eds.), *Handbook of sexual assault: Issues, theories, and treatment of the offender* (pp. 257-275). New York: Plenum.

Marshall, W. L., Champagne, F., Brown, C., & Miller, S. (1997). Empathy, intimacy, loneliness, and self-esteem in nonfamilial child molesters: A brief report. *Journal of Child Sexual Abuse, 6,* 87-98.

Marshall, W. L., Hamilton, K., & Fernandez, Y. (2001). Empathy deficits and cognitive distortions in child molesters. *Sexual Abuse: A Journal of Research and Treatment, 13,* 123-130.

Marshall, W. L., Hudson, S. M., Jones, R., & Fernandez, Y. M. (1995). Empathy in sex offenders. *Clinical Psychology Review, 15,* 99-113.

Marshall, W. L., Jones, R., Hudson, S. M., & McDonald, E. (1993). Generalised empathy in child molesters. *Journal of Child Sexual Abuse, 2,* 61-68.

Marshall, W. L., & Maric, A. (1996). Cognitive and emotional components of generalized empathy deficits in child molesters. *Journal of Child Sexual Abuse, 5,* 101-110.

Marshall, W. L., & Moulden, H. (2001). Hostility toward women and victim empathy in rapists. *Sexual Abuse: A Journal of Research and Treatment, 13,* 249-255.

Marshall, W. L., O'Sullivan, C., & Fernandez, Y. M. (1996). The enhancement of victim empathy among incarcerated child molesters. *Legal and Criminological Psychology, 1,* 95-102.

McGrath, M., Cann, S., & Konopasky, R. (1998). New measures of defensiveness, empathy, and cognitive distortions for sexual offenders against children. *Sexual Abuse: A Journal of Research and Treatment, 10,* 25-36.

Mehrabian, A., & Epstein, N. (1972). A measure of emotional empathy. *Journal of Personality, 40,* 525-543.

Merriam-Webster's Collegiate Dictionary. (2002). Retrieved on July 1, 2002, from http://www.m-w.com/cgi-bin/dictionary?empathy

Miller, P. A., & Eisenberg, N. (1988). The relation of empathy to aggressive and externalizing/antisocial behavior. *Psychological Bulletin, 103,* 324-344.

Moore, B. S. (1990). The origins and development of empathy. *Motivation and Emotion, 14,* 75-80.

Oxford English Dictionary. (2002). Retrieved on 1 July 2002 from http://dictionary.oed.com

Pithers, W. D. (1994). Process evaluation of a group therapy component designed to enhance sex offenders' empathy for sexual abuse survivors. *Behavior Research and Therapy, 32,* 565-570.

Pithers, W. D. (1999). Empathy: Definition, enhancement, and relevance to the treatment of sexual abusers. *Journal of Interpersonal Violence, 14,* 257-284.

Polaschek, D. L. L., Hudson, S. M., Ward, T., & Siegert, R. J. (2001). Rapists' offense processes: A preliminary descriptive model. *Journal of Interpersonal Violence, 16,* 523-544.

Polaschek, D. L. L., & Ward, T. (2002). The implicit theories of potential rapists: What our questionnaires tell us. *Aggression and Violent Behavior, 7,* 385-406.

Rice, M. E., Chaplin, T. C., Harris, G. T., & Coutts, J. (1994). Empathy for the victim and sexual arousal among rapists and nonrapists. *Journal of Interpersonal Violence, 9,* 435-449.

Rice, M. E., Harris, G. T., & Cormier, C. A. (1992). Evaluation of a maximum security therapeutic community for psychopaths and other mentally disordered offenders. *Law and Human Behavior, 16,* 399-412.

Salter, A. (1988). *Treating child sex offenders and victims: A practical guide.* Newbury Park, CA: Sage.

Schwartz, B. K., & Canfield, G. M. S. (1998). Treating the "sexually dangerous person": The Massachusetts Treatment Center. In W. L. Marshall, Y. M. Fernandez, S. M. Hudson, & T. Ward (Eds.), *Sourcebook of treatment programs for sexual offenders* (pp. 235-245). New York: Plenum.

Tavris, C. (1989). *Anger: The misunderstood emotion* (Rev. ed.). New York: Simon & Schuster.

Tierney, D. W., & McCabe, M. P. (2001). An evaluation of self-report measures of cognitive distortions and empathy among Australian sex offenders. *Archives of Sexual Behavior, 30,* 495-519.

Ward, T., Hudson, S. M., & Marshall, W. L. (1995). Cognitive distortions and affective deficits in sex offenders: A cognitive deconstructionist interpretation. *Sexual Abuse: A Journal of Research and Treatment, 7,* 67-83.

Ward, T., Keenan, T., & Hudson, S. M. (2000). Understanding cognitive, affective, and intimacy deficits in sex offenders: A developmental perspective. *Aggression and Violent Behavior, 5,* 41-62.

11

Research and Practice With Adolescent Sexual Offenders

Dilemmas and Directions

Robin Jones
University of Melbourne

This chapter selects some salient dilemmas relevant to research and practice with adolescent sex offenders, and suggests directions to help generate relevant knowledge in areas where it is most needed.

Two themes run through the material selected for this chapter. First is the oft-noted heterogeneity of the adolescent sex offender population, and the enormous implications this has for undertaking meaningful research. Three research areas have been chosen to illustrate and explore these implications: offender classification, etiology, and recidivism studies. The second theme is about the need to respond effectively to the developmental needs of adolescent sex offenders. Biological, intrapersonal, and social aspects are explored in the more clinically focused second half of this chapter, followed by a brief conclusion.

Research Issues

CLASSIFICATION OF ADOLESCENT SEX OFFENDERS

Given the heterogeneity of adolescent sex offenders, the need for empirically based typologies is acute. There is also an urgent need for taxonomic research to be integrated with empirical research on etiology. A combined approach could both identify (through classification) and explain (through etiological study) the multiple pathways to adolescent sexual offending, in turn rationalizing treatment planning. It is a real handicap to the field that research in both areas is still so rare and so fragmented.

A clinically derived typology developed by O'Brien and Bera (1986) is a case in point. Although it was first published more than 15 years ago, there has been no published empirical investigation of its utility, despite the wealth of clinical assistance it could provide, and the range of etiological pathways it suggests. Nor has it been systematically applied in clinical settings. While arguably this may be sensible in the absence of empirical validation, clinical applications could also stimulate the very research on this tool that is missing.

Knight and Prentky (1993) have proposed an empirically based typology of adolescent sex offenders as part of their groundbreaking research on the classification of adult sex offenders. Derived from retrospective data on adult sexual offenders who reported juvenile sex offending histories, two adolescent rapist subgroups and one child molester subgroup were identified. They were distinguished by factors including social competence, motivational intent, extent of fixation, and amount of sexual contact. The major drawback is that the study misses adolescent sex offenders who subsequently desisted and were therefore never picked up for sex offenses as adults. This problem is amplified by the observation in recidivism studies that the majority of adolescent sex offenders do not reoffend sexually, at least not within 5 to 10 years of their index offense. Therefore the "career" sex offenders who form the basis of Knight and Prentky's typology comprise a very restricted subgroup of (now mature) adolescent sex offenders. This limits the utility of the typology, since the sample upon which it is based is so unrepresentative of adolescent sex offenders overall.

Knight and Prentky's distinction between child molesters and rapists reflects the almost universal application of this broad typology in the adolescent literature, presumably because it has shown a great deal of utility in distinguishing subgroups of adults. Adolescent sex offenders have thus been grouped according to victim age, wherein those with victims significantly younger are classified as child molesters, and those with peer or adult victims are classified as rapists.

Although this has provided a simple and conceptually attractive starting point for adolescent sex offender classification, it has also been risky. The most basic understanding of developmental psychology indicates that tasks in such key areas as identity, social functioning, and sexuality are very different in adolescence than in adulthood. To ignore this difference or to assume it will not have a contaminating influence on offense-related variables is probably naïve. For example, there is evidence in the area of deviant sexual arousal that, compared to adults, adolescents show less correspondence between their sexual preferences and their offense histories, indicating that they are more fluid with respect to their sexual preferences, given their stage of psychosexual development (Hunter & Lexier, 1998). Therefore it can be expected that victim age and gender are less indicative of sexual preference for adolescent sex offenders than adults, which would draw into question the utility of the rapist-child molester distinction.

As it turns out, evidence is now emerging that the rapist-child molester distinction is insufficient for classifying adolescent sex offenders. Though "typical" characteristics such as poor social skills and antisocial attitudes have frequently been identified in adolescent offender samples, they tend not to cluster according the rapist-child molester distinction as predicted (Weinrott, 1996).

There are some exceptions, especially in studies with a more etiological focus; for example, a robust discriminator has been the high rates of physical abuse in the histories of adolescents classified as child molesters and the high rates of neglect in the histories of adolescents classified as rapists. Nevertheless, consistent findings are more the exception than the rule in adolescent research that utilizes the rapist-child molester typology. Although usually explained in terms of the ample methodological problems inherent in such studies, a recent and very promising study by Worling (2001) offers an alternative view.

Worling replicated and extended a study by Smith, Monastersky, and Deisher (1987) that sought to detect subtypes of adolescent offenders based on personality features (rather than victim selection or other factors). Using the California Psychological Inventory (Gough, 1987) with a sample of 112 adolescent offenders, Worling identified by cluster analysis four subgroups of adolescent sex offenders: (a) Antisocial/Impulsive, (b) Unusual/Isolated, (c) Overcontrolled/Reserved, and (d) Confident/Aggressive. The first two groups were considered the more "pathological," and recidivism data revealed higher rates of violent and nonviolent reoffenses (whether sexual or nonsexual) at a 6-year follow-up. The third and fourth groups were viewed as relatively healthy, and demonstrated lower rates of recidivism. Almost half the participants belonged to the antisocial/impulsive group. Notably, victim age and gender were not significantly related to subgroup assignment. Also, subgroup differences in sexual and physical victimization histories did not reach statistical significance.

These findings were very consistent with the original study by Smith et al. (1987), and suggest that personality factors may offer a more coherent classification framework than offense-related and victim variables. This contention is congruent with several other findings in the adolescent sex offender literature.

For example, the four-group typology may help identify which adolescent sex offenders will continue offending as adults (Groups 1 and 2) and who will desist (Groups 3 and 4). The typology also offers a more detailed understanding of why the adolescent sex offender recidivism rate is so much lower than for adults.

Further, Worling's typology may help explain the overlap between general delinquency and sexual offending. France and Hudson (in Barbaree, Marshall, & Hudson, 1993) have cautioned against simply superimposing a delinquency treatment model upon adolescent sex offender treatment, due to the delinquency model's lack of relevance to the offense histories of at least some adolescent sex offenders, and lack of clarity about which type of offending is primary when both are present. Others have recommended comparing delinquency models with offense-specific models of treatment, given the observation that, overall, nonsexual recidivism is at least twice as prevalent as sexual recidivism for this population (Weinrott, 1996). Worling's typology may help identify which subgroups of adolescent sex offenders need a delinquency-based treatment dimension (principally Group 1) and which need a more traditional sex offender-specific approach. One important clinical implication is that the assessment of adolescent sex offenders should routinely include personality measures.

ETIOLOGY AND DEVELOPMENTAL PATHWAYS

The heterogeneity of adolescent sex offenders makes it especially important for clinicians to understand the wide range of factors that cause and maintain offending. In keeping with taxonomic findings, it may be expected that a number of distinct developmental pathways exist. If these could be identified and used as a guide to determine treatment needs, more effective tailoring of interventions could occur, and the sometimes overwhelming heterogeneity of adolescent sex offender treatment groups could be reduced through empirically based partitioning.

While a range of clinically driven theories of etiology exists in the adolescent sex offender literature, some that have been extensively clinically applied (e.g., Ryan & Lane's sexual abuse cycle, 1991), empirical research has once again lagged behind. It appears that most clinicians are content to apply untested theory quite unquestioningly, rather than to use treatment contexts to test some of the core assumptions systematically. The sexual abuse cycle, for example, while containing many promising elements, is able to account for only two of the seven subtypes hypothesized by O'Brien and Bera's taxonomy of adolescent sex offenders, and cannot account for those who desist (Weinrott, 1996).

Adolescent sex offender treatment frameworks have therefore tended to be generated on the basis of clinical common sense but in the absence of a solid empirical base. Without a more scientific understanding of offender subtypes and the etiological pathways associated with each, treatment based on a generic model and applied to mixed groups can, by definition, be relevant to only a portion of adolescent sex offenders. Therefore, inconclusive or equivocal treatment outcomes (which abound) may misleadingly imply that adolescent sex offenders are not especially responsive to treatment, when instead the problem lies with the treatment model for not yet accurately identifying and meeting the full range of adolescent sex offender needs. The policy-related dangers and pitfalls of this situation are obvious.

There are, of course, at least some consistent research findings relevant to etiology. For example, the observation that many adolescents who offend against children have histories of childhood sexual victimization themselves has been found to be stronger for adolescent offenders who select male victims. This indicates that childhood sexual abuse is an important etiological factor in homosexual pedophilia (Weinrott, 1996). Due to the lack of prospective and longitudinal studies, however, many empirical findings relevant to etiology have been either small in scope, such as the above observation, or have been drawn from other populations.

For example Malamuth, Heavey, and Linz (1993) used undergraduate male volunteers to identify two pathways to sexual aggression against women. One presupposes delinquency, and identifies promiscuity as the link to sexual offending. The second pathway starts with proviolence attitudes, leading to hostile definitions of masculinity, in turn leading to adolescent or young adult sexual aggression. Both these pathways predicted sexual aggression 10 years later, which in some cases had expanded to include domestic violence and child abuse. This study sheds some light on how sexual violence unfolds developmentally, especially among older adolescent sex offenders who continue offending into adulthood. It also confirms the importance of key treatment targets such as restructuring proviolence cognitions, and redefining masculinity in positive ways. It tells us little, however, about adolescents who desist as adults, and also those who target children rather than peers or adult women.

Elliott (1994) undertook a large-scale longitudinal study of delinquents that measured a small number of variables specific to adolescent sex offending. The author identified an "early starter" path, beginning with involvement in a delinquent peer group and property crimes, then broadening to include aggravated assault and pressuring for sex, finally broadening again to include forcible rape. This study successfully tracks the development of sexual and nonsexual crime over time and suggests that delinquency must also be directly targeted in treatment for adolescent sex offenders who also commit nonsexual crimes. From an etiological perspective, however, the study tells us more about the "what" than the "why." Also, it is only relevant to adolescents whose sex offenses consist of forcible rape and who have coexisting delinquency.

Elliott's work illustrates how advanced juvenile delinquency research is compared to adolescent sex offender research. Longitudinal studies using adolescent sex offender samples rather than delinquents are desperately needed. Prospective studies that follow up very large numbers of randomly selected children into adulthood would also be valuable as a means of establishing the base rates for adolescent sex offending. A wide range of variables theoretically linked to sex offending could then be measured and investigated systematically. Large-scale studies of this kind would help overcome the very piecemeal approach to understanding adolescent sex offender etiology that dominates the field today.

At a practical level, two further issues warrant brief discussion in our efforts to encourage meaningful etiological research. First is the correct identification of relevant constructs to actually measure. It may be, for example, that important variables are yet to be identified that, if named and appropriately measured, would better delineate and discriminate between subgroups of adolescent sex offenders, and offer clearer etiological pathways than have been uncovered so far.

Weinrott (1996) highlights the need to explore the potential utility of empirically validated delinquency variables, such as those related to social cognition, community adjustment, family environment, and social (peer) bonding. In the area of social cognition, for example, attribution theory appears to offer some particularly rich possibilities for understanding cognitive processes that underlie offending, and to offer directions to address proviolence attitudes and beliefs effectively, and yet attribution theory is rarely mentioned in the adolescent sex offending literature.

The second issue is the reliable and valid measurement of known constructs, such as empathy, deviant sexual interests, and social competency. Beckett (1999) draws attention to the fact that much adolescent sex offender research fails to assess even the most obvious variables adequately, despite the availability of valid measurement tools. Beckett provides an excellent review of valid and reliable assessment tools to use in adolescent sex offender research and practice. This issue reflects the broader problem that serious methodological problems abound in adolescent sex offender research, of which Weinrott (1996) provides a comprehensive summary. Both Weinrott's and Beckett's contributions serve as sobering reminders that clinicians and researchers need to do a better job of practicing good science in their work with adolescent sex offenders.

Finally, Hudson and Ward (2001) suggest an excellent framework for theory building in the field of sexual offending, using a two-dimensional organizational system; according to explanatory level, on the one hand, and temporally, in terms of distal to proximal factors, on the other. Level I theories are multifactorial, using loosely grouped sets of constructs that serve as an integrated framework. Level II theories are single-factor theories, typically taking one variable of interest (such as empathy) and describing relevant processes and interrelationships. Level III consists of microtheories that build descriptive models of the offense process, such as relapse prevention or the sexual assault cycle. Comprehensive prospective and longitudinal studies could lead to theory building and empirical testing at all three levels in a way that is both coherent and integrated.

RECIDIVISM

The heterogeneity of adolescent sex offenders also has some important implications for recidivism. Common sense would dictate that with such a varied population, some subgroups of offenders would be quite likely to reoffend, whereas others would not. Research efforts to distinguish those who continue their offending into adulthood ("persisters") from those who subsequently desist, however, has given rise to some of the same difficulties identified in taxonomic and etiological research. Once again, knowledge in this area of the field is not expanding in a systematic, integrated way.

In some ways, popular wisdom about adolescent sex offender recidivism got off to a shaky start in the 1980s, when public awareness of adolescent sex offenders began to grow, at least partly from research reporting high rates of undetected adolescent sex offending in the histories of adult sex offenders (e.g., Abel, Mittleman, & Becker, 1985). From these data, it was often prematurely concluded that the risk of adolescent recidivism was therefore generally high. In the next decade, clinicians and researchers began to recognize that many adolescent sex offenders being referred for treatment were not just younger versions of the adult offenders they were treating: a wide range of recidivism potential seemed evident, rather than an inevitable trajectory into adult perpetration. It is now more generally understood that adult sex offenders with juvenile histories of sex offending represent only a portion of adolescent sex offenders. Understanding desistance therefore needs to be a major research focus.

For example, Weinrott (1996) in his comprehensive review of recidivism studies drew two firm conclusions from available research. First, the majority of adolescent sex offenders do not reoffend sexually within follow-up periods of 5 to 10 years. Thus, it is now evident that chronic sexual offending in adolescence is more the exception than the rule. Second, nonsexual recidivism occurs at double the rate, and much higher than that for some samples. Thus delinquency is a major issue for at least some subgroups of adolescent sex offenders.

Studies such as Worling (2001) are helping delineate differences between persisters and desisters. Knight and Prentky (1993), using retrospective data from adult sex offenders, established that those who began offending sexually in adolescence are more likely to have a history of antisocial behavior and poor social competence than those who did not begin offending until adulthood. Although this still does not tell us about adolescent sex offenders who subsequently desisted, it does support an observed link between antisocial characteristics and sexual recidivism risk for at least some adolescent sex offenders. This is consistent with Worling's typology (Group 1), and also the literature on the persistence of adolescent delinquency into general criminality in adulthood.

Here once again we are reminded of the need to consult the delinquency literature to see if it can enhance our understanding of adolescent sex offenders with delinquent histories. A number of large-scale studies (e.g., refer to review by Elkins, Iacono, Doyle, & McCue, 1997; see also Beckett, 1999) have identified robust predictors of persistence for general delinquency, principally low IQ, poor academic and behavioral adjustment in school, hostility, aggression, lifestyle impulsiveness, poor frustration tolerance, and substance abuse. Again, although this does not inform us about the persistence of sexual offending, it does give us a better understanding of risk characteristics and treatment needs of adolescent sex offenders who also engage in nonsexual crime.

Risk assessment research with adolescent sex offenders has been scarce, and this has contributed to the patchy nature of recidivism knowledge to date. Schram, Milloy, and Rowe (1991) undertook one of the few studies to report recidivism risk factors specific to adolescent sex offending. These were: (a) deviant arousal (clinically estimated), (b) cognitive distortions, (c) truancy, and (d) prior offenses. Prentky, Harris, Frizzel, and Righthand (2000) focused on risk assessment, and developed an actuarial instrument for assessing reoffense risk in adolescent sex offenders that comprises four subscales: sexual drive/preoccupation; impulsive, antisocial behavior; clinical/treatment; and community stability/adjustment. These studies again highlight the importance of antisocial characteristics, such as school problems and prior offenses in those who persist, and overall offer concepts and tools that can contribute to a more integrated understanding of recidivism in adolescent sex offenders.

Finally, an important gap in the recidivism literature is the long-term follow-up of adolescent sex offenders into middle adulthood. Little is yet known about their likelihood of reoffending when they have families of their own, because existing studies have not provided sufficiently long follow-up periods. Therefore, while we know that the majority of adolescent sex offenders desist in their early or mid-20s, we simply do not know if this remains the case. It is plausible that when confronted with the ample opportunity for offending afforded by family life, some individuals may lapse into incest offending if other vulnerability and triggering factors are brought into play. Hypotheses like these need to be investigated, and this echoes the aforementioned need for longitudinal studies of adolescent offenders that track a comprehensive range of variables.

Clinical Issues

This section reviews some of the more salient dilemmas and problems arising in the provision of clinical services to adolescent sex offenders. An emergent theme is that when working with an adolescent population, developmental considerations need to fundamentally inform and shape the nature of the service provided. Accordingly, clinical issues in this section are divided on the basis of relevance to biological, intrapersonal, and social domains.

THE BIOLOGICAL DOMAIN: SEXUALITY

Marshall and Barbaree (1990) note that the dramatic changes associated with sexual development constitute a critical period for young males, with respect to controlling their sexual behavior. Sex offending during adolescence points to problems negotiating these developmental changes. Studies of deviant sexual arousal in adolescent sex offenders (e.g., Hunter & Lexier, 1998) show less correspondence between measured arousal and offense histories than is observed in adults, which suggests that many adolescent sex offenders have not yet developed a consistent pattern of sexual arousal and interest. The impressionability of adolescents on sexual matters makes them especially receptive—and also vulnerable—to whatever sexual experiences and materials they gain access to during this critical period of their development.

Several important clinical implications follow from this. First is the ongoing controversy about the use of plethysmography. Proponents argue on the basis that deviant arousal is a clear risk factor for adolescents, and therefore, in the absence of a more valid and reliable physiological measure, plethysmography is necessary to provide the best standard of assessment data. In other words, the end justifies the means. Opponents contend that the potential gains are outweighed by reliability and validity problems, but more particularly by ethical concerns such as the risk of doing harm through exposing young offenders to deviant images to which they would not have otherwise had access. There is still no clear resolution on this matter, although the majority of adolescent sex offender programs do not routinely use plethysmography.

Another issue has to do with the provision of sex education in adolescent sex offender treatment. In view of developmental and learning considerations, building sex education into such programs makes good sense. Especially important, however, is the need to provide content that emphasizes interpersonal aspects of sexuality, such as values, dating skills, healthy relationships, and definitions of masculinity, in addition to more traditional topics such as anatomy, physiology, and sexual health (refer to Brown, 1993, for a good curriculum for at-risk youth). This broader approach would target the sexual aspects of social competence deficits that are so frequently seen in adolescent sex offenders.

Related to the need for a focus on positive sexuality in adolescent sex offender treatment is the issue of pornography use. Weinrott (1996) emphasizes the need for more research on the effects of pornography use on adolescent sex offenders. Adolescent males (whether or not they are offenders) typically name pornography as one of their more common sources of sexual information. It may be that those who sexually offend have a particular vulnerability to the messages portrayed in pornography (and also some aspects of mainstream media), constituting either a causal or a reinforcing link to their offending (Murrin & Laws, 1990). In any case, it is clear that the themes implicit in pornography, such as impersonal sex or fusion of sex with violence, would typically reinforce pro-offending cognitions, and that some adolescents may be especially vulnerable to such cues. Thus a programmatic focus on positive sexuality is important for counteracting these influences, especially during the impressionable years of adolescence.

THE INTRAPERSONAL DOMAIN: IDENTITY

Adolescence is also a crucial time for the development of personal identity. Cognitive abilities are expanding rapidly, and curiosity and risk-taking are the norm. Adolescents are preoccupied about who they are and who they want to become. Treatment programs need to be responsive to these priorities and developmental needs.

In the delinquency field, strengths-based models of treatment are well established; for example, Durrant (1993) provides an excellent philosophical framework for intervening with troubled youth in residential settings. This approach contextualizes the youth's problems, seeks opportunities to reframe problem behaviors, identifies existing competencies, and builds upon them in ways that help the youth develop a more positive view of self and the world. Similar approaches are now beginning to be articulated in adolescent sex offender treatment. For example, Jenkins (1990) proposes a strengths-based, responsibility-focused approach that seeks to empower abusive males in a range of ways. Although written with adult offenders in mind, many underlying principles and values in Jenkins's approach are compatible with the identity needs of adolescents.

Treatment models of this kind are especially appropriate for adolescents because they explicitly and implicitly address positive identity development and place the need for personal change within the context of an evolving and developing self. Offense-specific treatment components are still incorporated, but within a broader context that does not make assumptions about the young offender being on an inevitable trajectory toward adult offending.

The foregoing implies there needs to be something different about treatment philosophy and process in order to meet the developmental needs of adolescent sex offenders. What is being suggested here is not just the simplification of adult program material to match the cognitive level of adolescents. Rather it is the construction of programs that capitalize upon adolescent's sensibilities, and capture their imagination about their own capabilities and future lives. Programs that have been adapted to the needs of indigenous or other ethnic minority offenders often have a head start on these issues, because ethnicity is so integral to identity and sense of self (a volume by Lewis, 1999, provides a wide range of examples specific to sex offender treatment).

THE SOCIAL DOMAIN

A range of clinical issues arise in relation to the social transitions associated with adolescence. Developmentally, adolescents are beginning to separate from family, but are still dependent to some degree; peers are becoming a stronger influence, and various institutions have statutory obligations toward them: always the school, but often others such as social services, the courts, or mental health. A common source of difficulty is the capacity of treatment programs to effectively interact and communicate with the range of people and agencies involved with their adolescent clients.

Family. There is an immense need for treatment providers to work effectively with the families of adolescent sex offenders. Given that family is the first and most powerful agent of socialization, family problems or hardships have contributed in many instances to the adolescent's vulnerability to offending. For example, research clearly indicates an association between different kinds of adolescent sex offending and different kinds of family upheaval: More forceful and intrusive offending is associated with neglect in childhood, whereas molestation of younger children is associated with childhood physical and/or sexual abuse (Weinrott, 1996). These findings point to the need for family intervention, not only to identify and attempt to mitigate such influences, but also to increase the likelihood of change in adolescent behavior by facilitating change in some of the systems upon which they still depend.

Despite almost universal ideological acceptance of the need for it, family therapy is still not actually built into many adolescent sex offender programs. Funding constraints are often cited, but many programs are not actually developed on family-based models when funding is sought and secured. Although there are some welcome exceptions (e.g., refer to Cocoran, Miranda, Tenukas-Steblea, & Taylor, 1999, for an example of a family-based treatment model), it appears that many adolescent sex offender treatment programs are not particularly responsive to their clients' developmental needs in relation to family.

The fact that adolescent sex offender treatment models have developed largely as adaptations of adult programs, which have a lesser imperative to include the family in treatment, may help account for this. Traditional adult cognitive-behavioral programs have often downplayed systemic and contextual factors, often to their own detriment, but this restricted perspective has cost adolescent offenders even more. Urgently needed are adolescent sex offender programs that can investigate what kinds of family intervention will be most effective for what kinds of adolescent sex offenders.

For example, we could predict a need for intensive family work with sibling incest offenders, whereas an adolescent who has spent years in out-of-home placements and is convicted of raping peers may instead need work on trauma and loss issues in relation to family of origin, or joint work with protective services to assess the possibility of family reunification. This in turn reminds us of the need for informative research on adolescent sex offender classification and etiology, so family therapy approaches can be investigated in a systematic and integrated way. It also points to a need for clinicians to become more open and informed about family therapy, and to find out what the delinquency literature can teach us about this already.

Peers. It is quite amazing that the adolescent sex offender field has endorsed almost universally the idea that intensive, peer-group–based, offense-specific therapy is the intervention of choice for adolescent sex offenders, and yet, as Weinrott (1996) pointed out, "there is not yet a shred of evidence that supports this stance" (p. 85). These are the times when the lack of controlled and comparative outcome studies in the literature raises serious questions about whether we are yet doing the best we can do in the area of treatment.

Weinrott also points out that the only scientific evidence for therapeutic efficacy comes from a more general, delinquency-oriented intervention with adolescent sex offenders, wherein Borduin, Henggeler, Blaske, and Stein (1990) demonstrated lower recidivism for adolescent sex offenders who completed multisystemic therapy (MST), compared to those who completed individual therapy.

Again, developmental issues are at the core here. If we make clinical decisions that involve bringing troubled or delinquent young people together, we must be mindful of the fact that adolescents are especially strongly influenced by their peers at this stage of development. This has generally been used as a rationale in favor of offense-specific group therapy; for example, that groups can develop a positive peer culture to facilitate change. Yet treatment providers have tended to ignore evidence to the contrary, despite the fact that there is now a quite solid body of evidence from the delinquency literature cautioning practitioners against bringing antisocial youth together, due to the very real risk of reinforcing criminal behavior. Instead, it is recommended that treatment models establish ways to increase adolescent offenders' interactions with prosocial peers, improve school participation, and improve family communication (e.g., Henggeler & Borduin, 1990). The relevance of these findings specifically to adolescent sex offender treatment has been barely investigated at all, with the exception of Borduin's study.

Again, this gap in the treatment literature may be explained at least in part by the quite restricted interpretations of cognitive-behavioral therapy that abound in adult sex offender treatment, from which adolescent models of treatment have been developed. Many practitioners simply may not know how to transfer group treatment effectively to a family–based model, or how to develop interventions that safely put adolescent sex offenders in situations where they can learn from non-offending peers. Cost-effectiveness and logistics may also have a role, since it is clearly less expensive (and also just easier) to see adolescent sex offenders together in a group than to work with separate family systems, or with large groups that mix offenders with non-offending peers. It is noteworthy that Borduin's MST approach, which demonstrated utility with adolescent sex offenders, did not involve bringing them together in a group, but rather worked intensively with them in the contexts of family, school, and other activities, especially in ways that increased their involvement with prosocial peers and environments.

Clearly the adolescent sex offender field needs to adopt an investigative stance toward its current treatment of choice, again integrating lessons already learned in the delinquency field. A replication and extension of Borduin's study is especially urgently needed, in particular a comparison of offense-specific therapy with MST. A process evaluation of a community-based adolescent sex offender program in New York City takes a small step in this direction. Although limited by small sample size and lack of a control or comparison group, the program piloted a unique approach that mixed some elements of MST with traditional offense-specific treatment, and reported some encouraging preliminary results with an inner-city, predominantly African American client group. This program is described in detail by Jones, Winkler, Kacin, Salloway, & Weissman (1998).

School. The literature tells us that truancy, academic problems, and especially behavioral problems in school are associated with sexual and nonsexual recidivism for adolescent sex offenders, and also with the persistence of offending into adulthood. School is obviously also a large part of adolescent life, and is one of the most visible environments in which social competence can be assessed and encouraged. Therefore it follows that school-based interventions could be extremely beneficial for adolescent sex offenders. And yet, for reasons similar to above, explicit inclusion of the school in treatment planning is not routine for adolescent sex offenders unless they are residing in residential or detention facilities, where treatment and schooling are likely to occur at the same location.

Once again, reliable findings on offender typology and etiology could help establish sound clinical practice in this area. No doubt some adolescent offenders need school involvement more than others, and distinctly different forms of intervention would likely be indicated, depending on need. For example those with antisocial traits would need different intervention from those who are most socially isolated, and though truancy may need to be the key school-related target in one case, literacy problems may be primary for someone else. Community safety is yet another issue, wherein schools could benefit from being involved in relapse prevention plans, especially with school-age offenders who target peers as victims. Finally, in some cases school involvement might be strongly ill-advised, if for example it was likely to stigmatize the offender and if his (or her) problems and needs did not manifest in the school environment.

The problem is, adolescent sex offender research has not yet adequately investigated questions such as these. Effectively navigating large organizations (such as the public school system) is not generally a strength of cognitive-behavioral therapists, whose training better equips them to work at the individual and small-group level. Adapting sex offender treatment to the needs of adolescents poses a serious challenge to treatment providers to become more systems focused, and researchers need to build more systems-related variables into their investigations.

Other Agencies. In keeping with the above observations in relation to school involvement, Cellini (1997) and Worling (2001) both highlight the need for adolescent sex offender programs to integrate their services effectively with other agencies, such as social services and the courts. An explicit interagency policy of cooperation and information sharing is advocated. At an individual level, one such strategy is regular case conferencing with all involved parties represented. At a systems level, a strategy would be an interagency committee that meets regularly so that information sharing can occur without the gaps, duplication, or inconsistency so often reported. Once again, this requires a shift in focus and level of analysis for cognitive behavioral treatment providers, but in view of the developmental needs of adolescent offenders and the wide range of agencies typically involved in their lives, this shift is necessary. Obviously it needs to be accompanied by research to help evaluate the most effective approaches for different types of adolescent sex offenders.

Conclusion

In sum, it appears that both research and practice with adolescent sex offenders need to be approached with a more systematic and critical eye. The heterogeneity of the identified population, combined with the severe methodological problems in existing research, has put quite a low ceiling on what we can confidently conclude from the literature thus far.

Clinical applications appear, overall, to have focused on the role of sex offender-specific variables (as gleaned from the literature on adults), without sufficient attention to developmental variables. That is, there may have been too much reliance on adapting adult models of treatment, when youth-based interventions of other kinds could become an equally important reference point. Delinquency literature is one such avenue, but need not be the only one.

The problems and dilemmas in the adolescent sex offender treatment field extend far beyond those highlighted in this chapter. This may make the task of contributing meaningfully to the field seem daunting. However, if we examine closely the sources of the many problems identified, just a few axioms should help direct the reader toward making sound and relevant contributions. Researchers need to take more care to ensure their studies are methodologically defensible and conform to the basics of good social science. Clinicians need to learn more about systems-based interventions in order to maximize program responsiveness to adolescent developmental needs and circumstances. And we all need to read the literature critically, resist the temptation to accept untested clinical lore unquestioningly, and truly understand the gaps and priorities for knowledge building before we do another thing.

References

Abel, G. G., Mittleman, M. S., & Becker, J. V. (1985). Sexual offenders: Results of assessment and recommendations for treatment. In H. Ben-Aron, S. I. Hucker, & C. D. Webster (Eds.), *Clinical criminology* (pp. 191-205). Toronto: M. M. Graphics.

Barbaree, H. E., Marshall, W. L., & Hudson, S. M. (Eds.). (1993). *The juvenile sex offender.* New York: Guilford.

Beckett, R. (1999). Evaluation of adolescent sexual abusers. In M. Erooga & H. Masson (Eds.), *Children and young people who sexually abuse others: Challenges and responses* (pp. 204-267). New York: Routledge.

Borduin, C. M., Henggeler, S. W., Blaske, D. M., & Stein, R. J. (1990). Multi-systemic treatment of adolescent sex offenders. *International Journal of Offender Therapy and Comparative Criminology, 34,* 105-113.

Brown, S. (1993). *Streetwise to sex-wise: Sexuality education for high-risk youth.* Hackensack, NJ: Planned Parenthood of Greater Northern New Jersey, Center for Family Life Education.

Cellini, H. R. (1997). Assessment and treatment of the adolescent sexual offender. In B. K. Schwartz & H. R. Cellini (Eds.), *The sex offender: Correctional, treatment and legal practice* Vol. 2, (pp. 6-1—6-11). Kingston, NJ: Civic Research Institute.

Cocoran, C. L., Miranda, A. O., Tenukas-Steblea, K. W., & Taylor, B. (1999). Inclusion of the family in the treatment of juvenile sexual abuse perpetrators. In B. K. Schwartz & H. R. Cellini (Eds.), *The sex offender: Theoretical advances, treating special populations and legal developments* (Vol. 3, pp. 17-1—17-9). Kingston, NJ: Civic Research Institute.

Durrant, M. (1993). *Residential treatment: A cooperative, competency-based approach to therapy and program design.* New York: Norton.

Elkins, I. J., Iacono, W. G., Doyle, A. E., & McCue, M. (1997). Characteristics associated with persistence of antisocial behaviour: Results from recent longitudinal research. *Aggression and Violent Behavior, 2,* 101-124.

Elliott, D. S. (1994). *The developmental course of sexual and non-sexual violence: Results from a national longitudinal study.* Paper presented at the 13th Annual Research and Treatment Conference of the Association for the Treatment of Sexual Abusers, San Francisco.

France, K., & Hudson, S. M. (1993). The conduct disorders and the juvenile sex offender. In H. E. Barbaree, W. L. Marshall, & S. M. Hudson (Eds.), *The juvenile sex offender* (pp. 225-234). New York: Guilford.

Gough, H. G. (1987). *California Psychological Inventory: Administrator's guide.* Palo Alto, CA: Consulting Psychologists Press.

Henggeler, S. W., & Borduin, C. M. (1990). *Family therapy and beyond: A multisystemic approach to treating the behaviour problems of children and adolescents.* Pacific Grove, CA: Brooks/Cole.

Hudson, S. M., & Ward, T. (2001). Adolescent sexual offenders: Assessment and treatment. In C. R. Hollin (Ed.), *Handbook of offender assessment and treatment* (pp. 363-377). New York: John Wiley.

Hunter, J. A., & Lexier, L. J. (1998). Ethical and legal issues in the assessment and treatment of juvenile sex offenders. *Child Maltreatment, 3,* 339-348.

Jenkins, A. (1990). *Invitations to responsibility: The therapeutic engagement of men who are violent and abusive.* Adelaide, South Australia: Dulwich Centre Publications.

Jones, R. L., Winkler, M. X., Kacin, E., Salloway, W. N., & Weissman, M. (1998). Community based sex offender treatment for inner-city African American and Latino youth. In W. L. Marshall, Y. M. Fernandez, S. M. Hudson, & T. Ward (Eds.), *Sourcebook of treatment programs for sexual offenders* (pp. 457-476). New York: Plenum.

Knight, R. A., & Prentky, R. (1993). Exploring characteristics for classifying juvenile sex offenders. In H. E. Barbaree, W. L. Marshall, & S. M. Hudson (Eds.), *The juvenile sex offender* (pp. 45-83). New York: Guilford.

Lewis, A. (1999). *Cultural diversity in sexual abuser treatment*. Brandon, VT: Safer Society Press.

Malamuth, N. M., Heavey, C. L., & Linz, D. (1993). Predicting men's antisocial behaviour towards women: The interaction model of sexual aggression. In G. C. Nagayama Hall, R. Hirschman, J. R. Graham, & M. S. Zaragoza (Eds.), *Sexual aggression: Issues in etiology, assessment and treatment* (pp. 63-97). Washington, DC: Taylor & Francis.

Marshall, W. L., & Barbaree, H. E. (1990). An integrated theory of the etiology of sexual offending. In W. L. Marshall, D. R. Laws, & H. E. Barbaree (Eds.), *Handbook of sexual assault: Issues, theories and treatment of the offender* (pp. 343-361). New York: Plenum.

Murrin, M. R., & Laws, D. R. (1990). The influence of pornography on sex crimes. In W. L. Marshall, D. R. Laws, & H. E. Barbaree (Eds.), *Handbook of sexual assault: Issues, theories and treatment of the offender* (pp. 73-92). New York: Plenum.

O'Brien, M. J., & Bera, W. H. (1986). Adolescent sexual offenders: A descriptive typology. *Preventing Sexual Abuse, 1,* 1-4.

Prentky, R., Harris, B., Frizzel, K., & Righthand, S. (2000). An actuarial procedure for assessing risk with juvenile sex offenders. *Sexual Abuse: A Journal of Research and Treatment, 12,* 71-93.

Ryan, G., & Lane, S. (Eds.). (1991). *Juvenile sexual offending: Cause, consequences and correction*. San Francisco: Jossey-Bass.

Schram, D. D., Milloy, C. D., & Rowe, W. E. (1991*). Juvenile sex offenders: A follow-up study of reoffense behaviour.* Olympia: Washington State Institute for Public Policy.

Smith, W. R., Monsastersky, C., & Deisher, R. M. (1987). MMPI-based personality types among juvenile sex offenders. *Journal of Clinical Psychology, 43,* 422-430.

Weinrott, M. R. (1996). *Juvenile sexual aggression: A critical review*. Unpublished manuscript, Institute of Behavioural Sciences, University of Colorado.

Worling, J. R. (2001). Personality-based typology of adolescent male sexual offenders: Differences in recidivism rates, victim-selection characteristics and personal victimisation histories. *Sexual Abuse: A Journal of Research and Treatment, 13,* 149-166.

12

The Promise and the Peril of Sex Offender Risk Assessment

Stephen D. Hart
Simon Fraser University

D. Richard Laws
South Island Consulting

P. Randall Kropp
British Columbia Forensic Psychiatric Services Commission

Risk assessment is a cornerstone of effective offender management in contemporary corrections (Andrews & Bonta, 1998). It is crucial to identify the risks posed by offenders, the factors associated with these risks, and the interventions that could be taken to manage or reduce risk. This is as true for sexual offenders as for any other category of offenders.

AUTHORS' NOTE: Stephen D. Hart, Department of Psychology, Simon Fraser University; D. Richard Laws, South Island Consulting; P. Randall Kropp, Adult Forensic Outpatient Services, British Columbia Forensic Psychiatric Services Commission. Thanks to the usual suspects, and in particular to Dr. Caroline Logan, for contributions to the ideas expressed herein.

   Correspondence should be addressed to Professor Stephen D. Hart, Department of Psychology, Simon Fraser University, Burnaby, British Columbia, Canada, V5A 1S6 (e-mail: shart@arts.sfu.ca).

Assessment of risk for recidivistic sexual offending has, in the past 10 years, become a topic of great interest to researchers, sex offender therapists, and policymakers around the world (Association for the Treatment of Sexual Abusers [ATSA], 1993; Hanson, 1998; Janus & Meehl, 1997). One reason for this is, no doubt, increased awareness of the high incidence and harmful consequences of sexual violence. Research findings certainly sensitized people to the problem of sexual violence, but at the same time led to the establishment and maintenance of dangerous myths about sexual offenders; for example, the myths that sexual offenders as a group have a high recidivism rate, pose a risk to strangers, and are untreatable. A second reason is the occurrence of high-profile crimes—typically, the sexual homicide of a young child—committed by repeat sexual offenders that result in public outrage. These terrible crimes put pressure on governments to act immediately to restore public confidence by increasing social control over those convicted of sexual offenses. This has led in some jurisdictions to mandatory registration and community notification laws, longer sentences, denial of parole or probation, and indeterminate criminal or civil commitment for those convicted of sexual offenses (e.g., Fitch, 1998). A third reason is the recognition that mental health and criminal justice agencies face significant problems with respect to the community supervision of sexual offenders. As noted above, some jurisdictions deny parole to sexual offenders (or even to all offenders), with the result that people who reach the end of their custodial sentences are released directly into the community as "free" citizens. Other jurisdictions have reacted by imposing mandatory life-time probation for sexual offenders, a move that results in massive and steadily increasing caseloads for probation staff. Jurisdictions that have not changed their community supervision practices are faced with large and growing sex offender caseloads. Regardless, there exist few clear guidelines for delivering individualized and reliably effective treatment, supervision, and monitoring services for sexual offenders in the community.

Despite recent advances in research (or, perhaps more accurately, because of them) there is considerable debate concerning best practices with respect to sex offender risk assessment (Janus & Meehl, 1997). The optimistic view highlights the promise of risk assessment. The promise is that risk assessment procedures can identify who is likely to reoffend—in fact, they can identify the specific or absolute probability that any given offender will commit another sexual offense (e.g., ATSA, 2001; Doren, 2000; Epperson, Kaul, & Huot, 1995; Hanson & Thornton, 2000; Quinsey, Harris, Rice, & Cormier, 1998). The optimists believe that such prognoses are stable and accurate, and will assist in making important decisions about sexual offenders. In contrast, pessimists highlight the peril. Their primary concern is that mental health professionals who conduct risk assessments over-rely on methods of unknown or limited value, pretending a degree of scientific support and precision that has not been attained (Boer, Hart, Kropp, & Webster, 1997; Campbell, 2000; Hart, 2001b; Petrila & Otto, in press). One potential consequence is that important decisions will be based on professional opinions of questionable value; another is that decision makers are encouraged to think about management in very simplistic terms.

In this chapter, we discuss both the promise and the peril of sex offender risk assessment—more properly, sexual violence risk assessment. The first section defines key terms and concepts. The second section describes two major methods of sexual violence risk assessment, specifically, actuarial and structured professional judgment approaches. The third section discusses the evaluation of risk assessment procedures. The final section touches on some current controversies in the field.

Key Terms and Concepts

RISK

A *risk* is a hazard that is incompletely understood and whose occurrence therefore can be forecast only with uncertainty (Bernstein, 1996; National Research Council, 1989). The concept is multifaceted, referring to the nature of the hazard, the likelihood that the hazard will occur, the frequency or duration of the hazard, the seriousness of the hazard's consequences, and the imminence of the hazard; also, the concept of risk is inherently contextual, as hazards arise and exist in specific circumstances (Hart, 1998, 2001a; Janus & Meehl, 1997; Mulvey & Lidz, 1995; Otto, 2000).

SEXUAL VIOLENCE

A hazard must be defined to be discussed and studied clearly. For the purposes of this chapter, the relevant hazard is the commission of *sexual violence.* Unfortunately, the vagaries of language make it impossible to offer a precise definition of sexual violence. We offer the following definition, admittedly flawed but potentially useful: Sexual violence is actual, attempted, or threatened sexual contact with another person that occurs without that person's consent (e.g., Boer et al., 1997). Sexual contact may be construed broadly to include acts such as sexual battery (e.g., rape, sexual touching), communications of a sexual nature (e.g., exhibitionism, obscene letters or phone calls), and violating property rights for sexual purposes (e.g., voyeurism, theft of fetish objects). Consent may be considered absent if the sexual contact occurred without the victim's assent, or if a victim assented but was unable to appreciate the nature or consequences of sexual contact due to factors such as immaturity or mental disability.

ASSESSMENT

In the mental health professions, *assessment* is the process of gathering information about people for use in making decisions about them (American Educational Research Association/American Psychological Association/National Council on Measurement in Education, 1999). Assessment methods include personal interviews, psychological or medical testing, review of case records, and contacts with collateral informants. Mental health professions with forensic specializations have developed specialized assessment methods and procedures (e.g., Heilbrun, 1992, 2001).

INTEGRATION: SEXUAL VIOLENCE RISK ASSESSMENT

Putting these conceptual pieces together, then, *sexual violence risk assessment* is the process of gathering information about people to make decisions regarding their risk for perpetrating sexual violence. The primary decision to be made is what steps should be taken to minimize any risks posed by the individual (Hart, 1998, 2001a; Heilbrun, 1997; Monahan et al., 2001). It is important to note that sexual violence risk assessment does not necessitate a deterministic view of human behavior. The focus of the evaluation should be on the individual's decision making with respect to sexual violence; that is, on understanding what the individual was trying to accomplish. The task of the mental health professional is to speculate about how and why a person chose to commit sexual violence in the past and to determine whether the factors involved in those decisions (e.g., sexual deviation, antisocial attitudes, irrational beliefs, labile affect, interpersonal stresses) might lead the person to make similar choices in the future.

Approaches to Sexual Violence Risk Assessment

TWO BASIC APPROACHES

Mental health professionals use two basic approaches to reach opinions about sexual violence risk: *professional judgment* and *actuarial decision making.* These terms refer to how information is weighted and combined to reach a final decision, regardless of the information that is considered and how it was collected (Dawes, Faust, & Meehl, 1989; Meehl, 1954/1996). The hallmark of professional judgment procedures is that the evaluator exercises some degree of discretion in the decision-making process, although it is also generally the case that evaluators have wide discretion concerning how assessment information is gathered and which information is considered. It comes as no surprise that unstructured clinical judgment is also described as "informal, subjective, [and] impressionistic" (Grove & Meehl, 1996, p. 293). In contrast, the hallmark of the actuarial approach is that, based on the information available to them, evaluators make an ultimate decision according to fixed and explicit rules (Meehl, 1954/1996). It is also generally the case that actuarial decisions are based on specific assessment data, selected because they have been demonstrated empirically to be associated with sexual violence and coded in a predetermined manner. The actuarial approach also has been described as "mechanical" and "algorithmic" (Grove & Meehl, 1996, p. 293).

PROFESSIONAL JUDGMENT APPROACHES

The professional judgment approach comprises at least three different procedures. The first is *unstructured professional judgment*, also referred to by Hanson (1998) and others as *unaided clinical judgment*. This is decision making in the complete absence of structure, a process that could be characterized as "intuitive" or "experiential." Historically, it is the most commonly used procedure for assessing sexual violence risk and therefore is very familiar to mental health professionals, as well as to courts and tribunals. It has the advantage of being highly adaptable and efficient; it is possible to use intuition in any context, with minimal cost in terms of time and other resources. It is also very person-centered, focusing on the unique aspects of the case at hand, and thus can be of great assistance in planning interventions to manage risk for sexual violence. The major problem is that there is little empirical evidence that intuitive decisions are consistent across professionals or, indeed, that they are helpful in preventing sexual violence. As well, intuitive decisions are unimpeachable; it is difficult even for the people who make them to explain how they were made. This means that the credibility of the decision often rests on charismatic authority—that is, the credibility of the person who made the decision. Finally, intuitive decisions tend to be broad or general in scope, so that they become dispositional statements about the offender ("Offender X is a very dangerous person") rather than a series of speculative statements about what the offender might do in the future, assuming various release conditions.

The second professional judgment procedure is sometimes referred to as *anamnestic risk assessment* (e.g., Melton, Petrila, Poythress, & Slobogin, 1997). (*Anamnesis* is the process of history taking in medicine; roughly translated, it is Greek for "Remind yourself" or "Don't forget [what is known]."). This procedure imposes a limited degree of structure on the assessment as the evaluator must, at a minimum, identify the personal and situational factors that resulted in sexual violence in the past. The assumption here is that a series of events and circumstances, a kind of behavioral chain, resulted in the offender committing sexual violence. The professional's task, therefore, is to understand the links in this chain and suggest ways in which the chain could be broken (in this way, anamnestic assessment has much in common with relapse prevention or harm reduction approaches to treating sex offenders). However, there is no empirical evidence supporting the consistency or usefulness of anamnestic risk assessments. Anamnestic risk assessment also seems to assume that history will repeat itself—that violent people are static over time, so the only thing they are at risk to do in the future is what they have done in the past. Nothing could be further from the truth, or course; there are many different trajectories of sexual violence. Some sex offenders will escalate in terms of the frequency or severity of sexual violence over time, some change the types of sexual violence they commit, and some will de-escalate or even desist altogether.

The third procedure is *structured professional judgment*, or what Hanson (1998) and others call *guided clinical judgment*. Here, decision making is assisted by guidelines that have been developed to reflect the "state of the discipline" with respect to empirical knowledge and professional practice (Borum, 1996). Such guidelines—sometimes referred to as clinical guidelines, consensus guidelines, or clinical practice parameters—are quite common in medicine, although used less frequently in psychiatric and psychological assessment (Kapp & Mossman, 1996). The guidelines attempt to define the risk being considered; discuss necessary qualifications for conducting an assessment; recommend what information should be considered as part of the evaluation and how it should be gathered; and identify a set of core risk factors that, according to the scientific and professional literature, should be considered as part of any reasonably comprehensive assessment. Structured professional guidelines help to improve the consistency and usefulness of decisions, and certainly improve the transparency of decision making. However, they may require considerable time or resources to develop and implement. Also, some evaluators dislike this "middle ground" or compromise approach, either because it lacks the freedom of intuitive decision making or because it lacks the objectivity of actuarial procedures.

ACTUARIAL APPROACHES

There are at least two types of actuarial decision making. The first is the *actuarial use of tests*. Classically, tests are structured samples of behavior designed to measure a personal disposition, an attempt to quantify an individual's standing on some trait dimension. Research indicates that some dispositions—such as sexual deviation (Hanson & Bussière, 1998) or impulsivity (e.g., Prentky, Knight, Lee, & Cerce, 1995)—are associated with sexual violence risk. On the basis of research results, one can identify cutoff scores to use with, say, a particular plethysmographic evaluation that maximizes some aspect of predictive accuracy. This procedure has several strengths, the most important being its transparency and the empirical data supporting the consistency and utility of test-based decisions. One major problem is that the use of tests requires considerable discretion: Mental health professionals must decide which test(s) are appropriate in a given case, and judgment may also be required in test scoring and interpretation. Another problem is that reliance on a single test does not constitute a comprehensive evaluation and will provide limited information for use in developing intervention strategies. More generally, the actuarial use of tests focuses professional efforts on prediction rather than prevention efforts.

The second type of procedure is the use of *actuarial risk assessment instruments,* also known as *actuarial tests, tools,* or *aids.* In contrast to other tests, actuarial instruments are designed not to measure anything but solely to predict the future. Typically, they are high fidelity, optimized to predict a specific outcome in a specific population over a specific period of time. The items in the scale are selected either rationally (on the basis of theory or experience) or empirically (on the basis of their association with the outcome in past research). The items are weighted and/or combined according to some algorithm to yield a decision. In sexual violence risk assessment, the "decision" generally is the estimated likelihood of recidivism (e.g., rearrest for a specific category of sexual offenses) over some period of time. Like other tests, actuarial instruments have the advantage of transparency and direct empirical support; they also suffer many of the same weaknesses, including the need for discretion in selecting a test and interpreting its findings, as well as the limited use of test findings in planning interventions. There are additional problems with actuarial instruments that estimate the absolute likelihood or probability of recidivism. One is that they require tremendous time and effort to construct and validate. In cases where the time frame of the prediction is long, true cross-validation may require decades. Also, when constructing actuarial tests there is a classic bandwidth-fidelity trade-off between precision of estimated recidivism rates and generalizability: The same statistical procedures that optimize predictive accuracy in one setting will decrease that test's accuracy in others. Finally, it is easy to accord too much weight to information concerning the estimated likelihood of recidivism provided by actuarial tests. Most actuarial tests of sexual violence risk yield very precise likelihood estimates, proportions with two or three decimal places, but they do not provide the information necessary to understand the error inherent in these estimates. When one considers the fact that many of these estimates were derived from relatively small construction samples and have not been validated in independent samples, it is clear that the actuarial test results are only pseudo-precise. It is important for any professional who uses actuarial tests to understand and explain to others the limitations of absolute likelihood estimates of recidivism.

Some commentators (e.g., Hanson, 1998) have discussed another approach that sometimes is referred to as *adjusted actuarial decision making*. Here, evaluators start by using an actuarial risk assessment instrument and then adjust or reinterpret the findings intuitively in light of additional information. Its reliance on evaluator discretion means that this approach is properly considered a variety of structured or assisted professional judgment. Indeed, the term *adjusted actuarial* is somewhat oxymoronic: If there are fixed and explicit rules for adjusting the findings, then the procedure is actuarial; if there are not, then it is discretionary. Especially when an actuarial test was constructed on the basis of empirical research, it makes no sense to take test scores and then introduce guesswork (a "fudge factor") into the equation (see Grove & Meehl, 1996; Meehl, 1996/1954; Quinsey et al., 1998).

LIMITATIONS COMMON TO BOTH APPROACHES

All forms of risk assessment appear to share some problems or deficiencies. One is that they focus on negative characteristics or features—factors associated with increased risk—rather than personal strengths, resources, or "buffer" factors. A comprehensive risk assessment designed to assist in the development of intervention strategies must take into account these positive features. A second problem is that none of the existing risk assessment procedures is tied to the development of intervention strategies in a systematic or prescriptive manner. Once a risk assessment has been completed, decisions about risk management must be made using unstructured professional judgment. A third problem is one of quality assurance. Basic research to develop risk assessment procedures is important, but it is naïve to assume that any procedure will function similarly in the field. Evaluative research is required to monitor the implementation of risk assessment procedures, to determine whether they are functioning optimally, and what could be done to improve their use.

Evaluating Sexual Violence Risk Assessment Procedures

GENERAL ISSUES

The ultimate goal of sexual violence risk assessment is preventive. But a "good" risk assessment procedure should also accomplish secondary goals (Hart, 2001a). For example, it should yield consistent or replicable results. That is, mental health professionals should reach similar findings when evaluating the same offender at about the same time. It is highly unlikely that inconsistent or unreliable decisions can be of any practical use. Furthermore, a good risk assessment procedure should be prescriptive; it should identify, evaluate, and prioritize the mental health, social service, and criminal justice interventions that could be used to manage an offender's sexual violence risk. Finally, a good risk assessment procedure should be open or transparent. Put another way, as mental health professionals we are accountable for the decisions we make, and it is therefore important for us to make explicit, as much as is possible, the basis for our professional opinions. A transparent risk assessment procedure allows offenders and the public a chance to scrutinize our opinions. The transparency should protect mental health professionals when an offender commits sexual violence despite the fact that a good risk assessment was conducted, as it can be demonstrated easily that standard or proper procedures were followed. Contrariwise, transparency should protect offenders and the public when an improper risk assessment was conducted.

It is impossible for any single risk assessment procedure to achieve all these goals with maximum efficiency. Similarly, it is also impossible for the various parties interested in sexual violence risk assessment (mental health professionals, hospital administrators, offenders, lawyers, judges, victims, etc.) to reach a consensus regarding which procedure is "best" for all purposes and in all contexts (Hart, 2001a). Instead, mental health professionals should choose the best procedure—or set of procedures—for a particular assessment of a particular offender after considering explicitly the psycholegal context of the evaluation (e.g., sentencing, correctional intake or discharge, indeterminate civil commitment).

If all risk assessment procedures are imperfect in some way, then which procedures should be used by mental health professionals? Is it defensible to rely on a single procedure? Or is it better to rely on some combination or battery of procedures? Although it is impossible to provide simple answers to these questions—which depend in large part on nonscientific considerations such as law, social policy, and professional ethics—the following questions (synthesized from Boer et al., 1997; Hart, 2001a) may help mental health professionals to decide which procedure(s) they will choose:

1. Does the procedure gather information concerning multiple domains of the individual's functioning? A procedure should reflect the fact that sexual offenders are a heterogeneous group, and that sexual violence itself is a complex and multifaceted phenomenon.

2. Does the procedure use multiple methods to gather information? Each method of gathering information (interviews, questionnaires, case history review) is prone to certain weaknesses, and overreliance on a particular method can result in an evaluation that is incomplete and systematically biased.

3. Does the procedure gather information from multiple sources? Because people typically minimize or deny the sexual violence they have committed, overreliance on a particular source of information also can result in an evaluation that is incomplete and systematically biased.

4. Does the procedure gather information concerning both static and dynamic risk factors? Static (stable, historical) risk factors have, in general, the strongest empirical support with respect to prediction of future sexual violence, but evidence is accumulating that dynamic risk factors also are important, particularly with respect to evaluating short-term fluctuations in risk and in developing rational intervention programs.

5. Does the procedure allow users to evaluate explicitly the accuracy of information gathered? Because sexual violence risk assessments often are conducted for the purpose of forensic decision making, the procedure should allow evaluators to judge the credibility of various sources of information, reconcile contradictory information, and determine whether the information is sufficiently comprehensive to permit a valid decision.

6. Does the procedure allow reassessments to evaluate changes in risk over time? The status of risk factors, both static and dynamic, fluctuates over time. For people living in the community, these fluctuations can occur quite rapidly, and so sexual violence risk should be reassessed at regular intervals or whenever there is an important change in the status of a case.

7. Is the procedure comprehensive? The procedure should consider all the major risk factors, as well as allow for the consideration of case-specific risk and protective factors.

8. Is the procedure comprehensible to consumers? To be useful, the procedure should be comprehensible and, hopefully, acceptable to the people who must use the findings, including decision makers and the people being evaluated.

9. Can mental health professionals be trained to use the procedure in a consistent manner? Implementing a training program should be feasible in terms of time and money.

10. Does implementation of the procedure result in reduction of sexual violence? If prevention is the primary goal of sexual violence risk assessment, then the procedure or battery must go beyond the making of static predictions and assist in the planning and delivery of services.

No one has conducted a comprehensive evaluation of sexual violence risk assessment procedures in a way that attempts to answer the questions posed supra. Scientific research has, to date, relied exclusively on a rather narrow psychometric framework. The limitations of this framework for evaluating risk assessments have been discussed elsewhere (e.g., Douglas & Kropp, in press; Hart, 1998, 2001a). The primary problem is that it encourages researchers to conceptualize the goal of risk assessment in terms of predictive accuracy rather than preventive efficacy. In their impatience to get simple answers to complex questions, scientific studies ignore the reality of assessment contexts. Researchers examine single risk factors in isolation; they force evaluators to make static, quantitative predictions; they ignore changes in the psychological and environmental status of offenders over time; and they crudely conceptualize violence as a dichotomous outcome at some fixed time point rather than a time-dependent, transactional process.

THE STATE OF THE FIELD

Readers no doubt have intuited from our previous remarks that our overall evaluation of the "state of the field" with respect to sexual violence risk assessment is something less than sanguine. In this section, we comment briefly on the major approaches to sexual violence risk assessment as well as on the adequacy of specific procedures, where possible.

Professional Judgment Approaches. There has been very little systematic research on unstructured professional judgment approaches to sexual violence risk assessments. Hanson and Bussière (1998), in their meta-analysis of sex offender recidivism studies, reported that the validity of unstructured professional judgments was not much better than chance and lower than that of structured professional judgments and actuarial assessments. To be fair, however, most of these studies suffer from a lack of ecological validity that tends to underestimate the potential utility of unstructured professional judgment approaches.

To the best of our knowledge, there has been no research evaluating the reliability or validity of anamnestic approaches, either in isolation or in comparison to other approaches.

With respect to structured professional judgment, Hanson and Bussière (1998) reported that, on the basis of a small number of studies, such ratings had validity higher than those made using unstructured professional judgment; in fact, their validity approached that of actuarial approaches. Since the paper by Hanson and Bussière (1998), several sets of structured professional guidelines have been proposed, but at the time this chapter was written, no empirical evaluations of these guidelines have appeared in the peer-reviewed scientific literature.

Actuarial Judgment Approaches. In recent years, there has been relatively little interest in the use of individual tests with respect to assessing risk for sexual violence. There are two important exceptions to this general rule: Penile plethysmography (PPG; see Laws, Chapter 5 in this volume) and the Hare

Psychopathy Checklist-Revised (PCL-R; Hare, 1991). Resurgence of interest in the PPG was fuelled by the fact that it was, on average, the single best risk factor for recidivistic sexual violence according to the Hanson and Bussière (1998) meta-analysis. But the PPG is still a highly controversial procedure, and several problems seriously limit its practical utility. First, the PPG is most accurately considered a family of specific procedures. PPG is an umbrella term that covers a bewildering variety of measurement technologies, stimulus sets, testing protocols, and interpretive strategies. There is no consensus among professionals regarding best practices, so that there is no single cutoff that can be applied to test scores for decision-making purposes. Second, there is a lack of research supporting the utility of the PPG in certain subgroups, including children, adolescents, and the aged (obviously, it cannot be used at all with female sexual offenders). Third, there are ethical concerns about the propriety and potential negative consequence of exposing offenders to sexually deviant stimuli (for a more detailed critique of PPG evaluation, see Laws, Chapter 5 in this volume).

Interest in the PCL-R was fuelled by research indicating that it is the best single risk factor for serious and violent recidivism in diverse groups of correctional offenders and psychiatric patients, including sexual offenders (see Hart & Hare, 1997). There is, however, no good evidence that PCL-R scores are, on their own, predictive of sexually violent recidivism. In fact, because of competing hazards, PCL-R scores may be associated with a slightly decreased specific risk for sexual violence (i.e., because high scores are also associated with other risks, including risk for general criminality and nonsexual violence). It is important to note that neither the PPG nor the PCL-R was intended to assess risk for sexually violent recidivism, and there is no evidence that these tests can be used to make specific or absolute estimates of risk.

It is actuarial risk assessments that have been the primary focus of recent research. Ten years ago, no instruments of this sort existed; now there are literally dozens from which to choose. In the United States, their development and adoption have been motivated by sex offender registration and civil commitment laws, which require the state to prove, inter alia, that an individual is at elevated risk for reoffense before special controls can be imposed on him. A few actuarial instruments are used in multiple jurisdictions: the Rapid Risk Assessment for Sex Offense Recidivism (RRASOR; Hanson, 1997), developed on the basis of meta-analytic research by Hanson and Bussière (1998); the Static-99 (Hanson & Thornton, 2000), a revision of the RRASOR that also incorporates an English actuarial instrument, the SACJ-Min (Grubin, 1998); and the Minnesota Sex Offender Screening Tool-Revised (MnSOST-R; Epperson et al., 1995). Two other actuarial instruments, the Violence and Sex Offender Risk Appraisal Guides (VRAG and SORAG; Quinsey et al., 1998), are used in some jurisdictions, although they are intended to assess risk for any violence rather than sexual violence. Several other states have decided to develop their own actuarial instruments, including Colorado (English, Boyce, & Patzman, 1999) and Washington (Washington Department of Corrections, 1999). Most of these instruments are similar with respect to format. They are relatively brief checklists based primarily on static or background characteristics. Items are coded numerically and summed to form total scores that are then converted into estimates of the absolute likelihood of recidivism (typically defined as rearrest for a sexual offense) over some fixed time period. They were constructed using a known-groups or criterion-groups methodology, in which scoring rules were based on statistical analyses that maximized between-groups differences. Most of the tests are similar in terms of their limitations, as well. None of them has a proper manual that contains the information necessary for proper administration, scoring, and interpretation of the test. As a result, some jurisdictions have published their own versions of the test manuals—something that calls into question the generalizability of research findings based on the test. None of the tests has been evaluated systematically with respect to interrater reliability in the field. All were constructed on the basis of small samples of offenders, typically from a single jurisdiction (obtaining reasonably precise estimates of recidivism rates is something that requires large samples, typically 500 people or so per score category). Most important, however, there have been no replications (more technically, cross-validations or calibrations) of the test results. This is a critical issue, as actuarial tests constructed using statistical methods are mathematically optimized in the construction sample (sometimes referred to as the development sample), so that "predictive" accuracy is overestimated. A rough estimate of shrinkage on cross-validation can be estimated using statistical procedures, but this is no substitute for direct estimation of shrinkage via replication. To be blunt, the accuracy with which these tests make specific predictions of violence has never been evaluated: This was never done in the construction samples, as the tests were constructed *after* the outcomes were determined; and it has not been done since their development, using either retrospective or prospective methods in independent samples. The consequence of these limitations is that no one knows how well these actuarial tests actually work for their intended purposes. A few papers have appeared in the peer-reviewed scientific literature concerning these actuarial tests, including one describing the construction of the Static-99 (Hanson & Thornton, 2000) and others examining correlations between actuarial test scores and release failures (e.g., Barbaree, Seto, Langton, & Peacock, 2001)—although, as stated previously, none of the these articles cross-validates the accuracy of the absolute likelihood risk estimates made using the tests.

Current Controversies

SUPERIORITY OF ACTUARIAL RISK ASSESSMENT

Some researchers and professionals proclaim that the predictive accuracy of actuarial assessments of violence risk is superior to that of clinical assessments, that is, assessments made using professional judgment approaches (see Quinsey et al., 1998). Such proclamations have led to recommendations that sex offender risk assessment should be based, either in part or entirely, on the use of actuarial procedures (e.g., ATSA, 2001; Hanson, 1998; Quinsey et al., 1998). The simple truth is, there is no direct scientific evidence supporting proclamations or recommendations of this sort.

Narrative and quantitative reviews (e.g., Grove & Meehl, 1996; Grove, Zald, Lebow, Snitz, & Nelson, 2000) support the view that actuarial decision making is generally equal or superior to discretionary decision making in terms of reliability and validity. Focusing on the most comprehensive quantitative review (Grove et al., 2000), a crude summary of the findings is that there was a small but consistent trend favoring superiority of actuarial assessments. In about 40% of the direct comparisons, the actuarial approach was superior; in about 40% of the cases, the two approaches were equal; and in about 20%, the clinical approach was superior. Although it is correct to conclude from this that the actuarial approach was equal or superior 80% of the time, it is equally correct to conclude that the clinical approach was equal or superior 60% of the time. When actuarial was superior to clinical decision making, the typical increment in accuracy (hit rate) was about 10%.

Two things should be noted about the Grove et al. (2000) meta-analysis. First, most of the studies that directly compared the two decision-making approaches involved diagnosis or decisions about present state (e.g., studies that compare the human vs. mechanical interpretation of X rays with respect to the diagnosis of lung cancer), rather than prognosis or predictions about the future. Second, only a handful of studies compared actuarial versus clinical predictions of violence, and none examined predictions of sexual violence. In fact, a recent review of the more general literature of violence found only eight studies that directly compared actuarial versus clinical predictions of violence and found no evidence supporting the superiority of either method (Litwack, 2001). None of these eight studies examined sexual violence (see also Hanson & Bussière, 1998).

At present, then, the superiority of actuarial decision making is an article of faith rather than fact. Any claim of actuarial superiority is an inference based on evidence of questionable relevance, and should be acknowledged as such. It is entirely reasonable for mental health professionals to conclude that current scientific evidence is not sufficient to support the use of or reliance on actuarial procedures; indeed, it is entirely reasonable to conclude that the weight of the scientific evidence is sufficient to reject altogether the use of or reliance on actuarial procedures.

THE ROLE OF RISK ASSESSMENT IN SEX OFFENDER CIVIL COMMITMENT PROCEEDINGS

Many jurisdictions in the United States have passed laws permitting the indeterminate inpatient or outpatient commitment of sex offenders, following on the U.S. Supreme Court decision in *Kansas v. Hendricks* (1997). These laws are a relatively straightforward extension of traditional civil commitment: People who suffer from mental abnormality that impairs cognitive or volitional control and who pose a significant threat of violence may have their civil liberties restricted to protect public safety. Most statutes require that four conditions be met for a person to be committed (Janus, 2000): First, the person must have a history of sexual violence; second, the person must have a mental disorder; third, the person must have an elevated risk for future sexual violence; and fourth, the mental disorder must be at least partially responsible for (i.e., a cause of) the risk for future sexual violence. The definitions of key terms vary across jurisdictions (see Cohen, 1999, for a comparative analysis). For example, sexual violence may include any offense with a sexual motivation, or may be limited to contact sexual offenses against certain victims for certain motivations; the definition of mental disorder may be defined narrowly or broadly, with broad definitions including abnormalities such as sexual deviation and personality disorder; and the definition of elevated risk may be broad or narrow (e.g., "substantial likelihood" vs. "more likely than not"). Persons determined by the court to meet statutory criteria are typically committed to a secure facility for control and treatment, either in lieu of or subsequent to serving a criminal sentence for the predicate sexual offense, until they are considered no longer to pose an unacceptable risk for sexual reoffending.

Expert testimony regarding mental disorder and risk for sexual violence plays a key role in sex offender civil commitment hearings (Janus, 2000). In particular, it has been argued that actuarial risk assessment is the best—perhaps the only—means of forming scientifically and professionally defensible opinions regarding elevated risk (Doren, 2000; Quinsey et al., 1998). A common justification for this position is the "demonstrated" superiority of actuarial versus clinical approaches to sexual violence risk assessment, a point disputed previously. The Anglo American system of common law requires judges to act as gatekeepers for expert testimony so that the flow of the trial itself is not disturbed by opinions and research that are difficult to understand, of dubious relevance, and of questionable validity. The general legal criteria for the admissibility of expert opinion evidence include the following: (a) the evidence is relevant to some legal issue; (b) the evidence is outside the typical knowledge or understanding of laypeople; and, (c) the evidence is more probative than prejudicial, that is, more likely to help triers of fact reach a correct or proper decision than to mislead or confuse them (e.g., *Federal Rules of Evidence,* 1976). In the United States, additional specific legal criteria may be applicable in sex offender civil commitment proceedings. One important criterion is whether the theories or procedures underlying expert testimony are generally accepted in the relevant scientific or professional community (e.g., *Daubert v. Merrell Dow Pharmaceuticals,* 1993; *Frye v. United States,* 1923); others include the extent to which the theory is testable, whether the procedures have established error rates, and whether the theory or procedures have been subjected to peer review (e.g., *Daubert v. Merrell Dow Pharmaceuticals,* 1993). Although these legal criteria apply to all forms of expert testimony (e.g., *Kumho Tire Co. v. Carmichael,* 1999), they are especially relevant in cases where that testimony is based on scientific theory or procedures, as opposed to testimony based on training and experience, as triers of fact are likely to have difficulty weighing the probative value of scientific testimony due to its inherent complexity (Faigman, 1995).

Judged according to the relevant legal criteria, expert testimony proffered by mental health professionals in sex offender civil commitment hearings has a weak scientific foundation (Petrila & Otto, in press). Such testimony is on reasonably firm ground when it focuses on the assessment and diagnosis of mental disorder, which are core competencies of the mental health professions. There is an extensive scientific literature on descriptive psychopathology, as well as on the assessment and diagnosis of various mental disorders. Expert testimony regarding risk for sexual violence is shakier, as the scientific literature is relatively limited in scope and quality. Certainly professionals properly can opine, based on their assessments, about the existence of various risk factors and the nature of the risks posed in a given case. But notwithstanding some claims (e.g., those of actuarial superiority, as discussed in the preceding section), there is no body of scientific evidence supporting the view that it is possible to estimate the likelihood that an individual will commit an act of sexual violence with any reasonable degree of precision or certainty. Expert testimony is downright precarious when it comes to the issue of the causal nexus, that is, opinions regarding the extent to which the risks posed by an individual are attributable to a specific mental disorder. There are no accepted professional techniques or procedures for reaching such opinions, no relevant empirical studies—not even decent theory or speculation. Speculating about the possible causes of future behavior in a given case would appear to be an enterprise that is intrinsically professional rather than scientific.

In light of these arguments, it is perhaps unsurprising that the admissibility or scope of expert testimony regarding risk for sexual violence has been challenged, focusing primarily on actuarial procedures that estimate the absolute likelihood of future sexual violence. In cases where these challenges have been successful— that is, resulting in the exclusion of expert testimony based on actuarial procedures—judges have cited several reasons for their decisions (e.g., *In re Valdez et al.*, 2000): lack of relevance, as actuarial procedures may define sexual violence differently from the statute that is the basis for legal proceedings and also fail to address the causal nexus issue; potential for prejudice, as actuarial tests may give the false impression that they provide accurate and reliable information about the ultimate legal issue of risk; lack of general acceptance, as actuarial procedures are used and evaluated positively only by a minority of experts in the field of sexual violence; and lack of probative value, including an absence of independent, peer-reviewed, cross-validation research that establishes error rates.

Conclusion

Sexual violence risk assessments can be considered promising insofar as they have the potential to help people make informed and important decisions about sex offenders. But clearly they have not delivered on the promise that they can be used to make precise predictions about future sexual violence. Mental health professionals who conduct sexual violence risk assessments must be careful to appreciate and communicate the limits of their knowledge and practice, especially given the harm that may stem from bad decisions.

References

American Educational Research Association, American Psychological Association, and the National Council on Measurement in Education. (1999). *Standards for educational and psychological testing.* Washington, DC: American Educational Research Association.

Andrews, D. A., & Bonta, J. (1998). *The psychology of criminal conduct* (2nd ed.). Cincinnati, OH: Anderson.

Association for the Treatment of Sexual Abusers. (1993). *The ATSA practitioner's handbook.* Lake Oswego, OR: Author.

Association for the Treatment of Sexual Abusers. (2001). *Civil commitment of sexually violent offenders.* Retrieved July 8, 2002, from http://www.atsa.com/ppcivilcommit.html

Barbaree, H. E., Seto, M. C., Langton, C. M., & Peacock, E. J. (2001). Evaluating the predictive accuracy of six risk assessment instruments for adult sex offenders. *Criminal Justice and Behavior, 28,* 490-521.

Bernstein, P. L. (1996). *Against the gods: The remarkable story of risk.* New York: John Wiley.

Boer, D. P., Hart, S. D., Kropp, P. R., & Webster, C. (1997). *Manual for the Sexual Violence Risk-20.* Vancouver: British Columbia Institute Against Family Violence.

Borum, R. (1996). Improving the clinical practice of violence risk assessment: Technology, guidelines, and training. *American Psychologist, 51,* 945-956.

Campbell, T. W. (2000). Sexual predator evaluations and phrenology: Considering issues of evidentiary reliability. *Behavioral Sciences and the Law, 18,* 111-130.

Cohen, F. (1999). The law and sexually violent predators: Through the Hendricks looking glass. In A. Schlank & F. Cohen (Eds.), *The sexual predator: Law, policy, evaluation, and treatment* (pp. 1.1-1.13). Kingston, NJ: Civic Research Press.

Daubert v. Merrell Dow Pharmaceuticals (1993), 509 U.S. 579.

Dawes, R., Faust, D., & Meehl, P. (1989). Clinical versus actuarial judgment. *Science, 243,* 1668-1674.

Doren, D. (2000). Evidentiary issues, actuarial scales, and sex offender civil commitments. *Sex Offender Law Report, 1,* 65-66, 78-79.

Douglas, K. S., & Kropp, P. R. (in press). A prevention-based paradigm for violence risk assessment: Clinical and research applications. *Criminal Justice and Behavior.*

English, K., Boyce, E. J., & Patzman, J. (1999). *Sexually violent predator risk assessment screening instrument handbook: Background and instruction.* Denver: Colorado Division of Criminal Justice.

Epperson, D. L., Kaul, J. D., & Huot, S. J. (1995, October). *Predicting risk for recidivism for incarcerated sex offenders: Update on development of the Sex Offender Screening Tool (SOST).* Paper presented at the Annual Meeting of the Association for the Treatment of Sexual Abusers, New Orleans, Louisiana.

Faigman, D. L. (1995). The evidentiary status of social science under Daubert: Is it "scientific," "technical," or "other" knowledge? *Psychology, Public Policy, and Law, 1,* 960-971.

Federal Rules of Evidence. (1976). 28 United States Code §§ 101-1103.

Fitch, L. (1998). Sex offender commitment in the United States. *Journal of Forensic Psychiatry, 9,* 237-240.

Frye v. United States (1923), 293 F. 1013 (D.C. Cir.).

Grove W., & Meehl, P. (1996). Comparative efficiency of informal (subjective, impressionistic) and formal (mechanical, algorithmic) prediction procedures: The clinical-statistical controversy. *Psychology, Public Policy, and Law, 2,* 293-323.

Grove, W. M., Zald, D. H., Lebow, B. S., Snitz, B. E., & Nelson, C. (2000). Clinical versus mechanical prediction: A meta-analysis. *Psychological Assessment, 12,* 19-30.

Grubin, D. (1998). *Sex offending against children: Understanding the risk* (Police Research Series Paper 99). London: Home Office.

Hanson, R. K. (1997). *The development of a brief actuarial risk scale for sexual offense recidivism* (User Report No. 1997-04). Ottawa: Department of the Solicitor General of Canada.

Hanson, R. K. (1998). What do we know about sex offender risk assessment? *Psychology, Public Policy, and Law, 4*(3), 50-72.

Hanson, R. K., & Bussière, M. T. (1998). Predicting relapse: A meta-analysis of sexual offender recidivism studies. *Journal of Consulting and Clinical Psychology, 66,* 348-362.

Hanson, R. K., & Thornton, D. (2000). Improving risk assessments for sex offenders: A comparison of three actuarial scales. *Law and Human Behavior, 24,* 119-136.

Hare, R. D. (1991). *Manual for the Hare Psychopathy Checklist—Revised.* Toronto: Multi-Health Systems.

Hart, S. D. (1998). The role of psychopathy in assessing risk for violence: Conceptual and methodological issues. *Legal and Criminological Psychology, 3,* 123-140.

Hart, S. D. (2001a). Assessing and managing violence risk. In K. S. Douglas, C. D. Webster, S. D. Hart, D. Eaves, & J. R. P. Ogloff (Eds.), *HCR-20 violence risk management companion guide* (pp. 13-25). Burnaby, British Columbia: Mental Health, Law, & Policy Institute, Simon

Fraser University, and Department of Mental Health Law and Policy, Florida Mental Health Institute, University of South Florida.

Hart, S. D. (2001b). Forensic issues. In J. Livesley (Ed.), *The handbook of personality disorders* (pp. 555-569). New York: Guilford.

Hart, S. D., & Hare, R. D. (1997). Psychopathy: Assessment and association with criminal conduct. In D. M. Stoff, J. Brieling, & J. Maser (Eds.), *Handbook of antisocial behavior* (pp. 22-35). New York: John Wiley.

Heilbrun, K. (1992). The role of psychological testing in forensic assessment. *Law and Human Behavior, 16,* 257-272.

Heilbrun, K. (1997). Prediction versus management models relevant to risk assessment: The importance of legal decision-making context. *Law and Human Behavior, 21,* 347-359.

Heilbrun, K. (2001). *Principles of forensic mental health assessment.* New York: Kluwer Academic/Plenum.

In re Valdez et al. (2000). No. 99-000045CI (unpublished opinion, August 21, 2000).

Janus, E. S. (2000). Sexual predator commitment laws: Lessons for law and the behavioral sciences. *Behavioral Sciences and the Law, 18,* 5-21.

Janus, E. S., & Meehl, P. (1997). Assessing the legal standard for predictions of dangerousness in sex offender commitment proceedings. *Psychology, Public Policy, and Law, 3,* 33-64.

Kansas v. Hendricks (1997), 521 U.S. 346.

Kapp, M. B., & Mossman, D. (1996). Measuring decisional competency: Cautions on the construction of a "capacimeter." *Psychology, Public Policy, 33 and Law, 2,* 73-95.

Kumho Tire Co. v. Carmichael (1999), 526 U.S. 137.

Litwack, T. R. (2001). Actuarial versus clinical assessments of dangerousness. *Psychology, Public Policy, and Law, 7,* 409-443.

Meehl, P. E. (1996). *Clinical versus statistical prediction: A theoretical analysis and a review of the literature.* Northvale, NJ: Jason Aronson. (Original work published 1954)

Melton, G. B., Petrila, J., Poythress, N., & Slobogin, C. (1997). *Psychological evaluations for the courts: A handbook for attorneys and mental health professionals* (2nd ed.). New York: Guilford.

Monahan, J., Steadman, H. J., Silver, E., Appelbaum, P. S., Robbins, P. C., Mulvey, E. P., Roth, L. H., Grisso, T., & Banks, S. (2001). *Rethinking risk assessment: The MacArthur study of mental disorder and violence.* New York: Oxford University Press.

Mulvey, E. P., & Lidz, C. W. (1995). Conditional prediction: A model for research on dangerousness to others in a new era. *International Journal of Law and Psychiatry, 18,* 129-143.

National Research Council. (1989). *Improving risk communication.* Washington, DC: National Academy Press.

Otto, R. K. (2000). Assessing and managing violence risk in outpatient settings. *Journal of Clinical Psychology, 56,* 1239-1262.

Petrila, J., & Otto, R. (in press). Admissibility of expert testimony in sexually violent predator proceedings. In A. Schlank (Ed.), *The sexual predator.* Kingston, NJ: Civic Research Press.

Prentky, R. A., Knight, R. A., Lee, A. F., & Cerce, D. D. (1995). Predictive validity of lifestyle impulsivity for rapists. *Criminal Justice and Behavior, 22,* 106-128.

Quinsey, V. L., Harris, G. T., Rice, M. E., & Cormier, C. A. (1998). *Violent offenders: Appraising and managing risk.* Washington, DC: American Psychological Association.

Washington Department of Corrections. (1999). *Washington State Sex Offender Risk Level Classification Screening Tool-Revised.* Olympia: Author.

13

Treatment Models for Sex Offenders

A Move Toward a Formulation-Based Approach

Christopher R. Drake
Psychosexual Treatment Program,
Victorian Institute of Forensic Mental Health

Tony Ward
University of Melbourne

The sexual abuse of children and an awareness of its negative impact upon victims have become increasingly acknowledged by both the community and the judicial system as a serious public health concern requiring intervention (McMahon, 2000). Furthermore, the accumulation of evidence indicating that perpetrators frequently have large numbers of victims suggests that the treatment of offenders is a crucial step in reducing the risk of victimization to children and women. In response to these perceptions, there has been an increased focus on the treatment of sexual offenders. Research and clinical theory development have focused predominantly on determining the most appropriate interventions for sexual offenders and, related to this issue, the best way to implement such treatments (Marshall, 1996). Therefore, researchers and clinicians have been attempting to construct more adequate theories of sexual offending and have critically examined the issue of treatment delivery and structure (Ward & Siegert, in press).

Treatment models for sexual abuse are typically derived from a clinical theory that explains the development and maintenance of sexually abusive behavior. Such theories specify the psychological dispositions thought to play a role in sexual offenses and also outline the proximal causes that, in conjunction with these vulnerability factors, result in a sexually abusive act. For example, Finkelhor (1984) proposed that factors such as emotional congruence with children, deviant sexual preferences, and an inability to meet emotional and sexual needs in prosocial ways might motivate individuals to sexually abuse a child. Furthermore, he argued that the motivation to sexually abuse a child was the first step in a causal chain leading to an offense, followed by the overcoming of both the offender's and a child's inhibitions, circumventing external obstacles such as the presence of a watchful parent, and finally the occurrence of a sexual crime. Treatment guided by this etiological theory would focus upon reducing the motivation for offending, reducing the level of deviant sexual arousal, and increasing the offender's ability to achieve appropriate social goals.

Similarly, using Pithers's (1990) relapse prevention model, offenders would learn to understand their pattern of offending, more specifically, how they move from a state of abstinence or control over their sexually abusive behavior to high-risk situations, and ultimately a sexual offense. From the perspective of this model, treatment would focus on equipping individuals with the skills necessary to cope with negative affective states and to recognize and counter offense-supportive cognitions and desires.

Although these and other clinical theories have resulted in popular and broadly effective treatment interventions, they (and most other theories to date) suffer from a number of conceptual weaknesses that undermine their ability to adequately inform clinical work (Ward & Siegert, in press). The most serious shortcoming of all in the current etiological theories is the tendency to describe the offense and relapse processes as if they occurred in the same way for every offender (Ward & Hudson, 1998). However, work by Ward and his colleagues has indicated that there are quite distinct offense and relapse pathways, each associated with different psychological characteristics and clinical issues (Hudson, Ward, & McCormack, 1999; Ward, Louden, Hudson, & Marshall, 1995; Ward & Siegert, in press). In addition, others have described subtypes of child molesters and rapists who exhibit different kinds of psychological characteristics; for example, varying degrees of social skills (Knight, 1999; Knight & Prentky, 1990). This work points to the utility of developing theories that account for individual differences and enable clinicians to match treatment strategies to the specific developmental and relapse factors associated with each individual's pattern of offending.

In addition, there are a number of issues related to the delivery of treatment that may impact upon its effectiveness. Arguably the most popular mode of treatment for sex offenders involves the implementation of manual-based strategies in a group format. Despite the modest success of treatment programs using this approach, we have argued that there are situations where adopting a fixed set of interventions is unwarranted and likely to result in poor clinical outcomes (Ward, Nathan, Drake, Lee, & Pathé, 2000). Furthermore, although some authors advocate constructing a clinical formulation to guide the customizing of the program to the individual (e.g., Hudson, Wales, & Ward, 1998), there are few suggestions as to how this should be done.

Therefore, the present chapter sets the scene for the development of a more sophisticated approach to the problem of sexual deviance. It will be argued that a formulation-based approach using more adequate etiological and offense chain theories can overcome most of the above difficulties. A well-constructed theory-based formulation can assist in understanding the developmental factors giving rise to offending, identify the specific steps involved in the process of offending, and clarify how offending has been maintained over time for individuals. It can also provide clinicians with guidance when there is a paucity of treatment options for certain types of offenders or where previous treatment has been unsuccessful.

Formulation- Versus Manual-Based Treatments

Using a manual-based approach, treatment is provided depending on the categorization of an individual as an offender of a particular type, such as child molester (Marshall, 1996). This decision rests more on a concrete description of behavior or a diagnosis than on a clinical case formulation. Once allocated to a group, all individuals receive the same time-limited, structured, and standardized treatment components (Wilson, 1996). The assumption is that such individuals will share many of the same symptoms and problems and therefore have similar treatment needs. Because all individuals receive the same treatment, a detailed case formulation is not deemed to be necessary. Treatment manuals specify the content, sequencing, and delivery of different interventions, although there may be some flexibility with regard to these factors.

Evidence has accumulated suggesting that a small but stable treatment effect for sexual offenders in the form of reduced recidivism has been demonstrated using a relatively constant set of treatment modules (Grossman, Martis, & Fichter, 1999; Marshall, Jones, Ward, Johnston, & Barbaree, 1991). These include controlling deviant sexual preferences, social skill training, developing victim empathy, cognitive restructuring, mood regulation, and relapse prevention training (Marshall, Anderson, & Fernandez, 1999). Thus, it would appear on the surface that administering the above treatment modules in a relatively consistent manner decreases the need for complicated assessment and formulation regimes, and results in a reduction in recidivism.

However, it is likely that individual offenders have treatment needs that are not adequately addressed using the above approach. Clinical experience has revealed a small but important set of offenders who, having participated in such a treatment program, say, "It didn't cater to my needs" or, "My offense didn't happen the way they were trying to get me to say." Some are labeled deniers, not because they deny their offense, but because they don't admit to planning or fantasizing about their victim prior to the offense. The danger is that these types of offenders may then take up considerable amounts of (unproductive) therapeutic time. In addition, treatment providers sometimes suggest that although an individual has participated in and gained from treatment, he still represents a risk of reoffending, even after he has repeated elements of manual-based programs.

In light of the above difficulties, there must be a way to cater to the needs of these offenders. In doing so, however, the clinician risks being accused of departing from recommended treatment guidelines and not adhering to the demands of evidence-based practice. Thus, it can be asked whether there is room for a fine-tuning of the present treatment approaches based upon the successful elements of the present approaches and the explicit utilization of new theory. Sticking religiously with established treatment approaches runs the risk of not making changes that may prove beneficial.

In contrast to the manual-based approach, formulation-based approaches assume that in order to treat sexual offenders effectively, therapists need to develop a comprehensive understanding of their psychological vulnerabilities and problems (Ward, Vertue, & Haig, 1999). The result of this process is a conceptual model representing the client's various problems, the hypothesized underlying mechanisms, and their interrelationships. In essence, this clinical theory specifies how the symptoms or problems are generated by psychological mechanisms, for example, dysfunctional core beliefs or behavioral deficits. In one formulation model, the first phase of the clinical reasoning process aims to use various types of data to detect the existence of clinical phenomena (Ward et al., 1999). In the second phase, these phenomena become the focus of inquiry and an attempt is made to infer causes (i.e., hypothesized underlying mechanisms) for them. Third, the phenomena, their causal mechanisms, and factors that have contributed to the development of these mechanisms are fashioned into an integrated case formulation or clinical theory that has explanatory coherence. This then functions to guide subsequent therapeutic interventions; different interventions will follow different case formulations. It goes beyond diagnosis as two individuals may have the same diagnosis or cluster of difficulties, but different mechanisms may give rise to these particular problems.

A good case formulation for a sex offender should specify the developmental factors that made him vulnerable to committing a sexual offense. This may include factors such as inconsistent parenting, being a victim of sexual abuse, experimenting sexually at an early age, or compulsively masturbating as an adolescent. These may lead to dysfunctional mechanisms that later play a role in sexual offending. For example, inconsistent caring might lead to insecure attachment and resulting loneliness or difficulties in adult relationships. For another individual, a lack of capacity to modulate negative emotions or an inability to use social supports in times of emotional distress could play a role in subsequent sexual abuse. Strong negative mood states may result in a loss of control that, in conjunction with sexual desire, leads an individual opportunistically to use a child to meet his sexual needs. From a clinical perspective, the presence of different deficits or vulnerability factors requires the application of distinct therapeutic strategies, or at least the placement of different priorities on existing treatment approaches. For example, some individuals may need to acquire relatively greater levels of relationship skills to address attachment difficulties, whereas others would benefit from learning how to manage their moods more effectively.

Despite the apparent sophistication that the above approach appears to offer, there have been a number of well-documented criticisms of the formulation-based approach (for detailed criticisms see Ward et al., 2000). In general terms, inaccurate judgments, problems with interrater reliability, and undue reliance on decision-making heuristics have been noted (Ward et al., 2000). Therapists may develop habitual ways of making decisions, which, if relied upon excessively, results in clinical mistakes. Errors can also result from overconfidence in one's decisions, difficulty integrating large amounts of data, and the tendency to seek confirmatory rather than disconfirming evidence. Despite these difficulties we suggest that the above problems can be countered by the use of a systematic method for clinical reasoning, keeping issues such as the importance of base rates in mind, and developing multiple hypotheses to explain a set of phenomena (Ward et al., 1999).

Each approach to the treatment of sex offenders has its strengths and weaknesses. On the one hand, manual-based treatment has the advantages of standardization, less reliance on clinical judgment, and may be a more efficient use of scarce resources. On the other hand, formulation-based treatment has the advantages of greater flexibility, a more individualistic focus, and arguably is better equipped to deal with more complex clinical presentations. The extra time and energy spent on developing case formulations may be saved by the provision of more focused and directed treatment. Overall, we believe that formulation-based treatment is of immense value in tailoring treatment to the specific needs and problems evident in different sex offenders. There are several common clinical scenarios in which manual-based treatment is likely to be ineffective and where case formulations and an individualized approach may assist.

Situations Where Formulation-Based Approaches Are Useful

As outlined in a previous paper (Ward et al., 2000), the need for such a comprehensive understanding of an individual client is especially important in a number of clinical scenarios. The first is when an offender has such an array of problems that it is difficult to decide what the primary focus of treatment should be. For example, when an offender has a coexisting mental disorder such as Major Depressive Disorder, schizophrenia, or drug and alcohol abuse, it is useful to develop a formulation to provide a coherent conceptualization of the individual's problems and the interactions among the different causal mechanisms. Treatment would then focus upon the common causal mechanisms in order to ameliorate as many of the clinical phenomena as possible. In this clinical scenario, the complex interaction between the various causal factors and the subsequent clinical phenomena is the crucial issue and simply instituting a manual-based treatment for each of the above problems may be ineffective and inefficient (Ward et al., 2000).

The second situation in which formulation-based treatment may be beneficial is where a manual-based treatment program has been delivered but failed to result in significant clinical improvement. This may have occurred because important clinical features had not been identified or unique problems had not been adequately addressed by standard treatments. In these situations, case formulations can assist with the identification of problem areas and clarify how they relate to sexually abusive behavior. For example, clinical experience suggests that sexual dysfunctions can play an important role in the development of offending for some offenders. However, these are rarely, if at all, addressed adequately in present treatment approaches. If they are present and are related to subsequent sexual offending, such problems obviously require treatment. Other situations may also require a case formulation approach, for example, when few or no manual-based treatments exist for a particular group (female sex offenders and Internet child pornography users) or when there are problems in the therapeutic relationship (see Ward et al., 2000).

Theoretical Advancements
and Development of Treatment

More powerful and comprehensive theories of sexual offending can drive the development of improved treatment strategies and techniques. We are not suggesting a radical departure from the standard collection of treatment modules currently used in the majority of treatment programs, but more a question of the careful targeting of individual offenders' particular problems. We would like to advance our argument by suggesting that there are a number of distinct pathways leading to the sexual abuse of children, each associated with unique clusters of problems and issues. For example, offenders can differ in their degree of developmental disruption, capacity to self-regulate behavior, the intensity and presence of positive or negative emotions during the offense process, and the presence of elaborate deviant fantasies. In a nutshell, different offenders sexually abuse children for different reasons and therefore should receive treatment that is relevant to their particular problems.

From a clinical perspective, a current issue concerns the extent to which a therapist should use current manual-based approaches or use a more individual formulation-based approach. Answering this question depends somewhat upon the clinical competence of staff. Clearly, an individually tailored approach would require more highly trained and experienced clinicians. Related to this debate is the question of how an experienced clinician might adapt the current manual-based approaches to a more individualized approach. A final issue is what theoretical and treatment resources are available to help him or her? We argue that current theory is a good place upon which to base clinical innovations and, hence, there is room for recent theoretical developments to filter through to clinical practice. We now briefly describe two recent theories that can help therapists to focus treatment more effectively.

PATHWAYS MODEL

The first theory, the pathways model (Ward & Siegert, in press; Ward & Sorbello, Chapter 1 in this volume), outlines a general range of factors thought to play a role in sexual offending; specifically, differences in offenders' developmental progression toward offending. This theory clearly distinguishes between distal (long-term) and proximal (short-term) causes of offending and describes a process by which distal vulnerability factors result in a range of deficits that predispose a person to offend in a sexual manner. It also describes how different factors can lead to a sexual offense and can assist in the development of individual treatment goals.

According to the pathways model there are four distinct, and interacting, types of psychological mechanisms generating the clinical phenomena evident among child molesters: intimacy and social skill deficits; distorted sexual scripts; emotional dysregulation; and cognitive distortions. In the context of sexual need, all are arguably required for a sexual offense to occur. However, it is also suggested that each pathway has its own core dysfunctional psychological mechanisms. The emphasis on these distinct types of primary dysfunctions allows for an increased focus on individual vulnerability factors and their development, and directly leads to more individualized treatment. We now outline the five primary deficit areas, their possible development, and their suggested treatment foci.

Pathway 1. This describes those individuals who offend because they have primary deficits in intimacy and social skills. These are likely to be caused by various forms of insecure attachment that, in turn, cause difficulties in trusting others, problems in adult relationships, low self-esteem, and a reduced sense of personal autonomy. Although it is argued that sexual offenders must have some type of deficits in intimacy and social skills in order to offend, it is suggested that these deficits will be more marked in this group.

It is hypothesized that if intimacy and social deficits are the primary dysfunctional mechanisms, then treatment should focus on the underlying reasons for the above problems and the acquisition of the skills necessary to overcome such deficits. This may include exploring issues related to insecure attachment (e.g., difficulty in developing trust), identifying problems in adult relationships, and learning how to overcome them. For example, offenders can be encouraged to increase their engagement with others by involving themselves in more trusting relationships. This will arguably lead to greater satisfaction in relationships and a reduced sense of alienation from others.

Pathway 2. This pathway describes those who offend primarily because of deficits in one or more components of their underlying sexual scripts (Gagon, 1990). More specifically, seeking sex in inappropriate situations (e.g., when angry), having preferences for inappropriate partners (e.g., a child), or engaging in inappropriate or harmful activities (e.g., sadistic practices). Maladaptive scripts may result from early and inappropriate sexual experiences or deviant learning. Deviant sexual scripts may also be associated with victimization issues, such as offenders' believing that because they were abused as children it is acceptable to inflict the same behavior upon others, or deficits such as equating sex with intimacy. Finally, deviant sexual scripts may lead to a misreading of sexual cues and the interpretation of children's everyday behavior as revealing sexual intent (Ward, 2000; Ward & Keenan, 1999).

It would then follow that individuals with these primary deficits would require additional treatment to address the identified problems in their sexual scripts. This may include a specific focus on reducing deviant arousal, challenging the need for deviant sexual behaviors, and encouraging the engagement in more adaptive sexual behaviors, in appropriate contexts. For those offenders with victimization issues that relate to their offending behavior, it might be necessary to deal with these problems first in order to enable them to address their own offending behavior more effectively. Individuals who equate the need for intimacy with sexual desire can be taught to differentiate the two states and learn to achieve intimacy in more appropriate ways. Offenders with specific deficits in reading sexual cues represent a difficult area, but may be taught to discriminate the different meanings of sexual cues and to be cognizant of how they can be misread.

Pathway 3. This pathway describes offenders who offend primarily due to emotional dysregulation. These individuals may have problems recognizing and naming emotions or have difficulties resulting from inadequate coping skills or the inappropriate use of coping strategies. Consequently, sex can be used as a preferred coping strategy, and a sexual offense may be committed as a result of "acting out" emotional problems. This group is also likely to have problems with disinhibition.

Consequently, individualized treatment aimed at reducing the specific deficits in this group is likely to be beneficial. This may include assisting offenders to recognize and name emotions. Specific cognitive behavioral treatments for mood or anxiety disorders may also be useful (e.g., Barlow, 1993). Offenders can be taught to improve coping skills and to use these effectively when required. If they actually have good coping skills but choose not to use them in specific situations, this can also be addressed in more detail. Related treatment goals might be to increase appropriate social supports and use them more effectively in times of stress, and to develop improved anger management skills (Novaco, 1997).

Pathway 4. This accounts for those individuals who offend primarily as a result of cognitive distortions. These may consist of maladaptive implicit theories or schemas about the offender, potential victims, and the world that make someone vulnerable to behaving in a sexually abusive manner, and may also function to maintain offending after it has occurred. Alternatively, cognitive distortions may represent more general antisocial cognitions and behaviors. Those with this primary deficit may hold the belief that the world is a dangerous place and that they have to fight to have their needs satisfied. Others may have a sense of entitlement and believe that they have the right to have their needs met irrespective of the interests and desires of other people (Ward, 2000; Ward & Keenan, 1999). It is hypothesized that this group has a more entrenched set of cognitive distortions that make the offenders *vulnerable* to offending and to justifying their sexually abusive actions after they have occurred. In contrast, those in other pathways are proposed to have less entrenched distortions that function primarily to *justify* offending after it has occurred. For those with primary cognitive distortions, therefore, it is proposed that there are specific belief systems (or implicit theories) that are causally related to their sexual offenses. These should be a primary treatment target and require intensive and focused cognitive interventions. For those without entrenched distortions, treatment would more effectively focus primarily upon identifying and challenging excuse giving and the minimization of offending behavior.

Pathway 5. The final pathway is where an offender has deficits in all of the above areas. Thus there would be multiple maladaptive developmental processes, and all of the above factors would need to be addressed in depth in treatment.

THE SELF-REGULATION MODEL OF THE RELAPSE PROCESS

In addition to multifactorial theories of sexual offending, there are also fine-grained, micro-level, theories that attempt to describe what offenders actually do in the lead up to, and during, the commission of their offenses. These micro models typically specify the cognitive, behavioral, motivational, and social factors associated with the commission of a sexual offense. Pithers's relapse prevention model is a popular example of a micro-level theory that is used in treatment (Pithers, 1990). Despite the widespread use of this theory in treatment, it suffers from a number of conceptual and practical limitations (see Ward, Hudson, & Marshall, 1994). Also, the model emphasizes skills deficits in the progression toward relapse and fails to account for those who consciously decide to engage in sexually deviant behavior (Ward, 1999; Ward & Hudson, 1998).

Recent empirical research examining individual differences in the offense chains of sex offenders (Hudson et al., 1999; Ward et al., 1995) has lead to the development of a theory (Ward & Hudson, 1998) that can address the above limitations. Aspects of this model have also been empirically supported in a recent study (Bickley & Beech, 2002). Ward and Hudson's self-regulation model of the relapse/offence process explains differences in the manner in which individuals carry out their offenses in terms of their primary offense-related goal (to avoid or approach offending), self-regulation strategies, and dominant affective states.

The self-regulation theory proposes that certain life events lead to a desire for deviant sexual activity. The offender then decides upon a goal and how he should achieve it. These resulting goals and plans are conceptualized in terms of avoidance goals (a desire to avoid offending) or approach goals (a desire to offend) for the individual. These are classified as either active (conscious) or passive (unconscious or resulting from disinhibition). These constructs can be combined to yield four distinct offense pathways.

1. *Avoidance–Passive.* Some offenders wish to avoid offending but fail to actively attempt to prevent it from occurring. This represents underregulation or disinhibition. These individuals are likely to lack coping skills, be more impulsive, have low efficacy expectations, and to use covert planning.

2. *Avoidance–Active.* Some offenders wish to avoid offending and attempt to use strategies to reduce their risk of reoffending. However, their strategies are inappropriate (drug use or masturbating to deviant fantasies to reduce offending) and result in an increased risk of reoffending via factors such as disinhibition or inadvertent reinforcement of deviant sexual desires.

3. *Approach–Passive.* Some offenders wish to continue offending. However, their goals are not fully consciously acknowledged and their offenses tend to be activated by situational features. This could be conceived as a covert readiness to commit a sexual offence if the opportunity presents itself. Offenses committed under this pathway tend to be planned in a rudimentary manner and unfold rapidly with the input of limited cognitive resources.

4. *Approach–Active.* Finally, some offenders wish to offend and use conscious explicit planning and well-crafted strategies that result in a sexual offense. These include skills related to choosing a victim, grooming, and offending in a manner that decreases the chance of detection. Thus, there is intact self-regulation but harmful goals such as sex with children or abusive sex with women. Those offending using this pathway are likely to believe that their behavior is a legitimate way of achieving desirable ends.

Later in the offense chain the offender makes contact with the victim as a result of the earlier implicit planning or counterproductive strategies. All offenders then "switch" to an approach goal and desire sexual activity with the victim. They begin to engage in immediate preparatory activity to facilitate a sexual offense and carry it out. The final stage involves evaluation of the deviant sexual activity.

In terms of affective states, those who wished to avoid offending (avoidance goals) initially usually experience negative emotional states that are followed by positive emotions as the offense is about to be committed. Offenses tend to be followed by guilt and a desire to stop offending in the future. In contrast, those with a desire to offend (approach goals) are proposed to have more positive emotions throughout the offense chain. Early stages of the offense are characterized by positive emotions associated with the expectations of sexual contact and the period after each offense tends to be characterized by sexual satisfaction and a desire to continue offending in the future.

The distinct offending patterns noted above have clear implications for the assessment and treatment of sexual offenders. The first focus of assessment is determining whether offenders have approach or avoidance goals (Ward & Hudson, 1998) and the second is whether offenders have intact or otherwise self-regulation skills (Hudson & Ward, 2000).

ASSESSMENT

Clinicians can assess aspects of the above by gathering detailed offense data. Goals related to sexual offending can be assessed by asking questions such as, "In the period before you last offended, did you want to avoid offending or did you want to continue?" "When you realized that you were thinking of deviant sex, what did you want to happen?" and "When did you decide to have sex with the victim?" If offenders say that they wanted to avoid offending, they can be asked what strategies they used to prevent it from occurring. Conversely, if offenders say that they wanted to continue offending, they can be asked how they intended to continue their deviant sexual behavior. Further questions can be used to assess affective states and cognitive distortions at various points in the chain (Drake, Ward, Nathan, & Lee, 2001).

TREATMENT STRATEGIES

For those who wish to avoid offending but lack strategies to achieve this goal (avoidance-passive pathway), their avoidance goals require support and strengthening. Perhaps some may have partial avoidance goals that require strengthening to increase the chance they can cope with a wider range of more tempting high-risk situations. It is particularly important to note the way offenders in this group effectively disregard their original decision not to offend in the context of a high-risk situation and associated deviant sexual arousal. Increasing individuals' awareness of the way they shift their attention from the rightness and wrongness of their actions toward the satisfaction of the immediate goal of sexual satisfaction is likely to be helpful. It may be that those in this group do not believe that they can maintain their desire to refrain from offending in the context of opportunity and increased sexual arousal. For such individuals, it is necessary to learn appropriate strategies for exiting high-risk situations and also to increase their capacity to maintain preexisting commitment in the face of temptation (e.g., via role plays). If strong emotional states are implicated in the decision to offend, then increasing individuals' ability to recognize and manage these affective states would be beneficial. Some offenders may believe that they really have nothing to live for and therefore might be strongly inclined to capitalize on an offense opportunity despite a previous decision to avoid offending. For these offenders, increasing self-confidence and engaging in satisfying daily activities may assist. This will also increase the sense that they have something to lose if caught, thus strengthening their decision to refrain from sexual offending. Those with low efficacy expectancies may believe that they have no control over their sexual arousal and the resultant desire to engage in sexually deviant activity and could benefit from improved problem-solving skills that are practiced in vivo.

Individuals in this group are also likely to require more intensive treatment in the area of impulse control and dealing with unexpected high-risk situations. An aim of intervention would be to develop more explicit meta-cognitive control, that is, increase awareness of the selection, monitoring, and evaluation of actions as they occur (Ward & Hudson, 1998). This may be facilitated by increasing knowledge of the offense chain and the use of strategies to prevent progression toward offending. In a more general sense, increasing awareness of more general aspects of everyday behavior, its consequences, and associated emotional concomitants can also be generalized to sexual offending behavior. Similarly, emotional states that correspond with everyday events can be recognized and these may respond to emotional coping strategies. Finally, those with documented organic factors such as neurological disease, head injury, or major mental illness that may result in a more severe form of impulsivity and disinhibition may require more specialized intervention and high-intensity monitoring.

Those who wish to avoid offending but have inappropriate strategies to prevent this from occurring (avoidance–active pathway) should be supported to maintain their avoidance goals using some of the methods above. However, the tendency to use inappropriate strategies should be highlighted. Psycho-education linking alcohol abuse and masturbation to deviant fantasies eventually resulting in increased risk of sexual offending may be helpful. Similarly, these people may also require learning more effective coping strategies and effective self-control strategies.

Those who wish to offend but do not have well-formed strategies (approach–passive pathway) require initial challenging of their inappropriate goals. They are likely to have associated beliefs regarding the legitimacy of sexual contact with children, lack associated victim empathy, and require intensive intervention in these areas. Like the offenders in the avoidant passive pathway, these individuals are likely to require more intensive treatment in the domains

CASE ILLUSTRATION

The following case illustration highlights difficulties associated with adopting a single path theoretical model in a group format and how they can be effectively managed using the above theories in a formulation based manner.

ZB was a 23-year-old man with a history of exhibitionism since his early teens. He had been apprehended and sentenced several times but received little treatment prior to being placed in an adult sexual offender treatment program. He participated to the best of his capacity and was reported to have made important gains in admission of his level of sexual deviancy. He recognized and challenged his cognitive distortions, principally in the theme of females being attracted to his erect penis and wanting sex with him. He gradually accepted that females didn't really appreciate his behavior. He also made several gains in self-administering environmental management strategies aimed at reducing his exposure to high-risk situations. However, he reoffended soon after completion of the program and was referred for specialist treatment.

A comprehensive assessment was administered and a case formulation was constructed to understand the factors related to his offending and to develop a treatment plan. It was found that ZB had principal deficits in the area of deviant sexual scripts, and his cognitive distortions were centered on this deficit (hence his maladaptive beliefs about what women find attractive). As he found exposure so exciting, he had few opportunities to develop satisfying sexual relationships with females, despite expressing this desire. There was no history of other antisocial behavior, and he had a relatively stable family history and no history of abuse. A detailed examination of his offense chain revealed that most of the time he planned his offenses and carried them out in a systematic manner. However, he sometimes exposed himself in situations where he initially did not intend to do so. He reported high sexual arousal, acting "like a robot," and being unable to recall his thoughts around the time of the offenses. These situations tended to occur out of the blue, despite his attempts to avoid high-risk situations, and did not appear to be a result of "seemingly irrelevant decisions." When discussing his previous treatment, he said that this aspect of his offending was not acknowledged.

In planning treatment, it was decided to focus upon deviant sexual scripts as the primary deficit leading to his offending. As he wanted a girlfriend and had virtually exhausted the gains that could be made in social skill groups with male offenders, use was made of a carefully chosen community-based social skills group for non-offenders of both sexes. Another treatment target was challenging his desire to continue to offend. He still harbored the thought that it was legitimate to expose himself if lacking control in some situations and this cognition was effectively challenged. In terms of relapse prevention, recognition of the absence of planning in some offenses shifted the emphasis of this aspect of treatment to the management of more immediate urges to offend. This was achieved by administering covert sensitization techniques carefully adapted to his needs. ZB also completed thought, feeling, and behavior monitoring exercises aimed at assisting him to increase awareness of his feelings, behavior, and its consequences. At this point, the ultimate success of the above treatment plan is not clear, but in terms of its adequacy, it is superior to that previously developed (based on a simple manual-based assessment) and leads to intervention goals that had greater face validity.

of impulse control, mood management, and dealing with unexpected high-risk situations, as well as strategies to develop more explicit meta-cognitive control.

Finally, individuals who wish to offend and have conscious strategies to offend (approach–active pathway) also require challenging of their inappropriate goals. These offenders are likely to have more entrenched deviant sexual arousal and require treatment to reduce its intensity and frequency. Persistent offenders with deviant sexual arousal or urges they find difficult to control may require referral to medical personnel for sex-drive–reducing medication (Bradford, 1997).

It is evident that the application of the self-regulation model to clinical work with sex offenders differs in important respects from the use of Pithers's model. The attention to distinct offense chains and their associated clinical issues is particularly useful. Adoption of this model requires a shift in the way therapists evaluate, and respond to, offenders' verbal responses during therapy. For example, therapists following the standard model of the offense chain typically regard any attempt by an offender to deny a desire to offend, the existence of prior fantasies, or explicit planning as denial. This may lead to attempts to influence these offenders to falsely acknowledge these factors in their offenses. However, the present theory suggests that consistent and meaningful reports of absence of these factors be afforded more credibility, as there are specific interventions for this group that are likely to successfully reduce their chance of reoffending.

In the above case, the formulation-based approach allowed increased understanding of the primary deficits leading to ZB's offending and revealed the complexity of the actual offense process. His report of exposing himself with little planning was seen not necessarily as denial of implicit planning (it could have been), but as possibly indicating a different problem requiring more focused treatment for this individual.

Conclusions

In this chapter we have argued that most current treatment programs for child sexual offenders assume that they have a common set of dysfunctions that could be effectively treated by a comprehensive manual-based treatment approach. Certainly, recent research into the effectiveness of the treatment suggests there are enough commonalities among offenders to partially support treating the average offender with the standard cluster of interventions. We agree that there is merit in this position, but it does not tell the whole story. The relatively modest treatment effect of cognitive-behavioral programs for sex offenders indicates that present treatment is often poorly targeted. However, making changes to established treatment regimes involves real risks to therapists, offenders, and potential future victims. We argue that using presently available treatment modules as a starting point and adjusting them to fit the needs of individual offenders can minimize these risks. Furthermore, we argue that there are two major reasons to support a more tailored treatment approach.

First, the research and clinical literature in the general psychotherapy domain indicates that there is a range of situations that require more detailed assessment, formulation, and ultimately individualized treatment in order to result in the most effective outcome (Ward et al., 2000). As described above, in certain scenarios a formulation-based approach may be required and result in significant clinical improvement. Second, recent theory and research is focusing increasingly upon individual differences in the development of offense-related problems and vulnerabilities. These initiatives point to a variety of offense trajectories requiring distinct intervention strategies. We argue that these differences are too great to support the unqualified use of pure manual-based treatment approaches as they presently exist. It makes little sense to treat "expert" offenders (i.e., those with explicit goals and planning) in the same manner as the inadequate and impulsive ones (Ward, 1999).

Adopting a case formulation framework in conjunction with the application of multivariate etiological and offense models is likely to result in more precisely targeted treatment. We suggest that it is time to move away from a total reliance on manual-based or fixed interventions, and accept that knowledge of individual differences in sexual offending can be of immense clinical value. In time, the application of the combined model should lead to the development of more structured assessment and intervention strategies, allowing clinicians to benefit from the use of standardized and systematic procedures and yet still be attuned to the complexities of individual offenders.

References

Barlow, D. H. (1993). *Clinical handbook of psychological disorders: A step-by-step treatment manual.* New York: Guilford.

Bickley, J. A., & Beech, A. R. (2002). An investigation of the Ward and Hudson pathways model of the sexual offence process with child abusers. *Journal of Interpersonal Violence,* 17(4), 371-393.

Bradford, J. (1997). Medical interventions in sexual deviance. In D. R. Laws & W. O'Donohue (Ed.), *Sexual deviance* (pp. 449-464). New York: Guilford.

Drake, C. R., Ward, T., Nathan, P., & Lee, J. K. P. (2001). Challenging the cognitive distortions of child molesters: An implicit theory approach. *The Journal of Sexual Aggression, 7,* 35-45.

Finkelhor, D. (1984). *Child sexual abuse: New theory and research.* New York: Free Press.

Gagon, J. H. (1990). The explicit and implicit use of the scripting perspective in sex research. *Annual Review of Sex Research, 1,* 1-43.

Grossman, L. S., Martis, B., & Fichter, C. G. (1999). Are sex offenders treatable? A research overview. *Psychiatric Services, 50,* 349-361.

Hudson, S. M., Wales, D. S., & Ward, T. (1998). Kia Marama: A treatment program for child molesters in New Zealand. In W. L. Marshall, Y. M. Fernandez, S. M. Hudson, & T. Ward (Eds.), *Sourcebook of treatment programs for sexual offenders* (pp. 17-28). New York: Plenum.

Hudson, S. M., & Ward, T. (2000). Relapse prevention: Assessment and treatment implications. In D. R. Laws, S. M. Hudson, & T. Ward (Eds.), *Remaking relapse prevention* (pp. 102-122). Thousand Oaks, CA: Sage.

Hudson, S. M., Ward, T., & McCormack, J. C. (1999). Offence pathways in sexual offenders. *Journal of Interpersonal Violence, 14,* 779-798.

Knight, R. A. (1999). Validation of a typology for rapists. *Journal of Interpersonal Violence, 14,* 303-330.

Knight, R. A., & Prentky, R. A. (1990). Classifying sexual offenders: The development and corroboration of taxonomic models. In W. L. Marshall, D. R. Laws, & H. E. Barbaree (Eds.), *Handbook of sexual assault: Issues, theories and treatment of the offender* (pp. 23-52). New York: Plenum.

Marshall, W. L. (1996). Assessment, treatment, and theorizing about sex offenders: Developments during the past twenty years and future directions. *Criminal Justice and Behavior, 23,* 162-199.

Marshall, W. L., Anderson, D., & Fernandez, Y. (1999). *Cognitive behavioral treatment of sexual offenders.* New York: John Wiley.

Marshall, W. L., Jones, R., Ward, T., Johnston, P., & Barbaree, H. E. (1991). Treatment outcome with sex offenders. *Clinical Psychology Review,* 11, 465-485.

McMahon, P. M. (2000). The public health approach to the prevention of sexual violence. *Sexual Abuse: A Journal of Research and Treatment, 12,* 27-36.

Novaco, R. W. (1997). Remediating anger and aggression with violent offenders. *Legal and Criminological Psychology, 2,* 77-88.

Pithers, W. D. (1990). Relapse prevention with sexual aggressors: A method for maintaining therapeutic gain and enhancing external supervision. In W. L. Marshall, D. R. Laws, & H. E. Barbaree (Eds.), *Handbook of sexual assault: Issues, theories and treatment of the offender* (pp. 343-361). New York: Plenum.

Ward, T. (1999). Competency and deficit models in the understanding and treatment of sexual offenders. *The Journal of Sex Research*, 36, 298-305.

Ward, T. (2000). Sexual offenders' cognitive distortions as implicit theories. *Aggression and Violent Behavior*, 5, 491-507.

Ward, T., & Hudson, S. M. (1998). A model of the relapse process in sexual offenders. Journal of *Interpersonal Violence*, 13, 700-725.

Ward, T., Hudson, S. M., & Marshall, W. L. (1994). The abstinence violation effect in child molesters. *Behavior Research and Therapy*, 32, 431-437.

Ward, T., & Keenan, T. (1999). Child molesters' implicit theories. *Journal of Interpersonal Violence*, 14, 821-838.

Ward, T., Louden, K., Hudson, S. M., & Marshall, W. L. (1995). A descriptive model of the offence chain for child molesters. *Journal of Interpersonal Violence*, 10, 452-472.

Ward, T., Nathan, P., Drake, C. R., Lee, J. K. P., & Pathé, M. (2000). The role of formulation based treatments for sexual offenders. *Behavior Change*, 17, 251-264.

Ward, T., & Siegert, R. J. (in press). Toward a comprehensive theory of child sexual abuse: A theory knitting perspective. Psychology, Crime, & Law.

Ward, T., Vertue, F. M., & Haig, B. D. (1999). Abductive reasoning and clinical assessment in practice. *Behavior Change*, 16, 49-63.

Wilson, G. T. (1996). Manual-based treatments: The clinical application of research findings. *Behavior Research and Therapy*, 34, 295-314.

14

Responsivity Factors in Sexual Offender Treatment

Michael J. Proeve
Sexual Offender Treatment and
Assessment Program, Adelaide, South Australia

In the field of offender rehabilitation, three principles of classification of offenders for effective treatment have been widely adopted. The specific principles are risk, need, and responsivity (Andrews, Bonta, & Hoge, 1990). Risk, the first principle, refers to the risk of recidivism and, according to the risk-need model, offenders at higher risk of recidivism should be particularly targeted for intervention. The need principle refers to criminogenic needs, which are dynamic attributes of offenders. Changes in criminogenic needs are associated with changes in the likelihood of recidivism; therefore, criminogenic needs are targeted for intervention in the rehabilitation of offenders. The risk and need principles have also been adopted in treatment planning for sexual offenders (Nicholaichuk, 1996). Considerable attention has been given to the assessment of risk in sexual offenders (e.g., Hanson & Thornton, 1999), and to addressing the criminogenic needs of sexual offenders. Most current sexual offender treatment programs use a cognitive-behavioral approach, and their procedures for addressing criminogenic needs are similar. Common components of sexual offender treatment programs include addressing denial and minimization, addressing pro-offending thinking, modifying deviant sexual arousal, enhancing victim empathy, and preventing relapse (Marshall, 1996a).

In other words, there is a degree of agreement about how to address the criminogenic needs of sexual offenders.

The third principle of effective rehabilitation, responsivity, refers to the interaction of characteristics of offenders with the style and mode of service (Andrews et al., 1990). Addressing responsivity factors enhances the effective treatment of criminogenic needs and thereby reduces recidivism (Kennedy, 2000). Responsivity issues are referred to as process issues in the general psychotherapy literature. Just as the integration of process issues into the cognitive therapy of depression has been urged (Jacobson, 1989), there have also been recent calls to address process issues in the treatment of sexual offenders.

Marshall (1996b) has suggested that treatment processes and therapist characteristics should be targeted for research investigation and clinical development in order to enhance the treatment of empathy deficits, cognitive distortions, social skills deficits, problems in attaining relationship intimacy, and deviant sexual arousal. Kear-Colwell and Boer (2000) recognized the achievements that have been made in sex offender treatment, but suggested that significant improvements may be made by focusing on process issues. They proposed that it is important to concentrate on the interface between the clinician and the offender, and on engaging sexual offenders in treatment.

The focus of this chapter is on the relationship between client variables in sexual offender treatment with therapeutic style, and modes of service. The principle of responsivity is used to frame the topics addressed here. Kennedy (2000) has usefully divided forensic process issues into internal and external responsivity factors. Internal responsivity factors are offender characteristics and include motivation, personality characteristics, intellectual disability, and demographic variables. External responsivity factors include therapist characteristics, modes of program delivery, and setting characteristics such as institutional or community settings. He argues that external factors interact with offender characteristics to affect responsivity to treatment, positively or negatively.

The four internal responsivity factors discussed here apply to the majority of offenders in a standard treatment program. They are motivation, self-esteem, attachment, and shame. Two external responsivity factors and their interactions with the four internal responsivity factors are then discussed. These include therapist style and format of treatment. Finally, implications of the interaction between internal and external responsivity factors for practice and research are discussed.

Motivation

It is an often-repeated view that sexual offenders are poorly motivated to change their behavior (Garland & Dougher, 1991; Kear-Colwell & Pollock,

1997; Salter, 1988). Furthermore, enhancement of motivation for behavior change has been cited as a goal of sexual offender treatment (Allam, Middleton, & Browne, 1997). Despite the importance afforded to motivation for change, there has been little systematic investigation of this phenomenon with sexual offenders. Tierney and McCabe (2002) have described a variety of methods by which motivation for change in sexual offenders has been assessed. These include willingness to participate in treatment, measurement of cognitive distortions, measurement of self-efficacy, decisional matrices, and simple motivational ratings. These variables either do not show a strong relationship to treatment outcome or their relationship to motivation is unclear (Tierney & McCabe, 2002).

It has been suggested that motivation for change in sexual offenders may be better understood by adopting a view of motivation as a dynamic rather than a static concept, using constructs of the trans-theoretical model of behavior change (Garland & Dougher, 1991; Kear-Colwell & Pollock, 1997; Tierney & McCabe, 2002). The Stages of Change construct of the trans-theoretical model (Prochaska & DiClemente, 1982) identifies five stages: Precontemplation, where there is no intention to change behavior; Contemplation, where there is awareness of a problem but no commitment to action; Preparation, where there is intention to take action; Action, in which change occurs; and Maintenance, where people work to consolidate gains made during the action stage.

Garland and Dougher (1991) stated that sexual offenders present generally in the precontemplation or the contemplation stages, and fluctuate among the stages of change during treatment. Similarly, Kear-Colwell (1996) suggested that 75% of treatment time is spent in the precontemplation or the contemplation stages. However, he suggested that progress through the remaining stages might be swift once the preparation stage is reached.

Although the trans-theoretical model has yet to be investigated empirically with sexual offenders (Tierney & McCabe, 2002), its dynamic view of change processes and motivation suggests that motivation in these individuals might be influenced by the therapist. The relationship of therapist style to motivation is addressed in a later section. Here, direct interventions aimed at motivation enhancement are outlined. Van Beek and Mulder (1992) described an approach that involves the collaborative development, between therapist and client, of offense scripts covering the 6 hours prior to the offense. They argued that this task increases the offender's motivation. A more frequently described intervention for increasing motivation for change in sexual offenders is motivational interviewing (Garland & Dougher, 1991; Kear-Colwell & Pollock, 1997). This approach involves persuasive and supportive strategies aimed at increasing intrinsic motivation according to five principles: expressing empathy, developing discrepancy, avoiding argument, rolling with resistance, and supporting self-efficacy (Miller & Rollnick, 1991). Mann (1996) described the successful use of motivational interviewing in engaging a sexual offender, who denied he was guilty of the offense for which he was convicted, in a treatment program. The effect of motivational interviewing on engagement of sexual offenders into treatment requires systematic evaluation.

Self-Esteem

Marshall and colleagues (Marshall, Anderson, & Fernandez, 1999) have emphasized the importance of paying attention to self-esteem in the treatment of sexual offenders. The features held in common by people low in self-esteem and by sexual offenders led them to consider the relationship between self-esteem and sexual offending. They summarized the results of a series of studies that showed child sexual offenders obtained lower scores on a measure of social self-esteem than non-offenders. A similar result was obtained with a group of rapists (Marshall, Barbaree, & Fernandez, 1995). Furthermore, Marshall et al. (1999) examined several studies and concluded that there was a moderate correlation in child sexual offenders between self-esteem and personal characteristics, and added that these factors should be addressed in treatment. The identified characteristics included intimacy, loneliness, empathy for offender's own victim, and deviant sexual arousal.

Marshall, Anderson, and Champagne (1996) outlined the implications of the findings regarding self-esteem in sexual offenders: that self-esteem should be enhanced during treatment. In a series of studies, Marshall and colleagues have obtained support for their assertion that self-esteem should be a focus of treatment. An empathy training component that emphasizes the enhancement of self-esteem has been found to increase empathy (Marshall, O'Sullivan, & Fernandez, 1996). In addition, improvements in intimacy skills following an intimacy intervention, which has enhancement of self-esteem as a component, were associated with increased self-esteem (Marshall, Champagne, Sturgeon, & Bryce, 1997). Finally, Marshall (1997) demonstrated that increased self-esteem following treatment directly targeted at self-esteem was associated with reductions in deviant sexual arousal.

Self-esteem can be addressed by direct interventions and by attention to process issues (Marshall et al., 1999). Direct interventions include encouraging clients to increase social and pleasurable activities; having them write down positive and attractive features of themselves and pay frequent attention to these features; and encouraging clients to attend to their appearance and self-presentation. Process issues addressed by Marshall et al. (1999) in order to enhance self-esteem include distinguishing clients from their offensive behavior, therapist modeling of respect and empathy, and encouragement of respectful interactional behavior between clients in group therapy.

Attachment Style

Attachment theory offers a useful perspective for understanding the problems experienced by sexual offenders with intimate relationships. Marshall (1989, 1993) argued that the difficulties experienced by sexual offenders with interpersonal skills and self-confidence, necessary for achieving relationship intimacy, result from poor-quality attachments developed in childhood. Ward, Hudson, Marshall, and Siegert (1995) proposed that specific insecure attachment styles are linked to characteristic patterns of sexual offending. They drew on Bartholomew and Horowitz's (1991) model of adult attachment style and argued that sex offenders exhibit four adult attachment styles, each associated with distinct beliefs and interpersonal strategies. Individuals with a secure attachment style have a positive view of self and others. They are able to achieve high levels of intimacy in adult relationships. There are three insecure attachment styles: preoccupied (negative view of self, positive view of others), fearful (negative self, negative others), and dismissive (positive self, negative others). Preoccupied individuals have a profound sense of personal unworthiness and seek the approval of valued others. They are often sexually preoccupied and try to meet their needs through sexual interactions. Fearful individuals fear rejection and distrust others. They desire intimacy but keep their partners at a distance and may seek some degree of interpersonal contact through impersonal sex. Offenders with a dismissive attachment style are viewed by others as emotionally aloof and typically achieve low levels of intimacy in close relationships. They may seek impersonal contact that has a degree of hostility (Ward, Hudson, & McCormack, 1997). There is evidence that different insecure attachment patterns are associated with sexual offending. In a recent study, child sexual offenders were found to be more likely to have a preoccupied or fearful attachment style and less likely to have a dismissive style than were rapists (Ward, Hudson, & Marshall, 1996; Ward et al., 1997).

More recently, Sawle and Kear-Colwell (2001) compared pedophiles, nonoffending victims of sexual abuse, and a control group on a measure of attachment style. The pedophile group obtained lower scores for the secure attachment style and higher scores for an insecure attachment style. In addition, pedophiles who had an insecure attachment style experienced shorter-term adult sexual relationships than did victims and controls. Kear-Colwell and Boer (2000) outlined the implications of the findings of insecure attachment for the process of sexual offender treatment. Given pedophiles' disturbed early attachment experiences and subsequent difficulties with trusting adults and with forming close adult relationships, the authors advocated using principles of effective intervention derived from work with personality-disordered individuals. They described an approach to treatment in which considerable care is taken to build a therapeutic alliance. They also advocated giving attention to the client's developmental history. A combination of a more relationship-oriented approach with the usual cognitive-behavioral and relapse prevention techniques was advocated.

Shame

Relatively little attention has been given to the issue of shame in sexual offender treatment, although recently this has changed somewhat and become a focus of research interest (e.g., Bumby, 2000; Hudson, Ward, & Marshall, 1992; Proeve & Howells, in press).

Global negative evaluation of the self has been held to be a core feature of shame (Tangney, 1995). However, shame is not identical to low self-esteem, as shame involves "taking an 'other' perspective on the self" (Crozier, 1998, p. 273). According to Crozier (1998) and Deigh (1992), shame is commonly a response to the poor opinion of ourselves shown by others, and may occur when there is no loss of self-esteem. However, Taylor (1985) proposed that shame does not result unless there is a negative view of oneself through the eyes of others, and one identifies with that negative view.

Gilbert's (1998) model, which integrates the internal and external aspects of shame, provides a useful perspective for discussing this emotion in sexual offenders. In his model he described the cognitive domains of external and internal shame. External shame reflects a concern with how one is seen by others, a recognition that one is the object being looked at and judged by others (Sartre, 1958). The experience of shame depends on how important the views of others are to the self. Internal shame relates to an awareness of falling short of some internalized standard and is difficult to distinguish from low self-esteem, although it may be more transient. Gilbert (1998) stated that internal shame is often highly correlated with external shame, but need not always be. Using an example particularly pertinent to the present discussion, he cited the case of a pedophile who acknowledges that others see his actions as bad and experiences external shame, but has little internal shame.

Behaviors associated with shame include hiding oneself from others (Davitz, 1969; Tangney, Miller, Flicker, & Barlow, 1996) and externalizing strategies such as denying a negative action or blaming someone else for it (Fischer & Tangney, 1995; Tangney, Wagner, Fletcher, & Gramzow, 1992). Proneness to shame has also been found to be correlated negatively with empathy (Tangney, 1991).

The general shame and guilt literature has been applied to sexual offenders. Hudson et al. (1992) examined the role of shame in sex offending relapses from an attribution theory framework. They argued that a sexual offender who responds to a lapse with an internal uncontrollable attribution, experiencing shame, will give up attempts to cope and therefore increase his chances of relapsing. Shame has also been discussed in relation to the process of sexual offender treatment. Roys (1997), Hanson (1997), and Bumby (2000) suggested that shame inhibits victim empathy work because of the personal focus on threats to self-worth. Hanson (1997) noted that exposure to victim suffering can increase victim blaming and cognitive distortions among sexual offenders, and implicated shame reactions in this process. Bumby (2000) referred to an empirical study of sexual offenders in outpatient treatment in which there was a positive association between shame-proneness and measures of personal distress and externalization. Greater proneness to shame was linked to personal distress and externalizing of responsibility. Bumby proposed that the self-oriented distress of shame experienced by sexual offenders impedes the emotional recognition, perspective taking, and emotional replication components of empathy. Furthermore, the perceived negative evaluation by others and personal distress experienced in shame leads to externalization, such as blaming of the victim. This also impairs empathy for the victim.

Proeve and Howells (in press) suggest that personal characteristics empirically shown to be associated with shame-proneness, such as depression, a focus on personal distress, indirect hostility, blaming of others, and suicidal ideation (Lester, 1997; Tangney, 1991; Tangney, Wagner & Gramzow, 1992) also seem characteristic of child sex offenders (Bagley & Pritchard, 1999; Salter, 1995). Proeve and Howells also noted that other characteristics of child sex offenders observed anecdotally by therapists may reflect external shame, such as a preoccupation with other people knowing about their offenses, and apparent heightened distress following disclosure of the offenses at the time of court hearings, which bring increased awareness of the scrutiny of others.

There are contextual and personality-based reasons for expecting a high level of shame in child sexual offenders. Given that breaking social standards is a common antecedent to shame (Tangney et al., 1996), it is to be expected that sexual offending against a child in the context of a strong social prohibition against it would dispose a person toward the experience of (external) shame. Second, personality-based reasons to expect shame in child sexual offenders become apparent when shame is considered from the perspective of attachment theory. Child sexual offenders may be more likely to show a preoccupied (negative view of self, positive view of others) style or a fearful style (negative self, negative others). Given that the fearful and preoccupied attachment styles have been found to be positively correlated with shame (Gross & Hansen, 2000), it is to be expected that child sexual offenders would experience high levels of this emotion.

Relationship Among the Internal Responsivity Factors

In discussing the relationship between motivation, self-esteem, attachment, and shame, attachment should be considered first as it is arguably the most enduring and "trait-like" of the four concepts. The consistency and quality of attachment relationships affects our sense of self and provides the basis for subsequent self-appraisals and, relatedly, self-esteem (Anechiarico, 1998). Insecure attachment in the form of preoccupied and fearful styles is associated with low self-esteem (Bartholomew & Horowitz, 1991). Self-esteem is also closely connected to shame, as shame also concerns evaluation of the self. The link between preoccupied and fearful attachment styles and proneness to shame has already been discussed (Gross & Hansen, 2000). In circumstances where a person has committed sexually abusive behavior, and self-evaluation through the eyes of others occurs, the presence of an insecure attachment style is likely to result in the experience of significant shame. Shame and self-esteem can be considered to be intermediate between trait-like attachment style and transient motivation as understood in the trans-theoretical model (Prochaska & DiClemente, 1982). Shame may be associated with low motivation (Tierney & McCabe, 2002). If the cognitive dissonance between a sexual offender's self-image and his evaluation of his sexually deviant behavior is the fuel for motivating behavior change (Kear-Colwell & Pollock, 1997), then the relationship between shame and low motivation can be understood. In the experience of shame, cognitive dissonance is resolved in the direction of evaluating both the self and behavior negatively. The same relationship may apply between low self-esteem and low motivation.

Therapist Style

The quality of the therapist-client relationship is strongly related to treatment effectiveness, according to meta-analytic research (Martin, Garske, & Davis, 2000). There is no reason to expect that the quality of the therapist-client relationship is less important for sexual offender treatment. Factors related to the therapeutic relationship in psychotherapy and specifically in sexual offender treatment are described in this section. Their relationship to the four internal responsivity factors is outlined.

Marshall and colleagues (in press) reviewed the general psychotherapy literature for factors that have been found to facilitate or impede therapeutic change and argued for their relevance for sexual offender treatment. Factors that impede and facilitate change are considered in turn.

Of the factors that impede therapeutic change, confrontation has been the most discussed in relation to sexual offender treatment. Although the use of strong confrontation has been common in treatment of sexual offenders, recent opinion has been condemnatory of its use (Garland & Dougher, 1991; Kear-Colwell & Pollock, 1997; Marshall et al., in press). There is supportive evidence that confrontation is unhelpful. In group sexual offender treatment confrontation was associated with low cohesiveness, and this in turn was associated with less treatment change (Beech & Fordham, 1997).

When considering the four internal responsivity factors, the negative impact of confrontation is easily understood. A confrontational style by a therapist can directly threaten a client's self-esteem (DiClemente, 1991; Marshall et al., in press). In addition, it can be expected that confrontation would increase the level of shame experienced, particularly in clients so disposed. Confrontation can also be expected to decrease motivation for change. It has already been argued that sexual offenders spend considerable time in the precontemplation and contemplation stages of change. DiClemente (1991) has noted that confrontation at the precontemplation stage increases resistance, denial, and noncompliance. Consideration of attachment issues also points to the likely negative impact of confrontation. Sawle and Kear-Colwell (2001) suggested that insecurely attached pedophiles could perceive confrontation as another aversive experience with adult relationships, with the possible result of reinforcing pedophilic feelings and behavior.

A second factor that may impede client change (Marshall et al., in press) is therapist anger or hostility. Therapist hostility may be a source of increased external shame, and might affect the client's self-esteem. Clients with insecure attachment styles would be affected by therapist hostility. Those with a preoccupied style, holding others in high regard, might particularly experience lowered self-esteem and increased shame. Clients with a dismissive style may find their distrust of others vindicated as a result of the therapist's behavior.

Marshall et al. (in press) listed the following therapist features that facilitate change: empathy, genuineness, warmth, respect, support, therapist confidence, self-disclosure, encouragement of emotional expressiveness, open-ended questioning, directiveness, flexibility, rewardingness, and use of humor. Of this list, the client's motivation for change may be influenced positively by rewarding behavior on the part of the therapist. Warmth and respect expressed by the therapist, communicating acceptance of the client, are likely to be particularly important in decreasing clients' shame. It is also helpful for decreasing shame that therapists distinguish between clients and their offensive actions, approving of the person but disapproving of offending (Bumby, Marshall, & Langton, 1999; Marshall, 1996b).

The helpful therapist attributes listed by Marshall et al. (in press) all serve to develop the client-therapist relationship. They may positively influence the attachment style of the client so that a therapeutic alliance can be formed (Sawle & Kear-Colwell, 2001). Thus, these qualities are especially important for helping sexual offenders with insecure attachment styles develop trust, a consistent relationship, and a therapeutic alliance so that they can contemplate change (Kear-Colwell & Boer, 2000).

Format of Treatment

The choice of individual or group format is an important practical issue in the treatment of sexual offenders. In this section, the arguments for each type of treatment format with sexual offenders are reviewed. After this, the implications of the four client attributes of motivation, self-esteem, attachment, and shame for choice of treatment format are examined.

The group format is firmly established in the treatment of sexual offenders. Of 15 mainstream programs for adult male offenders described in a sourcebook of sexual offender treatment (Marshall, Fernandez, Hudson, & Ward, 1998), all offer group therapy. According to program descriptions, individual therapy is offered in addition to group therapy as a standard part of treatment in 9 of the 15 programs. Four of five programs in psychiatric settings and three of five community-based programs offer individual therapy. Individual therapy is offered in two of five prison-based programs. One other program offers limited individual therapy in order to assist group participation.

There are differing views regarding the appropriateness of individual treatment for sexual offenders. Marshall et al. (1999) advocated group therapy only, arguing that individual therapy is both less efficient and less effective than the group format. In contrast, Maletzky (1999) advocated a combination of group and individual treatment, arguing that some components of treatment, such as relapse prevention and modifying deviant sexual arousal, can be more effective on an individual basis. Cox (1996) noted that individual therapy is occasionally successful in cases where group therapy fails, but acknowledged that the opposite is also true. There is little evidence of differential treatment efficacy with adult sexual offenders that would provide a basis for advocating group or individual formats. DiFazio, Abracen, and Looman (2001) reported a comparison of two groups of comparable high-risk sexual offenders who underwent either a combination of group and individual treatment or individual treatment alone. There was no significant difference in the rates of recidivism of the two groups. Further comparisons of group and individual therapy formats are needed, extending evaluation to sexual offenders who present other levels of risk.

From the perspective of general clinical psychology practice, Beutler and Clarkin (1990) discussed the relative merits of individual and group formats. They proposed that the individual format offers greater confidentiality and greater comfort for the revelation of embarrassing issues. The group format has the advantage of cost efficiency. In addition, the group format provides support and encouragement from similar others, a means of reducing resistances encountered in an individual format, and an interpersonal setting in which interactional patterns can be examined. The advantages of group treatment seem to have particular relevance for sexual offenders, although the confidentiality and comfort advantages of the individual format are also important for sexual offender treatment.

Other authors have contrasted individual and group therapy formats in sexual offender treatment. Schwartz (1995) discussed the advantages and disadvantages of individual treatment for sexual offenders and noted that the individual format provides greater confidentiality and may help in establishing trust. However, she also argued that denial and secrecy are more easily perpetuated in an individual format, and that the therapist is more easily manipulated. Maletzky (1999) suggested that behavioral techniques can be applied more successfully on an individual basis, and that individual sessions allow more opportunity for specific attention to individual patterns of offending and relapse.

Marshall et al. (1999) outlined the advantages of group therapy. They proposed that groups of offenders are able to challenge each other with more credibility than the therapists are able to, and that they also understand their own offending better through challenging others. In addition, groups provide opportunities for vicarious learning and for mutual support. Fernandez and Marshall (2000) described an open treatment format in which new members are admitted as space becomes available. They argued that this format accelerates the progress of some offenders because of the more active participation of members who have been in the group longer. In addition, the open format allows treatment components to be customized according to individual client needs. Thus, the individual flexibility afforded by an individual format (Maletzky, 1999) may be available within the open group format.

In general, there seem to be strong reasons for advocating the general use of the group format in sexual offender treatment, and particularly the open format. However, the influence of internal responsivity factors on choice of treatment format should also be considered. The group format allows the active participation of members both to support and to challenge each other. Thus, an active group process may provide both enhancement of self-esteem as well as the cognitive dissonance needed to motivate change (Kear-Colwell & Pollock, 1997).

The internal responsivity factors of shame and attachment style may provide reason for more cautious consideration of the group format. Attending a group in which members are required to reveal past transgressions may be shame inducing (Dutton, van Ginkel & Starzomski, 1995). Therefore, offenders who experience a high level of external shame may be adversely affected by treatment in a group setting. On the other hand, shame may perhaps be offset by the careful encouragement of support within the group and a focus on the commonality of their inappropriate behavior rather than on clients as sexual offenders. Significant difficulties in attachment style may also lead to caution in considering group treatment. Arguing from an attachment theory framework, Kear-Colwell and Boer (2000) suggested that pedophiles may initially require individual treatment, as a group situation early on in treatment could lead to high anxiety and noninvolvement for some individuals.

Implications for Practice and Research

IMPLICATIONS FOR THERAPIST STYLE

The discussion of internal and external responsivity factors above leads to clear recommendations regarding therapist style in sexual offender treatment. First, the adoption of a confrontational therapist style is contraindicated. Confrontation is likely to impact negatively on client self-esteem, shame, and on clients who have an insecure attachment style. In addition, given the clinical opinion that sexual offenders tend to spend considerable time in the stages of precontemplation and contemplation (Garland & Dougher, 1991; Kear-Colwell, 1996), confrontation is also likely to decrease motivation for change (DiClemente, 1991). The contention that a confrontational style in group treatment is destructive for group cohesiveness and client change has received support (Beech & Fordham, 1997). Second, the expression of hostility by therapists is likely to have a negative impact on clients' self-esteem, shame, and trust for the therapist, especially clients with a dismissive attachment style.

At the same time they recommend against a confrontational therapist style, Marshall et al. (in press) also caution against responding to sexual offenders as victims and avoiding challenging their inappropriate views of offending. To maintain the ability to challenge distorted views of offending requires the therapist to be open to and aware of the damage to victims caused by sexual abuse. However, sexual offender therapists need to avoid their challenging being driven by hostility toward offending, and need to challenge carefully in the context of a supportive therapeutic relationship. To practice this approach as a therapist is a difficult task that requires maturity as well as supervision, adequate training, and ongoing support (Lea, Auburn, & Kibblewhite, 1999).

IMPLICATIONS FOR TREATMENT FORMAT

In the discussion of treatment format for sexual offender treatment, it was concluded that the group format is generally appropriate. Considering available research, clinical opinion, and the four internal responsivity factors of motivation, self-esteem, attachment, and shame, there seem to be no indications, should circumstances allow, for occasions in which group treatment is not appropriate, especially if an open group format is used. Rather, it is important to consider circumstances in which individual therapy in addition to group therapy is indicated. Adopting the perspective of each internal responsivity factor is useful for considering this issue.

Self-esteem may be addressed by both process, involving therapist style, and direct interventions, such as encouraging pleasurable activities, attending to self-presentation, and noting positive personal features (Marshall et al., 1999). The features of therapist style advocated by Marshall et al. (in press) are no less effective in a group than an individual format. They may be even more effective in a group format if group members adopt the supportive but challenging style of the therapist. The direct interventions aimed at increasing self-esteem are likewise quite suitable for a group format, where relevant homework assignments can be discussed in the session.

As raised in the discussion of motivation in sexual offenders, an active group in which both support and challenge are available may provide the motivational fuel for change. However, direct interventions for increasing motivation to change have also been advocated, including the offense script (van Beek & Mulder, 1992) and motivational interviewing (Garland & Dougher, 1991; Kear-Colwell & Pollock, 1997). The offense script approach requires collaboration between client and therapist. There seems no reason that it cannot be employed in a group format, using the collaborative efforts of group members. Motivational interviewing with sexual offenders, as described by Garland and Dougher (1991), is an individual intervention employed at the assessment stage, although they do suggest that motivational techniques may be used judiciously in groups by other offenders who are more advanced in treatment. It would be helpful to develop guidelines for recommending motivational interviewing as a formal individual intervention with sexual offenders, for example, when motivation is assessed as particularly low. In order to develop these guidelines, further research on motivation in sexual offenders is needed. Appropriate measures of motivation that reflect its dynamic and complex nature should be used (Tierney & McCabe, 2002) to guide decision making regarding the use of motivational interviewing.

No specific interventions have been described for addressing shame. Proeve and Howells (in press) emphasize the relevance of external as opposed to internal shame for child sexual offenders, and view shame as a process issue. Shame is likely to be increased by confrontation and hostility and decreased by a warm and respectful therapist style. The possibility that some individuals experience a level of shame likely to preclude their participation in group treatment was raised. However, research is needed to examine this issue seriously. The distinction between external and internal shame (Gilbert, 1998) should be a central concern in further research on shame in sexual offenders. Scenario-based measures of shame advocated by Tangney (1996) assess shame on the basis of evaluations made of oneself by oneself; internal shame in other words. For the purposes of incorporating assessment of shame in decisions about treatment, a measure of external shame may be more useful. The Other as Shamer scale (Goss, Gilbert, & Allan, 1994) may be an appropriate measure. Measurement of levels of external shame may yield guidelines regarding levels of shame at which individual therapy is indicated.

Recent work on attachment styles in pedophiles (Kear-Colwell & Boer, 2000; Sawle & Kear-Colwell, 2001) has implications for practice. Kear-Colwell and Boer (2000) advocated a specialized approach to treating pedophiles based on approaches used with personality-disordered individuals and informed by attachment theory. Their approach begins with unqualified, positive regard and nondirective questioning about the individual's history, and no requirement to discuss offending. The offender's psychosocial history and family of origin are examined prior to the introduction of motivational techniques, cognitive-behavioral techniques, and relapse prevention. In terms of treatment format, they state that some pedophiles may initially require individual treatment.

Research is required in which this approach is compared to the standard group-based treatment approaches for sexual offenders. In addition, guidelines are needed for deciding who should be assigned to this approach rather than to a standard set of interventions. For these purposes, the attachment research that informs the proposed approach to treatment requires further development.

There does not appear to be consistency in findings regarding attachment styles and sexual offending. For example, whereas Ward et al. (1996) found that pedophiles were more likely to have a preoccupied or fearful attachment style and rapists a dismissive style, Sawle and Kear-Colwell (2001) found that participants in their pedophile sample had Relationships as Secondary (dismissive) attachment style.

IMPLICATIONS FOR RESEARCH

Outcome research in treatment with sexual offenders should include responsivity issues. As suggested by Marshall et al. (in press), within-treatment client changes should be monitored together with specific therapist characteristics. In addition, measurement of the internal responsivity variables of motivation, self-esteem, shame, and attachment would assist the process of matching therapist style and treatment format to client characteristics to increase treatment effectiveness. Further development and investigation of appropriate measures of internal responsivity are needed.

References

Allam, J., Middleton, D., & Browne, K. (1997). Different clients, different needs? Practical issues in community based treatment for sex offenders. *Criminal Behaviour and Mental Health, 7,* 69-84.

Andrews, D. A., Bonta, J., & Hoge, R. D. (1990). Classification for effective rehabilitation: Rediscovering psychology. *Criminal Justice and Behavior, 17,* 19-52.

Anechiarico, B. (1998). A closer look at sex offender character pathology and relapse prevention: An integrative approach. *International Journal of Offender Therapy and Comparative Criminology, 42,* 16-26.

Bagley, C., & Prichard, C. (1999). Completed suicide in men accused of sexual crimes involving children: Implications for a humanistic approach. In C. Bagley & K. Mallick (Eds.), *Child sexual abuse and adult offenders: New theory and research* (pp. 285-289). Aldershot, UK: Ashgate.

Bartholomew, K., & Horowitz, L. (1991). Attachment styles among young adults: A test of a four-category model. *Journal of Personality and Social Psychology, 61,* 226-244.

Beech, A., & Fordham, A. S. (1997). Therapeutic climate of sexual offender treatment programs. *Sexual Abuse: A Journal of Research and Treatment, 9,* 219-237.

Beutler, L. E., & Clarkin, J. F. (1990). *Systematic treatment selection: Toward targeted therapeutic interventions.* New York: Brunner/Mazel.

Bumby, K. M. (2000). Empathy inhibition, intimacy deficits, and attachment difficulties in sex offenders. In R. D. Laws, S. M. Hudson, & T. Ward (Eds.), *Remaking relapse prevention with sex offenders: A sourcebook* (pp. 143-166). Thousand Oaks, CA: Sage.

Bumby, K. M., Marshall, W. L., & Langton, C. (1999). A theoretical model of the influences of shame and guilt on sexual offending. In B. K. Schwartz (Ed.), *The sex offender: Theoretical advances, treating special populations and legal developments* (pp. 1-12). Kingston, NJ: Civic Research Institute.

Cox, M. (1996). Dyn amic psychotherapy with sex offenders. In I. Rosen (Ed.), *Sexual deviation* (3rd ed., pp. 300-336). Oxford, UK: Oxford University Press.

Crozier, W. R. (1998). Self-consciousness in shame: The role of the "other." *Journal for the Theory of Social Behaviour, 28,* 273-286.

Davitz, J. R. (1969). *The language of emotion.* New York: Academic Press.

Deigh, J. (1992). Shame and self-esteem: A critique. In J. Deigh (Ed.), *Ethics and personality: Essays in moral psychology* (pp. 133-153). Chicago: University of Chicago Press.

DiClemente, C. C. (1991). Motivational interviewing and the stages of change. In W. R. Miller & S. Rollnick (Eds.), *Motivational interviewing: Preparing people to change addictive behavior* (pp. 191-202). New York: Guilford.

DiFazio, R., Abracen, J., & Looman, J. (2001). Group versus individual treatment of sex offenders: A comparison. *Forum on Corrections Research, 13,* 56-59.

Dutton, D. G., van Ginkel, C., & Starzomski, C. A. (1995). The role of shame and guilt in the inter-generational transmission of abusiveness. *Violence and Victims, 10,* 121-131.

Fernandez, Y. M., & Marshall, W. L. (2000). Contextual issues in relapse prevention treatment. In R. D. Laws, S. M. Hudson, & T. Ward (Eds.), *Remaking relapse prevention with sex offenders: A sourcebook* (pp. 225-235). Thousand Oaks, CA: Sage.

Fischer, K. W., & Tangney, J. P. (1995). Self-conscious emotions and the affect revolution: Framework and overview. In J. P. Tangney & K. W. Fischer (Eds.), *Self-conscious emotions: The psychology of shame, guilt, embarrassment, and pride* (pp. 3-21). New York: Guilford.

Garland, R. J., & Dougher, M. J. (1991). Motivational interventions in the treatment of sex offenders. In W. R. Miller & S. Rollnick (Eds.), *Motivational interviewing: Preparing people to change addictive behavior* (pp. 303-313). New York: Guilford.

Gilbert, P. (1998). Shame and humiliation in the treatment of complex cases. In N. Tarrier, A. Wells, & G. Haddock (Eds.), *Treating complex cases: The cognitive behavioural therapy approach* (pp. 241-271). London: Wiley.

Goss, K., Gilbert, P., & Allan, S. (1994). An exploration of shame measures—I: The Other as Shamer scale. *Personality and Individual Differences, 17,* 713-717.

Gross, C. A., & Hansen, N. E. (2000). Clarifying the experience of shame: The role of attachment style, gender, and investment in relatedness. *Personality and Individual Differences, 28,* 897-907.

Hanson, R. K. (1997). Invoking sympathy: Assessment and treatment of empathy deficits among sexual offenders. In B. K. Schwartz & H. R. Cellini (Eds.), *The sex offender: New insights, treatment innovations, and legal developments* (pp. 1-11). Kingston, NJ: Civic Research Institute.

Hanson, R. K., & Thornton, D. (1999). *Static-99: Improving actuarial risk assessments for sex offenders* (User Report 99-02). Ottawa: Department of the Solicitor General of Canada.

Hudson, S. M., Ward, T., & Marshall, W. L. (1992). The abstinence violation effect in sex offenders: A reformulation. *Behavior Research and Therapy, 30,* 435-441.

Jacobson, N. S. (1989). The therapist-client relationship in cognitive-behavior therapy: Implications for treating depression. *Journal of Cognitive Psychotherapy, 3,* 85-96.

Kear-Colwell, J. J. (1996). Guest editorial: A personal position on the treatment of individuals who commit sex offenses. *International Journal of Offender Therapy and Comparative Criminology, 40,* 259-262.

Kear-Colwell, J., & Boer, D. P. (2000). The treatment of paedophiles: Clinical experience and the implications of recent research. *International Journal of Offender Therapy and Comparative Criminology, 44,* 593-605.

Kear-Colwell, J., & Pollock, P. (1997). Motivation or confrontation: Which approach to the child sex offender? *Criminal Justice and Behavior, 24,* 20-33.

Kennedy, S. M. (2000). Treatment responsivity: Reducing recidivism by enhancing treatment effectiveness. *Forum on Corrections Research, 12,* 19-23.

Lea, S., Auburn, T., & Kibblewhite, K. (1999). Working with sex offenders: The perceptions and experiences of professionals and paraprofessionals. *International Journal of Offender Therapy and Comparative Criminology, 43*, 103-119.

Lester, D. (1997). The role of shame in suicide. *Suicide and Life-threatening Behavior, 27*, 352-361.

Maletzky, B. M. (1999). Editorial: Groups of one. *Sexual Abuse: A Journal of Research and Treatment, 11*, 179-181.

Mann, R. E. (1996). Motivational interviewing with a sex offender who believed he was innocent. *Behavioural and Cognitive Psychotherapy, 24*, 127-134.

Marshall, W. L. (1989). Intimacy, loneliness, and sexual offenders. *Behavioral Research and Therapy, 27*, 491-503.

Marshall, W. L. (1993). The role of attachment, intimacy, and loneliness in the etiology and maintenance of sexual offending. *Sexual and Marital Therapy, 8*, 109-121.

Marshall, W. L. (1996a). Assessment, treatment, and theorizing about sex offenders. *Criminal Justice and Behavior, 23*, 162-199.

Marshall, W. L. (1996b). The sexual offender: Monster, victim, or everyman? *Sexual Abuse: A Journal of Research and Treatment, 8*, 317-335.

Marshall, W. L. (1997). The relationship between self-esteem and deviant sexual arousal in non-familial child molesters. *Behavior Modification, 21*, 86-96.

Marshall, W. L., Anderson, D., & Champagne, F. (1996). Self-esteem and its relationship to sexual offending. *Psychology, Crime, and Law, 3*, 81-106.

Marshall, W. L., Anderson, D., & Fernandez, Y. (1999). *Cognitive behavioural treatment of sexual offenders.* Chichester, UK: Wiley.

Marshall, W. L., Barbaree, H. E., & Fernandez, Y. (1995). Some aspects of social competence in sexual offenders. *Sexual Abuse: A Journal of Research and Treatment, 7*, 113-127.

Marshall, W. L., Champagne, F., Sturgeon, C., & Bryce, P. (1997). Increasing the self-esteem of child molesters. *Sexual Abuse: A Journal of Research and Treatment, 9*, 321-333.

Marshall, W. L., Fernandez, Y. M., Hudson, S. M., & Ward, T. (1998). *The sourcebook of sex offender treatment programs.* New York: Plenum.

Marshall, W. L., Fernandez, Y. M., Serran, G. A., Mulloy, R., Thornton, D., Mann, R. E., & Anderson, D. (in press). Process variables in the treatment of sexual offenders: A review of the literature. *Aggression and Violent Behavior: A Review Journal.*

Marshall, W. L., O'Sullivan, C., & Fernandez, Y. M. (1996). The enhancement of victim empathy among incarcerated child molesters. *Legal and Criminological Psychology, 1*, 95-102.

Martin, D. J., Garske, J. P., & Davis, M. K. (2000). Relation of the therapeutic alliance with outcome and other variables: A meta-analytic review. *Journal of Consulting and Clinical Psychology, 68*, 438-450.

Miller, W. R., & Rollnick, S. (Eds.). (1991). *Motivational interviewing: Preparing people to change addictive behavior.* New York: Guilford.

Nicholaichuk, T. (1996). Sex offender treatment priority: An illustration of the risk/need principle. *Forum on Corrections Research, 8.*

Prochaska, J. O., & DiClemente, C. C. (1982). Transtheoretical therapy: Toward a more integrative model of change. *Psychotherapy: Theory, Research, and Practice, 19*, 276-288.

Proeve, M., & Howells, K. (in press). Shame and guilt in child sexual offenders. *International Journal of Offender Therapy and Comparative Criminology.*

Roys, D. T. (1997). Empirical and theoretical considerations of empathy in sex offenders. *International Journal of Offender Therapy and Comparative Criminology, 41*, 53-64.

Salter, A. (1988). *Treating child sex offenders and their victims: A practical guide.* Newbury Park, CA: Sage.

Salter, A. (1995). *Transforming trauma: A guide to understanding and treating adult survivors of child sexual abuse.* Thousand Oaks, CA: Sage.

Sartre, J. P. (1958). *Being and nothingness: An essay on phenomenological ontology.* London: Methuen.

Sawle, G. A., & Kear-Colwell, J. (2001). Adult attachment style and pedophilia: A developmental perspective. *International Journal of Offender Therapy and Comparative Criminology, 45,* 32-50.

Schwartz, B. K. (1995). Group therapy. In B. K. Schwartz & H. R. Cellini (Eds.), *The sex offender: New insights, treatment innovations, and legal developments* (pp. 1-15). Kingston, NJ: Civic Research Institute.

Tangney, J. P. (1991). Moral affect: The good, the bad, and the ugly. *Journal of Personality and Social Psychology, 61,* 598-607.

Tangney, J. P. (1995). Shame and guilt in interpersonal relationships. In J. P. Tangney & K. W. Fischer (Eds.), *Self-conscious emotions: The psychology of shame, guilt, embarrassment, and pride* (pp. 114-139). New York: Guilford.

Tangney, J. P. (1996). Conceptual and methodological issues in the assessment of shame and guilt. *Behavior Research and Therapy, 34,* 741-754.

Tangney, J. P., Miller, R. S., Flicker, L., & Barlow, D. H. (1996). Are shame, guilt, and embarrassment distinct emotions? *Journal of Personality and Social Psychology, 70,* 1256-1269.

Tangney, J. P., Wagner, P., Fletcher, C., & Gramzow, R. (1992). Shamed into anger: The relation of shame and guilt to anger and self-reported aggression. *Journal of Personality and Social Psychology, 62,* 669-675.

Tangney, J. P., Wagner, P., & Gramzow, R. (1992). Proneness to shame, proneness to guilt, and psychopathology. *Journal of Abnormal Psychology, 101,* 469-478.

Taylor, G. (1985). *Pride, shame, and guilt: Emotions of self-assessment.* Oxford, UK: Clarendon.

Tierney, D. W., & McCabe, M. P. (2002). Motivation for behavior change among sex offenders: A review of the literature. *Clinical Psychology Review, 22,* 113-129.

van Beek, D. J., & Mulder, J. R. (1992). The offense script: A motivational tool and treatment method for sex offenders in a Dutch forensic clinic. *International Journal of Offender Therapy and Comparative Criminology, 36,* 155-167.

Ward, T., Hudson, S. M., & Marshall, W. L. (1996). Attachment style in sex offenders: A preliminary study. *Journal of Sex Research, 33,* 17-26.

Ward, T., Hudson, S. M., Marshall, W. L., & Siegert, R. J. (1995). Attachment style and intimacy deficits in sex offenders: A theoretical framework. *Sexual Abuse: A Journal of Research and Treatment, 7,* 317-335.

Ward, T., Hudson, S. M., & McCormack, J. (1997). Attachment style, intimacy deficits, and sexual offending. In B. K. Schwartz & H. R. Cellini (Eds.), *The sex offender: New insights, treatment innovations, and legal developments* (pp. 1-14). Kingston, NJ: Civic Research Institute.

15

Integrating Pharmacological Treatments

William Glaser
University of Melbourne

The "magic pill" for sex offenders has always been an attractive idea. Courts, the community, and health professionals remain fascinated with the idea of instant "fixes": "Chopping off their balls" appeals as both a suitable form of revenge and a treatment (of sorts), and it is easy to become enthusiastic about medications that might offer the benefits of castration without its grisly and disfiguring sequelae. In contrast, one needs to have a fair degree of psychological sophistication to understand the subtle effects of cognitive-behavioral techniques that, all too often, can be dismissed as yet another wimpish form of "counseling."

This sometimes-unjustified enthusiasm for pharmacological agents has had two unfortunate consequences. First, they have often been seen as being the main, or even the only, efficacious treatment for sex offenders (which is clearly not the case). Second, there has been an increasing divide between medically trained professionals, such as psychiatrists, who are generally more familiar with medication treatments for mental health problems (and hence tend to advocate pharmacological treatment for sex offenders) and other professionals, such as psychologists or social workers who use other treatment modalities such as cognitive-behavior therapy, family therapy, and so on.

This is a great pity because it has repeatedly been shown that the best chance of success of any treatment program for sex offenders rests on its being both eclectic and comprehensive. Pragmatic considerations, rather than ideology or training, should dictate what is offered to offenders in these programs.

To this end, therefore, this chapter attempts to describe both the advantages and the shortcomings of pharmacological agents against the background of the sometimes-unrealistic claims made about them. It then attempts to place them in the context of integrated treatment programs for sex offenders and show how, in particular, lessons learned from the application of cognitive-behavioral techniques can guide us in introducing these agents, encouraging compliance with them, and monitoring their effects. Finally, ethical and legal issues are discussed, particularly with respect to the growing preoccupation of sex offender treatment programs with the interests of the community, rather than those of the offender.

The Ideal Pill

There seems little doubt that biology determines human sexual behavior, but controversy has always surrounded the extent of this influence. After the Second World War, learning, socialization, and environmental stimuli were thought to be more important determinants than hormones or the central nervous system, the effects of which were really confined to animals and clinical rarities (Bancroft, 1989). More sophisticated recent studies, however, have lead to the recognition of a complex important biological substrate for much human sexual behavior, including the feelings, fantasies, and urges that accompany it; this work is discussed further below.

Nevertheless, the place of biological agents in the control of aberrant sexual behavior remains unclear. The current literature gives little guidance as to the properties of the ideal agent, although it implies that they exist. Such properties need to be formally defined to guide further research and practice:

1.   *Side effects should be minimal and/or easily reversible.* Many offenders are required to take medication treatments under ethically dubious conditions: Their consent may be only partly voluntary (particularly if the use of such medication is an actual or implied condition of a court or parole board order), confidentiality is often limited, and they may be under coercion in other ways (e.g., be forced to confess their misdeeds, be required adopt values espoused by the therapeutic program). In this sort of setting, the provision of medication with unpleasant or even dangerous side effects adds insult to injury. From another angle, offenders are often unwilling participants in treatment anyway and may use even trivial side effects to justify their withdrawal from treatment.

2. *The agent should preferentially suppress "deviant" sexual activity while leaving "normal" sexual functioning unaffected.* Allowing for the difficulties in defining "normal" sexual functioning, it is clear that a pharmacological agent should selectively affect deviant fantasies and activities that involve the targeting of vulnerable victims and various forms of nonconsensual sexual activity. Some would argue that this selective effect might also be useful in cases where the sexual deviation involved has significantly affected a person's occupational or social functioning (e.g., compulsive masturbation).

3. *There should be an appropriate way of monitoring an offender's compliance.* It would be even better if the measure of compliance (whether biological or otherwise) had some correlation with frequency and intensity of fantasies and behaviors likely to produce recidivism.

4. *The treatment must be effective.* As amply discussed elsewhere in this book, there are ongoing problems in assessing the outcomes of sexual offender treatment programs, and biological agents are no exception. These problems include the lack of proper control groups, skewed samples, insufficient periods of follow-up, and the use of measures that may not correlate with "gold standard" outcome indicators such as recidivism rates (see, for example, Marshall, 1996). Unfortunately, proper clinical trials of any form of treatment need huge amounts of resources and money and may not be ethically appropriate in this group (e.g., using untreated controls who then remain at high risk of reoffending).

5. *The treatment must be ethically and socially acceptable.* Castration, although proven in large-scale studies to have considerable success in reducing recidivism rates (see, for example, Heim & Hursch, 1979), is seen as repugnant in many societies. In most jurisdictions based on the English common law tradition, there are limits as to the nature and extent of punishments that can be used, whether they are labeled punishment, treatment, or something else. Thus, for example, the use of a medication that required the restriction of an offender's liberty for a period longer than that commensurate with the crime that had been committed would usually not be allowed.

So far, none of the pharmacological treatments currently in use measures up to all five of these criteria, although some seem to come closer than others. Most probably, an agent that even approximates these ideals will not become available for some time. Emotion and prejudice often color the evaluation of treatment effectiveness, however, and the following brief discussion is an attempt to compare and contrast agents currently in use in the light of these guidelines.

Pharmacological Treatments

ANTIPSYCHOTIC MEDICATIONS

Although antipsychotic medications are rarely used for sex offender treatment these days, they were in vogue during the 1970s, being said to be as effective as hormonal preparations in reducing self-reported sexual interest and associated deviant behaviors (Bartholomew, 1968; Tennent, Bancroft, & Cass, 1974). Their effects on human sexual functioning include erectile difficulties, delay or failure of ejaculation, and increased production of prolactin, which is known to be associated with decreased libido (Bancroft, 1989, pp. 604-605).

The main limitation to their use currently is that of their side effects, common troublesome ones including drowsiness, dry mouth, constipation, blurred vision, postural hypotension, skin rashes, liver problems, weight gain, blood count abnormalities, and occasionally breast milk production. Some produce acute and frightening neurological side effects and, more seriously, long-term neurological effects such as tardive dyskinesia.

Thioridazine, which has some effectiveness in violent offenders, produces ECG abnormalities associated with sudden cardiac death and long-term ocular changes (Therapeutic Guidelines, 2000, pp. 4-7). Nevertheless, antipsychotic agents like thioridazine may be useful in the treatment of the small proportion of sex offenders who suffer from major psychiatric disorders such as schizophrenia, having the dual effect of treating the psychotic symptoms as well as reducing deviant sexual preferences.

SEROTONERGIC DRUGS

By contrast, drugs that modify the serotonin transmitter system in the central nervous system have relatively few side effects. Their effectiveness, however, is yet to be properly assessed. They include antidepressants such as clomipramine, fluoxetine, sertraline, and fluvoxamine, all of which selectively inhibit serotonin re-uptake at the presynaptic neuron terminal, and buspirone, an anti-anxiety agent that is largely a serotonin agonist, although its mechanism of action is still somewhat obscure. Low levels of serotonin in the central nervous system are associated with a range of psychopathology, including depressive, anxiety, and obsessive-compulsive symptoms as well as aggression (Kaplan & Sadock, 1998, pp. 116, 158-159), and it is possible that these agents modify sexual behaviors that have a "compulsive" component to them, for example, exhibitionism.

Serotonin re-uptake inhibitors combined with psychosocial interventions produce a greater reduction in the frequency and intensity of sexually deviant fantasies and urges than psychosocial interventions used alone, with the therapeutic effect lasting for up to a year following the cessation of treatment. There appear to be no differences in efficacy among sertraline, fluvoxamine, and fluoxetine. Because, unlike the hormonal agents, they have no effects on genital and bone growth, they could be considered as first-line agents for the pharmacological treatment of teenagers (Galli, Raute, McConville, & McElroy, 1998; Greenberg & Bradford, 1997; Greenberg, Bradford, Curry, & O'Rourke, 1996; Kafka, 1994).

Their relatively mild side effects include nausea, "nervousness," diarrhea, constipation, headaches, and insomnia, and there are interactions with other medications, particularly other antidepressant drugs. Clomipramine has additional side effects, including sedation, postural hypotension, dry mouth, and weight gain. All have additional effects on sexual functioning, including loss of libido, anorgasmia, and inhibition of ejaculation; some cynics might argue that these effects, rather than the central nervous system serotonergic effects, are the real reasons for their success (Kaplan & Sadock, 1998, pp. 1087-1090; Therapeutic Guidelines, 2000, pp. 11-12). There may be a case for using them in combination with hormonal agents, particularly where the sexually deviant behaviors are both "compulsive" and pose a considerable risk of victim harm (e.g., some forms of ritualized sadistic rape).

HORMONAL MEDICATIONS

Hormonal medications are the much-vaunted agents of "chemical castration," and their use has probably received undue prominence precisely because of the social and emotional connotations of this term. In fact, they are probably neither as effective as some of their advocates would claim, nor, on the other side of the coin, are they as harmful as feared by their detractors. They include *anti-androgens,* currently represented by cyproterone acetate (CPA); *progesterone-like agents,* particularly medroxy-progesterone acetate (MPA, which, because of better absorption, is usually administered in its depot injectable form known as Depo-Provera); and *gonadotropin-releasing hormone analogues* (GnRH analogues), which include leuprolide, nafarelin, goserelin, and triptorelin. *Estrogen-like compounds* have not been used since the 1960s, despite their efficacy, because of major side effects, which include nausea and substantial breast growth.

TESTOSTERONE AND MALE SEXUAL ACTIVITY

All of the above hormonal preparations act in various ways to suppress production of testosterone, the key hormone implicated in much of male human sexual behavior. The reader is referred to more detailed discussions of the testosterone production chain (see, for example, Bancroft, 1989, chap. 2), but to summarize very crudely: Hormones from the hypothalamus, at the base of the brain, stimulate the production of other hormones by the pituitary gland, just below the hypothalamus, which in turn stimulate the production of testosterone by the testicles and (to a small extent) by the adrenal glands. Testosterone is transported around the body attached to blood proteins, with only 2% being in the biologically active free form, and can attach to receptor sites in a number of locations, particularly the genitals, spinal cord, and hypothalamus. At these sites, testosterone is converted via an enzyme to a more potent version, and there are complicated feedback loops by which excessive levels of the various hormones being produced inhibit the production of themselves as well as hormones farther down the line.

The physiological effects of testosterone are now well known and include sexual differentiation of the male fetus and the characteristic changes of puberty (enlargement of the sex organs, increase in body hair and muscle mass, deepening of the voice, more frequent and intense erections, ejaculations, and orgasms, etc.). In contrast, the effect of testosterone on male sexual fantasies, behavior, and preferences is less well understood. Males with low levels of testosterone can still achieve full erections in response to specific erotic stimuli (such as movies), but need testosterone replacement in order to increase their low levels of sexual interest and their ability to achieve spontaneous erections or erections in response to erotic fantasies (Hucker & Bain, 1990; McConaghy, 1993). In normal men, there appears to be no good correlation between testosterone levels and the intensity of sexual interests and activity, although a "threshold" level of testosterone is probably required and this, although different in different individuals, is probably well above the low level needed simply to maintain satisfactory erections. Episodes of sexual arousal are associated with transient increases in testosterone levels, although it is unclear as to which causes what. In any case, the association is weaker with increasing age, supporting the popular stereotype that teenagers are much more at the mercy of their hormones than older men (Bancroft, 1989; Hucker & Bain, 1990; McConaghy, 1993).

Even less clear is the influence of testosterone on deviant sexual behavior. The relevant studies are plagued by small sample sizes and limited validity of measures used (e.g., self-report measures of sexual aggression). Generally, sexually violent offenders do not have higher serum testosterone levels compared with nonviolent sexual offenders or nonviolent non-offenders. Pretreatment testosterone levels may be useful predictors of recidivism in offenders treated with hormonal agents, however (Kravitz et al., 1996; Meyer, Cole, & Emory, 1992). There also may be subtle differences in dynamic hormone responses.

For example, one study has demonstrated that pituitary hormone production increases more rapidly in response to stimulation by hypothalamic hormone stimulation in pedophiles than in normal controls. Perhaps this implies a greater sensitivity in such offenders to hormones that may be produced initially in response to deviant fantasies or urges (Gaffney & Berlin, 1984).

There are, nevertheless, well-documented cases of offenders with low testosterone levels who have exhibited considerable and ongoing sexual violence. In one case known to the author, an offender with Klinefelter's syndrome (a chromosomal abnormality associated with low testosterone levels and a range of physical abnormalities) had a long history of stalking and brutally raping, or attempting to rape, teenage girls. There were, however, nonbiological explanations for this offending behavior, including social isolation caused by his odd appearance, low intelligence (which is often associated with Klinefelter's syndrome), childhood neglect, and recurrent alcohol abuse.

EFFECTS AND SIDE EFFECTS OF CPA AND MPA

Both CPA and MPA produce dramatic and fairly rapid (within a few weeks) lowering of serum testosterone levels, often to prepubescent levels, with consequent reductions in the frequency and intensity of spontaneous erections and ejaculation; decreased sperm production; and marked diminution of self-reported deviant sexual urges, fantasies, and behaviors (Kravitz et al., 1996). Nevertheless, offender self-report, as already noted, remains an unreliable measure; in one study where self-report was checked with penile plethysmography (laboratory measurement of penile responses to erotic stimuli), offenders who were hoping to be released from indeterminate incarceration tended to report equal responses to both MPA injections and placebo injections of saline (Kiersch, 1990).

The vagaries of self-report have also troubled attempts to ascertain whether CPA and MPA preferentially reduce deviant sexual arousal. This may possibly occur, leaving normal arousal relatively unaffected (see, for example, Kravitz et al., 1995), but it is more likely that the reduction takes place globally. The maritime metaphor used 25 years ago by Laschet and Laschet (1975) to describe the phenomenon when reporting on the effects of CPA is quaint but still apt:

> With (CPA) one can reduce the "wind force" or create a "sexual calm"; the "wind direction" remains basically unchanged. It is, however, obvious that torn sails can be repaired more easily in a calm than in a storm: the "sexual calm," the reduction in the driving force created by (CPA) provides more favourable starting conditions for sexual pedagogical or psycho- and socio-therapeutic measures. (p. 821)

The ultimate "gold standard" measure of effectiveness remains that of recidivism reduction (Marshall, Anderson, & Fernandez, 1999, p. 147). Although there seems to be some agreement that CPA and MPA are as effective as cognitive-behavioral techniques in reducing reoffending, there are flaws in the relevant research. One study that purported to show an 18% reoffending rate in offenders treated with MPA, compared to 58% in untreated controls, excluded offenders who had "severe dissocial tendencies e.g. brutal physical assault" and those who could not afford treatment. As well, those who accepted treatment seemed to be more motivated than the untreated group; they were more likely to be self-referred or referred by other health practitioners rather than the legal system (Meyer et al., 1992). Clearly, more studies are needed that at least try to approximate the ideal of double-blind control studies.

The *side effects* of CPA and MPA are still the subject of myths and stereotypes. Although one would not wish to minimize the impact of these substances on those who are using them, there is the danger that the presence of even trivial discomfort will be used by an offender to justify noncompliance with the medication. A female colleague who was being treated with CPA for medical problems once ruefully told this author that she had suffered most of the known side effects of the medication but no one had treated her complaints particularly seriously, a sad tribute indeed to the gender biases of our culture.

Furthermore, many of these side effects are dose dependent. There are quite striking differences between doses of MPA used in various jurisdictions (much higher doses are used in the United States). This is illogical because, as we have seen, it may not be necessary to suppress testosterone to levels where erectile functioning is affected in order to achieve a reduction of deviant arousal (Kravitz et al., 1996). Thus a proactive approach, using the least necessary dose of these agents, may well achieve a substantial reduction in side effects.

The following is an attempt to place the significance of the side effects reported for MPA and CPA in some sort of rational perspective, using the relevant literature and some impressions from the writer's own experience (Cooper, 1995; Glaser, 1996; Kravitz et al., 1995; Robinson & Valcour, 1995; Rosler & Witztum, 2000):

1. *Effects that are life threatening or pose serious threats to health.* These are rare and include thrombo-embolic events (e.g., stroke, blood clots in the lungs, loss of vision due to vascular causes, etc.). Very rarely, liver failure can develop. The medications are thus contraindicated in those with a history of the thrombo-embolic disorders mentioned above or severe liver disease (which might well include the growing number of offenders suffering from full-blown AIDS). Routine liver function tests should be performed on all offenders,

although these nearly always, at worst, show only transient and mild increases in the relevant enzymes.

Both CPA and MPA affect genital and bone growth and thus should not be given to boys under the age of 18.

2. *Clinically significant (but treatable) side effects.* These include a rise in blood pressure, reduced glucose tolerance, breast changes (tenderness, swelling, nodules, and breast milk production, especially with CPA), skin changes (especially stretch marks), gallstone development, and significant depressive symptoms. The rise in blood pressure is usually not clinically significant; when it is, it can be treated by the usual means. Increases in blood sugar are often secondary to weight gain and will respond to dietary measures; those offenders suffering from diabetes usually retain good control over blood sugar levels provided they comply with their usual treatment regime, although severe brittle diabetes is said to be a contraindication to the use of hormones. Breast and skin changes, which place incarcerated offenders at substantial risk of sexual assault, respond to dose reduction, switching to MPA, or other strategies such as weight reduction. Depressive symptoms (which may be reactive to legal proceedings and social stressors) respond to standard therapies.

3. *Troublesome but mild and generally transient side effects.* These include drowsiness, fatigue, sleeplessness, dizziness, headaches, nausea, sweating, leg cramps, and occasional allergic reactions (mainly skin rashes). All of these generally resolve with time. Weight gain, however, can be quite substantial and is usually caused not so much by fluid retention but by specific carbohydrate craving. Consumption of low-calorie drinks and foods and high-protein snacks for afternoon "munchies" are useful interventions.

GONADOTROPIN-RELEASING HORMONE ANALOGUES (GnRH ANALOGUES)

These preparations, which have a variety of medical uses, have recently been studied in uncontrolled trials. They initially act to stimulate the pituitary to dramatically increase its production of luteinizing hormone, thus causing a rapid rise in testosterone levels. Subsequently, through negative feedback, the pituitary is "down-regulated" and testosterone secretion decreases to castration levels. Completion abolition of deviant sexual fantasies, urges, and behavior has been reported in offenders who had failed to respond to CPA or serotonergic drugs. GnRH analogues are ineffective orally and are administered by depot injections (Rosler & Witztum, 1998, 2000).

The side effects include significant pain at the injection site, persistent hot flushes, reduced body hair, reduction in testicular volume, and, more ominously, progressive loss of bone calcium, particularly in the lumbar spine. This last effect needs careful monitoring via bone densitometry and the provision of calcium and vitamin D supplements (Rosler & Witztum, 1998). Cover with an anti-androgen such as CPA may be needed during the initial period of raised testosterone levels before down-regulation starts to occur (Bradford, 1998). Because of limited, although promising, experience with these preparations, their use should be regarded as experimental at present.

Assessment and Management: Integrating Pharmacological and Other Approaches

Given that pharmacological agents are probably of some use, how can they be incorporated into comprehensive treatment programs? Integrated approaches to sex offender treatment are not new, and several models have been outlined over the years. For example, a "bimodal" approach has been advocated combining psychodynamic and cognitive-behavioral orientations (Travin & Potter, 1993). Nevertheless, even in "multimodal" programs, the medically trained member of the treatment team (usually a psychiatrist) often sees the offender in splendid isolation, with very little input (apart from the biased self-report of the offender) from the rest of the program. Though psychiatrists are certainly in scarce supply in offender treatment programs, there are ways of using their expertise more efficiently. In particular, the skills and concepts used by other therapeutic approaches (particularly cognitive-behavior therapy and relapse prevention) can be adapted in order to monitor medication effects, encourage compliance, and reinforce what the offender is learning in other parts of the program.

THE TARGET OF PHARMACOLOGICAL MANAGEMENT

Although the risk management model of sex offender treatment has been increasingly questioned (Ward & Stewart, Chapter 2 in this volume), there is reasonable evidence that many sex offenders are troubled by areas of inadequate or inappropriate psychosocial functioning, which needs to be specifically targeted. These areas include cognitive distortions, empathy deficits, poor social skills, deviant sexual preferences, lack of sexual knowledge, and difficulties in predicting and controlling behaviors likely to lead to relapse. It is almost trite to say that the use of pharmacological agents will not, in and of itself, enhance social skills or modify cognitive distortions (although it may provide a psychological environment more conducive to the application of such interventions). Rather, where these agents appear to be most useful is in the reduction and modification of deviant sexual arousal, which, even though it may not be truly as important in offending behaviors as was once thought (see, for example, Marshall et al., 1999), still remains a central target for treatment.

WHO SHOULD BE CONSIDERED
FOR PHARMACOLOGICAL THERAPY?

These considerations should lead to more rational guidelines for selecting candidates for pharmacological treatment. Too often, pharmacological interventions are used only when other treatment modalities have failed or, conversely, they are introduced without adequate attention being paid to the other areas of poor psychosocial functioning described above. A useful rule of thumb is to prescribe medication when there is obvious evidence of continuing high levels of deviant arousal that may impact on the offender's ability (or willingness) to comply with other aspects of the treatment program. This implies the following selection criteria:

1. Those who experience high levels of deviant arousal not responsive to other measures.

2. Offenders whose behaviors are characterized by considerable violence, since there is suggestive (but not substantial) evidence that hormonal agents, in particular, may reduce aggression.

3. Offenders who are unwilling or unable to comply with other forms of treatment; for example, those living in rural or isolated areas without access to a practitioner skilled in the use of cognitive-behavioral techniques. There are also a few offenders who, paradoxically enough, resist any form of counseling-based therapy (probably due to high levels of denial) but are happy to take medication.

Medical contraindications to the use of hormonal agents have been discussed above.

For those offenders who are unable to provide informed consent (e.g., those with intellectual disability or mental illness), an application to appoint a guardian to consent on their behalf is usually necessary. The argument that is usually put to the relevant court or tribunal is that the offender's best interests are better served by treatment that will help him avoid contact with the criminal justice system (O'Neil, 2000). However, this seems to be a little hypocritical, as the real aim of treatment is often more that of community protection. The legal and ethical bases of such decisions remain contentious; indeed cynics might argue that, in this jurisdiction, an offender's best interests would be better served by teaching him how to reoffend without being detected.

ASSESSMENT AND MONITORING PROCESSES IN AN INTEGRATED TREATMENT ENVIRONMENT

In most cases where pharmacological therapy is being considered (particularly hormone therapy), a full medical history, physical investigation, and relevant investigations need to be carried out by appropriately qualified medical personnel. A full discussion of these is beyond the scope of this chapter, but clearly non-medically trained members of the treatment program need to be aware of the side effects of various medications discussed above and should be able to communicate any concerns rapidly to the prescribing physician.

Assessment issues in general are covered more fully in other chapters of this volume. What needs to be highlighted here are the pitfalls of assessing and monitoring deviant sexual arousal, which, as just noted, is the main target of medication therapy.

With hormonal agents, levels of serum testosterone certainly provide an objective way of checking compliance, but, as noted above, there is only a limited correlation with the degree of sexual arousal. In any case, the threshold level of testosterone to maintain sexual interest may be considerably higher than that needed to achieve erections, and these levels will differ in different individuals.

Compliance with serotonergic medications can be checked using blood or urine assays, but these will usually only confirm the presence of the drug or its metabolites and will not give any indication as to whether the prescribed dose is being taken.

Penile plethysmography (measuring penile responses to various forms of erotic and nonerotic stimuli in the laboratory) has been advocated as a seemingly more objective measure of deviant arousal. Its limitations are discussed in detail in another chapter of this volume and include a lack of standardization of the procedures used, easily faked responses, and poor validation in some types of offenders (e.g., rapists compared to pedophiles). In addition it seems undesirable to encourage sex offenders, who routinely abdicate responsibility for their actions anyway, to believe (as would be implied by repeated testing) that their lives are under the control of their willful and independently minded penis.

Offender self-report is, as we have seen, also unreliable, particularly if couched merely in terms of the presence or absence of deviant thoughts or activities. A more sophisticated approach is to incorporate the offender's understanding of other therapeutic techniques (particularly relapse prevention) and the judicious use of motivational interviewing techniques (Ryder, 1999; Towl & Crighton, 1996). Essentially, the clinician assumes that deviant thoughts and fantasies are present and asks the offender, using real or hypothetical scenarios, how he is going to deal with them. Such techniques are an extraordinarily useful practical test of how strongly an offender's deviant arousal is influencing his capacity to think through the relevant coping strategies (and how well he has learned them). Furthermore, the therapist does not have to confront the offender's glib denial of deviant thoughts.

The most accurate assessment of deviant fantasies, however, is still that of behavioral observation. Friends, relatives, carers, other health professionals, correctional staff, and outreach workers all can play a part in checking for signs of deviant arousal, such as staring at potential victims (especially children) in the street; inappropriate attempts to become friendly with potential victims; hoarding of pornography (particularly with violent or deviant themes); seeking out pornography on the Internet; frequenting venues such as parks, schools, and playgrounds in search of potential victims; exposure to other high-risk situations (e.g., voyeurs walking the streets at night), and so on. More motivated offenders can be persuaded to self-report such activities by means of a diary, checking in with trusted people via the phone, and so on. As well as serving as objective (if indirect) indicators of arousal, such behaviors can then be discussed with the offender as part of an ongoing risk-management program.

USING RELAPSE PREVENTION TECHNIQUES IN ONGOING PHARMACOLOGICAL MANAGEMENT

Although classic relapse prevention models have recently come under fire (Ward & Stewart, Chapter 2 in this volume), they still are useful in managing compliance with treatment for any long-term disorder. Thus they can be used in chronic conditions such as high blood pressure, diabetes, and dyslipidaemias where the risk of nontreatment (e.g., a major cardiovascular event) seems remote and there are no immediate rewards for compliance (National Heart Foundation, 2001). This is, of course, precisely the situation in which many offenders undertaking treatment, both pharmacological and nonpharmacological, find themselves.

The metaphor of a chronic non–life-threatening medical disorder that nevertheless requires treatment to avert a disastrous outcome is thus often a useful way of introducing the notion of pharmacological treatment. Other themes can then be raised, including the idea that treatment is "control not cure," the importance of lifestyle and environmental changes to help avoid relapse (just as the diabetic must avoid certain foods, so too must the pedophile avoid certain high-risk environments), and the importance of considering long-term risk (relapse, like a heart attack, may not happen for years, even without treatment, but will definitely be disastrous when it does occur). Cognitive reframing can be used to redefine treatment success: Just as the person with diabetes should feel pride in the lifestyle changes that have produced a stable and normal blood sugar level, so too should the sex offender be proud of lifestyle changes that minimize exposure to situations where he might be at high risk of relapse.

Ethical and Legal Issues

The recent decision by the California legislature requiring repeat sex offenders to undergo compulsory treatment with Depo-Provera as a condition of parole has reignited the debate about the use of pharmacological therapy in sex offenders. Broadly speaking, the debate has focused on the conflict between the state's duty to protect its citizens from serious criminal activity and the preservation of an individual's rights, particularly those concerning bodily autonomy, procreative freedom, freedom of speech and communication, and protection against cruel and unusual punishment (Meisenkothen, 1999; Mellela, Travin, & Cullen, 1989). Yet, despite a large amount of literature in the area (some of it, regrettably, penned by those who have clearly never encountered a real live sex offender), the arguments remain unidimensional; they simply vacillate between the two extremes of allowing the state unlimited powers to protect civil society and prohibiting even the slightest infringement on individual rights.

The issues are really more complex than this. A fundamental point is that treatment with pharmacological agents is subject to the same ethical rules as any other form of treatment used in sex offender treatment programs, including therapies based on cognitive-behavior principles. As I have demonstrated elsewhere (Glaser, 2002), these rules are constantly being broken, with consequences at least as harmful as (say) the side effects of hormonal medication. In order to deal with the psychosocial deficits mentioned above (e.g., cognitive distortions, poor social skills, deviant sexual arousal, etc.), treatment programs have become stricter and more dogmatic, keen to exercise as much control as possible over an offender's thoughts, feelings, and activities. An offender is required, in many cases, to submit to involuntary treatment, allow breaches of confidentiality, accept unquestioningly therapist-dictated attitudes and values, incriminate himself (particularly in group settings), and give up his right to the therapist or mode of therapy of his choice (see, for example, Kaden, 1998; O'Connell, Leberg, & Donaldson, 1990; Salter, 1988).

The justification for all these breaches of the traditional ethics of mental health care is that of the protection of society, and, indeed, this is now stated as being the primary aim of many sex offender treatment programs, taking precedence over the interests of the offender (Association for Treatment of Sexual Abusers [ATSA], 1996). Furthermore, these breaches are considered to be not only desirable but also necessary for the efficacy of the program, this efficacy being assessed in terms of the protection of current and potential victims and the reduction of social and economic costs to the community. "Good" therapists are those who abandon their interest in the offender's welfare (except to the extent that it is necessary to ensure offender compliance; Glaser, 2002).

Pharmacological treatment of sex offenders thus is no longer a special case. It is part of a major ideological change in the explicit values underpinning and justifying sex offender treatment programs generally. This fact, in and of itself, does not allow the indiscriminate use of medication therapies. Nevertheless, the legal and ethical framework governing their use is now more complex and more dependent on situational factors.

Thus, in the criminal jurisdiction, societal protection is achieved by punishments determined by the courts in accordance with sentencing policies and guidelines laid down by legislation and case law. In most Western jurisdictions, there are limits to punishment, irrespective of whether the rights of individual offenders are also protected. For example, punishment must be proportional to the crime and must be the least necessary to achieve its purpose. Such principles, in and of themselves, may prevent the court's ordering medication treatment for those committing minor sex offenses, even though such treatment could well be effective.

However, the protection of society can be achieved in other ways. In the United States, following the 1997 Supreme Court decision in *Kansas v. Hendricks*, the civil commitment of sex offenders has now been resurrected. The relevant laws allow for the indeterminate detention of those with an alleged "mental abnormality" or "personality disorder" who are likely to engage in "predatory acts of sexual violence" (see the discussion in Slovenko, 1997). Medication treatment of a sex offender detained under this type of legislation would be aimed both at curing the mental abnormality (vaguely defined) and also reducing the offender's dangerousness. If it did not succeed on either count, then there would be little justification for its use, even though the offender himself might feel that he is deriving benefit from it.

Yet another way of achieving the aim of protecting society's interests is through public health legislation that allows for the isolation of, or other restrictions on the liberty of, those suffering from infectious diseases. This is probably the clearest example of society's interests taking precedence over those of the individual; whatever the extent of individuals' suffering, they must remain in quarantine until the risk of their spreading the disease (including behavioral or lifestyle risks) is eliminated (see, for example, the *Health Act,* Victoria [Australia], 1973). There would thus appear to be a specific and clear mandate for programs offering treatment to sex offenders suffering from sexually transmitted diseases, but even here matters can be complicated, as the following case example shows:

F was a 40-year-old man with advanced but relatively well-controlled acquired immune deficiency syndrome who had committed numerous rapes (involving anal, oral, and vaginal penetration) on a range of victims including prepubertal children. After release from jail he complied only intermittently with a treatment program based on cognitive-behavioral techniques and admitted to ongoing strong deviant fantasies. The severe liver damage caused by the AIDS was an absolute contraindication to his receiving hormone therapy, even though he had consented to its use, and he spent the last 2 years of his life under 24-hour quarantine.

As this case poignantly demonstrates, the ethical dilemmas of sex offender treatment are rarely simple, even when the interests of society and the offender seem to coincide.

To summarize the central issues, therefore: Sex offender treatment programs generally have now become focused on victims and society at large; indeed, it is debatable as to whether (ethically speaking) they now carry out "treatment" at all. "Social control" or even "social defense" might be more accurate (and less hypocritical) definitions of their aims. Medication treatment (particularly hormone treatment) of sex offenders is simply following this wider trend and hence needs to be considered in a broader context than the traditional dichotomy between community protection and individual rights. The relevant legal and ethical issues are now much more complex and need to be considered in relation to the jurisdiction or setting in which the aims of social control are being pursued.

Conclusion

Pharmacological treatment plays an important role in the therapy of sex offenders. To date, its usefulness has been limited not so much by the lack of effective agents but rather by its lack of integration with other elements of comprehensive treatment programs. There is certainly a need to develop preparations that can specifically suppress deviant sexual arousal and that are also more acceptable to both offenders and society at large. Nevertheless, a greater challenge, and one that can be overcome now, is to ensure that the existing agents in use are more effectively introduced, monitored, and complied with using well-proven techniques derived from other aspects of sex offender treatment. In doing so, there may well be pleasant surprises for those who truly wish to provide effective and comprehensive therapy for this most complex group of clients.

References

Association for Treatment of Sexual Abusers (ATSA). (1996). Reducing sexual abuse through treatment and intervention with abusers. Retrieved September 19, 2001, from http://www.atsa.com/pptreatment.html

Bancroft, J. (1989). *Human sexuality and its problems.* Edinburgh: Churchill Livingstone.

Bartholomew, A. A. (1968). A long-acting phenothiazine as a possible agent to control deviant sexual behavior. *American Journal of Psychiatry, 124,* 917-923.

Bradford, J. M. W. (1998). Treatment of men with paraphilia. *New England Journal of Medicine, 338,* 464-465.

Cooper, A. J. (1995). Review of the role of two antilibidinal drugs in the treatment of sex offenders with mental retardation. *Mental Retardation, 33,* 42-48.

Gaffney, G. P., & Berlin, F. S. (1984). Is there hypothalamic-pituitary-gonadal dysfunction in paedophiles? *British Journal of Psychiatry, 145,* 657-660.

Galli, V. B., Raute, N. J., McConville, B. J., & McElroy, S. L. (1998). An adolescent male with multiple paraphilias successfully treated with fluoxetine. *Journal of Child and Adolescent Psychopharmacology, 3,* 195-197.

Glaser, B. (1996). Sex Offenders. In W. Brookbanks (Ed.), *Psychiatry and the law: Clinical and legal issues.* Wellington, NZ: Brooker's.

Glaser, B. (2002). *Therapeutic jurisprudence: An ethical paradigm for therapists in sex offender treatment programs.* Manuscript submitted for publication.

Greenberg, D. M., Bradford, J. M., Curry, S., & O'Rourke, A. (1996). A comparison of treatment of paraphilias with three serotonin re-uptake inhibitors: A retrospective study. *Bulletin of the American Academy of Psychiatry and the Law, 24,* 525-532.

Greenberg, D. M., & Bradford, J. M. W. (1997). Treatment of the paraphilic disorders: A review of the role of the selective serotonin reuptake inhibitors. *Sexual Abuse: A Journal of Research and Treatment, 9,* 349-360.

Heim, N., & Hursch, C. J. (1979). Castration for sexual offenders: Treatment or punishment? A review and critique of recent European literature. *Archives of Sexual Behavior, 8,* 281-300.

Hucker, S. J., & Bain, J. (1990). Androgenic hormones and sexual assault. In W. L. Marshall, D. R. Laws, & H. E. Barbaree (Eds.), *Handbook of sexual assault.* New York: Plenum.

Kaden, J. (1998). Therapy for convicted sex offenders: Pursuing rehabilitation without incrimination. *Journal of Criminal Law and Criminology, 89,* 347-368.

Kafka, M. P. (1994). Sertraline pharmacotherapy for paraphilias and paraphilia-related disorders: An open trial. *Annals of Clinical Psychiatry, 6,* 189-195.

Kaplan, H. I., & Sadock, B. J. (1998). *Synopsis of psychiatry.* Baltimore, MD: Williams and Wilkins.

Kiersch, T. A. (1990). Treatment of sex offenders with Depo provera. *Bulletin of the American Academy of Psychiatry and the Law, 18,* 179-187.

Kravitz, H. M., Haywood, T. W., Kelly, J., Wahlstrom, C., Liles, S., & Cavanaugh, J. L. (1995). Medroxyprogesterone and treatment for paraphiliacs. *Bulletin of the American Academy of Psychiatry and the Law, 23,* 19-33.

Kravitz, H. M., Haywood, T. W., Kelly, J., Wahlstrom, C., Liles, S., & Cavanaugh, J. L. (1996). Medroxyprogesterone and paraphiles: Do testosterone levels matter? *Bulletin of the American Academy of Psychiatry and the Law, 24,* 73-83.

Laschet, U., & Laschet, L. (1975). Anti-androgens in the treatment of sexual deviations of men. *Journal of Steroid Biochemistry, 6,* 821-826.

McConaghy, N. (1993). *Sexual behavior: Problems and management.* New York: Plenum.

Marshall, W. L. (1996). Assessment, treatment, and theorizing about sex offenders: Developments over the past 20 years and future directions. *Criminal Justice and Behavior, 23,* 162-199.

Marshall, W. L., Anderson, D., & Fernandez, Y. (1999). *Cognitive behavioural treatment of sexual offenders.* Chichester: Wiley.

Meisenkothen, C. (1999). Chemical castration—Breaking the cycle of paraphiliac recidivism. *Social Justice, 26,* 139-156.

Mellela, J. T., Travin, S., & Cullen, K. (1989). Legal and ethical issues in the use of anti-androgens in treating sex offenders. *Bulletin of the American Academy of Psychiatry and the Law, 17,* 223-231.

Meyer, L., Cole, C., & Emory, E. (1992). Depo provera treatment for sex offending behavior: An evaluation of outcome. *Bulletin of the American Academy of Psychiatry and the Law, 20,* 249-259.

National Heart Foundation of Australia/The Cardiac Society of Australia and New Zealand. (2001). Treatment of dyslipidaemias. *Medical Journal of Australia, 175*(Suppl.), 557-585.

O'Connell, M., Leberg, E., & Donaldson, C. (1990). *Working with sex offenders: Guidelines for therapist selection.* Thousand Oaks, CA: Sage.

O'Neil, N. (2000). Capacity to be criminal, the criminal justice system and the protection of adults with an intellectual disability for the benefit of themselves and others. In T. Shaddock, M. Bond, I. Bowen, & K. Hales (Eds.), *Intellectual disability and the law: Contemporary Australian issues.* Callaghan, New South Wales: Australian Society for the Study of Intellectual Disability.

Robinson, T., & Valcour, F. (1995). The use of Depo-provera in the treatment of child molesters and sexually compulsive males. *Sexual Addiction and Compulsivity, 2,* 277-294.

Ryder, D. (1999). Deciding to change: Enhancing client motivation to change behaviour. *Behavior Change, 16,* 165-174.

Rosler, A., & Witztum, E. (1998). Treatment of men with paraphilia with a long-acting analogue of gonadotropin-releasing hormone. *New England Journal of Medicine, 338,* 416-423.

Rosler, A., & Witztum, E. (2000). Pharmacotherapy of paraphilia in the next millennium. *Behavioral Sciences and the Law, 18,* 43-56.

Salter, A. C. (1988). *Treating child sex offenders and victims: A practical guide.* Newbury Park, CA: Sage.

Slovenko, R. (1997, Winter). Highlights in the history of law and psychiatry with focus on the United States. *Journal of Psychiatry and Law,* pp. 445-579.

Tennent, G., Bancroft, J., & Cass, J. (1974). The control of deviant sexual behaviour by drugs: A double-blind controlled study of benperidol, chlorpromazine and placebo. *Archives of Sexual Behavior, 7,* 417-428.

Therapeutic Guidelines: *Psychotropic.* (2000). Version 4. North Melbourne: Therapeutic Guidelines Ltd.

Towl, G. J., & Crighton, D. A. (1996). *The handbook of psychology for forensic practitioners.* London: Routledge.

Travin, S., & Potter, B. (1993). *Sexual perversions: Integrated treatment approaches for the clinician.* New York: Plenum.

16

Harm Reduction and Sexual Offending

Is an Intraparadigmatic Shift Possible?

D. Richard Laws
South Island Consulting
Victoria, British Columbia, Canada

It is not really possible to be for or against harm reduction. Harm reduction is what we do all the time.

—P. Denning (2000),
Practicing Harm Reduction Psychotherapy

What Is Harm Reduction?

The classical model of relapse prevention (RP; Daley, 1991; Laws, 1995b; Marlatt & Gordon, 1985; Wanigaratne, Wallace, Pullin, Keaney, & Farmer, 1990) has its roots in the drug and alcohol field. RP has now been applied to a variety of behavioral disorders in addition to drugs and alcohol (e.g., Wilson, 1992). The application to sex offenders has been under way since the mid-1980s (Pithers, Marques, Gibat, & Marlatt, 1983), and the treatment has become extremely popular. Unfortunately, its popularity and uncritical acceptance has effectively insulated it from serious empirical evaluation. Recently, questions have been raised about the comprehensiveness of its application to sex offenders (Hanson, 2000; Laws, in press; Laws, Hudson, & Ward, 2000a; Marshall & Anderson, 2000; Ward & Hudson, 2000).

Harm reduction is a concept that also has roots in the drug and alcohol field and is closely related to relapse prevention (Marlatt, 1998b; Denning, 2000). Stoner and George (2000) have described the overlap between the two approaches. Harm reduction has gained considerable popularity in drug and alcohol work due to the recognition that, in many cases, clients cannot be persuaded to give up drinking or drug use completely. There are numerous views of its application in these areas (Canadian Centre on Substance Abuse, 1996; Denning, 2000; Denning & Little, 2001; DesJarlais, 1991; Duncan, Nicholson, Clifford, Hawkins, & Petosa, 1994; Gunn, White, & Srinivasan, 1998; Marlatt, 1994, 1998b; Marlatt & Tapert, 1993; Marlatt, Larimer, Baer, & Quigley, 1993; Riley, 1993).

Harm reduction (although it was not so called) has a long history dating back to the 18th century. Levine (1979) noted that "colonials did not make major distinctions among the poor and deviant. . . . [They] did not expect society to be free from crime, poverty, insanity or drunkenness—from deviance" (p. 3). He cites Rothman's (1971) *The Discovery of the Asylum* in which he stated that colonial Americans

> did not interpret its presence as symptomatic of a basic flaw in community structure or *expect to eliminate it.* They would combat the evil, warn, chastise, correct, banish, flog or execute the offender. *But they saw no prospect of eliminating deviance from their midst.* (p. 15, italics added)

How is this related to a contemporary view of harm reduction? It means that 250 years ago, American society recognized that there were some elements of human behavior that probably could not be changed. Instead of ostracizing socially deviant people, instead of medicalizing, legalizing, or psychologizing their problems, they kept them in the human community and treated them as best they could. This theme will recur throughout this chapter.

As nearly as I can determine, the idea of harm reduction as such dates to the time of the American Revolution. Marlatt et al. (1993) state that its basic structure was first advanced by Dr. Benjamin Rush, who is generally accredited with being the father of American psychiatry. In 1785, Rush published a diagram that he called "A Moral and Physical Thermometer." Figure 16.1 shows this diagram.

The thermometer is intended to show the progressive perils of alcohol indulgence. Marlatt et al. (1993) state that Rush referred to alcoholism as "intemperance" or "inebriety" but, unlike the contemporary disease model, did not view the condition dichotomously, where one is either an alcoholic or one

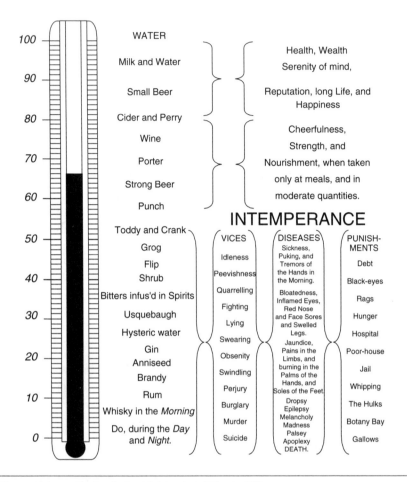

Figure 16.1   Benjamin Rush's Moral and Physical Thermometer

is not. He viewed severe intemperance as a disease, they say, but "he also endorsed an underlying continuum and included nonabstinence or moderate drinking as a component of temperance" (Marlatt et al., 1993, p. 46). Examination of this continuum would suggest that this is so. It ranges (top of figure) from total abstinence from alcohol to total indulgence (lower portion). Rush listed various types of drink, presumably in increasing potency, and, opposite these, he listed the consequences of increasing indulgence. This notion of a continuum ranging from abstinence through moderation to total indulgence is a hallmark of contemporary harm reduction thinking. Marlatt et al. (1993) have not gotten it completely right. While Rush proposed a continuum as seen in the figure, Levine (1979) stated that he was a fanatic about the dangers of drink and is more properly seen as the founder of the 19th century Temperance Movement. For Rush, movement on the continuum was in one direction—from sobriety to total indulgence.

However it was intended, Rush's thermometer is the first clear statement of a possible continuum of harm in socially deviant behavior. Marlatt et al. (1993), as well as many other writers, suggest that harm reduction methods are intended to facilitate movement along this continuum toward less harmful effects. They view abstinence as the "anchor point of minimal harm" (p. 46) but see any movement toward reduced harm as desirable. It is clear that there are risks of harm at all points of the continuum as one moves away from abstinence. The more the client can be moved away from excess toward moderation, the more harm is reduced. This belief is embodied in the harm reduction slogan, "Any steps toward decreased risk are steps in the right direction" (Marlatt & Tapert, 1993, pp. 245-246).

Laws (1995a) has stated, and this is quite consistent with Rothman's (1971) observations on practices in the American colonial era:

> Adopting this approach to troublesome human behavior requires the normalization of some behaviors that we may find socially unacceptable, offensive, or even criminal. From a public health perspective it requires bringing these behaviors into the larger arena of public discourse. It also means discovering ways to deal with these behaviors such that persons who engage in them are not punished or ostracized. It amounts to acknowledging the imperfections of fellow citizens and encouraging them to moderate their behaviors to an extent that does less harm to themselves and others, yet keeps them within the human community. (Laws, 1995a, pp. 244-245)

So, in practice, what is harm reduction? It is both a belief system, a philosophy, if you will (e.g., Marlatt, 1998a) and a treatment approach (Denning, 2000; Denning & Little, 2001).

HARM REDUCTION AS A BELIEF SYSTEM

This perspective has been described by DesJarlais (1991, pp. 10-12) and Marlatt (1998a, pp. 49-58). Marlatt notes the following basic principles, assumptions, and values. In what follows I have modified Marlatt's text (pp. 49-58) somewhat to suggest the possibility of a broader application beyond alcohol and drug abuse.

   1.   *Harm reduction is a public health alternative to the moral/criminal/ disease models of deviant behavior.* Harm reduction, rooted in the philosophy

of pragmatism and a public health approach, shifts the focus away from the deviant behavior itself and toward the consequences or effects of that behavior. The effects are evaluated in terms of whether they are helpful or harmful to the deviant and to the larger society, not on the basis of whether the behavior is viewed as morally right or wrong. Harm reduction accepts the obvious fact that many people engage in socially deviant and high-risk behaviors, and that idealistic visions of a deviance-free society are unlikely to become reality.

2. *Harm reduction recognizes abstinence as an ideal outcome but accepts alternatives that reduce harm.* Moral and disease models share one strong common value: They insist upon total abstinence as the only acceptable goal of either incarceration or treatment. This is the zero tolerance position, so familiar from alcoholism, drug abuse, and family violence treatment (the zero tolerance position in sex offender programs is discussed below). Zero tolerance establishes a dichotomy between no deviant behavior at all and any deviant behavior whatsoever. This dichotomy labels all deviant behavior as equally criminal (or mentally ill) and does not distinguish between mild, moderate, or heavy engagement in those behaviors, or the degrees of harm associated with each. Contrary to much contemporary belief, harm reduction is not antiabstinence. Rather, harmful effects of deviant behavior are recognized as being distributed along a continuum much like Rush's (Figure 16.1). The harm reduction approach would encourage individuals to adopt a step-down approach. Persons showing excessive deviant behaviors would be encouraged to gradually reduce the harmful consequences of their behavior, taking it one step at a time. Miller and Page (1991) described a stepped approach that they called "warm turkey."

3. *Harm reduction has emerged primarily as a bottom-up approach based on client advocacy, rather than a top-down approach often promoted by correctional or treatment policymakers.* This principle is clearly linked to the harm reduction approach to alcohol and drug abuse. It states that the movement rejects bureaucratic interference and directives from above that define policy without consideration for the needs of the consumers themselves. A top-down approach is obviously related to the zero tolerance position. On the other hand, harm reduction efforts are more likely to emerge at the local level through grassroots advocacy for clients. This is a community-based public health approach that supports deviants and their communities in reducing harm.

4. *Harm reduction promotes low-threshold access to services as an alternative to traditional, high-threshold approaches.* It is important to get people involved in treatment and harm reducing activities rather than setting high-threshold preconditions for obtaining services. This is highly important

because many deviants will not come forward and make their needs known if highly stringent preconditions must first be met. In many cases, sex offender clients are met with a list of "Thou Shalt Nots" when entering treatment. These preconditions may take the form of: "Immediately stop whatever it is you're doing. Stop fantasizing, stop masturbating, stop cruising, get rid of pornography, stay away from deviant peers," and so on. The idea of low-threshold access is to reach out to achieve a partnership with the clientele by adopting a normalized approach to deviant behavior. Clients are encouraged to "come as you are" rather than "come after you do what I tell you to do." Clients are accepted as capable of assuming responsibility for making personal changes in their behavior. When the focus is toward reducing harm associated with deviant behavior and away from labeling the problem as criminal or immoral, it is believed that persons seeking help are more likely to come forward.

5. *Harm reduction is based on the tenets of compassionate pragmatism versus moralistic idealism.* As a pragmatic approach, harm reduction accepts the fact that harmful behavior is going to occur no matter what; it has always been that way. Pragmatism does not ignore empiricism; it simply says: Use what works. Any approach is acceptable, and the validity of the approach is evaluated by its results. It either reduces harm or it does not. Acknowledging that harmful behaviors occur, however, does not mean accepting them. The question is: What can be done to reduce harmful consequences? Based on acceptance and compassion for the client, harm reduction bears close resemblance to various schools of humanistic psychology.

This is not to say that harm reduction is value free. The values that it does embrace are realistic, not moralistic ones. Traditional disease and moral models attempt to cloak treatment with those values without considering the processes of behavior change. They are therefore unlikely to work. Harm reduction, on the other hand, is considerably more flexible and responsive to the complexities of deviant human behavior as well as the nature of behavior change. In addition, harm reduction is empirically sensitive. It takes into account that behavior change is more likely to be incremental than dramatic. It constantly seeks the reduction of harmful consequences, and it respects individual choice and human agency. Harm reduction's values center around increasing benefits to people rather than being concerned solely with right or wrong, good or bad.

HARM REDUCTION AS A TREATMENT APPROACH

The words *treatment* and *intervention* appear in many writings about harm reduction, but statements about how these might be implemented are often broad, vague, and imprecise. Recently Denning (2000; Denning & Little, 2001) described a treatment approach called Harm Reduction Psychotherapy. Even though she would embrace all of the basic principles described above, Denning is primarily a substance abuse therapist and has designed a system of treatment based on a sort of marriage of dynamic psychotherapy and cognitive-behavioral therapy. As with Marlatt (1998a), I have modified her text some-what to reflect application to deviant behavior in general.

As a basic framework for this model, Denning (2000, pp. 57-61) adopts Prochaska, DiClemente, and Norcross's (1992) description of stages of change. The stages are:

1.   *Precontemplation.* She calls this the "Who, me?" stage of change. There is no intention to change behavior at this point. This stage is often seen as one of denial. She believes that it is actually a lack of information.

2.   *Contemplation.* Clients begin to acknowledge that they have a prob-lem and might wish to do something about it. She states that the therapist's job is to encourage this ambivalence rather than label it as resistance or denial.

3.   *Preparation.* Here people have decided to make a change and are exhibiting behaviors that demonstrate this.

4.   *Action.* Behavior changes begin to become evident. Time and effort is devoted to deciding upon the details of the change process.

5.   *Maintenance.* This is an extended stage in which persons learn new behaviors and coping strategies to maintain the changes that they have achieved. Denning states that 6 months with no relapse is required for consi-dering that a person is in the maintenance stage. Relapses are likely to occur here, she warns, but clients can learn from them.

6.   *Termination.* Denning is rather vague about this stage. "People do, in fact, reach a point in time where the behavior no longer threatens to intrude on daily life," or "Symptom reduction or elimination, increased performance and satisfaction with work and relationships . . . are indicators that the person's work is near finished. . . . [T]he therapist can now join with the patient in an evaluation and celebration of change" (Denning, 2000, p. 61).

The work of harm reduction psychotherapy, she says, is keeping a close watch on the stage in which the client is currently occupied. Duncan and Little (2001) recommend keeping the client engaged through use of Miller and Rollnick's (1991) five principles of motivational interviewing:

1.   *Express empathy.* The therapist must see the world from the client's point of view and communicate to the client, "I get it."

2. *Develop discrepancy.* The client needs to see the discrepancy between . . . (his/her) . . . goals and the reality of . . . (his/her) . . . situation in order to create pressure to change. *Note: it is the client's job to see the discrepancy, not the therapist's to point it out.*

3. *Avoid argumentation.* The client has the right to tell his own story and is always right.

4. *Roll with resistance.* Resistance to change is natural; it is the mind's way of saying, "wait a minute, how do I know I am going to be better off if I . . . ?"

5. *Support self-efficacy.* Self-efficacy is the sense that one can accomplish one's goals. The therapist must take every effort to build self-efficacy in the client by supporting all efforts the client makes toward healthy change. (Denning & Little, 2001, p. 9)

If these are the general guidelines, what is the treatment? Denning's writings reveal a strong commitment to dynamic psychotherapy but, on the other hand she is also a Marlattian compassionate pragmatist. She will use what works. She uses a primary technique called the Decisional Balance (Denning, 2000, p. 4), which is a virtual replica of Marlatt and Gordon's (1985) and Jenkins-Hall's (1989) Decision Matrix. Denning and Little (2001, p. 10) state that the Decisional Balance is

the primary tool used to explore the client's ambivalence . . . and behavior change. The pros and cons of change are compared to the pros and cons of maintaining the same behavior. (Looking from both points of view increases the complexity of the change process—and makes it more real) . . . The therapist must remain neutral in the decisional balance. The client's own life issues and investment in each issue will provide sufficient weight to give the therapist plenty to explore. (p. 10)

However, the therapist is obliged to provide information when needed: "This information must be balanced, correct, and not based on generalizations . . . on myths . . . or on the therapist's wish to frighten the client into abstinence." It is easy to see how the Decisional Balance and the principles of motivational interviewing can be fitted into the framework of Prochaska et al.'s (1992) stages of change. This is not all. Other specific interventions include: "stress reduction and coping skills training, nutrition, psychiatric medication, relapse prevention, family therapy" (Denning & Little, 2001, p. 10). Marlatt (1998a) states that behavior therapy and cognitive behavior therapy are well suited to harm reduction treatment.

A recent paper by Ward and Stewart (2001) proposes more attention to human needs and quality of life, a position not dissimilar to what is attempted in harm reduction in general and harm reduction psychotherapy in particular. Ward and Stewart acknowledge that the notion of "criminogenic needs" proposed by Andrews and Bonta (1998) has come to be the standard that guides programming in much correctional and rehabilitative treatment. Criminogenic needs refer to dynamic risk factors such as impulsiveness, pro-offending attitudes, poor problem-solving skills, high hostility and anger, and so on. These factors are targeted in treatment because empirical research has indicated that these are the ones predictive of recidivism. Needs not associated with recidivism—low self-esteem, anxiety, personal distress—are not considered worthy of attention. This approach may work toward keeping society safer (reducing harm), but it does nothing to improve the inter- and intrapersonal life of the offender. Ward and Stewart (2001) conclude:

> The rehabilitation of offenders should be driven by an enhancement model, not a harm avoidance one. This does not entail ignoring the needs of the community for security and safety; it simply reminds us that all human lives should reflect the best possible outcomes rather than the least worst possibilities. (pp. 41-42)

Dwyer's (2000) notion of "negativity reduction" is related to the preceding. The qualities of harm reduction that she finds appealing are its sensitivity to the client and overall nonjudgmental approach. She would take it a bit farther:

> To employ sensitivity and nonjudgment in a treatment model means the language used is respectful of the client . . . terms . . . such as: molester, . . . predator, deviant, or pervert are not helpful either for our client or for the public to get beyond their rage and look at treatment possibilities. (pp. 10-11)

I have considered the general principles of harm reduction as well as the basic operations of harm reduction psychotherapy at some length to suggest that there is an extremely close resemblance between this approach and both classical relapse prevention and its application to sex offenders. It is to these issues that I now turn.

RELAPSE PREVENTION AND HARM REDUCTION

The classical, substance abuse view of relapse prevention (RP; Marlatt & Gordon, 1985) acknowledged that the ultimate goal of treatment, abstinence, was highly desirable but not always achievable. It recognized the certainty of lapses and the possibility of relapses, and tried to build skills to combat both. In that model, following a lapse or relapse, one could still return to abstinence. When the classical model was applied to sex offenders (Laws, 1989; Laws, Hudson, & Ward, 2000b) these terms had to be redefined. In this model, *lapse* referred to any deliberate sexual fantasizing with deviant themes or "returning to sources of stimulation associated with the sexual offense pattern but short of performance of the offense behavior," and *relapse* as any occurrence of sexual offense "thus constituting full scale reestablishment of the problematic behavior" (George & Marlatt, 1989, p. 6). Note this well; it says that lapses are manageable but relapses must never occur. Relapse prevention applied to sex offenders holds a zero tolerance position. The problem, says Riley (1993), is that "the 'ideal' of zero tolerance excludes all compromise and sets impossible goals" (p. 10).

Harm reduction would view sexual deviation as a chronic, entrenched disposition to engage in deviant behavior, a condition that is incurable but one that could be managed, probably imperfectly. Marlatt and Tapert (1993) have summarized this viewpoint:

> With ongoing relapse problems, RP programs are designed for relapse management: to reduce the frequency and intensity of relapse episodes, to keep the client involved in the treatment process and to motivate renewed efforts toward behavior change. Applied to relapse management, RP represents a tertiary prevention approach to harm reduction, designed to reduce the magnitude of relapse. (p. 267)

That is in direct opposition to the zero tolerance position of sex offender RP. If we are to adopt a harm reduction perspective, then we must acknowledge that lapses and relapses are likely inevitable and that the job of treatment is to eliminate them if possible, but at least to reduce the frequency and intensity of these instances. Elsewhere (Laws, 1999) I have suggested that

> it may be more realistic to give less emphasis to something called *treatment* and more emphasis to *management,* i.e., more attention to *reducing harm* rather than *eliminating harm,* more attention to *containing evil* than *eradicating evil.* I suggested this because it is actually what we do. (p. 234)

This statement has, understandably, horrified and disgusted some clinicians (e.g., Maletzky, 1998; Paré, 1997a, 1997b). It is understandable because, as harm reduction teaches us, it is very difficult to let go of entrenched beliefs and attitudes. How dramatic would it be to shift the emphasis of intervention from *relapse prevention* to *relapse management* or *relapse minimization*? It would certainly not mean abandoning RP as a treatment or abandoning the effort to forestall lapses and prevent relapses. As I have shown in the treatment of the typical harm reduction approaches above, there are great similarities to what we are already doing. Shifting the emphasis to harm reduction would require little more than shifting our perspective to make it more congruent with what we actually do in practice. In his book *The Structure of Scientific Revolutions,* Kuhn (1970) describes what he calls "paradigm shifts." The word *paradigm* refers in this sense to accepted ways of conducting scientific inquiry or practice (RP is a paradigm for conducting treatment; Laws, 1989). Eventually, contradictory evidence accumulates or insoluble theoretical problems expose a paradigm's inadequacies (RP is a constrictive, "one size fits all" treatment that lacks generality; Ward & Hudson, 2000; harm reduction may fit the problems better). Kuhn wrote of sweeping paradigmatic shifts such as the overthrow of Newtonian mechanics by quantum physics and general relativity. Nothing so broad is being proposed here. What we need is an "intraparadigmatic shift," more a change in attitude *within* the relapse prevention paradigm than a change in practical therapeutic efforts.

MISCONCEPTIONS ABOUT HARM
REDUCTION AND SEX OFFENDERS

Harm reduction examples are all around us, but we take these for granted and typically do not have a generic label for them. In recent years harm reduction has gained increasing acceptance in the substance abuse field. This has often led to the belief that it applies *only* to that field. That being so, if one suggests that harm reduction might equally apply to the treatment of sex offenders (Laws, 1995a, 1999), some predictable misconceptions arise (Paré, 1977a, 1997b; Laws, 1999, pp. 235-238; Maletzky, 1998). I will treat each of these in turn.

1.   *Harm reduction applies only to alcohol and drug abuse and not to anything else.* Everyday examples of harm reduction may be seen in seat belts, collapsible bumpers on vehicles, air bags, gun control legislation, recommended use of condoms in sexual intercourse, transdermal patches to control smoking, medication to reduce obsessive-compulsive behavior, or antiandrogenic drugs to reduce excessive sexual arousal. None of these have anything to do with substance abuse.

2.   *Harm reduction is most often associated with alcoholism and drug abuse. Therefore, harm reduction refers only to harm to oneself, not harm to others.* All of the major impulse control disorders, sexual deviation included, involve harm to the self and harm to others, primarily partners and family. Other problematic behaviors that come to mind are: compulsive gambling, problem drinking (but not alcoholism), compulsive sexual behavior (but not sexual deviance), compulsive spending, shoplifting, or domestic violence. In all of these areas, a single individual's misbehavior can affect scores of other persons.

3.   *Normalizing any aspect of deviant sexual behavior is unacceptable.* The normalization of the previously forbidden is an insidious historical process

that moves along very slowly until no one notices anymore that something was once seen as deviant. For example, 30 years ago homosexuality was not only seen as deviant, it was illegal. Today, homosexuality is tolerated, accepted by most people and, in some circles, seen as trendy. It is easy for us to accept harm reduction, decriminalization, and normalization when we are speaking of alcohol or drug abuse, compulsive gambling, or compulsive eating. It is much less easy to do so when we are speaking of deviant sexual behavior where someone gets hurt. We have essentially already normalized socially unacceptable behaviors such as drug dealing, prostitution, and gambling because they can only be contained, not eliminated. Similarly, we do not have the resources to deal with minor paraphilias such as voyeurism, fetishism, exhibitionism, or obscene telephone calling. Many aspects of sexual deviation are simply part of the contemporary societal landscape. "Normalizing," as I am using the word, does not mean ignoring that the school bus driver may be an exhibitionist or that the choirmaster may be a bit too interested in his charges. Rather it means that distasteful things go on around us all the time, and we have very limited ability to intervene against most of them. Some amount of deviant behavior is present all the time. Because we cannot prevent it, we ignore it; by ignoring it, we normalize it.

4. *People will not accept that a person is simply less dangerous than he used to be.* We continuously accept the fact that people are different than they used to be—less obnoxious, less foolish, less sexy, why not less dangerous? For example, consider a man who used to expose himself 100 times per year completes a treatment program and reduces the frequency to 10 times per year. He is still deviant but he has dramatically reduced his capacity for doing harm. This is an outcome that most people would accept. It is a clear example of harm reduction.

5. *In the world of offender treatment, relapse is treatment failure.* There is an argument in the alcoholism literature that says that there is no such thing as relapse. A person who has achieved some degree of self-management, but fails to keep the problem behavior changed, is not the same person who entered treatment. The relapse could be viewed as an experience that provided additional information on how to control one's behavior. Marlatt (1985) referred to this as a "prolapse." Prochaska et al. (1992) argue that many attempts may be needed before a behavior can finally be brought under control. If relapse is an expected part of treatment, why should this not be so for sexual deviants? However, those who believe that one more victim is one too many will not find this argument persuasive. The fact remains, nonetheless, whether using the classical model or the sex offender model, that lapsing and recovering are the very essence of relapse prevention.

6.   *It is not possible to measure the extent to which harm has been reduced.* If we have not measured the extent of harm reduction it is because we have not looked. It is sadly typical that most treatment programs do not follow up treatment completers to determine the extent, if any, of reoffending. In recent years researchers have begun examining the behaviors of relapsers and survivors in an attempt to learn which portions of treatment contribute most to the prevention of relapse (R. E. Mann, personal communication, June 2000). This type of activity can tell us much about the extent to which harm has been reduced.

7.   *There is a large difference on the continuum between merely offensive behavior and devastating behavior.* We all put up with the troublesome behaviors of others on a daily basis. It is obvious that rape or molestation of children is devastating behavior and not to be tolerated. Some critics (e.g., Maletzky, 1998, p. 79) are concerned that acceptance of a harm reduction approach will encourage and be accepting of devastating deviant behavior. Relapse prevention to reduce harm is what we do. We should always strive to eliminate deviant thinking and deviant behavior to the extent possible. The brutal fact is that we are not going to be entirely successful.

8.   *Harm reduction does more harm than good because it says that some deviant behavior is okay.* This is the major misconception about harm reduction. Harm reduction *does not* say that deviant sexual behavior is okay. A little bit of child molesting or a little bit of rape is not okay. Laws (1999) put it this way:

> The reality, which the harm reduction position openly acknowledges, is that a little bit of sexual offending is whatever category is going to happen no matter what we do, no matter how hard we try, no matter how good the treatment. This is simply a fact and we should have the courage to wake up to it. (p. 238)

I believe that many people misinterpret harm reduction because they fail to make the distinction between working with individual clients and overall therapeutic policy. The goal of working with clients is always abstention, albeit realizing that this may be a very long incremental process and that not everyone will be a successful abstainer. Treatment policy, on the other hand, is to reduce as much harm as possible. We need to distinguish between intention and actual outcome. Our goal is to eliminate sexual offending. However, actual reduction in recidivism and in the severity of offending is an obvious reduction in harm and should be viewed as an acceptable outcome. The zero tolerance position confuses this point. The mistake that opponents of harm reduction make is to think that, if you view harm reduction as a good outcome, this must mean that all you were aiming for all along was reduction rather than abstinence. This mistaken belief then leads to the conclusion that harm reduction is itself harmful, unethical, and irresponsible.

Where Do We Go From Here?

Adopting a harm reduction perspective means accepting the fact that sexual abuse and all forms of interpersonal violence are, at bottom, public health issues. Sexual abuse is not a criminal justice issue (although justice is meted out); it is not a medical or psychiatric issue (although medications are dispensed); it is not a psychological issue (although interventions are applied); and it is not a political issue (even though protests might fill the streets). Rather, deviant behavior and sexual abuse are everybody's business. Reduction of sexual harm from a public health perspective requires a reframing of the problem, an intraparadigmatic shift of attitude. Freeman-Longo (1997) has stated the basic issues that are consistent with the classical harm reduction approach:

> Sexual abuse prevention requires a national campaign to recognize sexual abuse as a public health problem. If society expects people who are prone to act out sexually and abuse others to get help for their problem and stop their behavior, then society must offer the opportunity for sexual abusers and persons prone to act out sexually, to come forward and get help. All of the other prevention programs provide hope and the opportunity for treatment, even when there is not a "cure" for the particular problem. To prevent sexual abuse from becoming a more widespread epidemic, we must provide the potential abuser and the currently active abusers the same opportunities for hope and recovery. (p. 3)

Conclusion

We cannot go on waging an endless war on sexual abuse, because it is a battle that we are not going to win. We must recognize sexual abuse as a pandemic public health problem. We must acknowledge sex offenders as imperfect and faulted human beings, our fellow persons who are deserving of our consideration and care. Harm reduction is a public health alternative to the current disease, immoral, or criminal models of sexual deviance. It recognizes abstinence as an ideal goal but accepts alternatives that reduce harm to self and others. It promotes low-threshold access to services to encourage the fearful and reluctant to come forward. It is based on an approach of humanitarian pragmatism; it uses whatever works to achieve the best possible outcomes in the individual case.

From 1992 to 1993 I served as the President of the Association for the Treatment of Sexual Abusers (ATSA). Early in that term the Executive Board was attempting to design a logo and a slogan for the organization. I asked for suggestions for a slogan. One of the Board members said, "How about 'Making Society Safe'?" I countered, "What about 'Making Society Safe*r*'?" The slogan was adopted. ATSA has now abandoned this slogan, and that is unfortunate because it clearly says that harm reduction is what we are all about in sex offender treatment.

References

Andrews, D. A., & Bonta, J. (1998). *The psychology of criminal conduct* (2nd ed.). Cincinnati, OH: Anderson.

Canadian Centre on Substance Abuse. (1996). Harm reduction: Concepts and practice. Retrieved June 23, 2001, from the World Wide Web: http://www.ccsa.ca/plweb-cgi/fastweb.exe? getdoc+view1+Genera

Daley, D. C. (1991). *Kicking addictive habits once and for all.* Lexington, MA: Lexington Books.

Denning, P. (2000). *Practicing harm reduction psychotherapy: An alternate approach to addictions.* New York: Guilford.

Denning, P., & Little, J. (2001). Harm reduction in mental health: The emerging work of harm reduction psychotherapy. *Harm Reduction Communication, 11,* 7-10.

DesJarlais, D. C. (1991). Harm reduction: A framework for incorporating science into drug policy [Editorial]. *American Journal of Public Health, 85,* 10-12.

Duncan, D. F., Nicholson, T., Clifford, P., Hawkins, W., & Petosa, R. (1994). Harm reduction: An emerging new paradigm for drug education. *Journal of Drug Education, 24,* 281-290.

Dwyer, S. M. (2000). Harm reduction: A good debate. Leading to a new theory of negativity reduction. *The Forum, XII,* No. 2, 10-11.

Freeman-Longo, R. E. (1997). Challenging our thoughts. *The Forum, IX,* No. 2, 3.

George, W. H., & Marlatt, G. A. (1989). Introduction. In D. R. Laws (Ed.), *Relapse prevention with sex offenders* (pp. 1-31). New York: Guilford.

Gunn, N., White, C., & Srinivasan, R. (1998). Primary care as harm reduction for injection drug users. Retrieved June 23, 2001, from the World Wide Web: http://www.ama-assn.org/sci-pubs/msjama/articles/vol_280/no_135/jms81007.htm

Hanson, R. K. (2000). What is so special about relapse prevention? In D. R. Laws, S. H. Hudson, & T. Ward (Eds.), *Remaking relapse prevention with sex offenders* (pp. 27-38). Thousand Oaks, CA: Sage.

Jenkins-Hall, K. D. (1989). The decision matrix. In D. R. Laws (Ed.), *Relapse prevention with sex offenders* (pp. 159-166). New York: Guilford.

Kuhn, T. (1970). *The structure of scientific revolutions* (2nd ed.). Chicago: University of Chicago Press.

Laws, D. R. (1989). *Relapse prevention with sex offenders.* New York: Guilford.

Laws, D. R. (1995a). Relapse prevention or harm reduction? *Sexual Abuse: A Journal of Research and Treatment, 8,* 243-247.

Laws, D. R. (1995b). A theory of relapse prevention. In W. O'Donohue & L. Krasner (Eds.), *Theories of behavior therapy: Exploring behavior change* (pp. 445-473). Washington, DC: American Psychological Association.

Laws, D. R. (1999). Harm reduction or harm facilitation? A reply to Maletzky. *Sexual Abuse: A Journal of Research and Treatment, 11,* 233-240.

Laws, D. R. (in press). The rise and fall of relapse prevention. *Australian Psychologist.*

Laws, D. R., Hudson, S. H., & Ward, T. (2000a). The original model of relapse prevention with sex offenders: Promises unfulfilled. In D. R. Laws, S. H. Hudson, & T. Ward (Eds.), *Remaking relapse prevention with sex offenders* (pp. 3-24). Thousand Oaks, CA: Sage.

Laws, D. R., Hudson, S. H., & Ward, T. (2000b). *Remaking relapse prevention with sex offenders.* Thousand Oaks, CA: Sage.

Levine, H. C. (1979). The discovery of addiction: Changing conceptions of habitual drunkenness in America. *Journal of Studies on Alcohol, 15,* 493-506. Retrieved June 27, 2001 from the World Wide Web: http://www.lindesmith.org/library/tlclevin.html

Maletzky, B. (1998). Harm facilitation. *Sexual Abuse: A Journal of Research and Treatment, 10,* 77-80.

Marlatt, G. A. (1985). Relapse prevention: Theoretical rationale and overview of the model. In G. A. Marlatt & J. R. Gordon (Eds.), *Relapse prevention* (pp. 3-70). New York: Guilford.

Marlatt, G. A. (1994). A public health approach to addictive behavior. *American Psychological Association: Division on Addictions, 2,* 1-3.

Marlatt, G. A. (1998a). Basic principles and strategies of harm reduction. In G. A. Marlatt (Ed.), *Harm reduction: Pragmatic strategies for managing high-risk behaviors* (pp. 49-66). New York: Guilford.

Marlatt, G. A. (1998b). *Harm reduction: Pragmatic strategies for managing high-risk behaviors.* New York: Guilford.

Marlatt, G. A., & Gordon, J. R. (1985). *Relapse prevention.* New York: Guilford.

Marlatt, G. A., Larimer, M. E., Baer, J. S., & Quigley, L. A. (1993). Harm reduction for alcohol problems: Moving beyond the controlled drinking controversy. *Behavior Therapy, 24,* 461-504.

Marlatt, G. A., & Tapert, S. F. (1993). Harm reduction: Reducing the risks of addictive behaviors. In J. S. Baer, G. A. Marlatt, & R. J. McMahon (Eds.), *Addictive behaviors across the life span* (pp. 243-273). Newbury Park, CA: Sage.

Marshall, W. L., & Anderson, D. (2000). Do relapse prevention components enhance treatment effectiveness? In D. R. Laws, S. H. Hudson, & T. Ward (Eds.), *Remaking relapse prevention with sex offenders* (pp. 39-55). Thousand Oaks, CA: Sage.

Miller, W., & Page, A. (1991). Warm turkey: Other routes to abstinence. *Journal of Substance Abuse Treatment, 8,* 227-232.

Miller, W. R., & Rollnick, S. (1991). *Motivational interviewing: Preparing people to change addictive behavior.* New York: Guilford.

Paré, R. (1997a). *Relapse prevention or harm reduction? Making the case for relapse prevention.* Unpublished manuscript.

Paré, R. (1997b, October). *Making the case for relapse prevention: Holding the line in an age of compromise.* Paper presented at the meeting of the Association for the Treatment of Sexual Abusers, Arlington, VA.

Pithers, W. D., Marques, J. K., Gibat, C. C., & Marlatt, G. A. (1983). Relapse prevention with sexual aggressives: A self-control model of treatment and maintenance of change. In J. G. Greer & I. R. Stuart (Eds.), *The sexual aggressor* (pp. 214-239). New York: Van Nostrand Reinhold.

Prochaska, J. O., DiClemente, C. C., & Norcross, J. C. (1992). In search of how people change: Applications to addictive behaviors. *American Psychologist, 47,* 1102-1114.

Riley, D. (1993). The harm reduction model: Pragmatic approaches to drug use from the area between intolerance and neglect. Retrieved June 23, 2001 from the World Wide Web: http://www.ccsa.ca/harmred.htm

Rothman, D. J. (1971). *The discovery of the asylum: Social order and disorder in the new republic.* Boston: Little, Brown.

Stoner, S. A., & George, W. H. (2000). Relapse prevention and harm reduction: Areas of overlap. In D. R. Laws, S. H. Hudson, & T. Ward (Eds.), *Remaking relapse prevention with sex offenders* (pp. 56-75). Thousand Oaks, CA: Sage.

Wanigaratne, S., Wallace, W., Pullin, J., Keaney, F., & Farmer, R. (1990). *Relapse prevention for addictive behaviors.* Oxford, UK: Blackwell.

Ward, T., & Hudson, S. H. (2000). A self-regulation model of relapse prevention. In D. R. Laws, S. H. Hudson, & T. Ward (Eds.), *Remaking relapse prevention with sex offenders* (pp. 79-101). Thousand Oaks, CA: Sage.

Ward, T., & Stewart, C. (2001). *Criminogenic needs or human needs? A theoretical critique.* Unpublished manuscript.

Wilson, P. H. (1992). *Principles and practice of relapse prevention.* New York: Guilford.

17

Sexual Offending
Is a Public Health Problem

Are We Doing Enough?

D. Richard Laws

South Island Consulting, Victoria, British Columbia

Elsewhere I have argued that the concept of harm reduction is a public health approach to serious social problems (see Laws, Chapter 16 in this volume). The principles of harm reduction (see Marlatt, 1998, pp. 49-57) assert that it (a) is a public health alternative to moral, criminal, or disease models of social misbehavior; (b) recognize abstinence from deviant behavior as an ideal, but accept reduced harm as an alternative; (c) promote client advocacy; (d) promote low-threshold access to treatment services; and (e) are based on a philosophy of compassionate pragmatism; harm reduction uses what works. Although this is not the language of public health, these goals are clearly within the general mission of public health efforts. The purpose of this chapter is to examine the general public health approach and how it may be applied in the management of sex offenders, and whether it can be effective.

Looking at the problem of sexual deviance from a general public health point of view, Mercy (1999) has stated its nature concisely:

AUTHOR'S NOTE: The author thanks Fran Henry of STOP IT NOW! for helpful critical comments. Thanks also to Carmen Gress for preparation of Figure 17.1.

Imagine a childhood disease that affects one in five girls and one in seven boys before they reach 18 . . .: a disease that can cause dramatic mood swings, erratic behavior, and even severe conduct disorders among those exposed; a disease that breeds distrust of adults and undermines the possibility of experiencing normal sexual relationships; a disease that can have profound implications for an individual's future health by increasing the risk of problems such as substance abuse, sexually transmitted diseases, and suicidal behavior . . .; a disease that replicates itself by causing some of its victims to expose future generations to its debilitating effects.

Imagine what we, as a society, would do if such a disease existed. We would spare no expense. We would invest heavily in basic and applied research. We would devise systems to identify those affected and provide services to treat them. We would develop and broadly implement prevention campaigns to protect our children. Wouldn't we?

Such a disease does exist—it's called child sexual abuse. (p. 317)

Two observations follow from that quotation. First, Mercy (1999) is speaking of child sexual abuse, but much of what he says applies equally well to all forms of sexually abusive behavior. His remarks capture the pervasiveness and insidious nature of the problem. Second, the final paragraph of Mercy's remarks describes a classical public health approach to the problem. This approach has worked very well against smallpox, tuberculosis, polio, and to a lesser extent against drunk driving, smoking, and HIV/AIDS. It has not worked in the area of sexual offending because, for the most part, it has not been tried.

Levels of Prevention in Public Health

The classical public health approach identifies three levels of prevention: (a) primary, (b) secondary, and (c) tertiary (Henry, 1996; Laws, 2000; McMahon, 1997, 2000). Laws (2000, pp. 31-32) has described how this approach may be applied to sexual deviance.

The *primary* level of prevention is the classic public health approach. The goal is to prevent deviant behavior from ever starting. As McMahon (2000) has noted, the public health approach to sexual violence focuses upon primary prevention rather than treatment. Many people believe that this approach is exemplified in so-called just-say-no programs that teach potential victims, children or adults, how to avoid being victimized. Although that approach is primary prevention of a sort, it puts the onus of prevention upon actual or potential victims rather than upon perpetrators. Using public health methods for primary prevention would mean targeting adults generally about sexual abuse, its magnitude, who is at risk for abusing and being abused, and how to intervene or confront abusers if needed.

The *secondary* level of prevention is an intervention approach. Here the concern is with persons who have begun to engage in deviant sexual behavior. It is devoted to early identification and intervention. The secondary level would target children, adolescents, and adults. For example, adults would be made aware of signs of unusual sexual interest or activity in children. These might include inappropriate sexual talk, exhibitionism, masturbation, use of pornography, sexual precocity, antisocial attitudes or beliefs, or outright sexual aggression. Such signs should be viewed as deviant sexual behavior that requires intervention. Similarly, adolescent sexual behavior that exceeds accepted social boundaries should be viewed with some alarm and intervention considered. Situational (incest) or opportunistic offenders would fit into this level. At the secondary level of prevention it is acknowledged that deviant sexual behavior has occurred. A further assumption is that the behavioral pattern is not stable or chronic and that the individual may be amenable to treatment.

The *tertiary* level of prevention is the criminal justice approach. Here we are dealing with chronic offenders who very likely have deeply entrenched patterns of deviant sexual behavior and who have been offending for many years. These are the persons seen in medium- and maximum-security prisons, mental hospitals, and in the community postrelease. The word *prevention* is used here in the sense of preventing offending from occurring again, or at least occurring at a much lower frequency and intensity. McMahon (2000) has said that "one limitation of this approach is that there is no direct attempt to alter the conditions or attitudes that led the abuser to the point of abuse" (p. 28).

Persons seen at the tertiary level are usually candidates for intensive relapse prevention treatment, behavior therapy to modify deviant sexual arousal, or anti-androgenic treatments. The goal is always to stop the behavior now and keep it stopped.

Figure 17.1 summarizes the situation graphically. Although this figure was taken from the alcohol abuse literature, the message is equally applicable to sexual abuse. The triangle represents a spectrum of possible interventions. The area from the broad base of the triangle to the dotted line below "Mild" would represent no known sex offending. The focus here would be exclusively primary prevention. The area from "Mild" to the dotted line below "Substantial" would represent the secondary level. Identification and brief intervention would be applied here. From "Substantial" to the apex of the triangle is the area of tertiary intervention. Several things are noteworthy in this figure. First, primary and secondary prevention never stop. Second, fewer and fewer people are involved in intervention as the triangle narrows. Third, "specialized treatment," which is what most of us provide, is serving the smallest number of clients who have the most serious, perhaps intractable problems.

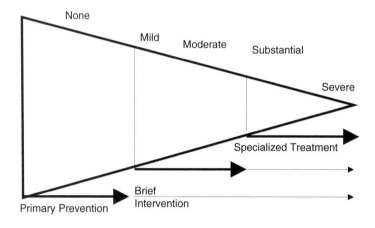

Figure 17.1   A Spectrum of Public Health Responses to Sexual Abuse
SOURCE: Reproduced from Marlatt (1998). Reprinted with permission.

Laws (2000) has summarized current efforts to prevent or alter sexual abuse in a classic public health model:

> In considering sexual violence in a public health perspective it would certainly be ideal if we could focus most of our efforts on primary prevention. While there is much room to exert effort at this level and effort is being exerted, it is far from adequate and much that could be done is simply ignored or put off as not urgent. Most of our efforts are applied at the secondary and tertiary levels and in the main [are] directed to the tertiary level where [they are] least likely to succeed. (p. 32)

The Public Health Approach to Sexual Violence

There are four major steps in the general public health approach (McMahon, 1997, 2000; Mercy, Rosenberg, Powell, Broome, & Roper, 1993) that may be equally applied to the problem of sexual violence (Laws, 2000). McMahon (2000, p. 30) describes the four steps:

   1. *Public health surveillance.* This is defined as "the ongoing, systematic collection, analysis, and interpretation of health data." Surveillance involves the tracking of trends in a public health problem. The data are then provided to policymakers who are in a position to do something about the problem.

2. *Risk factor research.* This step focuses upon "which factors place an individual at higher risk for an unhealthy consequence." Identification of a risk factor does not mean that all persons exposed to it will develop the consequence. It does say that the unhealthy consequence is more likely if a person is exposed to a specified factor.

3. *Development and evaluation of programs.* "The likelihood of having effective prevention programs . . . is increased if development of such programs is based on knowledge about modifiable risk factors identified in step two . . . and if the programs are evaluated and modified as suggested by evaluation results."

4. *Dissemination of information on what works.* The public health approach requires wide dissemination of information. This includes "conferences, journal publications, and networks and can be accompanied by direct consultation and technical assistance."

I turn now to an examination of how these steps have thus far been applied toward the goal of controlling deviant sexual behavior.

SURVEILLANCE

The dimensions and magnitude of the problem of sexual abuse are not well understood. Such information as we have does not neatly conform to the model presented by McMahon (2000). Rather, the information is scattered and comes from many sources. Following are some typical examples:

a. Macrolevel estimates such as the FBI Uniform Crime Reports are based on crimes known to the police; most sexual crimes are never reported.

b. Abel and his colleagues (Abel et al., 1987; Abel & Rouleau, 1990) have reported individual sex offenders having an enormous number of distinct paraphilias. These data are based on a highly deviant and unrepresentative sample.

c. Marshall and Barbaree (1988) examined unofficial sources such as complaints, police reports not resulting in charges, and social service investigations to assess the likelihood that a known offender might have committed an unadjudicated crime. They improved on the official record by a factor of 2.7.

d. STOP IT NOW! (2000a) reports that one in five girls and one in seven boys have been sexually abused before the age of 18. Ninety percent of these victims know their abusers (fathers, mothers, siblings, relatives, and other caretakers).

e. The Centers for Disease Control and Prevention (CDC; 2001) conducts the biennial Youth Risk Behavior Survey to assess the prevalence of health risk behaviors in high school students. Four of the sexual behaviors that were queried showed improvement in the period from 1991 to 1999. None of them dealt with sexually abusive behaviors.

f. CDC (2000) also publishes the Rape Fact Sheet based in part of the National Crime Victimization Survey, National Women's Study, and the Uniform Crime

Report. This report provides some limited information on prevalence and incidence, risk factors, and consequences.

These are not extreme examples but rather common ones that one finds in the literature. The message is quite clear: There is a huge problem of sexual abuse but even a reasonably accurate estimate of the incidence and prevalence is simply unknown. The preceding examples should be considered snapshots of the problem.

RISK FACTOR RESEARCH

Here we are faring better. The abovementioned rape fact sheet from the CDC is highly informative, but it is unsystematic and assembled from a variety of sources. In the sexual abuse field itself, and quite apart from public health issues, risk factor research has developed considerable momentum in recent years. First, the identification of risk factors is a main feature of relapse prevention treatment, the approach most favored with sex offenders (Laws, 1989, 1995; Laws, Hudson, & Ward, 2000; Marlatt & Gordon, 1985). The treatment centers on identification of high risk factors and the use of self-management strategies to deal with them. This is a fairly clear application of a secondary or tertiary level of prevention. Second, there has been a movement to develop risk assessment procedures to predict sexual offense recidivism. There are two types of assessment, actuarial risk assessment and structured professional guidelines to assess risk. Actuarial risk assessments are typically based on static (unchangeable) risk factors (prior offenses, age, victim gender, substance abuse, etc.). They attempt to predict the probability that an individual bearing certain factors will reoffend in a given time period (5 or 10 years). This approach is exemplified by the work of Quinsey, Harris, Rice, and Cormier (1998) and Hanson and Thornton (2000). Structured professional guidelines combine static and dynamic (changeable) risk factors. This approach, like the PCL-R (Hare, 1991), uses highly specific descriptors and instructions for scoring items. Rather than a probability statement, this approach makes the judgment that a person bearing the risk factor(s) is a low, moderate, or high risk for reoffense. This approach is exemplified in the work of Boer, Hart, Kropp, and Webster (1997) and Laws, Hart, and Kropp (2000). Risk factor research per se is another separate endeavor. Hanson and Bussiere (1998), in a meta-analysis of 67 sex offender recidivism studies, outlined a series of reoffense risk factors that has begun to have an impact on treatment design. Andrews and Bonta (1998) have been instrumental in tying risk facts to treatment goals. This approach has recently been subject to stringent review and critical analysis (see below; also Ward & Stewart, in press).

DEVELOPMENT AND EVALUATION
OF TREATMENT PROGRAMS

Although things have begun to change in recent years, the useful clinical yield in this area has been extremely low. From the mid-1970s to the late 1980s the National Institute of Mental Health (NIMH) rather lavishly funded a number of treatment demonstration projects. After 15 years it was apparent that the informational yield of these various programs was extremely low, and NIMH abandoned funding of these projects. This can now be seen, overall, as a misguided decision. A crucial and quite critical evaluation of sex offender treatment was published in 1989 by Furby, Weinrott, and Blackshaw. The review reported that early efforts at treatment were unsuccessful due to poor methodology and evaluation. These results were taken by many to indicate that sex offender treatment did not work. In fact, the authors offered specific suggestions for making things better, and these have largely been adopted in the succeeding 10 years. In 1985 the State of California took a chance and funded a major project for 10 years. This project examined the latest technology of cognitive-behavioral treatment conducted within a valid experimental design with a matched no-treatment control (Marques, 1984). The program terminated in 1995 and follow-up continued to 2000. The results were disappointing to many; they appeared to show that treatment might delay but not totally eliminate reoffense. Within the past decade there has been an incremental development of more positive results. Gordon and Nicolaichuk (1996) reported highly positive results for a prison-based program in Canada. The advent of meta-analysis has been a blessing for the evaluation of treatment outcome studies. Hall (1995) reported an analysis of treatment outcome studies over a 15-year period that showed a slight but positive effect. I think that we can safely state that even more positive results will be forthcoming in this decade. The problem in this area is that this work is being performed by single programs (Gordon & Nicolaichuk, 1996) or by individual researchers (Hall, 1995).

More recently, a promising approach was reported by Hanson et al. (2000, 2001). The Association for the Treatment of Sexual Abusers (ATSA) has established the Collaborative Outcome Data Project to examine treatment outcome data from multiple sites. Hanson et al. (2000, 2001) performed a meta-analysis of data from 43 studies (combined $n = 9,454$). Averaged across all studies, the sexual offense recidivism rate was 12.3% for the treated groups and 16.8% for the comparison groups (38 studies, unweighted average). For general recidivism the rates were considerably higher (treatment = 27.9%, comparison = 39.2%, 30 studies). Cognitive behavioral treatment ($k = 13$) and systemic treatment ($k = 2$) showed the greatest reductions in both sexual recidivism (from 17.4% to 9.9%) and general recidivism (from 51% to 32%). Forms of treatment operating before 1980 had little effect. It is ATSA's intent to report these data on an annual basis. In a general public health sense, this is indeed an encouraging approach.

There is, as yet, no coordinated national or international effort to fund this type of research and that is what is required for a true public health approach to this problem.

DISSEMINATION OF INFORMATION ON WHAT WORKS

There has thus far been no large-scale effort in the sexual abuse field to collate and disseminate information on exactly which assessment and treatment strategies appear to be most effective in maintaining treatment gains and reducing recidivism. What we have instead are rather persuasive meta-analyses that inform us about treatment outcome (Hall, 1995) or the risk factors predictive of recidivism (Hanson, 2000; Hanson & Bussiere, 1998). The latter is a truly impressive piece of work that targeted 61 treatment programs with a total of 23,393 participants. It is impossible to know if the risk factors identified by Hanson and Bussiere will be translated into specific treatment goals, particularly since some currently favored targets (e.g., victim empathy) were not shown to be predictive of recidivism. Presently the most impressive program worldwide is offered by HM Prison Service in the United Kingdom. It offers an integrated cognitive-behavioral treatment program implemented at 28 sites throughout the country. It has been under way for 10 years and probably has the largest database on sex offenders ever assembled. Unfortunately, this program has thus far published very little of its results and its impact is yet to be felt in North America where the information is most needed.

A controversy regarding what works and what does not has been ongoing in criminology for more than 25 years. Gendreau (1996) has cited the famous "nothing works" review by Martinson (1974) as kicking off the battle. He states that this paper was highly influential in justifying "abandoning rehabilitation and redirecting American correctional philosophy and practice to a new era of deterrence and 'doing justice'" (p. 145). In his view, severe deterrence policies (e.g., "Three Strikes You're Out") have come to dominate U.S. correctional policy. On the other hand, he says, during this same period an impressive number of studies have demonstrated effective treatment services in corrections. Gendreau cites in particular the meta-analysis of Lipsey (1992) as a review of all treatment studies that had control group comparisons. This was a review of 443 treatment programs. Sixty-four percent of the studies reported reductions in recidivism in favor of the treatment group. He summarizes Lipsey's (1992) findings:

> The average reduction in recidivism was 10%. . . . [W]hen the results were categorized by the general type of program . . . reductions in recidivism were as high

as 18%. . . . However, one must sort out those characteristics that differentiate between programs that reduced recidivism and those that did not. When that was done the results became even more impressive. Reductions in recidivism routinely ranged from 25% to 60%, with the greatest reductions found for community-based rather than prison programs. (Gendreau, 1996, pp. 148-149)

Gendreau (1996, pp. 149-150) then compared the characteristics of programs that reduced recidivism with those that did not. Keeping in mind that this is information from the correctional literature, note the similarity of the various approaches to sexual abuse treatment.

Characteristics of programs that reduced recidivism were:

1. The service was intensive, usually of a few month's duration.

2. The programs were behavioral, primarily of the cognitive and modeling type, targeting the criminogenic needs of high-risk offenders.

3. Programs were delivered in a manner that facilitated the learning of prosocial skills.

4. The program contingencies (rules) were enforced in a firm but fair manner.

5. Program structure and activities reached out into the offenders' real-world social network and disrupted the delinquency network by placing offenders in situations (i.e., among people and in places) where prosocial activities predominated.

It is worth noting that Item 5 is highly consistent with the general public health approach to social problems.

Programs that did not reduce recidivism contained some of the following items:

1. Used traditional psychodynamic or nondirective/client-centered therapies

2. Strategies based on subcultural and labeling perspectives on crime

3. "Punishing smarter" programs or any that concentrated on punishment/sanctions, such as boot camps, drug testing, electronic monitoring, restitution, or shock incarceration ("Scared Straight")

4. Any program, including behavioral ones, that targeted low-risk offenders or noncriminogenic needs or failed to focus upon multiple causes of offending

It is readily apparent that many of the above are present in sexual abuse treatment programs.

The work of Andrews and Bonta (1998) has been highly influential in the correctional field. They have developed a criminological theory based on three factors: risk, need, and responsivity. *Risk* in this sense refers to identifying those factors that are highly predictive of recidivism. These high-risk offenders are the ones believed to profit most from intensive treatment. Treatment, they say, must target "criminogenic needs" (i.e., those factors most likely to generate criminal behavior). Typical criminogenic needs include antisocial attitudes and behavior, impulsivity, delinquent peers, and so on. *Responsivity* refers to the principle that the treatment delivered must be relevant and responsive to the needs and abilities of the offenders. The notion of criminogenic need has filtered into the sexual abuse field through meta-analyses that identified specific risk factors (e.g., Hanson & Bussiere, 1998) and the development of actuarial risk predictors (e.g., Hanson & Thornton, 2000; Quinsey et al., 1998).

Ward and Stewart (in press) have subjected the Andrews and Bonta (1998) theory to a stringent critical analysis. They claim that the concepts of risk and need are confounded and that, overall, the theory delivers considerably less than it promises. These authors are particularly distressed that treatment goals consistently focus upon criminogenic risk factors and simply ignore noncriminogenic needs such as low self-esteem, anxiety, and personal distress. They argue that sex offenders are, after all, human beings who may desire and have a right to fulfilling personal lives. They state,

> when offenders agree to enter a rehabilitation programme they are implicitly asking therapists: "How can I live my life differently?" This requires clinicians to offer concrete possibilities for living [a] good or worthwhile life that takes into account each individual's abilities, circumstances, interests, and opportunities. Ethical questions involve clinicians in the consideration of what constitutes a worthwhile life and are not exhausted by issues related to their conduct. There is no discretion here, every therapeutic intervention is buttressed by assumptions about what constitutes a desirable outcome, and therefore points to [a] vision of human well being and fulfillment. The rehabilitation of offenders should be driven by an enhancement model.

Does this view signal a potential retreat back to the old, psychodynamic methods of treatment? I do not think so. Ward is a powerful cognitive-behaviorist voice in the sexual abuse field and he is calling for a broadening of treatment goals, not restriction, not retreat.

So where does this end? An aggressive public health model would agree with Ward and Stewart's (in press) recommendations. That model would urge the maximum effort to make offenders' lives better and more fulfilling while not removing the focus upon risk factors associated with interpersonal violence, abuse, and recidivism. However, until such time as what works is conceptualized, tested, and marketed on a far broader scale than anything imaginable today, we will remain right where we are—not stuck, but moving forward ever so slowly.

Sexual Abuse as a Public Health Issue

In a recent article McMahon and Puett (1999), speaking of child sexual abuse, have stated that, while violence per se is seen as a major public health issue, the abuse of children (or for that matter, any sexual abuse) has not received attention as a public health issue. They note, as I have above, that independent studies have provided some information on the epidemiology of the problem, have discovered risk factors for abuse, and have developed some promising programs. However, they say, there has been no systematic effort to target sexual abuse as a primary prevention goal.

In 1997, McMahon and Puett (1999) report, the CDC assembled a panel to advise the agency on developing a national response to child sexual abuse. This broadly based group represented federal and state agencies concerned with health issues, clinicians, former abusers, and victims of abuse. Their charge was to determine how to raise awareness of child sexual abuse as a public health problem and suggest how the federal government might respond to it. Three work groups were formed: (a) research, surveillance, and evaluation; (b) public awareness and education; and (c) public policy. In what follows I summarize the major findings of this panel (McMahon & Puett, 1999, pp. 260-265). The issues raised by this panel apply equally well to sexual violence and sexual abuse of all kinds. Where necessary, I have altered the authors' text to reflect this. Not all of the recommendations are included here.

RESEARCH, SURVEILLANCE, AND EVALUATION

This work group recommended the following:

1. Develop a standardized surveillance system that reports to state agencies. The goal is to capture both reported and unreported cases of abuse.

2. Identify risk factors for perpetration of sexual abuse. This could be accomplished through prospective studies comparing persons who become abusers with those who do not. Define treatment modalities and match these with abuser type.

3. Conduct research to determine the parameters of normative sexual behaviors and fantasies at various developmental stages.

4. Develop techniques that permit early identification and treatment of victims.

5. Encourage universities to offer courses on sexual abuse.

PUBLIC EDUCATION AND AWARENESS

This work group recommended the following:

1. Quickly disseminate research findings to the public and policymakers. What are the most promising practices for early intervention? Outcome studies are needed to determine treatment effectiveness. Cost/benefit issues must be examined.

2. Create a public health agency that deals only with sexual abuse.

3. Develop powerful, person-oriented messages about sexual abuse that will allow people to understand it free of defensiveness and denial.

4. Create a framework for the media to address sexual abuse frankly. The media's focus on sensational cases leads many middle-class people to believe that sexual abuse is not their problem.

5. Develop a consensus among experts on how to prevent and intervene in cases of sexual abuse. This should be framed as a community issue involving experts from various disciplines.

6. Target educational efforts toward medical and mental health professionals, the public, and the media.

POLICY ISSUES

To some extent, many of these recommendations overlap with the preceding. The work group recommended the following:

1. Elevate the position of sexual abuse on the national public health agenda. The CDC should encourage public health departments at the state and federal levels to address the issue. States should hold annual research and training meetings and disseminate information on promising programs.

2. Fund a nationwide study of the problem by the prestigious National Academy of Sciences.

3. Encourage collaboration among agencies dealing with sexual abuse.

4. Encourage foundations to support prevention and research activities.

5. Increase federal funding for research and evaluation.

6. Increase career development incentives in the sexual abuse area. These would be career development grants for clinicians/researchers working in this area.

7. Develop a strategy to increase political activism among adult survivors and their families.

In examining these recommendations one can easily see that this is an enormous task that would require determined involvement of the central government. McMahon and Puett (1999, p. 264) state that there are many barriers to the realization of these recommendations. There is no common reporting system across states, so there is no surveillance system. There is currently no spokesperson in public health to become the voice for this issue. Foundations do not typically support sexual abuse prevention. The media cover the sensational cases, not the everyday abuse that is the norm. The sociolegal attitude toward sex offenders assures them that, if they step forward and ask for treatment, what more likely awaits them are highly punitive sanctions. Finally, I might add, is the negative, denying attitude of the public in general. To the ordinary citizen, sexual abuse is something that is happening to someone else, on another street, in another town, anywhere but in his or her own backyard.

STOP IT NOW!: The Campaign to Prevent Child Sexual Abuse

STOP IT NOW! (2000a) is a community-based, public health organization that broadly considers all three levels of prevention. It is not a treatment program but is able to make appropriate referrals. Their position is that adults, not children or other victims of sexual abuse, are responsible for stopping sexual violence. Their goals are to increase awareness and knowledge about sexual abuse in both offenders and the general public. They encourage abusers to come forward, report their abuse, and make themselves accountable so they may be referred for treatment. In addition, they work with families, peers, and friends of abusers, helping them learn to confront the abusers. The main goal is to bring sexual abuse out of the shadows and make it a central object of community concern. STOP IT NOW! conducts media campaigns to educate the general public and to change governmental policy regarding sexual abuse. The organization is aware that there is a large and growing social science literature on sexual abuse. They note, however, that very little of that literature addresses sexual abuse from a public health point of view. Therefore, they conduct their own research through correspondence with recovering sex offenders, Internet-based questionnaires, and through focus groups. Their contacts with social scientists working in the sexual abuse area ensure that the organization's public health messages are received by professionals.

Chasan-Taber and Tabachnick (1999; CDC, 2001) have reported on a pilot program that STOP IT NOW! conducted in Vermont. The purpose of the pilot program was to "make an assessment of public attitudes and beliefs . . . in Vermont to identify facilitators and barriers to adult-targeted child sexual abuse prevention." The research was conducted by a market research group using what the authors call a "social marketing campaign."

Information was initially gathered by a telephone survey in 1995, then followed up in a second survey in 1997. Using random-digit dialing, they generated a representative sample of 200 Vermont residents; 67.3% agreed to participate. The researchers then asked the participants if they were familiar with the term *child sexual abuse,* what they thought it was, and to identify characteristics or warning signs of sexually abusive behavior. The results indicated that most adults were familiar with the term. However, only about half could define the term. Two thirds of the families believed that sex offenders lived in their communities but were unsure of what signs might indicate who was an abuser. Slightly less than one third believed that abusers could stop their behavior.

The researchers also formed two small focus groups for each of three target audiences: adult male abusers, friends and families of adult abusers, and parents of adolescent abusers. This approach was conducted within treatment groups and support groups, and was supplemented by interviews and questionnaires. The work with the focus groups was based on a public health research procedure that enables researchers to organize information into a framework that will guide the choice of intervention strategies. Table 17.1 shows the results of the work with the focus groups. Chasan-Taber and Tabachnick (1999) describe the information in the table:

> This framework suggests the assessment of predisposing, enabling, and reinforcing factors. Predisposing factors deal with a person's knowledge, attitudes, beliefs, values, and perceptions. These are the social and psychological forces that may motivate or inhibit an individual or group to participate in child sexual abuse prevention programs. . . . Enabling factors refer to the availability and accessibility of specific resources or skills and policies and procedures that enhance or inhibit appropriate preventive action. . . . Reinforcing factors are those elements that appear subsequent to the behavior and provide continuing incentives for the behavior to become persistent. (pp. 282-283)

STOP IT NOW! then began their social marketing program. The goal was to (a) increase adult awareness and knowledge about sexual abuse, and (b) to have an impact on abusive behavior. They blanketed the media, providing information on radio, cable and network television, editorials and stories in newspapers, bus advertising, an interactive Web site, and advertising banners. All of this was directed toward the three target audiences. They established one-to-one outreach through treatment providers and other professionals, parent groups, victim advocacy groups, public agencies, and nonprofit

Table 17.1   Factors Influencing Adults to Prevent Child Sexual Abuse

Facilitator	Barrier
Predisposing factors: Knowledge, attitudes, beliefs, values, and perceptions	
Universal familiarity with the term child sexual abuse	More than 50% do not know the characteristics of an abuser
Over 75% agree that child sexual abuse is a serious problem	Fear of bringing more harm to a child by reporting the abuse
Over 50% believe that abusers live in their communities	Fear of confronting family members who may be abusing
Those abused as a child or those college educated are more likely to know an abuser or victim	Adults over 55 less likely to know an abuser or victim
Almost all residents agree that children are most likely abused by someone they know	35% cannot give any definition of *child sexual abuse*
Enabling factors: Resources, skills, or policies that affect appropriate preventive actions	
Over 90% said they would act if they were definitely sure an adult was abusing	Only 75% would act if they were unsure an adult was abusing
70% would contact police or protective services if they were definite about the abuse	Only 27% would contact police or protective services if they were unsure of the abuse
Media accessible for public service message	59.5% do not know where to refer someone with sexual behavior problems
Responsive child protection system	Lack of technique for confronting someone
Mandatory reporting to ensure children's report reaches appropriate agency	who may be sexually abusing a child
Significant investment of policy makers in prevention programs	Mandatory reporting might inhibit friends and families from seeking help
Reinforcing factors: Incentives for behaviors to become persistent	
Model program in Vermont for treatment of abusers, victims, and family members	Public perception that sexual abusers cannot be cured
Support groups for family members	Isolation felt by those who have experienced sexual abuse
Small communities where people's actions have consequences	47% did not talk about sexual abuse in the last year

SOURCE: L. Chasan-Taber & J. Tabachnick (1999, p. 282). Reproduced with permission.

organizations. They also set up workshops, conferences, and training, and provided informational materials. A toll-free help line was established to enable offenders to self-report as well as to receive information and, if necessary, a referral to treatment providers. Abusers were given a confidential ID number. Using the code, the abuser could telephone a clinician and be evaluated without being reported to the police or child protective organizations.

The success of the first 2 years of the program was evaluated in 1997. This included a second telephone survey, interviews with a number of "key decision makers and leaders" in Vermont, and an analysis of the effectiveness of the telephone help line. The telephone survey revealed a 20% increase in recognition of the term child sexual abuse. There was a 10% increase in the belief that sex offenders probably live in one's community. People were still uncertain that offenders could stop their behavior but thought that treatment might be effective. Interviewees were less certain of what to do if confronted with a situation of sexual abuse. The community leaders were able to accurately describe the nature of the STOP IT NOW! program. They identified an increase in public awareness, getting abusers into treatment programs, and advancing the concept that abusers are human as the main contributions of the program. By late autumn 1997 the help line had received 241 calls. Twenty-three percent were from abusers and half from persons who were aware of abuse. The balance was primarily requests for information.

In 2000, STOP IT NOW! (2000b) reported on a 1999 follow-up of the social marketing program. They summarized the results of the second follow-up under four major headings:

1. *Abusers will call for help.* In the first 4 years there were 657 calls to the help line. Fifteen percent of the calls came from abusers and 50% from persons who were acquainted with an abuser or a victim. About 25% heard of the help line through the media, 29% from the STOP IT NOW! Web site, and 25% from professionals or other help lines or agencies.

2. *There was an increase in adults who can talk about sexual abuse.* Citizens who could explain what child abuse is almost doubled in 4 years. Overall awareness of the problem was high.

3. *Adults need better skills to stop abuse.* By 1999, 38% of citizens could name at least one warning sign of sexual abuse. Eighty-eight percent said that they would take direct action if they "definitely" were aware of sexual abuse. However, this fell to 66% if abuse was merely "suspected." Sixty-six percent of respondents said that they had never reported their own abuse. Only 54% of respondents knew where to refer a sexual abuser, compared with 77% who knew where to refer someone with a drinking problem. Only 19% agreed that abusers could stop if they wanted to, but 69% agreed that they could stop with appropriate treatment. When presented with scenarios, 43% of respondents either did not know if the case was sexual abuse or "might be" abuse. The

authors state (STOP IT NOW!, 2000b), "Adults do not seem aware of their potential role in preventing . . . abuse: identifying emerging problems, confronting difficult situations, reporting suspicions of sexual abuse, or referring someone to a qualified treatment provider" (p. 4).

4. *Abusers stopping the abuse.* The program identified 118 people who voluntarily sought assistance for sexual behavior problems (20 adults, 98 adolescents). Through states attorneys and victim advocates, the program identified 15 adults and 10 adolescents who turned themselves in to the legal system.

The two evaluations of the pilot program of STOP IT NOW! tell us several things. First, they show that a community-based grassroots effort can succeed in promoting a general public health effort aimed at an extremely serious social problem. In a very real sense, STOP IT NOW! has done what the U.S. government, with its vast array of resources, has not had the courage to undertake.

Second, considering the amount of effort and high skill level that went into the social marketing campaign, the results are quite encouraging but, in overall impact, they will be somewhat disappointing to some. However, this began as a pilot program and the evaluations report results from only the first 4 years. These data will undoubtedly improve over time. Third, and perhaps the most important message, is that Vermont is one of the smallest of the U.S. states. If, in 4 years of intensive campaigning, it remains difficult to get STOP IT NOW!'s very important social message across, imagine the task of getting it out to the remaining 49 states.

Conclusion

As clinicians and researchers in the area of sexual abuse we like to pride ourselves on the fact that, unlike most people, we have voluntarily undertaken the fight against a pervasive social menace. And so we should. It is often forgotten that, in reality, we are holding our fingers in the dike, struggling to hold back the inexorable flood of sexual abuse. That is admirable, to be sure, but it is a battle that we are not winning. As I attempted to show in the brief discussion of Figure 17.1, most of our therapeutic efforts are focused at the tertiary level, and to a lesser extent, at the secondary level. This is perfectly understandable because here reside the identified offenders who are available to us. If we are ever to have a major impact upon the problem of sexual abuse, we must focus intense effort on primary prevention, stopping the behavior before it ever gets started.

We must not wait for anybody's central government to do something about this problem. That might or might not happen. Governments may acknowledge that sexual abuse is indeed a public health problem, but given the intensely negative social climate concerning sexual offending, they are far more likely to leave it up to the police, the courts, and the correctional system to address the problem. That this approach has not been very successful is manifestly evident.

If we are to do enough, if we are to make a difference that makes a difference, I suggest that we adopt a model such as that pioneered by STOP IT NOW! They have already done much of the research on how to make social marketing work, and they are willing to share that information with anyone. If enough centers undertook this public health model and reported their results to a central organization such as STOP IT NOW!, The Association for the Treatment of Sexual Abusers (ATSA), or the American Professional Society on Abuse of Children (APSAC), an enormous database could be compiled within a very few years. Armed with this information we could confidently approach federal and state governments and demand an endorsement of a public health approach to sexual abuse. We should never abandon the efforts in which we are now engaged. But it will only be when we commit ourselves to a primary prevention approach that we will be able to confidently say that we have done enough.

References

Abel, G. G., Becker, J. V., Mittelman, M. S., Cunningham-Rathner, J., Rouleau, J. L., & Murphy, W. D. (1987). Self-reported sex crimes of nonincarcerated paraphiliacs. *Journal of Interpersonal Violence, 2,* 3-25.

Abel, G. G., & Rouleau, J.-L. (1990). The nature and extent of sexual assault. In W. L. Marshall, D. R. Laws, & H. E. Barbaree (Eds.), *The handbook of sexual assault* (pp. 9-21). New York: Plenum.

Andrews, D. A., & Bonta, J. (1998). *The psychology of criminal conduct* (2nd ed.). Cincinnati, OH: Anderson.

Boer, D. P., Hart, S. D., Kropp, P. R., & Webster, C. D. (1997). *Manual for the Sexual Violence Risk—20.* Vancouver: The British Columbia Institute Against Family Violence.

Evaluation of a child sexual abuse prevention program—Vermont, 1995-1997. (2001, March 7). *Journal of the American Medical Association, 285,* 1147-1148. (Reprinted from Centers for Disease Control and Prevention *Morbidity and Mortality Weekly Report,* 2001)

Centers for Disease Control and Prevention (CDC), National Center for Injury Prevention and Control. (2000). Rape fact sheet: Prevalence and incidence. Atlanta, GA: Author. Retrieved June 16, 2001, from http://www.cdc.gov/ncipc/factsheets/rape.htm

Centers for Disease Control and Prevention (CDC), National Center for Chronic Disease Prevention and Health Promotion. (2001). Fact sheet: Youth risk behavior trends. Atlanta, GA: Author. Retrieved July 11, 2001, from http://cdc.gov/nccdphp/dash/yrbs/trend.htm

Chasan-Taber, L., & Tabachnick, J. (1999). Evaluation of a child sexual abuse program. *Sexual Abuse: A Journal of Research and Treatment, 11,* 279-292.

Furby, L., Weinrott, M. R., & Blackshaw, L. (1989). Sex offender recidivism: A review. *Psychological Bulletin, 105,* 3-30.

Gendreau, P. (1996). Offender rehabilitation: What we know and what needs to be done. *Criminal Justice and Behavior, 23,* 144-161.

Gordon, A., & Nicolaichuk, T. (1996). Applying the risk principle to sex offender treatment. *Forum on Corrections Research, 8,* 36-38.

Hall, G. C. N. (1995). Sexual offender recidivism revisited: A meta-analysis of recent treatment studies. *Journal of Consulting and Clinical Psychology, 63,* 802-809.

Hanson, R. K. (2000). *Risk assessment.* Beaverton, OR: Association for the Treatment of Sexual Abusers.

Hanson, R. K., & Bussiere, M. T. (1998). Predicting relapse: A meta-analysis of sexual offender recidivism studies. *Journal of Consulting and Clinical Psychology, 66,* 348-362.

Hanson, R. K., Gordon, A., Harris, A. J. R., Marques, J. K., Murphy, W., Quinsey, V. L., & Seto, M. C. (2000, November). *The effectiveness of treatment for sexual offenders: Report of the Association for the Treatment of Sexual Abusers Collaborative Data Research Committee.* Plenary presented at the meeting of the Association for the Treatment of Sexual Abusers, San Diego.

Hanson, R. K., Gordon, A., Harris, A. J. R., Marques, J. K., Murphy, W., Quinsey, V. L., & Seto, M. C. (2001). *First report of the Collaborative Outcome Data Project on the effectiveness of psychological treatment of sexual offenders.* Manuscript submitted for publication.

Hanson, R. K., & Thornton, D. (2000). Improving risk assessment for sex offenders: Comparison of three actuarial scales. *Law and Human Behavior, 24,* 119-135.

Hare, R. D. (1991). *Manual for the Psychopathy Checklist—Revised.* Toronto: Multi-Health Systems.

Henry, F. (1996, November). *Creating public policy through innovative prevention strategies.* Plenary address at the annual meeting of the Association for the Treatment of Sexual Abusers, Chicago.

Laws, D. R. (Ed.). (1989). *Prevention of relapse in sex offenders.* New York: Guilford.

Laws, D. R. (1995). A theory of relapse prevention. In W. O'Donohue & L. Krasner (Eds.), *Theories of behavior therapy* (pp. 445-473). Washington, DC: American Psychological Association.

Laws, D. R. (2000). Sexual offending as a public health problem: A North American perspective. *The Journal of Sexual Aggression, 5,* 30-44.

Laws, D. R., Hart, S. D., & Kropp, P. R. (2000, November). *Structured professional guidelines for assessing risk in sex offenders.* Symposium presented at the meeting of the Association for the Treatment of Sexual Abusers, San Diego, CA.

Laws, D. R., Hudson, S. M., & Ward, T. (Eds.). (2000). *Remaking relapse prevention with sex offenders.* Thousand Oaks, CA: Sage.

Lipsey, M. W. (1992). Juvenile delinquency treatment: A meta-analytic inquiry into the variability of effects. In T. D. Cook, H. Cooper, D. S. Cordray, H. Hartmann, L. V. Hedges, R. J. Light, T. A. Louis, & F. Mosteller (Eds.), *Meta-analysis for explanation* (pp. 83-127). New York: Russell Sage.

Marlatt, G. A. (1998). *Harm reduction: Pragmatic strategies for managing high-risk behaviors.* New York: Guilford.

Marlatt, G. A., & Gordon, J. R. (1985). *Relapse prevention: Maintenance strategies in the treatment of addictive behaviors.* New York: Guilford.

Marques, J. K. (1984). *An innovative treatment program for sex offenders: Report to the Legislature in response to 1983/84 Budget Act Item.* Sacramento: California Department of Mental Health.

Marshall, W. L., & Barbaree, H. E. (1988). The long-term evaluation of a behavioral treatment program for child molesters. *Behaviour Research and Therapy, 26,* 499-511.

Martinson, R. (1974). What works? Questions and answers about prison reform. *The Public Interest, 35,* 22-54.

McMahon, P. M. (1997, October). *The public health approach to the prevention of sexual violence.* Plenary presented at the meeting of the Association for the Treatment of Sexual Abusers, Arlington, VA.

McMahon, P. M. (2000). The public health approach to the prevention of sexual violence. *Sexual Abuse: A Journal of Research and Treatment, 12,* 27-36.

McMahon, P. M., & Puett, R. C. (1999). Child sexual abuse as a public health issue: Recommendations of an expert panel. *Sexual Abuse: A Journal of Research and Treatment, 11,* 257-266.

Mercy, J. A. (1999). Having new eyes: Viewing child sexual abuse as a public health problem. *Sexual Abuse: A Journal of Research and Treatment, 11,* 317-321.

Mercy, J. A., Rosenberg, M. L., Powell, K. E., Broome, C. V., & Roper, W. L. (1993). Public health policy for preventing violence. *Health Affairs, 12,* 7-29.

Quinsey, V. L., Harris, G. T., Rice, M. E., & Cormier, C. A. (1998). *Violent offenders: Appraising and managing risk.* Washington, DC: American Psychological Association.

STOP IT NOW! (2000a). About STOP IT NOW! Haydenville, MA: Author. Retrieved July 6, 2001 from the World Wide Web: http://www.stopitnow.com/about.htm

STOP IT NOW! (2000b). Four year evaluation: Findings reveal success of STOP IT NOW! VERMONT (Report #5). Haydenville, MA: Author.

Ward, T., & Stewart, C. (in press). Criminogenic needs and human needs: A theoretical model. *Psychology, Crime, & Law.*

18

Enhancing Relapse Prevention Through the Effective Management of Sex Offenders in the Community

Astrid Birgden

Karen Owen

Bea Raymond
Sex Offender Programs, CORE-the Public
Correctional Enterprise, Dept. of Justice, Victoria, Australia

M ost state-of-the-art sex offender intervention programs are based on the theoretical assumption that relapse is a chain of behavior occurring across time influenced by cognitive, affective, and contextual factors. Relapse prevention was originally developed by Marlatt and colleagues in relation to drug and alcohol addiction (Marlatt, 1985). Rather than prevent the occurrence of problematic behavior, relapse prevention aims to prevent the recurrence of such behavior (Hanson, 2000; Ward & Hudson, 1998). The model is based on cognitive-behavioral/social learning theory and is influenced by notions of learned habits, attributional biases, self-efficacy, situational influences, and decision chains (Hanson, 2000). In this context, relapse prevention can best be described as a package of self-management strategies and skills to manage threats to drug or alcohol abstinence (Laws, Hudson, & Ward, 2000).

The relapse prevention model was later adapted to sex offenders by Pithers, Marques, Gibat, and Marlatt (1983). The model closely reflects Marlatt's behavioral chain from abstinence to relapse and has since become the treatment of choice (Laws et al., 2000). Essentially, relapse prevention with sex offenders aims to (a) instill the capacity to recognize the factors and situations that initiate the offense chain; (b) help identify the steps in the offense chain and associated thoughts, feelings, and behaviors; (c) provide coping skills to deal with future problems that can place sex offenders at risk; and (d) generate a relapse prevention plan to reduce the likelihood of being in future high-risk situations (Marshall & Anderson, 2000). An urge to sexually offend (i.e., a lapse) is viewed not as a permanent feature but as a personal choice, and therapists should demonstrate to sex offenders that they have the capacity to be offense-free.

Nevertheless, Laws et al. (2000) warn that relapse prevention's popularity has also been its undoing. Its broad acceptance, ease of implementation, and good face validity have meant that little research to determine its efficacy has been conducted. A number of conceptual and empirical problems with the original relapse prevention model have been highlighted (Ward & Hudson, 1996). First, relapse prevention was originally designed to manage addictive drug- and alcohol-related behaviors that may be generalized to impulse control disorders such as the paraphilias, but no farther. Therefore, indiscriminate application to all sex offenders results in treatment poorly matched to needs. Second, a variety of posttreatment interventions have been described as relapse prevention but do not necessarily reflect the original model. Third, the model fails to understand why some offenders desist from reoffending. Fourth, it is assumed that sex offenders are highly motivated to change behavior and that they provide accurate accounts of their behavior. Furthermore, Laws et al. (2000) recommend that sex offending should be viewed as a public health problem within the purview of the community, not just the province of law, psychology, or medicine.

This chapter addresses relapse prevention in the context of a service delivery model in Victoria, Australia. The assumptions that the model is based on are (a) relapse prevention is applied after cognitive-behavioral intervention; (b) relapse prevention plans are based on such interventions, which in turn are based on individualized case formulations regarding offense pathways; and (c) motivation to change sex offending behavior is not necessarily present. A difference from accepted relapse prevention practice is that greater emphasis is placed on the external supervision component of the relapse prevention model. This emphasis is enhanced by the application of stages of change readiness, motivational principles, and dramatherapy techniques. Within this context, motivation to change is seen as adaptational; the way sex offenders respond to the criminal justice system is normal under the circumstances.

External Supervision in Relapse Prevention

Motivation to change sex offending is both internal and external. Therefore, successful relapse prevention programs require internal and external components (Marshall & Anderson, 2000; Pithers, 1990). The internal self-management component involves training in the language and concepts of relapse prevention, identification of risk factors, identification of offense chains, and assistance to develop relapse prevention plans. The external supervisory component involves extensive postdischarge supervision to maintain change. In order to reduce reoffense rates, it is recommended that treatment services be combined with community supervision (Cumming & McGrath, 2000; English, Pullen, & Jones, 1996). It is our view that the external component in relapse prevention has received less attention in service delivery models in the sex offender field. As a reflection of this, accreditation criteria for sex offender treatment programs in the United Kingdom and Canada appear to focus on aspects of intervention strategies delivered by therapists to enhance self-management to the detriment of management strategies delivered by correctional staff, and other agencies, to maintain self-management.

One recent study has considered the external component. Marques, Nelson, Alarcon, and Day (2000) have determined reoffending rates in sex offenders who have received intensive supervision and community treatment for up to one year postrelease in California. The authors report that whether offenders skilled in relapse prevention are at lower risk of reoffense cannot yet be determined. Marshall and Anderson (2000) postulated that the intensity of the postrelease supervision might have convinced sex offenders that they were unable to manage relapse prevention plans on their own. However, Marshall and Anderson failed to consider that aftercare support was provided by numerous private clinicians, and adequate housing, employment, and social support were not available (i.e., no coordinated approach). Marques et al. are yet to determine whether subsequent changes to include state-provided aftercare treatment and greater transitional support will improve outcomes.

As outlined above, relapse prevention has an internal and external component. Cumming and McGrath (2000) indicate that sex offender programs in the United States initially relied upon an internal self-management component alone, which resulted in offenders not providing full disclosure to community corrections officers upon release for fear of being returned to prison. As a result, an external supervisory dimension was developed. The elements include community corrections officers being trained in relapse prevention to supervise a caseload of sex offenders and increased collaboration with therapists.

Sex Offender Programs in Victorian Corrections

Treatment programs for sex offenders have existed for a decade within the Victorian correctional system, commencing in 1991-1992. In prison, a moderate-intensity sex offender treatment program was delivered and follow-up support in the community was provided by appropriate government and nongovernment agencies. In community corrections, one sex offender treatment group cofacilitated by a psychologist and a community corrections officer was piloted. Training in community corrections focused upon typologies and characteristics of sex offenders and the relapse prevention model. Training was not skill based nor did it involve ongoing clinical supervision.

By 1996, community corrections officers had begun to rely upon relapse prevention workbooks developed by Freeman-Longo and Bays (1994a, 1994b) to guide individual intervention with sex offenders. This meant that relapse prevention plans were being developed with offenders in the absence of cognitive-behavioral intervention. This is despite the fact that motivation is an important precondition for relapse prevention strategies, and relapse prevention in itself cannot induce motivation (Hanson, 2000). Such an approach served to reinforce assumptions about relapse prevention challenged earlier, namely, that offenders would be motivated to change and that offense processes followed a particular pathway. However, at the time, as outlined by Laws et al. (2000) in a different context, this approach may have offered correctional staff "a model and a language that reduced treatment providers' anxieties with respect to what they were attempting to do" (p. 21). In summary, the prison-based and community-based approaches in Victoria largely functioned as parallel services rather than a coordinated statewide approach within the Department of Justice.

In 1996, a "continuum of care" approach across the public correctional system was initiated. It involved a statewide coordinated assessment, intervention, and management approach to all convicted male sex offenders (perpetrators against both adults and children). Sex offenders accommodated in private prisons are transferred to the public prison system for intervention toward the end of their sentence. The result has been that numerous cognitive-behavioral treatment programs of moderate and high intensity and maintenance programs after treatment are delivered by CORE Sex Offender Programs to sentenced prisoners, offenders sentenced to community dispositions, and parolees. At any one time (i.e., "snapshot" data), an average of 723 convicted sex offenders are in the public correctional system, with 55% of these being managed on community dispositions (12- or 24-month orders; Birgden & Langthaler, 2001). After 4 years, the Program was reviewed by Professor Stephen M. Hudson, guided by the U.K. accreditation criteria (Hudson, 1999). The program is consequently undergoing refinement.

We believe the Program has placed greater emphasis than other jurisdictions on the external supervisory component of relapse prevention; therapists assist offenders to develop internal self-management, and community correction officers provide the external supervisory component to assist offenders with their relapse prevention plans. Relapse prevention support is delivered within the context of environmental management throughout the sentence to assist sex offenders to develop healthy lifestyles and positive coping strategies rather than merely learn avoidance strategies (as recommended by Cumming & McGrath, 2000). To further enhance a continuum of care approach, inter-agency protocols and working relationships have been developed with the Victorian Adult Parole Board, child protection authorities, forensic psychiatry services, specialist police squads, and community-based victim/survivor support agencies. In his review of the CORE Sex Offender Programs, Hudson (1999) noted that, "[T]he existence of the 'continuum of care' framework is exemplary . . . the sheer number of agencies involved that are both aware of what sex offender treatment is about and what [the Program] can provide, is amazing" (p. 4). The Program trains and consults to correctional staff and other agencies to facilitate the model of service delivery.

THE CHANGING ROLE OF CORRECTIONAL STAFF

In reconsidering a training approach to the effective management of sex offenders, a needs analysis for community correction officers was conducted by the Program (Owen & Keogan, 1996). An analysis of the 100 respondents indicated that the officers used work practices that were drawn from the previous model of training. The belief had been incorporated that offender denial and minimization were deliberate strategies used by offenders to avoid responsibility for offenses. This view can be described as the criminogenic model, where the sex offender is a "bad" person in a "bad" situation who is acting "badly" in being uncooperative (Rogers & Dickey, 1991). As a result, confrontation techniques were used with the goal that the offender was to "confess" to the offense and then develop a relapse prevention plan. Again, this was in the absence of prior cognitive-behavioral interventions. Often the outcome was an unproductive supervisory relationship between officers and sex offenders. Staff expressed concern that they had not received skill-based training in sex offender management.

As a result of the needs analysis, a statewide training strategy was devised to address these issues. Change in offending behavior is equally affected by the motivation of sex offenders and the skill of staff. Before we outline the model to train correctional staff in the effective management of sex offenders, theoretical work concerning behavior change in clients and required skills in staff is considered.

Enhancing Motivation to Change

Motivation to change as a treatment factor has been addressed with addictive behaviors such as substance abuse, although the efficacy of interventions to address this issue remains unclear. As outlined previously, there are theoretical difficulties with the adaptation of the relapse prevention model to sex offenders centered on assumptions about motivation. A major difference from addictive behaviors is the greater level of denial and minimization exhibited by sex offenders due to the nature of the offenses. Because of this presentation, sex offenders are often considered unmotivated to change. However, denial and minimization are seen as important clinical factors to be treated as risk indicators of future offences (Hogue & Peebles, 1997). Essential preconditions for behavior change are that the client is motivated, has positive expectations regarding the outcome, and a warm trusting relationship with the therapist(s) has been established (Miller, 1985; Prochaska & DiClemente, 1982; Prochaska, DiClemente, & Norcross, 1992). As with treatment programs, staff training should be based on theoretical assumptions about what underpins motivation to change and how an individual will deal with unpleasant states and situations, make free choices, and make informed decisions.

Three psychological theories underpin techniques in the development and maintenance of change in clients with behavioral problems. *Cognitive dissonance* occurs when contradictory behavior and attitudes create an unpleasant state. The individual therefore seeks to reduce this state through attitude change, removal and replacement of inconsistent attitudes, or trivialization of the dissonant element. Free choice is important in this process as it improves the efficacy of the outcome (Draycott & Dabbs, 1998). *Self-efficacy* (or self-appraisal about how well one can perform actions to deal with a situation) influences emotions, cognitions, and behavior (Bandura, 1997). Self-efficacy increases as individuals gain new skills to manage situations that threaten them. *Decisional balance* is also required when individuals weigh the gains and losses associated with a particular course of action when decisions are required (Janis & Mann, 1977). These psychological theories underpin theories and techniques to enhance and maintain behavior change in clients with addictive behavior problems, including relapse prevention.

STAGES AND PROCESSES OF CHANGE

An empirically based theory for behavior change in addictive behaviors has been provided by Prochaska and his colleagues. Based upon the comparison of 18 leading psychological therapies, Prochaska developed a general explanatory model in order to determine how individuals change addictive health-related behaviors (Prochaska & DiClemente, 1982; Prochaska, DiClemente, & Norcross, 1992; Prochaska & Norcross, 1994; Prochaska & Prochaska, 1999). The transtheoretical (or across theories) model incorporates psychological theories outlined above to explain how individuals motivate themselves to change behavior.

Briefly, the identified stages of change readiness are: (a) Precontemplation: lack of awareness of a problem and no intention to change; (b) Contemplation: awareness of a problem and thoughts about change; (c) Preparation: small behavioral changes; (d) Action: modification of behavior and the environment to reach an acceptable criterion; and (e) Maintenance: the consolidation of gains and effort to prevent relapse. The model can be described as a cognitive-behavioral approach integrating verbal processes and environmental management. Clients change emotions, cognitions, and behavior as they move through stages of change readiness.

In addictive behaviors, relapse is considered a rule rather than an exception, and clients can potentially return to the Contemplation Stage or Preparation Stage. The factors that determine relapse are influenced by the strength of the behavior, strength of commitment, environmental contingencies, and adequacy of maintenance strategies or skills. Relapse is also influenced by self-efficacy; the more clients feel they are able to deal with internal and external pressures, the more likely they will be able to resist relapse. Behavior change occurs when clients attain maximum self-efficacy and minimum temptation to engage in problem behaviors across risky situations.

MOTIVATIONAL INTERVIEWING

Motivational interventions increase the likelihood that clients will enter, continue, and comply with active change strategies (Miller, 1985; Miller & Rollnick, 1991). Motivational interviewing is a brief, client-centered intervention for eliciting behavior change. As outlined above, the client is assisted to explore and resolve ambivalence about health-related behavioral change (Rollnick & Miller, 1995). It is a technique founded on motivational psychology and complements the stages of change readiness model (Lawendowski, 1998). In essence, motivational interviewing involves a therapeutic relationship; it relies upon client articulation of goals and motives for present or potential problems, and emphasizes freedom of choice. Strategies used are persuasive and supportive rather than coercive or argumentative (Miller & Rollnick, 1991).

In this form of intervention, client resistance or denial is seen as a defense mechanism in response to therapist behaviors of diagnostic labels, threats, coercion, confrontation, and argumentation. Wagner and Conners (2002) warn of "traps" that therapists may experience when dealing with resistant clients that may induce a client to argue, interrupt, deny the problem, or ignore the therapist. Potential traps include the following: question/answer eliciting client passivity, confrontation/denial with the client countering with arguments against change, being an expert providing premature direction, diagnostic labeling, premature focus on problems, and the view that the client is to blame. Miller and Rollnick list five principles of motivational interviewing to be delivered by therapists to defuse resistance: (a) Express empathy: listen reflectively and accept ambivalence as normal; (b) Develop discrepancy: highlight differences between present drug use and goals to motivate change, discuss consequences, and encourage the client to present a case for change; (c) Avoid argumentation: disagreements are counterproductive, labels are unnecessary, and resistance is a signal to change strategies; (d) Roll with resistance: the client is a valuable resource for solutions, and new perspectives can be invited but not imposed; and (e) Support self-efficacy: belief in the possibility of change as a motivator, client choice from a range of alternatives, and client mastery of behavioral change.

APPLICATION TO SEX OFFENDERS

The stages of change readiness, motivational interviewing, and a combination of both have recently been applied to offenders (e.g., Garland & Dougher, 1991; Harper & Hardy, 2000; Mann, 1996, 2000; Serin & Kennedy, 2002). In Victoria, stage of change readiness was specifically applied to sex offenders in an evaluation of the Program (Tierney, 2001). As with relapse prevention, it is again the application of strategies designed for addictive and other health-related behaviors. Both stages of change readiness and motivational interviewing complement the relapse prevention model because it allows offenders to be guided in a nonconfrontational manner to arrive at their own source of motivation (Marques et al., 2000).

Together, motivational interviewing and the transtheoretical model encourage change in clients in relation to addictive behaviors; stage of change readiness provides the theoretical underpinning and motivational interviewing the technique. In relation to sex offenders, Mann (2000) indicates that this link requires three preconditions: (a) offenders have made the decision to stop sex offending; (b) offenders accept the relapse prevention model; and (c) offenders believe that high-risk situations can be managed through self-monitoring, cognitive control, and behavioral strategies on a lifelong basis. Cognitive-behavioral intervention is therefore required first, to increase the likelihood of its success. In applying relapse prevention principles to sex offenders, considerable effort is required to maintain offender motivation (Hanson, 2000; Mann, 2000; Marques et al., 2000) particularly after treatment. In this context it is proposed that community corrections officers provide relapse prevention support through the use of motivational techniques.

DRAMATHERAPY TECHNIQUES

A more useful explanation than the criminogenic model outlined is the adaptational model where sex offenders perceive themselves to be in an adversarial position, that they have something to lose from disclosure, and that denial and minimization are the most effective means to respond (Rogers & Dickey, 1991). That is, the sex offender is neither "mad" nor "bad," but has weighed up the costs and benefits. Marques et al. (2000) indicate that relapse prevention strategies can be enhanced by greater emphasis on beliefs and attitudes that underlie motivational deficits. In the criminal justice system, dramatherapy has been used as a method to change offending attitudes and behaviors in serious offenders. As with the transtheoretical model and motivational interventions, dramatherapy is client centered. In addition, it is a group-based, interpersonal, interactive, and educational technique (Reiss, Quayle, Brett, & Meux, 1998). The premise of dramatherapy is that offenders make active choices and have individual volition. This concept sits well with the application of psychological theories that underlie the transtheoretical model (i.e., self-efficacy and decisional balance). Theatrical exercises are integrated with cognitive-behavioral principles with a particular emphasis on responsibility for behavior, denial, and minimization, and the practice of coping skills and relapse prevention strategies. For instance, the use of theatrical masks highlights discrepancies between the existing image presented to the world and inner feelings (i.e., cognitive dissonance).

Reiss et al. (1998) indicate that dramatherapy may have an advantage over other therapies in that it works at both a cognitive *and* an affective level. Sex offenders have implicit theories and rigid attitudes about their behavior that are not conducive to healthy lifestyles, and dramatherapy techniques assist to challenge their core beliefs (Bergman, 2001; Ward, 2000). Sex offenders hide behind masks of intimidation, passive resistance, fear, or self-pity; each mask reflects a particular attitude and is simple enough for offenders to recall (Bergman, 2001; Bergman & Hewish, 1996). Through therapeutic intervention, the masks are identified and activated to reveal the real self so that the sex offender can be heard and can be seen to be honest. This method is particularly useful to test relapse prevention plans and whether change has been genuinely incorporated (Bergman, 1995). Examples of masks that offenders are encouraged to raise in order to "catch sight of behaviors" and experience a new state include intimidation (The Fist), innocence (The Good Guy), and those that tune out while still enraged (The Stone Wall) (Bergman & Hewish, 1996).

Staff Attitudes Toward Sexual Offenders

In enhancing motivation to change, community corrections officers are expected to have a supportive and persuasive approach to offenders. However, the propensity for offender denial and minimization can cause considerable frustration (Lea, Auburn, & Kibblewhite, 1999). Although correctional staff are considered integral in the process of change in sex offenders, Weekes, Pelletier, and Beaudette (1995) indicate that it is "curious" that few systematic attempts have been made to understand how attitudes of staff will impact upon the effectiveness of relapse prevention. Lea et al. (1999) describe the tension between the need for professionals to develop a relationship with offenders and demonstrate tolerance while they simultaneously abhor the offenses. In turn, this professional-personal dilemma is reinforced by the broader social context within which attitudes of intolerance and prejudice toward sex offenders are implicitly set up as the norm, which impacts upon the way sex offenders are treated by professionals, who in turn may be stigmatized by society. Moreover, for community corrections officers there is the added tension between their community protection and treatment functions (McGrath, Cumming, & Holt, 2002).

Attitudes toward sex offenders can be measured on quantitative scales and are particularly valuable for measures of pre- and post training. Weekes et al. (1995) found that sex offenders were perceived by prison officers to be more dangerous, harmful, violent, tense, bad, unpredictable, mysterious, unchangeable, aggressive, weak, irrational, and afraid than non–sex offenders. This was most likely a means to insulate staff from being too closely aligned with sex offenders. The need for training to manage sex offenders better was identified by two thirds of the prison officers assessed. Hogue (1993) administered the Attitudes Towards Sexual Offenders Scale, and community corrections officers scored halfway between the police (most negative attitudes) and sex offenders (most positive attitudes). Staff attitudes changed positively after completion of a training course and at 6-month follow-up. It is expected that community correction officers in Victoria also have a range of attitudes toward offenders. Lee, Bartholomew, and Holgate (2002) found that 118 officers could be divided between rehabilitative (36%), retributive (20%), or a combination of both orientations (43%). On the basis of semi-structured interviews with 23 participants, including 6 community corrections officers, Lea et al. (1999) found that participants could hold both negative and positive attitudes simultaneously. Those participants with less training and experience tended to use stereotypes more, used these stereotypes as theories that informed practice, and tended not to reflect on their validity. Lea et al. postulated that without training, prejudicial and pessimistic attitudes would prevail and be communicated and therefore impede the progress of sex offenders in treatment.

Most important, the ability of professionals to develop effective working relationships with sex offenders was found to be a function of attitude as well as training and experience (Lea et al., 1999). We believe that positive staff attitudes that provide environmental support for changes in offending behavior are required for relapse prevention strategies to succeed. Although motivational interviewing techniques and the stages of change model together provide an excellent means to empower correctional staff to assist in relapse prevention, it is crucial that beliefs and attitudes are addressed first in order to ensure that support by community corrections officers is motivational rather than confrontational.

A praxis approach underpins training to change staff beliefs and attitudes. This approach provides new ideas that then become incorporated into implicit theories held by staff, which in turn informs practice on a day-to-day basis. In order for this form of training to be successful, staff need to reflect upon their beliefs and attitudes to reinform their theories. Most correctional staff are unaware of how their beliefs and attitudes influence their interactions with offenders. Dramatherapy techniques have been applied to access beliefs in a conscious way, and to encourage attitude change in correctional staff. An evaluation of the effectiveness of such a method in creating a culture change within a Victorian juvenile justice center has recently occurred (Bergman, 2000).

A Model for Training Correctional Staff

Interest by the Program in staff attitudes and how they impact upon denial and resistance in sex offenders commenced in 1995 with a joint graduate research project conducted by Owen and Raymond (supervised by Birgden). Subsequently, a competency-based staff training package to enhance relapse prevention was developed by Owen and Raymond and training to community corrections officers commenced in 1997. Competency-based training is designed to train staff to a standard at which they are considered able to perform the task independently (Australian National Training Authority, 1994). The training is delivered by CORE Sex Offender Programs staff, at least one of whom has a Category 4 qualification and so recognition as a workplace trainer and assessor (National Training Board, 1992).

A three-dimensional model has been developed by the Program based upon theories and techniques provided by Prochaska, DiClemente, and Norcross (stages of change), Miller and Rollnick (motivational interviewing), and Bergman (masks and personas). The model takes into account the principles of relapse prevention and addresses (a) the degree of denial and minimization expressed by sex offenders, (b) the skills required of correctional staff, and (c) correctional staff beliefs and attitudes that impact upon responses to sex offenders. The goal is to raise the possibility that a nonconfrontational approach to supervisory relationships with sex offenders is possible in order to initiate and maintain change. Emphasis is placed on activity-based learning because it allows staff to enact significantly different versions of their work-related behavior, it is more responsive to different adult learning styles, and it stimulates affective responses and real-time testing of skills (Bergman, 2000). Although the training has recently been extended to prison officers and different offender types, the following information focuses on community corrections officers and their management of sex offenders.

LEVEL 1: ADDRESSING ATTITUDES TOWARD SEX OFFENDERS

Level 1 training attendance is mandatory for community corrections officers because they will all have contact with sex offenders at some stage in offenders' sentences. The training session runs for one day and is provided to groups of 15 to 20 staff. In Level 1 training, beliefs and attitudes about sex offenders are explored in the context of myths and theories about sex offending. Officers are first provided with a series of vignettes. For example, an offender with intellectual disability who offends against a child in a public toilet is questioned by the officer in an "intake interview" and responds with statements that minimize and victim blame. Officers are then asked to brainstorm what they believe may be the causes of the sex offending. Rather than focus on the disability alone, other risk factors and precursors to offending are generated. Sex offender typologies and characteristics are then linked to underlying theories—biological, environmental, developmental, sociocultural, and possible transitory states.

Sex offender personas are introduced to officers by the trainers to demonstrate what attitudes they may hold toward them. Sex offenders present a mask to community corrections officers in order to resist change. Depending upon the officers' attitudes, the mask may or may not trigger a response. If a negative response is triggered and officers respond to the mask, they will "fall into the trap" of nonproductive interaction, and offenders will not address their offending behavior. Nonproductive traps such as labeling, being the expert, and blaming are the roles officers may find themselves in if they react to the persona being presented. In recognition of this, the officer is to "get behind the mask" in a nonconfrontational manner. On the basis of the adaptational model outlined above, the message to officers is: "Sex offender denial and minimization are normal responses to the situation, and a productive relationship depends on how you respond to the decision the offender has made." Therefore, it is important for officers to be aware of their attitudes toward different types of sex offenders and to recognize their potential traps.

The following six personas are based upon anecdotal information provided by community corrections officers in relation to their day-to-day interactions with male sex offenders. These masks may serve to avoid the real work of managing relapse. It is expected that sex offenders may also shift between these personas.

Mr. Dependent presents as unable to do anything for himself and very needy, although he may be covertly engaged in sabotage. Mr. Dependent says, "I can't possibly do this, you have to help me." The officer may cater to his needs and engage in parental behavior.

Mr. Slippery presents to male officers as a "mate" and to female officers as "slimy." He attempts to use personal familiarity and searches for common interests. He tends to talk about the officer rather than himself. Mr. Slippery says, "That's a lovely perfume you're wearing, what fragrances do you like?" The officer may engage in conversations of a personal nature.

Mr. Know-It-All presents as having all the answers to his offending and will also closely question the officer about qualifications, skills, and understanding of sex offending. Mr. Know-It-All says, "You're too young to possibly understand . . . and your qualifications would be . . .?" The officer may engage in battles to prove adequate skills or allow the offender to control the intervention process because of self-doubt created about the capacity to provide competent supervision.

Mr. Angel Face presents as compliant, motivated, agreeable, and honest. He will attempt to split staff and agencies. Mr. Angel Face will say, "I'm so lucky to have you, it's about time I had someone who understands me, not like the last one." The officer may accept the information without question.

Mr. Angry presents as verbally and/or physically aggressive. He will puff himself up and say, "The last officer I had ran out of here screaming." The officer may either respond aggressively or tread gingerly in order to avoid an outburst.

Mr. Joker presents himself as affable, always has a witty story to tell, and does not take the situation seriously. He says, "Saw something on TV the other day that was a real hoot, did you see it?" The officer may join in the distraction or become confrontational out of frustration.

Each persona with the accompanying mask is role-played by the trainers, and the officers then reflect on its application to their own caseloads. Officers are to work with what they hear, not what they want the sex offender to say or be (Bergman, 2001). The use of masks has become a popular and valuable feature of the training.

LEVEL 2: INTRODUCING STAGES OF CHANGE AND MOTIVATIONAL INTERVIEWING

Level 2 training is more intensive and optional for staff that wish to manage sex offenders on an ongoing basis. It is a 2-day training provided to groups of 7 to 10 staff. In Level 2, the aim is for correctional staff to integrate stages of change readiness and motivational interviewing principles to enhance sex offender motivation to commence and maintain change. Principles of motivational interviewing, rather than training in motivational interviewing techniques per se, are presented.

As a refresher from the Level 1 training, a Sale of the Century (more recently The Weakest Link) game is played to test retention of knowledge regarding theories of sex offending and the generalization of knowledge to the workplace. Stages of change readiness theory is then presented. For example, officers are asked to choose a behavior that they may or may not wish to change (and are prepared to talk about!). The stages of change readiness with descriptors are placed around the training room and the officers are to stand at the most appropriate stage and explain to the group the rationale for that choice. In turn, statements by sex offenders are provided on cards and again officers place themselves at the most appropriate stage of change and explain the rationale. The response is then linked back to theories of sex offending. For example, a sex offender has phoned an officer to state that he is experiencing a high-risk situation. If the officer stands at the Relapse Stage, the group discusses why, according to relapse prevention principles, it is the Maintenance Stage.

The training then returns to the use of masks to question which personas officers have found are "traps" for them. Stages of change readiness is combined with motivational principles to present officers with a framework to respond appropriately to particular sex offenders who may trigger a negative reaction *in them* rather than blaming the offenders. The use of appropriate skills at the appropriate time will thus enhance the supervisory relationship. Examples regarding this approach are shown in Table 18.1 and detailed below.

Two examples are Mr. Dependent and Mr. Know-It-All. If a Mr. Dependent is at the Precontemplation Stage and triggers parental behavior in the officer, this means that the motivational principles to be used are developing discrepancy, avoiding argumentation, rolling with resistance, and supporting

Table 18.1   Stages of Change Readiness and Motivational Principles

	Express Empathy	Develop Discrepancy	Avoid Argumentation	Roll With Resistance	Support Self-efficacy
Precontemplation		Mr. Dependent	Mr. Dependent	Mr. Dependent	Mr. Dependent
Contemplation					
Preparation			Mr. Know-It-All	Mr. Know-It-All	
Action					
Maintenance					
Relapse					

self-efficacy. In this instance, expressing empathy would be inappropriate because the officer may become trapped. Therefore, the officer needs to focus on the goals and gradually express empathy once Mr. Dependant starts to move forward toward the Action Stage. Alternatively, if a Mr. Know-It-All is at the Contemplation Stage and triggers competitiveness in the officer, this means that the avoid argumentation and roll with resistance principles, in particular, need to be adhered to, otherwise the officer may again become trapped.

In summary, the three-dimensional staff training model developed addresses (a) the degree of denial and minimization expressed by sex offenders, (b) the skills required of correctional staff, and (c) beliefs and attitudes that impact upon staff responses to sex offenders. In other words, the training assists staff to recognize personas, deal with masks, and avoid traps.

Evaluation

As of August 2002, 480 community corrections officers have completed Level 1 training, and 50% of these staff have decided to manage sex offenders on their caseloads and so have returned to complete Level 2 training. To date, evaluations have consisted of feedback from course participants who consistently score it as "extremely useful" on a number of dimensions. Revisions to the training package have been made according to the written feedback. Two reports have anecdotally touched on the training strategy. Upon inspection of the training package, the review of the Program noted that the training achievements in the community were excellent (Hudson, 1999). Likewise, Purvis (2001) conducted a study of the attributions of 87 Victorian community corrections officers regarding child sexual offending. The respondents understood the complexity of issues and the range of variables that

What skills
are required by
staff?

Motivational Interviewing

What stage of
change readiness
is the offender?

Stages of Change

Sex Offender

Management

Personas, Masks, and Traps
What are staff beliefs and attitudes?

Figure 18.1

contributed to sex offending. The author cited the possible explanation as being that community corrections officers

> may have conformed to their organization's culture, which in turn may have influenced their thoughts about sexual offending and their responses . . . [all staff] have been educated with the same set of guidelines and objectives . . . receive the same sex offender training which educates [all staff] on how to manage, respond to, and challenge the sex offenders they supervise. (p. 39)

Raymond is currently conducting an empirical evaluation to determine whether the training delivered provides correctional staff with the skills to address relapse prevention strategies using a goal-oriented approach (as outlined by Cumming & McGrath, 2000). The three dimensions of the model will be measured by the administration of the Attitudes Towards Sex Offenders Scale (Hogue, 1993) to measure beliefs and attitude change. An additional questionnaire will be administered to measure acquired knowledge in stages of change readiness and motivational interviewing principles. These assessments have occurred pre- and post Level 1 and Level 2 training and data are being collated. Preliminary findings indicate that those who have completed both levels of training have maintained knowledge and report greater confidence in developing strategies to manage sex offenders.

In addition, an individually based competency assessment has been developed by Raymond adapted from key competencies developed by the Programme Development Section (n.d.) in the U.K. Prison Service. The competencies have been revised to measure key learning outcomes and assessment criteria for Australian competencies in sex offender management. Competencies include demonstration of the following: use of feedback, warmth and empathy, flexibility of style, discussion-leading and questioning skills, maintenance of boundaries, and understanding of cognitive-behavioral techniques. Recently, Owen and Raymond conducted 3-day training courses in the Northern Territory, and participants are currently completing exercises on videotape to demonstrate these competencies.

Future Directions

The model of stages of change readiness, motivational interviewing principles, and focus on beliefs and attitudes has provided the opportunity for application to other areas in an effort to motivate and maintain change in offenders. Motivational interviewing *principles* rather than *techniques* have been applied as a method to shift correctional staffs' attitudes in their day-to-day interactions with offenders. We believe that the next step is to train both community corrections officers and prison officers in motivational interviewing techniques for all moderate- to high-risk and need offenders who have committed a range of offenses.

Recently, Birgden revised the model by combining the Precontemplation, Contemplation, and Preparation Stages with specific motivational interviewing techniques for nonclinicians such as defense lawyers and correctional staff (e.g., Birgden, 2002; Birgden, in press; Birgden & Ward, 2002). Clinicians can then provide cognitive-behavioral interventions at the Action Stage for a range of offending behaviors. Once intervention has been provided, motivational techniques can be used to support the Maintenance and Relapse Stages. Again, this approach is useful for encouraging approaches that are persuasive and supportive rather than coercive or argumentative.

Conclusion

Since mid-1996, CORE Sex Offender Programs has provided a coordinated and integrated system of assessment, management, and intervention to male sex offenders in the public correctional system in Victoria, Australia. The external supervisory component of relapse prevention designed to manage sex offenders and protect the community is considered of equal importance to sex offender treatment; intervention without systemic support is considered ineffective. As a consequence, the understanding of sex offending as a public health problem is reinforced by the equal participation of all disciplines in the support of relapse prevention. The training of community corrections officers in providing effective offender management is an example of one of these strategies.

Effective offender management requires that community corrections officers recognize the stage of change readiness in sex offenders and apply appropriate motivational interventions while being aware how their own core beliefs and attitudes may impact negatively on the supervisory relationship. Relapse prevention is appropriately applied only after cognitive-behavioral interventions; those interventions require individualized case formulations regarding offense pathways, and sex offenders need to be motivated. A three-dimensional model based upon theories and techniques provided by stages of change readiness, motivational interviewing, and masks and personas presented by offenders has been described. The model takes into account the principles of relapse prevention and addresses (a) the degree of denial and minimization expressed by sex offenders, (b) the skills required by correctional staff, and (c) beliefs and attitudes that impact upon staff responses to sex offenders. The adaptational approach is underpinned by psychological theories that explain how offenders deal with unpleasant states and situations, make free choices, and make informed decisions. We believe that the Program has made a serious attempt to address the external supervisory component of relapse prevention and has given correctional staff the means to manage the professional-personal dilemma in working with a client group that is stigmatized by society.

A strength of the relapse prevention model is that it provides a framework for close collaboration between therapists and the criminal justice system (Hanson, 2000), and community safety is further enhanced when therapists and community corrections officers collaborate (McGrath et al., 2002). In this instance, the Program's continuum of care model manages relapse prevention in sex offenders in a coordinated and systemic manner; therapists provide treatment and community corrections officers provide supervision. It is hoped that the training model outlined above that assists staff to recognize personas, deal with masks, and avoid traps is one means to avoid the difficulties as outlined by Marques et al. (2000) in terms of generalization of relapse prevention skills in the community.

References

Australian National Training Authority. (1994). *National vocational and educational training: Australian system priorities for 1999.* Canberra: Australia.

Bandura, A. (1997). *Self-efficacy: The exercise of control.* New York: Freeman.

Bergman, J. (1995). Life, the life event, and theater—A personal narrative on the use of drama therapy with sex offenders. In B. K. Schwartz & H. R. Cellini (Eds.), *The sex offender: Corrections, treatment and legal practice* (Vol. 1, pp. 1-24). Kingston, NJ: Civic Research Institute.

Bergman, J. (2000). Creating new cultures: Using drama therapy to build therapeutic communities in prisons. In P. Lewis & D. R. Johnson (Eds.), *Current approaches in drama therapy* (pp. 303-330). Springfield, IL: Charles C Thomas.

Bergman, J. (2001). Using drama therapy to uncover genuineness and deception in civilly committed sexual offenders. In A. Schlank (Ed), *The sexual predator: Vol. 2. Legal issues, clinical issues, and special populations* (pp. 1-15). Kingston, NJ: Civic Research Institute.

Bergman, J., & Hewish, S. (1996). The violent illusion: Dramatherapy and the dangerous voyage to the heart of change. In M. Liebmann (Ed.), *Arts approaches to conflict* (pp. 92-117). Bristol, PA: Jessica Kingsley Publishers.

Birgden, A. (in press). Therapeutic jurisprudence and "good lives": A rehabilitation framework for corrections. *Australian Psychologist, 37*(3).

Birgden, A. (2002). Dealing with the resistant criminal client: A psychologically-minded strategy for more effective legal counseling. *Criminal Law Bulletin, 38*(2), 225-243.

Birgden, A., & Langthaler, L. (2001). SOP Redevelopment Project: Document 1: Background report. CORE-the Public Correctional Enterprise. Melbourne: Australia.

Birgden, A., & Ward, T. (in press). Pragmatic psychology through a therapeutic jurisprudence lens: Psycholegal soft spots in the criminal justice system. *Psychology, Public Policy, and Law.*

Cumming, G. F., & McGrath, R. J. (2000). External supervision: How can it increase the effectiveness of relapse prevention? In D. R. Laws, S. M. Hudson, & T. Ward (Eds.), *Remaking relapse prevention with sex offenders: A sourcebook* (pp. 236-253). Thousand Oaks, CA: Sage.

Draycott, S., & Dabbs, A. (1998). Cognitive dissonance I: An overview of the literature and its integration into theory and practice in clinical psychology. *British Journal of Clinical Psychology, 37,* 343-353.

English, K., Pullen, S., & Jones, L. (1996). *Managing adult sex offenders on probation and parole: A containment approach.* Lexington, KY: American Probation and Parole Association.

Freeman-Longo, R., & Bays, L. (1994a). Who am I and why am I in treatment? A guided workbook for clients in evaluation and beginning treatment (SOS Series-Number One). Brandon, VT: Safer Society Press.

Freeman-Longo, R., & Bays, L. (1994b). Why did I do it again? Understanding my cycle of problem behaviors: A guided workbook for clients in treatment (SOS Series-Number Two). Brandon, VT: Safer Society Press.

Garland, R. J., & Dougher, M. J. (1991). Motivational intervention in the treatment of sex offenders. In W. R. Miller & S. Rollnick (Eds.), *Motivational interviewing: Preparing people to change addictive behavior* (pp. 303-313). New York: Guilford.

Hanson, R. K. (2000). What is so special about relapse prevention? In D. R. Laws, S. M. Hudson, & T. Ward (Eds.), *Remaking relapse prevention with sex offenders: A sourcebook* (pp. 3-26). Thousand Oaks, CA: Sage.

Harper, R., & Hardy, S. (2000). An evaluation of motivational interviewing as a method of intervention with clients in a probation setting. *British Journal of Social Work, 30,* 393-400.

Hogue, T. E. (1993). Attitudes towards prisoners and sexual offenders. *Issues in Criminological and Legal Psychology, 19,* 27-32.

Hogue, T. E., & Peebles, J. (1997). The influence of remorse, intent and attitudes toward sex offenders on judgments of a rapist. *Psychology, Crime and Law, 3,* 249-259.

Hudson, S. (1999). CORE Sex Offender Program review. CORE-the Public Correctional Enterprise. Melbourne: Australia.

Janis, I. L., & Mann L. (1977). *Decision-making: A psychological analysis of conflict, choice and commitment.* New York: Free Press.

Lawendowski, L. A. (1998). Motivational interviewing for adolescent smokers. *Preventive Medicine, 27*(5 Part 3), A39-A46.

Laws, D. R., Hudson, S. M., & Ward, T. (2000). The original model of relapse prevention with sex offenders: Promises unfulfilled. In D. R. Laws, S. M. Hudson, & T. Ward (Eds.), *Remaking relapse prevention with sex offenders: A sourcebook* (pp. 3-26). Thousand Oaks, CA: Sage.

Lea, S., Auburn, T., & Kibblewhite, K. (1999). Working with sex offenders: The perceptions and experiences of professionals and paraprofessionals. *International Journal of Offender Therapy and Comparative Criminology, 43*(1), 103-119.

Lee, E., Bartholomew, T., & Holgate, A. (2002). The relationship between correctional orientation and community correctional officers' implementation of actuarial penological initiatives in Victoria, Australia. Manuscript submitted for publication.

Mann, R. (1996). Motivational interviewing with sex offenders. A practice manual. The National Association for the Development of Work with Sex Offenders. London: National Association for the Development of Work With Sex Offenders.

Mann, R. (2000). Managing resistance and rebellion in relapse prevention intervention. In D. R. Laws, S. M. Hudson, & T. Ward (Eds.), *Remaking relapse prevention with sex offenders: A sourcebook* (pp. 187-200). Thousand Oaks, CA: Sage.

Marlatt, G. A. (1985). Relapse prevention: Theoretical rationale and overview of the model. In G. A. Marlatt & J. R. Gordon (Eds.), *Relapse prevention* (pp. 3-70). New York: Guilford.

Marques, J. K., Nelson, C., Alarcon, J., & Day, D. M. (2000). Preventing relapse in sex offenders: What we learned from SOTEP'S experimental treatment program. In D. R. Laws, S. M. Hudson, & T. Ward (Eds.), *Remaking relapse prevention with sex offenders: A sourcebook* (pp. 39-55). Thousand Oaks, CA: Sage.

Marshall, W. L., & Anderson, D. (2000). Do relapse prevention components enhance treatment effectiveness? In D. R. Laws, S. M. Hudson, & T. Ward (Eds.), *Remaking relapse prevention with sex offenders: A sourcebook* (pp. 39-55). Thousand Oaks, CA: Sage.

McGrath, R. J., Cumming, G., & Holt, J. (2002). Collaboration among sex offender treatment providers and probation and parole officers: The beliefs and behaviors of treatment providers. *Sexual Abuse: A Journal of Research and Treatment, 14*(1), 49-65.

Miller, W. (1985). Motivation for change: A review with special emphasis on alcoholism. *Psychological Bulletin, 98*, 84-107.

Miller, W. R., & Rollnick, S. (1991). *Motivational interviewing.* New York: Guilford.

National Training Board. (1992). National competency standards: Policy and guidelines. Canberra: Australia.

Owen, K., & Keogan, C. (1996). CORE community correction officers key competencies in sexual offender intervention: Training needs analysis. Sex Offender Programs, CORE-the Public Correctional Enterprise. Melbourne: Australia.

Pithers, W. D. (1990). Relapse prevention with sexual aggressors: A method for maintaining therapeutic change and enhancing external supervision. In W. L. Marshall, D. R. Laws, & H. E. Barbaree (Eds.), *The handbook of sexual assault: Issues, theories and treatment of the offender* (pp. 363-385). New York: Plenum.

Pithers, W. D., Marques, J. K., Gibat, C. C., & Marlatt, G. A. (1983). Relapse prevention with sexual aggressives: A self-control model of treatment and the maintenance of change. In J. G. Greer & I. R. Stuart (Eds.), *The sexual aggressor* (pp. 214-234). New York: Van Nostrand Reinhold.

Prochaska, J. O., & DiClemente, C. C. (1982). Transtheoretical therapy: Towards a more integrated model of change. *Psychotherapy: Therapy, Research and Practice, 19*, 276-288.

Prochaska, J., DiClemente, C. C., & Norcross, J. C. (1992). In search of how people change: Applications to addictive behaviors. *American Psychologist, 47*, 1102-1114.

Prochaska, J., & Norcross, J. C. (1994). *Systems of psychotherapy: A transtheoretical analysis.* New York: Brooks/Cole .

Prochaska, J. O., & Prochaska, J. M. (1999). Why don't continents move? Why don't people change? *Journal of Psychotherapy Integration, 9*(1), 83-102.

Programme Development Section. (n.d.). SOTP managers' manual. London: UK Prison Services.

Purvis, M. (2001). Working with sex offenders: Victorian community correctional officers' attributions for sexual offending against children. Unpublished master's thesis, Melbourne University, Melbourne, Victoria, Australia.

Reiss, D., Quayle, M., Brett, T., & Meux, C. (1998). Dramatherapy for mentally disordered offenders: Changes to level of anger. *Criminal Behavior and Mental Health, 8,* 139-153.

Rogers, R., & Dickey, R. (1991). Denial and minimization among sex offenders: A review of competing models of deception. *Annals of Sex Research, 4,* 46-93.

Rollnick, S., & Miller, W. R. (1995). What is motivational interviewing? *Behavioral and Cognitive Psychotherapy, 23*(4), 325-334.

Serin, R., & Kennedy, S. (2002). Treatment readiness and responsivity: Contributing to effective correctional programming: Correctional Services of Canada. Retrieved June 14, 2002, from http://www.csc-scc.gc.ca/text/rsrch/reports/r54/r54e.shtml

Tierney, D. (2001). An evaluation of CORE's treatment programs for sex offenders. Unpublished manuscript, School of Psychology, Deakin University, Melbourne, Australia.

Wagner, C., & Connors, W. (2002). Motivational interviewing: Resources for clinicians, researchers, and trainers. Retrieved June 14, 2002, from http://www.motivationalinterview.org/clinical/traps.html

Ward, T. (2000). Sexual offenders' cognitive distortions as implicit theories. *Aggression and Violent Behavior, 5,* 491-507.

Ward, T., & Hudson, S. M. (1996). Relapse prevention: A critical analysis. *Sexual Abuse: A Journal of Research and Treatment, 8,* 177-200.

Ward, T., & Hudson, S. M. (1998). A model of the relapse process in sex offenders. *Journal of Interpersonal Violence, 13,* 24 7-725.

Weekes, J. R., Pelletier, G., & Beaudette, D. (1995). Correctional officers: How do they perceive sex offenders? *International Journal of Offender Therapy and Comparative Criminology, 39*(1), 55-61.

19

The Risk-Need Model of Offender Rehabilitation

A Critical Analysis

Tony Ward

Mark Brown
University of Melbourne

Over the past two decades empirical evidence has increasingly supported the view that it is possible to reduce reoffending rates by treating or rehabilitating offenders rather than simply punishing them (Andrews & Bonta, 1998; Gendreau & Andrews, 1990). In fact, renewed interest in a rehabilitation model is arguably one of the most significant events in modern correctional policy, although it must be noted that the impact of this model has been uneven and it often has been co-opted into broader programs of offender control (Garland, 2001).

The rehabilitation perspective rests on a number of important assumptions about crime and the characteristics of offenders. First, that crime is caused by distinct patterns of social and psychological factors that increase the chances a given individual will break the law. Second, that targeting these factors will decrease reoffending rates. Third, that individuals vary in their predisposition to commit deviant acts and this should be taken into account when planning rehabilitation programs; treatment should be tailored to meet each offender's unique needs (Andrews & Bonta, 1998; McGuire, 2000).

In this chapter we critically analyze the risk-need model as expounded in the work of correctional psychologists and researchers. We focus our analysis on arguably the most influential theory of risk-need currently available, namely that developed by the Canadian psychologists Don Andrews and James Bonta (1998). In outlining this model we also draw upon the work of a number of other researchers and clinicians who are broadly sympathetic with the Andrews and Bonta perspective (e.g., Blackburn, 2000; Hanson, 2001; McGuire, 2000). After outlining the model, we critically examine its underlying assumptions and conceptual adequacy. Although much of this discussion is based on offender rehabilitation in general, it also applies directly to the treatment of sex offenders (see Hanson & Harris, 2000).

The Risk-Need Model

GENERAL COMMENTS

Andrews and Bonta formulate four general principles of classification to guide effective correctional treatment. First, the *risk* principle, which is concerned with the match between level of risk and the amount of treatment warranted. For example, according to this principle high-risk individuals should receive the most treatment, typically at least 100 hours of cognitive-behavioral interventions over a 3- to 4-month period (Hollin, 1999). Second, according to the *need* principle, programs should target criminogenic needs—that is, dynamic offender characteristics that, when changed, are associated with reduced risk of recidivism. These include pro-offending attitudes and values, aspects of antisocial personality (e.g., impulsiveness), poor problem solving, substance abuse, high hostility and anger, and criminal associates (Andrews & Bonta, 1998). In fact, criminogenic needs should be detected for each type of crime rather than simply for crimes in general. For example, Hanson and Harris (2000) identified a number of criminogenic need factors for sexual offending that included deviant sexual arousal, intimacy deficits and loneliness, and problems with emotional regulation. Third, the *responsivity* principle is concerned with a program's ability to reach and make sense to the participants for whom it was designed. In other words, will offenders be able to absorb the content of the program and subsequently change their behavior? Examples of factors that if not taken into account may impede learning include gender, learning styles, ethnicity, and treatment motivation. Finally, the principle of *professional discretion* states that clinical judgment should override the above principles if circumstances warrant it. This principle allows for treatment flexibility and innovation under certain circumstances.

Criminogenic needs are a subset of factors predictive of recidivism. They are identified empirically through the careful detection of variables that covary with criminal conduct. Subsequent research and intervention programs that seek to effect changes in these factors can provide further evidence for the utility of targeting them and their functional role in criminal offending. Other risk factors include static (or unchanging) factors such as gender, age, and offending history (Andrews & Bonta, 1998). Although static factors play an important role in determining background levels of risk, they are of lesser value in guiding treatment. The fact that they are unmodifiable means they fail to reveal whether a person has changed as a result of treatment, by how much, what has changed, or to inform us under what conditions an offense is likely to occur. Therefore, the usefulness of static risk factors is limited once an initial risk assessment has been performed. By way of contrast, dynamic risk factors (i.e., criminogenic needs) should be able to provide clinicians with information concerning the impact of treatment on an individual's level of risk and also indicate where change has occurred. Noncriminogenic needs are dynamic attributes of offenders and their circumstances that, when changed, have not yet been associated with reduced recidivism. For example, low self-esteem, anxiety, personal distress, or group cohesion (Andrews & Bonta, 1998), for reasons to do with the stability of the need state or the duration and quality of the evaluated interventions, have not been reliably associated with reduced offending. Andrews and Bonta acknowledge the importance of noncriminogenic needs but argue that priority should be given to targeting criminogenic needs because of their positive demonstrated impact on recidivism rates. Though they do not explicitly state this, the implication is that noncriminogenic needs are therefore *discretionary* intervention targets.

It is clear that from Andrews and Bonta's perspective risk and need are closely related; in fact, criminogenic needs are treated simply as dynamic risk factors. Arguably, therefore, risk and need are essentially the same thing, with the former denoting an overall risk category or numerical value and the latter the *type* of risk factor. The tendency to collapse the concepts of risk and need into the hybrid category risk-need appears to make sense from the perspective of offender rehabilitation. A rehabilitation model that is oriented around the principle of risk-need focuses interventions on risk management, and also underlines the necessity of adjusting the intensity and duration of therapy in accordance with offenders' level of risk.

Thus, according to the model, risk assessment should drive need assessment and the treatment process. That is, offenders' level of risk should determine the required intensity and duration of treatment. Furthermore, the severity of risk (i.e., whether low, medium, or high) is assumed to covary with the number of criminogenic needs, and in addition, the severity or strength of each need.

That is, low-risk offenders will have few, if any, criminogenic needs whereas high-risk offenders will display a significant range of such needs. Relatedly, it is assumed that risk factors are discrete, quantifiable characteristics of offenders and their environment that can be identified and measured. A final claim of the risk-need model is that the identification of risk factors and/or criminogenic needs is an empirical and therefore value-free process.

The Concepts of Risk and Need

THE CONCEPT OF RISK

Blackburn (2000) states that "risk assessment is the process of determining an individual's potential for harmful behavior. It entails consideration of a broad array of factors related to the person, the situation, and their interaction" (p. 179). Furthermore, in the developmental psychopathology literature a risk factor increases the chances of an individual developing a particular disorder or problem. In addition, risk factors may change over a person's life and their influence will vary across people, situations, and development (Mrazek & Haggerty, 1994).

Thus the concept of risk is complex and contains a number of distinct features. The crucial thing to note from Blackburn's definition (see also Hanson, 2001; McGuire, 2000) is that risk involves an estimate or prediction of the possibility of harm to the self or others. This focus strongly points to a value component in the sense that what benefits or harms individuals is a question of specific types of goods and their presence or absence. In addition, the above definition suggests that there are a number of risk factors ranging from personal dispositions to environmental factors that should be canvassed in a comprehensive risk assessment. Some of these factors are causally related to offending behavior in a fundamental way (e.g., antisocial attitudes) and others may simply function as disinhibitors or triggers that precipitate an offense, for example intoxication (Hanson, 2001). Thus risk factors range from those that causally generate problematic behaviors to others that function simply as markers or indicators that a problem behavior exists or is likely to exist in the future (Mrazek & Haggerty, 1994). The latter type of risk factors frequently emerges out of deep-seated psychological dispositions such as anger or from interpersonal relationships and events.

Risk factors tend to fall within four broad domains: (a) dispositional factors such as psychopathic or antisocial personality characteristics, cognitive variables and demographic data; (b) historical factors such as adverse developmental history, prior history of crime and violence, prior hospitalization, and poor treatment compliance; (c) contextual antecedents to violence such as criminogenic needs (risk factors of criminal behavior), deviant social networks, and lack of positive social supports; and (d) clinical factors such as diagnosis, poor level of functioning, and substance abuse (Andrews & Bonta, 1998; Blackburn, 2000; Hollin, 1999; McGuire, 2000).

Therefore, a comprehensive risk assessment will seek to determine the presence or absence of each category of risk factor (McGuire, 2000). The presence of a risk factor will increase chances of an offense occurring in the future, while its absence and/or the existence of protective factors that insulate individuals from the effects of high-risk events will function to decrease the odds of offending behavior. In order to arrive at an accurate estimate of risk it is therefore necessary to gather information on the following areas: the cognitive, affective, behavioral, and contextual factors associated with an offense (i.e., the offense chain); the psychological dispositions of an offender that have predisposed him or her to commit an offense (e.g., maladaptive core beliefs and values, interpersonal skills deficits, self-regulatory deficits, and substance abuse); an offender's developmental and socialization history; the proximal or triggering factors resulting in an offense (e.g., the presence of criminal peers and stressful events); sociocultural factors and norms relevant to an offender and his or her social environment (e.g., values that support the use of violence or legitimize the sexual abuse of women or children); and finally, an account of general social and economic conditions in the local community (McGuire, 2000). It is clear that according to rehabilitation theorists and researchers such as Blackburn, Hanson, and McGuire, an adequate risk assessment is a comprehensive and time-consuming process culminating in a case formulation or clinical theory that explains why an offender committed the offenses he or she did and also specifies the future conditions that are likely to increase or decrease the risk of recidivism.

THE CONCEPT OF NEED

To have a need typically indicates a lack or deficiency of some kind, a lack of a significant good, or at least indicates that such a lack would be harmful. From a psychological perspective, Deci and Ryan (2000) have developed the self-determination theory of needs. We have found their theory particularly useful for thinking about needs in the correctional context. Self-determination theory states that human beings are inherently active, self-directed organisms who are naturally predisposed to seek autonomy, relatedness, and competence (basic human needs). *Autonomy* refers to individuals' propensity to self-regulate and organize their experiences and to function as unified, integrated beings. *Relatedness* refers to individuals' propensity to establish a sense of emotional connectedness to other human beings and to seek the subsequent goals of feeling loved and cared for. *Competence* refers to the propensity to establish a sense of mastery in one's environment, to seek challenges and increasingly to master them. They define need as "innate psychological nutriments that are essential for ongoing psychological growth, integrity, and well-being" (p. 229). Human needs outline the conditions essential for psychological well-being and fulfillment, and individuals can flourish only if they are met. The failure to meet the three basic needs for autonomy, relatedness, and competence will inevitably cause psychological distress and result in the acquisition of maladaptive defenses. In other words, thwarted basic needs result in stunted lives, psychological problems, and social maladjustment. Under these circumstances individuals acquire *substitute needs* that give them at least some degree of relatedness, competence, and autonomy. However, the goals associated with these proxy needs are likely to result in a poorly integrated self, ultimately frustrating and unsatisfying relationships, self-esteem disturbances, and a sense of personal helplessness (for research evidence see Deci & Ryan, 2000). Deci and Ryan argue that in order to experience a sense of enduring well-being, all three needs have to be fulfilled; social conditions that pit one need against another are likely to result in defensive motives and the development of substitute needs. The outcome of this forced accommodation is reduced levels of well-being.

Basic needs require *external* and *internal* conditions for their fulfillment, for example, adequate parenting, opportunities to learn and make independent decisions, and the possession of skills necessary to establish intimate relationships. Knowledge of the internal and external conditions for need fulfillment is arrived at from what we know about basic human dispositions and the circumstances necessary for their cultivation and development—for example, the capacity to be self-directive or to establish close, supportive, friendships. The various goods or valued activities that typically make up a life (e.g., health, knowledge, creativity, and friendship) are possible only if basic needs are being met (Braybrooke, 1987; Thompson, 1987; Willard, 1987).

Critical Comments

We now critically examine the risk-needs model by focusing on the way it uses the key concepts of risk and need. However, before considering these components of the model we make some general critical comments.

GENERAL POINTS

A key question concerning the risk-need model is whether estimates of risk should determine the type and extent of treatment offenders receive. Although there is a limited amount of empirical evidence that supports such a strategy in general, we caution against it as a routine assumption. We have two major reasons for this view. First, if need is simply defined as a subset of risk factors, then the risk-need principle is misleading. This is because criminogenic needs are simply dynamic risk factors, changes which reduce recidivism rates. And if needs are simply subsets of risk factors, then you really have only risk factors and therefore the term "risk-need" is misleading and basically tautological.

Second, if risk and need are truly independent constructs referring to real phenomena, then there are a number of possible relationships between them, some of which would violate the above assumption. More specifically, it may be that high-risk individuals exhibit high levels of clinical need or problems that merit intensive and sustained treatment, as assumed by the risk-need model. Under this interpretation, risk level is a marker for need severity and that therefore someone assessed as high risk will display high needs and those with low risk display low needs, and so on. Thus while they are thought to exist independently, they are associated in some way (risk *and* need). However, it is also possible that individuals who are assessed as low risk may display high needs, or clinical problems. These needs may not be criminogenic needs, but could still require therapeutic attention and have an impact on rehabilitation (e.g., low mood, relationship problems, etc.). Another possibility is that they may be high need, in the criminogenic sense, with respect to another criterion, for example physical violence as opposed to sexual. Moreover, it is possible to be confronted with individuals who are high risk, but in fact exhibit low needs. Such individuals could have quite circumscribed problems that may put them at risk for reoffending, but do not display a *wide range* of problems. For example, a sex offender who has deviant sexual preferences but possesses good social skills and demonstrates no obvious interpersonal or self-regulatory deficits (Ward & Siegert, in press). In other words, the relationship between level of risk (an estimate or prediction) and level of need is a complex one and not exhausted by the symmetry implied in the risk-need principle. Thus, in order to allocate offenders to treatment streams it is necessary to be acquainted with the range and severity of their clinical problems, and also to be clear about the relationship between such factors and criminal acts. Need should determine treatment allocation, not risk. And if risk and need are collapsed into the same category, that of risk factors, then the fact they do so is unremarkable and merely a question of semantics.

Relatedly, the evidence indicating that matching offenders' intensity of treatment to level of need results in better outcomes does not necessarily indicate a simple linear interpretation between risk and need. The assumption that there is a linear relationship between the degree of risk and amount of treatment required is not unambiguously supported by research evidence. Treating high-risk offenders with high intensity treatment may be effective for a number of reasons. First, they may have a small number of intense or severe needs that require prolonged treatment to shift. Alternatively, they may have a wide range of needs of varying intensity or severity and thus require broadband or comprehensive treatment of sufficient duration to ensure all the needs are likely to be targeted. The key point is that there may be quite distinct mechanisms generating similar outcomes. We need to be wary of the assumption that it is intensive treatment itself, rather than the quality and theoretical sophistication of the assessment leading to it, that is most important in addressing high-risk offenders' needs.

The notion of basing treatment on risk management is problematic as it implies that the major task of rehabilitation is to reduce the chances of harm to community *and* that this is best achieved by managing risk. However, this simply begs the question: How can an approach dedicated to preventing something harmful occurring recruit individuals in the task of changing their lives? Relatedly, what is the relationship between offending behavior and basic human goods? Focusing on criminogenic needs is arguably not helpful to clinicians (and offenders) because it tells them only what to eliminate or modify. Negative goals are extremely difficult to achieve, as they do not specify what is being sought, but merely what is absent. Therefore, any therapeutic approach based on a risk management model needs to be supplemented by additional theories that specify what goods or goals are to be sought and how this is to happen (see Ward & Stewart, Chapter 2 in this volume). For example, a treatment goal that focuses on the acquisition of relationship skills is more useful than one that simply aims to reduce intimacy deficits. And motivational concepts like that of need, which entail specific goals and valued outcomes, provide exactly this type of guidance. Therefore, basing a treatment model on risk factors alone is insufficient. If we are to be guided by the clinical literature, it is clear that treatment should focus on *enhancing* positive capabilities rather than *suppressing* dysfunctional ones (Emmons, 1999). The focus of risk-needs analysis upon negative aspects of offenders' personal capacities and development thus appears markedly out of step with established clinical principles and practice.

A final general point concerns the different roles risk and need concepts play in the correctional psychology domain. The assessment of risk enables clinicians and criminal justice workers to predict offending behavior whereas the detection of offenders' needs helps to explain why they behaved antisocially. Risk assessments are based on statistical associations between offender characteristics and types of offending behavior, whereas need ascriptions are typically embedded in a theory of human agency in which causal links are drawn between intrapersonal and external factors. The treatment of an offender requires the development of a case formulation in which psychological constructs such as that of need are used to explain why he or she finds certain goals compelling and seeks to achieve them. Therefore, collapsing the concept of need into that of risk effectively undermines the construction of clinical explanations, and also defeats any attempt to construct an accurate estimate of risk (as this is based on a case formulation).

RISK

It is important to note that risk can be conceptualized in different ways: Current psychological representations are not the only theoretically grounded conception of risk operating in the justice process. Indeed, one of us has argued elsewhere that

> rather than thinking of risk as a phenomenon that has been similarly conceptualized [across time and discipline] but differently measured, risk could more profitably be thought of as varying in its conceptualization.... Seen in this light, risk emerges as a label to denote the presence of particular circumstances of interest, circumstances that may differ considerably depending upon what view of the markers of threat and danger are being invoked by the risk assessor. (Brown, 2000, p. 95)

Brown distinguishes between *fluid risk* and *categorical risk,* two quite different, yet theoretically grounded, ways in which criminal justice professionals think about and analyze individual propensities to commit crime. Fluid risk is viewed as consisting of discrete individual characteristics associated with offending behavior, and this risk is construed as existing on an identifiable underlying behavioral continuum. The core idea is that individuals are basically a bundle or cluster of properties that are in principle observable and measurable. The methods used to assess risk are analytic and reductionist, enabling clinicians to examine the relationship of specific characteristics to criminal behavior. Risk factors are thought to be susceptible to manipulation and management; therefore rehabilitation programs set out to target identified risk factors and to teach the offender new, prosocial ways of thinking and acting. The idea is to give individuals the skills necessary to cope with problems in socially acceptable ways. Brown states that it is this fluid risk model that underlies psychological and psychiatric estimates of risk.

According to the categorical model, on the other hand, risk can best be assessed and described by reference to the categories of human virtue and character, so that risk, measured in this way, is categorical rather than continuous in nature. Individuals are viewed as autonomous agents who act upon the world in a manner that expresses aspects of their character. Because of the transcendent nature of personal agency it is possible to identify risk only indirectly, by way of individuals' actions as they reflect aspects of human character and virtue. Thus, risk markers in the categorical view of risk are not the disembodied and atomized "factors" of the fluid risk assessment, but carefully considered features of human individuality. Brown cites remorse as an example of a human virtue that assists decision makers whose thinking about risk is grounded in an ethical and value-based consideration of the human condition. For example, an offender's recognition of the singularity of his or her behavior, that "wrong done and wrong experienced are *sui generis*" (Brown, 2000, p. 106), is an important moral and ethical exercise. It must capture and regard what it is for the offender to be that wronging person and to have done a wrong: to have changed the balance of human relations in a way that can never be recovered. Therefore, risk cannot be "measured" (or if so, only spuriously, from an ethical point of view, since the individual is a null set) but only assessed through systematic and careful judgment, a holistic and partly intuitive process. Risk can be managed or manipulated, yet what is required is not a packaged cognitive or skills program but assistance in the personal developments that would allow for an evaluation of his or her individual character and the experience of the appropriate moral emotions. The primary focus of rehabilitation is on values or beliefs rather than skill acquisition, although this is certainly of some importance. According to Brown, it is the categorical risk model that frequently underlies the assessments of judicial decision makers and other criminal justice practitioners who eschew the reductive analyses of the fluid risk paradigm.

The problem is that typically these models of risk are unacknowledged by their proponents and exert their influence silently, without argument or discussion. In fact, the arguments between clinical researchers and judicial and criminal justice personnel are often fueled by these fundamentally different ways of conceptualizing risk and the nature of persons. It is clear to us that the risk-need model assumes the validity of the fluid conception of risk and therefore is most concerned with issues of management, and is not interested in questions of value or character (unless the latter are viewed as sources of antisocial behavior that can be measured). Both models have their basis in broader conceptualizations of the world and of the nature of people. It would be fruitful to open this issue to critical debate because the refusal of advocates of the risk-need model to consider the role of values in the rehabilitation of offenders is a major problem (see the discussion of needs below). We do not assume that one model is more valid than the other, but would simply like to point out that each has its domain of application and should be a focus of critical inquiry. Failure to consider alternative ways of understanding risk and rehabilitation is likely to hinder the effective treatment of offenders rather than facilitate the process.

In our discussion of risk factors we concluded that they varied from variables that were simply associated with criminal actions to those that causally produced such actions. It was also apparent in this outline of risk factors that some dynamic variables were more fundamental than others. While acute dynamic risk factors such as negative mood may trigger an offense, they do not cause it in any meaningful sense. Rather, we suggest that deeply rooted belief systems or psychological processes generate such acute mental states, for example, antisocial attitudes or fears of intimacy, which in turn cause someone to commit a crime (stable dynamic factors). Therefore, dispositional or vulnerability factors, and acute factors that emerge from the activation of the latter, represent two distinct types of risk factors. It is arguably the former type that constitutes criminogenic needs in the sense that Andrews and Bonta refer to them, that is, they are enduring propensities to engage in harmful or antisocial behavior. Because dispositional factors are causally related to crimes, they should be the primary targets in rehabilitation.

We argue that while collapsing or merging the constructs of risk and need may prove beneficial in some respects, it is also deeply problematic. Basically, the focus on risk at the expense of clinical need shifts attention away from the underlying fundamental causes of criminal offending and results in interventions that are superficial, simplistic, and misconceived. In a nutshell, risk factors vary in level and type from variables that are simply associated with offending (risk markers) to those that are functionally or causally related (primary causal factors). It is the latter, not the former, that are of crucial importance in developing an effective treatment program. Needs, in the dispositional sense, underlay and generate risk, and the rehabilitation of offenders should be driven by a need or dispositional model. Unfortunately, this distinction is seldom recognized, leaving the position where essentially distracting risk markers are targeted while more fundamental causal problems tend to be overlooked or ignored.

Risk assessment, as it is popularly conceived, reflects the process of detecting markers or indicators of the potential to inflict harm on others. Such indicators are relatively easily detected and typically form the basis of brief measures of risk. For example, the Rapid Risk Assessment for Sexual Offence Recidivism contains only four items: age less than 25; any male victim; any victims unrelated to the offender; and prior sexual offences (Hanson, 2001). The characteristics tapped by these items are indicators or markers of sexual offending rather than underlying vulnerability factors such as intimacy deficits, emotional/sexual disregulation, or offense supportive attitudes (Hanson, 2001). By way of contrast, the presence of psychological dispositions or vulnerability factors can be detected only by a more comprehensive assessment process involving a battery of scales, a structured clinical interview, and the incorporation of file data. In other words, a risk assessment that aims to assess an individual's degree of vulnerability is basically equivalent to a thorough clinical assessment. The problem is that these are two contrasting methods for detecting risk and it is unclear which type of risk assessment underlies the risk-need model. However, a careful reading of Hanson (2001), Blackburn (2000), McGuire (2000), and Andrews and Bonta (1998) suggests that the dispositional model should be the preferred one. And if this is the case, then the relationship between need (i.e., dispositional factors) and risk becomes muddy. Should the primary focus be on need (as defined as dispositions) or risk?

NEED

We now critically examine the concept of criminogenic need. It should be clear from the preceding discussion of risk that a clear risk-need distinction is almost impossible to sustain. What follows here, then, is a critique of the concept of need as it is more broadly defined and construed within psychology. Our critique in this section draws upon an extensive investigation of need contained in a recently completed paper (see Ward & Stewart, in press).

The term *criminogenic need* is itself a little odd in that risk factors are not needs in the usual sense. As discussed above, to have a need indicates a lack or deficiency of some kind, a lack of a valued good. Needs are concerned with the attainment of objective goods that sustain or enhance an individual's life; their absence will harm a person in some way or increase the chances of harm occurring in the future. However, in what sense can criminogenic needs such as impulsivity be said to involve objective goods? It is strange to speak of a need to behave impulsively. We suggest that this may not be an insurmountable problem for the theory of criminogenic needs if they are viewed as instrumental needs. Under this interpretation, impulsivity would be instrumentally related to criminal actions and therefore provide a means to the goals associated with a particular crime. Furthermore, if impulsivity is transposed to self-control or self-regulation, then the substantive therapeutic need an offender requires is that of autonomous functioning. Self-regulation then becomes instrumentally related to the more basic need for autonomy, and is then a condition for this need to be met or, if you like, an intermediate need related to the more basic one. Therefore, it may be perfectly legitimate and meaningful to speak of criminogenic needs if it is accepted that such talk is merely shorthand for an expanded analysis. Of course, what such an analysis indicates is that if it is meaningful to construe criminogenic needs as *needs,* then it must be possible to ground them in categorical or basic human needs. It is not clear that Andrews and Bonta's approach is capable of this, indicating a serious problem in their theory.

Andrews and Bonta appear to conflate (or equivocate between) two senses of need and therefore run the risk of not appreciating their important differences and possible contributions to the process of offender rehabilitation. These are instrumental needs and basic or categorical needs (Wiggins, 1991). *Instrumental needs* refer to those needs whose value depends entirely on their contribution to a further goal or end. For example, "The Melbourne Storm need to strengthen their defense if they are to win the league," or "Peter will need to learn how to control his anger if he is to be paroled." The requirement to act depends on the motivational force, or value, of the end for which the need is necessary. On the other hand, *categorical needs* derive their value from the needs themselves; they are not means to a further, more fundamental, end. When a categorical need exists, then in the circumstances there is no realistic alternative but to act in a certain way. For example, "Peter needs to eat now because he is starving," or "Mary needs to be loved." To fail to meet a categorical need would result in harm to a person. The need itself provides powerful reasons for certain actions and the value of fulfilling a categorical need is overriding. Categorical needs are derived from the nature of human beings and in a sense express our basic potentialities and properties. They are essentially the kind of needs described by Deci and Ryan (2000) as innate or basic needs.

The claim that a criminogenic need such as impulsivity is instrumentally related to further offending suggests that individuals choose to act in an impulsive manner in order to achieve the further goal of offending. However, it is a confusion to view what is essentially a loss of behavioral control as an intentional object; individuals do not choose to behave impulsively, they fail to inhibit problematic impulses or desires. A more accurate way of understanding the relationship between criminogenic needs and offending behavior is to say that they are necessary conditions for offending to occur. Thus they are not needs in an instrumental or categorical sense but rather *obstacles* to need fulfillment.

The relationship between needs and risk is not really explained by Andrews and Bonta. Although we acknowledge that assessment of an individual's level of risk is initially determined by consideration of static and dynamic variables, once treatment has commenced criminogenic needs are the major factors of interest. Unfortunately, Andrews and Bonta's formulation of the theory underpinning their four principles of treatment is incomplete, and they fail to clarify what determines an individual's range and depth of need. We suggest that offenders' level of risk is plausibly determined by the severity and/or the range of their criminogenic needs (see above). This indicates that criminogenic needs exist at a more fundamental level, and in some sense generate (e.g., by being related to the distortion of fundamental needs) offending behavior. If this is not the case, then arguably risk and need are essentially the same thing, with the former simply denoting an overall risk category or numerical value and the latter simply the *type* of risk factor. And if they are collapsed in this way, then the notion of need becomes interchangeable with that risk, and the utility of Andrews and Bonta's theory is severely restricted.

Relatedly, the Andrews and Bonta model does not really provide a conceptually integrated account of the relationships *between* offenders' criminogenic needs. Essentially, each risk factor has its own (statistical) relationship to reoffending and functions somewhat in isolation from the others. There is no real attempt at integration at the level of criminogenic need; needs are simply deficiencies or characteristics, changes which reduce reoffending. Andrews and Bonta do state via their general personality and social psychological perspective that each of the major criminogenic needs have their own causal relationship to offending behavior, or, more accurately, to the positive appraisal of offending behavior. However, the relationship of these factors to each other is not considered, just their convergence on crime supportive appraisals. What is missing is clarification of how needs are embedded in individuals and/or related to individual lives.

Another criticism concerns the relationship of criminogenic needs to values or normative issues. Needs are concerned with the attainment of personal goods that sustain or enhance an individual's life (Braybrooke, 1987; Thompson, 1987; Willard, 1987). Failure to meet such needs is likely to result in harm and/or increase the chances of harm occurring in the future. Needs thus reflect values: They are constitutive of personal goods in the sense of the valued goals of relatedness, autonomy, and competence. True, genuine needs also point to the conditions necessary to achieve goods and their associated goals, but if you accept that need is at least partially a normative concept and does not directly refer to a psychological state (although it may have a factual basis), then *needs* are not identified through empirical research, even on an instrumental reading of need. Rather, researchers detect dynamic characteristics that appear to be associated with disvalued outcomes (crime) and make normative judgments that such risk factors or predictors are needs. Thus there are independent value judgments that the factors in question are related to harmful outcomes; and that if needs are viewed in the categorical sense, failure to meet such needs will ultimately result in serious harm and contribute to social maladjustment and antisocial behavior. In other words, needs reflect both factual and normative judgments and also an understanding of the fundamental architecture of the human mind. If these further judgments are not made, the concept of criminogenic needs again simply collapses into that of risk. If need is partially normative and reflects personal and social values, then it should be explicitly tied to a theoretical base of some kind—either to a further end (non-offending) or to human nature.

A suitable candidate in this respect is the categorical risk model described earlier. Favored by judicial decision makers because of its clear links to the moral foundations upon which law is based, the categorical risk model provides a coherent, if not yet well developed, base of ethical values upon which to ground risk assessment and conceptualize risk-reduction strategies. The needs identified in the categorical risk model are elementary faculties or aspects of individual character. The task before psychologists is to capitalize upon their focus on human goodness and flourishing and to translate the largely philosophical descriptions and logical structures that surround them into practical and meaningful strategies for intervention with offenders.

We argue therefore that the current crop of empirically derived criminogenic needs are for the most part little more than range riders—they tell you that there is a problem but do not tell you what to do or how to go about it. For this, substantive theories about the need in question (e.g., impulsiveness) are required. Such theories will spell out how to bring about change in the relevant mechanisms that cause impulsiveness and how it relates to other needs. It will also explain how the particular criminogenic need in question is generated and what mechanisms are currently contributing to its maintenance. A policy that simply states that criminogenic needs should be primary treatment targets without invoking additional theory and clinical models will not result in effective treatment. Although Andrews and Bonta have recognized this and tried to construct a broad psychological theory of criminal conduct, their theory is essentially a framework and does not provide clear descriptions of the relevant causal mechanisms that generate criminogenic needs.

Conclusions

The risk-need model of offender rehabilitation represents a considerable achievement. The explicit aim of treating problems associated with offending makes clinical sense and has led to the identification of the features of effective programs. However, confusion concerning the different types of risk factors and risk assessment and the failure to clarify the nature of criminogenic needs are major problems. We acknowledge the demonstrated treatment effects of this approach. But we argue that the problems identified above may lead people to think in a simplistic and cursory manner about offender treatment and that such difficulties may, together with the unfortunate focus on range-rider type factors, account for the quite modest impacts of such interventions. In addition, we suggest that addressing the problems evident in the risk-need model along the lines outlined in this chapter may result in interventions that are more successful.

References

Andrews, D. A., & Bonta, J. (1998). *The psychology of criminal conduct* (2nd ed.). Cincinnati, OH: Anderson.

Blackburn, R. (2000). Risk assessment and prediction. In J. McGuire, T. Mason, & A. O'Kane (Eds.), *Behavior, crime and legal processes: A guide for legal practitioners* (pp. 178-204). Chichester, UK: Wiley.

Braybrooke, D. (1987). *Meeting needs.* Princeton, NJ: Princeton University Press.

Brown, M. (2000). Calculations of risk in contemporary penal practice. In M. Brown & J. Pratt (Eds.), *Dangerous offenders: Punishment and social order* (pp. 94-108). London: Routledge.

Deci, E. L., & Ryan, R. M. (2000). The "what" and "why" of goal pursuits: Human needs and the self-determination of behavior. *Psychological Inquiry, 11,* 227-268.

Emmons, R. A. (1999). *The psychology of ultimate concerns.* New York: Guilford.

Garland, D. (2001). *The culture of control: Crime and social order in contemporary society.* Chicago: University of Chicago Press.

Gendreau, P., & Andrews, D. A. (1990). Tertiary prevention: What the meta-analyses of the offender treatment literature tell us about what works. *Canadian Journal of Criminology, 32,* 173-184.

Hanson, R. K. (2001). Sex offender risk assessment. In C. R. Hollin (Ed.), *Handbook of offender assessment and treatment* (pp. 86-96). Chichester, UK: Wiley.

Hanson, R. K., & Harris, A. J. R. (2000). Where should we intervene? Dynamic predictors of sex offense recidivism. *Criminal Justice and Behavior, 27,* 6-35.

Hollin, C. R. (1999). Treatment programs for offenders: Meta-analysis, "what works" and beyond. *International Journal of Law and Psychiatry, 22,* 361-372.

McGuire, J. (2000). Explanations of criminal behavior. In J. McGuire, T. Mason, & A. O'Kane (Eds.), *Behavior, crime and legal processes: A guide for legal practitioners* (pp. 135-159). Chichester, UK: Wiley.

Mrazek, P. J., & Haggerty, R. J. (1994). *Reducing risks for mental disorders: Frontiers for preventive intervention.* Washington, DC: National Academy Press.

Thompson, G. (1987). *Needs.* London, UK: Routledge & Kegan Paul.

Ward, T., & Stewart, C. A. (in press). Criminogenic needs and human needs: A theoretical model. *Psychology, Crime, & Law.*

Ward, T., & Siegert, R. (in press). Toward a comprehensive explanation of child sexual abuse: A theory knitting perspective. *Psychology, Crime, & Law.*

Wiggins, D. (1991). *Needs, values and truth.* Oxford, UK: Blackwell.

Willard, L. D. (1987). *Needs and rights.* Dialogue, XXVI, 43-53.

Index

Abel, G. G., 93, 98, 136, 158, 160, 161, 183, 185, 301
Abracen, J., 254
Abstinence, xviii, 79, 283, 284, 288, 292
Actuarial assessment instruments, 212-214, 217-221, 223
Addictive behavior, 66, 67-68
Adolescent sex offenders, xiv-xvii, 11, 16
    adolescence, critical period of, 121-122, 191-192
    biological domain/sexuality, 198-199
    childhood sexual abuse and, 194
    classification of, 190-193
    clinical issues, 198-204
    delinquency model and, 193, 197
    diagnosis of, 160
    etiological pathways of, 193-196
    family and, 200-201
    interpersonal domain/identity, 199-200
    peers and, 201-203
    penile plethysmography and, 198-199
    personality features and, 192-193
    pharmacological treatments, 266
    pornography, vulnerability to, 199
    recidivism rate for, 193, 196-198
    research issues, 190-198
    school environment and, 203
    social domain of, 200-204
    social services for, 203-204
    treatment frameworks, 194, 199-200, 201-204, 299
Adult mating strategies, 49-51, 54-55, 57
Adversarial Sexual Beliefs scale, 141
Affective dyscontrol, 9, 10
Aggression, 11, 13-14, 140, 141
Alarcon, J., 319, 325
Anderson, D., 148, 247, 253, 254, 319

Andrews, D. A., 288, 302, 305, 306, 339, 340, 350
Antecedents. *See* Developmental antecedents
Antisocial cognitions, 17, 121
Archer, M. S., 25
Arnhart, L., 26
Arousal reconditioning, 39-40
Assessment process, xii, xiv, xvi
    formula-based approach, xvii-xviii
    good lives model and, 31-37
    pharmacological treatments, 273-274
    See also Behavioral economics; Penile plethysmography (PPG); Risk assessment
Association for the Treatment of Sexual Abusers (ATSA), 88, 96, 208, 276, 303
Attachment theory, xviii, 7, 248-249, 255, 257-258
Attitudes. *See* Beliefs; Corrections staff
Attitudes Towards Prisoners Scale, 332
Attitudes Towards Sexual Offenders Scale, 326
Attribution theory, 195, 250
Auburn, T., 326

Baer, J. S., 281, 282, 283
Blackburn, R., 341
Bancroft, J. H. J., 83
Barbaree, H. E., 3, 10-14, 56, 89, 91, 97, 98, 121, 184, 198, 247, 301
Barlow, D. H., 85, 91, 93
Barlow gauge, 85
Bartholomew, K., 248
Bartlett, F. A., 139
Bays, L., 320
Beaudette, D., 326
Beck, A. T., 136, 139, 140

355

Becker, J. V., 98
Beckett, R., 183, 195
Beech, A., 178, 180, 183, 185
Behavioral economics, xiv, 65
    constraint on access/treatment, 72-73,
        73-74 (figures), 75 (table),
        76 (figure)
    definition of, 66
    demand assessment, 70-71, 71 (figure)
    demand, law of, 68-69, 69-70 (figures)
    help-seeking implications, 77-79
    hyperbolic discounting function/impulsiv-
        ity, 73-79, 76 (figure)
    impulse control, 67-68
    reinforcement, matching law and, 66-67
    sexual interest assessment, 70-71,
        71 (figure)
    treatment implications, 77, 79
    See Change; Motivation to change
Behavior pathology, 139
Beliefs, xii
    children-as-sexual-beings, 130, 137
    corrections staff, 326-327, 328-330
    critical reflection and, 115-116
    dangerous world beliefs, 130-131, 137
    dysfunctional core beliefs, xvii
    entitlement beliefs, 130, 137, 142-143, 144
    harm reduction, 283-285
    harm reduction perspective, 283-285
    locus of control belief, 131, 137
    schemas, xv-xvi, 147
    See also Cognitive therapy theory;
        Implicit theories
Benson, C., 103
Bera, W. H., 191
Berlin, S. B., 104
Bickel, W. K., 66, 69, 73, 77
Biological variables, xii, 18, 59-60,
    119, 198-199
Blackburn, R., 341, 349
Blackshaw, L., 303
Blanchard, E. B., 93
Boer, D. P., 245, 249, 255, 257, 302
Bonta, J., 288, 302, 305, 306, 339, 340, 350
Bordieu, P., 105, 106
Brett, T., 325
Brown, C., 180
Browne, K., 178, 180, 185
Brown, L. M., 141, 142
Bumby, K. M., 185, 250
Burt, M. R., 141, 183

Buss, D. M., 51
Bussière, M. T., 93, 217, 218, 302

California Psychological Inventory, 192
Calmas, W., 166
Cann, S., 178, 181
Case formulation, xii, 32, 162-164,
    231, 241-242
Castration, 264
Cellini, H. R., 203
Champagne, F., 180, 247
Change:
    behaviors, 246-247
    decisional balance and, 287, 322, 325
    stages of, 286, 323
    See also Motivation to change
Chaplin, T. C., 179
Chasan-Taber, L., 309, 310, 311
Check, J. V. P., 141
Child Empathy Test (CET), 176, 180
Child Molester Empathy Measure (CMEM),
    176, 177, 180
Children-as-sexual-beings belief, 130, 137
Child sexual abuse, xiii, 3
    entitlement belief and, 142-143
    integrated theory of, 10-14
    meta-theoretical framework and, 3-4
    offender self-report interest
        measures, 92, 159-160
    offender typology, 166-167, 250-251
    pathways model of, xiii, 4, 14-18
    pedophile index, recidivism prediction
        and, 93
    precondition theory of, 4-8
    public health response to, 307-309
    quadripartite theory of, 8-10
    See also Pedophilia
Choice. See Behavioral economics
Cicchetti, D., 120
Circumferential strain gauge, 83, 85
Civil commitment proceedings, 221-223, 276
Classification models. See Sex offender classifi-
    cation models
Clinical practice, xii-xiii
    cultural-reflective model and,
        113-116, 114 (figure)
    formula-based assessment/treatment and,
        xvii-xviii
    group vs. individual treatment formats,
        253-255, 256-258
    interpretation process and, 115

open treatment format, 254
power effects and, 116
risk-need model and, xiii-xiv, 21-23
social control effect in, 277
See also Case formulation; Cultural factors;
    Empathy; Pathways model;
    Responsivity factors; Sex offender
    classification models; Therapy goals
Coercive sexual behaviors, 54-56
Cognitive behavioral model, xv-xvi,
    76-77, 135, 317
    antisocial cognitions, 17
    cognitive dissonance, 322
    cognitive distortions, 129-130, 136-138,
        234-235
    cognitive variables, 10
    See also Cognitive therapy theory; Relapse
        prevention; Schemas; Social
        cognition theory; Treatment
        programs
Cognitive distortions, 129-130,
    136-138, 234-235
Cognitive motivation, 8, 9
Cognitive therapy theory, xv-xvi, 139
    aggressive cognitive scripts and, 140
    cognitive restructuring, 38-39, 148
    interpersonal interactions and, 140
    schema concept in, 139-140, 148-149
    sexual offending, schema-based model
        of, 145-147, 146 (figure)
Cohen, M. L., 166
Coherency, 33
    cognitive restructuring and, 39
    horizontal coherence, 33-34
    primary goods, selection of, 34-35
    vertical coherence, 34
Coleman, E. M., 24, 142
Collaborative Outcome Data Project, 303
Community interests, xviii, 21-22,
    163, 276-277
    See also Relapse prevention
Conduct disorder, 17
Connors, W., 324
Context. *See* Environmental factors
CORE Sex Offender Programs, 320-321, 324,
    327, 331, 333
Cormier, C. A., 302
Correctional psychology. *See* Risk-need model
Corrections staff, 320
    attitudes/beliefs of, 326-327, 328-330
    change stages, motivational interviewing

and, 330-331
    confrontation techniques of, 321
    external supervisory role, 321
    training, evaluation of, 331-333,
        332 (figure)
    training model for, 327-331, 331 (table)
    See also Criminal justice approach; Relapse
        prevention
Cosmides, L., 50
Coutts, J., 179
Cox, M., 253
Criminal justice approach, xvii, 21-22, 207,
    299, 304-306
    continuum of care, 320-321, 334
    See also Corrections staff; Relapse
        prevention
Criminogenic needs, 287-288, 306,
    321, 339, 349
Critical reflection, 114-116
Critical threshold, 8, 9, 10
Cross-cultural communication. *See* Cultural
    factors
Crozier, W. R., 249
Cultural factors, xii, xv
    case study, 108-112
    child sexual abuse and, 17-18
    critical reflection, 114-116
    cultural-reflective model, 113-116, 114
        (figure)
    nontransparent reflexivity, 110-112
    personal self and, 105-106, 107, 113
    practice context and, 103-105
    professional self and, 106, 107, 114
    reflexive reactions, locations of, 105-107
    transparent reflexivity, 108-110
Cumming, G. F., 319
Cummins, R. A., 26
Cunningham-Rathner, J., 98

Dangerous world belief, 130-131, 137
Daubert v. Merrell Dow Pharmaceuticals,
    95, 97, 222
Day, D. M., 92, 319, 325
Deci, E. L., 342, 343, 350
Decisional Balance, 287, 322
Deigh, J., 249
Deisher, R. M., 192
Demand, 68-69, 69-70 (figures)
    constraints on access/treatment, 72-73,
        73-74 (figures), 75 (table),
        76 (figure)

sexual interest assessment, 70-71,
71 (figure)
Denning, P., 286, 287
DesJarlais, D. C., 283
Developmental antecedents, 119-120, 230
adolescence, transition into, 121-122
implicit theories and, 127-131
self-regulation, sexual offending
and, 122-124
theory of mind and, 124-127
See also Developmental psychopathology
Developmentally adverse events, 11, 12
Developmentally disabled offenders, 24
Developmental psychopathology, xv, 120
adolescence and, 121-122
adult mating strategies and, 55, 56
equi/multifinality and, 121, 132
life-span approach, 121
risk factors, 341-342
tenets of, 120-121
See also Developmental antecedents
Deviant sexual behavior, xii, xiv
harm reduction perspective, xviii, 27, 40
impulse control and, 67-68
sexual script deficits and, 14-15, 18,
233-234
See also Demand; Sex offender
classification models
Diagnosis. *See* Sex offender classification
models
*Diagnostic and Statistical Manual of
Mental Disorders, Fourth Edition*
(DSM-IV), xvi, 155, 157-161
DiClemente, C. C., 252, 286, 287, 291, 323
DiFazio, R., 254
Disabled offenders, 24
Disinhibition, 5, 6, 7, 9
dysfunctional self-regulation, 123
emotional dysregulation and, 234
sex offending and, 12
Donovan, D. M., 66, 68, 77, 78
Dougher, M. J., 246, 256
Drake, C. R., 163
Dramatherapy techniques, 325-326
Durrant, M., 199
Dutton, D. G., 140
Dwyer, S. M., 288
Dysfunctional mechanisms, 17

Eagleton, T., 106
Economics. *See* Behavioral economics

Elliott, D. S., 194
Ellis, B. J., 51-54
Emmons, R. A., 26, 34
Emotional congruence, 4, 5, 7, 227
Emotional dysregulation, 16, 234
Empat-A scale, 176, 177, 181
Empat-G scale, 176, 178, 179
Empathy, xvi, 173
caring and, 174
deficits in, 124, 125, 172, 184
four-stage model of, 175
general empathy measures, 175-176, 177,
178-179 (table)
good lives model and, 40-41
interventions, empathy-based,
179, 181-183
measurement of, 175-177
models of, 173-175
offense process, victim-specific deficits
and, 184-186
self-esteem enhancement and, 247
shame/guilt and, 182, 250
theory development in, 186-187
victim-specific measure of, 176-177, 179,
180-181 (table)
Empathy for Women Test (EFWT), 176, 180
Entitlement belief, 130, 137, 142-143, 144
Environmental factors:
culture, role of, 17-18
personal identity construction and, 27, 30,
34-35, 36
reinforcement, matching law and, 66-67
ultimate/proximate causation, 48-49,
60-61
Ethical issues, xii, xviii
human desires and, 26-27
pharmacological treatments, 275-277
Etiological theories, xii-xiii, xvi, 227
See also Adolescent sex offenders; Child
sexual abuse;
Developmental antecedents;
Developmental psychopathology
Evans, I. M., 91
Evolutionary psychology, xii, 45-46
adaptation/selection and, 46-47, 58
coercive behaviors, evolutionary-based
model, 54-56
definition of, 47-49
empirical research and, 60
human mating strategies, 49-51,
54-55, 57

information processing
    mechanisms, 47-48
rape, evolutionary theory of, 56-59
reductionism and, 60-61
synthesized theory on rape and, 51-54
ultimate/proximate causation, behavior
    patterns and, 48-49, 60-61
External locus of control belief, 131, 137
External responsivity factors.
    See Responsivity factors

Fantasies, 16, 17
Farkas, G. M., 91
Feminist theory, 55, 59
Fernandez, Y. M., 89, 96, 148, 176, 180, 182,
    183, 184, 185, 186, 247, 253, 254
Finkelhor, D., 3, 4-8, 136
Fisher, D., 178, 180, 183, 185
Fishman, N., 173
Fiske, S. T., 139
Folk psychological theories. See Implicit
    theories
Fook, J., 115
Formulation-based assessment, xvii-xviii,
    229-231, 241-242
Freed, D. E., 66, 67
Freeman-Longo, R. E., 293, 320
Frenzel, R. R., 89
Freud, S., 107
Frizzel, K., 197
Frye v. United States, 95, 222
Fulfillment. See Good lives model
Furby, L., 303

Garland, R. J., 246, 256
Garmezy, N., 120
Gaulin, S. J. C., 49
Gender:
    child sexual abuse offender, 18
    competitive male behaviors, xii
    hostile masculinity, 55, 141-142
    human mating strategies, 49-51
    low-commitment sex, 57, 58
    male sexual activity, testosterone
        and, 266-268
    rape, adaptive strategy of, 57-58
Gendreau, P., 304, 305
George, W. H., 281
Gibat, C. C., 318
Giddens, A., 105
Gilbert, P., 249

Gizzarelli, R., 142
Gladstein, G. A., 173
Good lives model, 23, 24, 42-43, 149
    arousal reconditioning and, 39-40
    assessment process, 31-37
    case formulation, 32
    cognitive restructuring in, 38-39
    coherence and, 33-34
    internal/external conditions and, 36-37
    mood management, 41
    needs fulfillment, 33
    norm-building, 38
    personal identity, context dependency and,
        27, 30, 34-35, 36
    primary goods and, 25-27, 32-33
    principles of, 24-25
    rehabilitation concept within, 27-29
    relapse prevention and, 42
    relationship skills, development of, 41
    therapy goals in, 35-37
    traditional treatment framework, 29-31
    treatment phase in, 37-42
    victim impact/offender empathy, 40-41
Gordon, A., 303
Gordon, J. R., 287
Green, L., 66, 67
Greenbaum, P. E., 92
Grove, W. M., 220
Grubin, D. H., 161, 164
Gulayets, M. J., 89
Gunn, J., 161

Haaven, J. L., 24
Hagstrom, A., 158, 159
Hall, G. C. N., 3, 8-10, 303
Hamilton, K., 180, 186
Handy, L., 178
Hanson, R. K., 92, 93, 138, 142, 174,
    176, 180, 211, 212, 217, 218,
    250, 302, 303, 339, 349
Harm reduction perspective, xviii, 27, 40, 79
    belief system of, 283-285
    client advocacy-based approach of, 284
    continuum of harm, 283
    criminogenic needs and, 287-288, 306
    history of, 281-283, 282 (figure)
    low-threshold access to services,
        xviii, 284-285
    misconceptions about, 290-293
    psychotherapeutic approach
        of, 285-288

public health perspective,
283-284, 293, 297
relapse prevention and, 280-281, 288-290
Harm risk, xvii, 131, 137
Harris, A. J. R., 303, 339
Harris, B., 197
Harris, G. T., 179, 302
Hart, S. D., 302
Hayashino, D. S., 178
Haynes, M. R., 142
Heavey, C. L., 194
Helmreich, R., 141
Help-seeking, 77-79
Herrnstein, R. J., 66, 67
Hildebran, D., 181
Hirschman, R., 3, 8-10
Hogan Empathy scale, 175
Hogue, T. E., 326
Holahan, C. K., 141
Hollin, C. R., 143, 144
Holmen, M. L., 97
Homosexual pedophilia, 194
Horowitz, L., 248
Hostile masculinity, 55, 141-142
Hostility Toward Women scale, 141
Howells, K., 250
Howes, R. J., 87, 92
Hudson, S. M., 79, 139, 178, 184, 185, 196,
248, 250, 320, 321
Huesmann, L. R., 140, 141
Human mating strategies, 49-51, 54-55, 57
Hursh, S. R., 67
Hyperbolic discounting function, 73-77,
76 (figure)
help-seeking implications, 77-79
research/treatment implications, 77

Identity construction, 24, 27-28
adolescence, 199-200
human goal coherency and, 33-35
intentional actions and, 39
norm-building and, 38
Implicit theories, xv, 127-128
children-as-sexual-objects, 130, 137
cognitive distortions, 129-130
dangerous world belief, 130-131, 137
entitlement beliefs, 130, 137
harm, nature of, 131, 137
scientific theories and, 128-129
uncontrollable world, 131, 137
See also Schemas

Impulse control, 67-68, 73-77, 76 (figure)
Incest offenders, 1, 8, 142-143
Information processing, 139, 142
Inhibition. See Disinhibition
In re Valdez et al., 223
Integrated theory of child sexual abuse, 10-14
Internal responsivity factors. See Responsivity
factors
Interpersonal Reactivity Index (IRI),
175, 176, 178, 179
Interventions, xii, xvii, 299
approach-goal-oriented intervention, 24
empathy-based, 179, 181-183
low-threshold access to, xviii, 284-285
reconditioning interventions, 18
See also Good lives model; Therapy goals
Intimacy deficits, 12, 15
attachment style and, 248-249
relationship skill development, 41
sexual gratification, 39-40
sexual offending schemas, 141, 233

Jackson, H. J., 161
Jenkins, A., 200
Jenkins-Hall, K. D., 287
Johnston, L., 139
Jones, H. C., 83
Jones, J. H., 107
Jones, R., 18, 178, 184, 185
Josselson, R., 173
Just-say-no programs, 298

Kahn, M., 167
Kalmar, D. A., 4
Kansas v. Hendricks, 221, 276
Kaszniak, A., 167
Kear-Colwell, J., 245, 246, 248, 252, 255, 257
Keenan, T., 126, 137, 140
Kekes, J., 26
Kennedy, H. G., 164
Kennedy, S. M., 245
Kerem, E., 173
Kibblewhite, K., 326
Kinsey, A. C., 107
Klebe, K. J., 178
Klinefelter's syndrome, 268
Knight, R. A., 165-167, 191, 197
Konopasky, R., 178, 181
Koss, M. P., 141
Krop, H., 136
Kropp, P. R., 302

Kuhn, T., 289, 290
Kumho Tire Co. v. Carmichael, 222

Lalumiere, M. L., 55
Langevin, R., 178
Larimer, M. E., 281, 282, 283
Laschet, L., 268
Laschet, U., 268
Laws, D. R., 78, 89, 91, 92, 93, 97, 283, 292, 300, 302, 320
Lea, S., 326
Lee, J. K. P., 161, 163
Legal issues, xviii
    civil commitment proceedings, 221-223, 276
    penile plethysmography, 94-97
    pharmacological treatments, 275-277
    See also Criminal justice approach
Letourneau, E., 87, 89, 90, 92, 93, 96
Levine, H. C., 281, 283
Life satisfaction, 26-27
Lightbody, S., 176, 180
Linville, P. W., 139
Linz, D., 194
Lipsey, M. W., 304
Little, J., 287
Looman, J., 254

Madden, G. J., 66, 69, 73, 77
Malamuth, N. M., 54-56, 141, 142, 194
Maletzky, B. M., 253, 254
Mann, R. E., 24, 42, 89, 143, 144, 247, 324
Manual-based interventions, xvii, 30, 228-229, 241
Maric, A., 178
Marlatt, G. A., 66, 68, 77, 78, 79, 281, 282, 283, 286, 287, 289, 291, 300, 318
Marques, J. K.., 303, 318, 319, 325
Marshall, L. E., 89
Marshall, W. L., 3, 10-14, 53, 89, 96, 121, 139, 148, 160, 176, 178, 180, 181, 182, 183, 184, 185, 186, 198, 245, 247, 248, 250, 252, 253, 254, 256, 301, 319
Martinson, R., 304
Massachusetts Treatment Center, 165-167
Masturbation, 8, 11, 13, 16, 39, 40
Matching law, 67
Mating strategies, 49-51, 54-55, 57
Mavissakalian, M., 93
McBurney, D., 49
McCabe, M. P., 179, 246

McDonald, E., 178
McFall, R. M., 141
McGrath, M., 178, 181
McGrath, R. J., 319
McGuire, J., 349
McHugh, J., 98
McMahon, P. M., 298, 299, 300, 301, 307, 309
Meaning. *See* Coherency; Good lives model
Medication. *See* Pharmacological treatments
Mehrabian-Epstein empathy scale, 175, 178, 179
Mental disorders, 156-158, 231
Mental health professionals, xvii
    expert testimony of, 221-222
    risk assessment procedures, 211-214
Mental states. *See* Theory of mind
Mercy, J. A., 297, 298
Meux, C., 325
Miller, G., 50
Miller, S., 180
Miller, W. R., 286
Milloy, C. D., 197
Mind reading, 125, 127
Mind. *See* Theory of mind
Miner, M. H., 92
Minnesota Sex Offender Screening Tool-Revised (MnSOST-R), 218
Monsastersky, C., 192
Mood management, xiii, 16, 41
Motivational interviewing, 246-247, 257, 286-287, 323-324, 330-331
Motivation to change, xviii, 8, 9, 136, 245-247, 256-257
    change stages/processes, 286, 323
    cognitive dissonance and, 322
    decisional balance in, 287, 322
    enhancement of, 322-326
    motivational interviewing and, 323-324, 330-331
    self-efficacy and, 322
    sex offenders and, 324-325
    See also Relapse prevention
Moulden, H., 181
Mulder, J. R., 246
Multidimensional Assessment of Sex and Aggression (MASA), 166
Multiphasic Sex Inventory (MSI), 92
Murphy, J., 92
Murphy, W., 303
Murphy, W. D., 89, 91, 97, 98, 142, 148
Myers, R., 143

Nathan, P., 163
National Crime Victimization Survey, 301
National Women's Study, 301
Naturalistic model, xii, 59-60
Need. See Risk-need model
Negative blindness hypothesis, 142
Negative Masculinity scale, 141
Neidigh, L., 136
Nelson, C., 319, 325
Nicolaichuk, T., 303
Norcross, J. C., 286, 287, 291, 323
Nussbaum, M. C., 26, 105

O'Brien, M. J., 191
O'Donohue, W., 87, 89, 90, 92, 93, 96, 158, 159
Offender management. See Motivation to
    change; Relapse prevention;
    Risk-need model
Offense supportive attitudes, 136-137, 138
Osborn, C. A., 91, 92, 161
O'Sullivan, C., 176, 180, 182, 183
The-Other-as-Shamer scale, 257
Overperception hypothesis, 142

Palmer, C. T., 56-59
Paraphilia, 155
    mental disorder and, 156-158
    pedophilia, 159-160
    rape, exclusion of, 160-161
Pathé, M., 163
Pathways model, xiii, 4, 14, 232-233
    antisocial cognitions, 17
    cognitive distortions, 234-235
    culture, role of, 17-18
    emotional dysregulation, 16, 234
    intimacy deficits, 15, 233
    multiple dysfunctional mechanisms, 17
    psychological mechanisms in, 14-15
    sexual scripts deficits, 15-16, 233-234
    victims, subsequent abuse by, 17
Patriarchal attitudes, 17
Pattison, P., 161
Pedophilia, 159-160, 194
    attachment styles and, 248-249, 257-258
    confrontation, impact of, 252, 255
Pelletier, G., 326
Penile plethysmography (PPG), xiv-xv, 83, 273
    adolescent sex offenders and, 198-199
    age/gender assessment, 86, 89
    art of, 87-90
    construct validity of, 90-92

faking phenomenon, 97
future of, 99
legal challenges to, 94-97
multisite assessment of, 89-90, 99
norm-referenced vs. criterion-referenced
    test, 92-93
recidivism prediction and, 93-94, 217-218
self-report measures, 91-92, 99, 268
sexual activity assessment, 86-87
standardization in, 88-90
suppression effect, 83
technological definition of, 85-86
utility of, 97-98
Personal identity. See Identity construction
Personality deficits, 8, 249
Personal striving, 26-27, 33
Persons, J. B., 162
Petry, N. M., 66, 69, 73, 77
Pharmacological treatments, xviii, 262-263
    antipsychotic medications, 265
    assessment/monitoring processes, 273-274
    candidates for, 272-273
    castration, 264
    compliance with, 264
    effectiveness measures, 268-269
    ethical/legal issues in, 275-277
    hormonal treatments, 266, 268-271
    ideal criteria for, 263-264
    management target, 271-272
    recidivism reduction and, 269, 274-275
    self-report measures, 268, 273-274
    serotonergic drugs, 265-266
    side effects, 263, 269-271
    testosterone, male sexual activity
        and, 266-268
Pithers, W. D., 178, 179, 181, 182, 183,
    184, 227, 235, 318
Practice. See Clinical practice; Cultural factors;
    Treatment programs
Precondition theory, 4-8
Preferential offenders, 8-9, 12
Premack principle, 66-67
Prentky, R. A., 165-167, 191, 197
Prevention. See Public health perspective;
    Relapse prevention
Primary goods. See Good lives model
Prochaska, J. M., 323
Prochaska, J. O., 286, 287, 291, 323
Proeve, M., 250
Psychiatric diagnosis, xvi, 155-156, 167-168
    mental disorder, paraphilias and, 156-158

pedophilia, 159-160
rape, exclusion of, 160-161
See also Sex offender classification models
Psychological processes, xii
deficits and, 8, 9
developmental adversity, 11, 12
offender symptomology and, xvii
primary goods and, 26-27, 33
See also Developmental antecedents; Good
lives model; Pathways model;
Risk-need model; Theory of mind
Psychopathology. *See* Developmental
psychopathology
Psychopathy Checklist-Revised (PCL-R),
218, 302
Public health perspective, xviii, xix, 297-298
child sexual abuse, 307-309
harm reduction and, 283-284, 293, 297
outcome information, dissemination
of, 304-307
prevention, levels of, 298-300,
300 (figure)
recidivism rates, 303-305
risk factor research, 302
sexual violence, remedies for, 300-307
social vs. individual interests, 276-277
STOP IT NOW! Campaign, 309-313,
311 (table)
surveillance of data, 301-302
treatment programs, development/
evaluation of, 303-304
Puett, R. C., 307, 309
Pullan, B. P., 83
Purvis, M., 331

Quadripartite theory, 8-10
Quayle, M., 325
Quigley, L. A., 281, 282, 283
Quinsey, V. L., 55, 302, 303

Rape, xvi
acquaintance rape, 141
adaptive strategy of, 57-58
coercive behaviors, evolutionary-based
model of, 54-56
diagnosis of, 160-161
evolutionary theory of, 56-59
forced copulation threshold, 52, 53-54
rapist typology, 165-166
standard social science model of, 59
synthesized theory of, 51-54

ultimate/proximate causation,
48-49, 60-61
See also Sexual offending
Rape Fact Sheet, 301, 302
Rape Myth Acceptance scale, 183
Rapid Risk Assessment for Sex Offence
Recidivism (RRASOR), 218, 348
Rapist Empathy Measure (REM), 176, 177,
179, 180, 181
Recidivism, 21
criminogenic needs and, 340
good lives model and, 23
penile plethysmography, prediction and,
93-94
pharmacological treatments, 269
See also Adolescent sex offenders; Relapse
prevention; Risk assessment
Reconditioning interventions, 18
Regev, L. G., 158, 159
Rehabilitation, xiii-xiv, 338
classification principles, 244-245
enhancement model and, 27, 29
risk management and, 21, 23, 29-30
wellness and, 23-24, 25
See also Good lives model; Risk-need
model
Reinforcement, 66
matching law and, 67
See also Behavioral economics
Reiss, D., 325
Relapse prevention model, xii, xiii, xix, 227,
317-318, 334
correctional staff, roles of, 321-322,
326-327
dramatherapy techniques, 325-326
external supervision in, 319-320, 333-334
good lives model and, 24, 25, 42
internal self-management
component, 319
motivation to change, 320, 322-326, 333
pharmacological treatment and, 274-275
prison/community-based sex offender
programs, 320-322
research and, 318
service delivery model, 318-319
staff attitude effects and, 326-327
staff training model, 327-333, 331 (table),
332 (figure)
treatment framework and, 29-30, 235
See also Corrections staff; Harm reduction
perspective; Motivation to change

Relationship, xiii, 11
  deviant sexual scripts and, 15-16, 141
  primary good of, 26
  self-other relationship schemas, 140
  skill development, 41
  See also Cognitive therapy theory; Social
    cognition theory; Theory of mind
Relativity theory of reinforcement, 66-67
Reproductive behavior. *See* Human mating
    strategies
Responsivity factors, xviii, 245
  attachment style, 248-249, 253,
    255, 257-258
  confrontation and, 252, 255
  individual vs. group treatment formats,
    253-255, 256-258
  motivation to change, 245-247, 256-257
  outcome research and, 258
  self-esteem, 247-248
  shame, 249-251, 252, 255, 257
  therapist style, 246, 251-253, 255-256
Rice, M. E., 179, 302
Righthand, S., 197
Riley, D., 289
Risk assessment, xvi, xvii, 22-23, 197, 207
  actuarial approaches, 212-214,
    217-221, 223
  civil commitment proceedings and,
    221-223, 276
  evaluation, assessment
    procedures, 214-219
  limitations of, 214
  predictive power of, 219, 220-221
  professional judgment procedures,
    211-212, 217, 221-223
  recidivistic sexual offending, 208-209
  sexual violence risk assessment, 209-210
  transparency of, 215
  See also Risk-need model
Risk factor research, 302
Risk-need model, xii-xiv, xix, 339
  categorical risk model, 346-347, 352
  correctional psychology domain
    and, 345-346
  criminogenic needs and, 339, 340,
    349, 351, 352
  critical analysis of, 343-352
  dispositional factors, 348-349
  fluid vs. categorical risk, 346-347
  instrumental needs and, 350
  need concept, 342-343

needs, normative issues and, 351-352
  offender needs, 21-22
  principles of, 22-23
  risk assessment, 348-349
  risk concept, 341-342, 348
  risk-need relationship, 344, 348,
    350-351
  treatment process in, 340-341,
    342, 344-345
  See also Good lives model
Rollnick, S., 286
Rothman, D. J., 281, 283
Rouleau, J. -L., 160, 161
Rowe, W. E., 197
Roys, D. T., 250
Rubin, H. B., 97
Rush, B., 281, 282
Rutter, M., 120
Ryan, R. M., 342, 343, 350

Safer Society Foundation, Inc., 97
Saffran, J. D., 140
Sales, B., 167
Salter, A. C., 147, 183
Satiation training, 39
Satisfaction index, 26-27
Sawle, G. A., 248, 252
Schemas, xv-xvi
  aggressive cognitive scripts, 140
  cognition, schema-based model
    of, 145-147, 146 (figure)
  cognitive distortions and,
    137-138, 234-235
  dysfunctional relationship schemas,
    14-15, 18
  sexual offending schemas, 138, 141-144
  treatment implications of, 147-150
  See also Cognitive therapy theory; Sexual
    offending; Social cognition theory
Schofield, C., 24, 42
Schram, D. D., 197
Schwartz, B. K., 254
Scott, H., 142, 174, 176, 180
Segal, Z. V., 139
Seghorn, T. K., 166
Self, 26
  cultural thinking, locations of, 105-107
  global negative evaluation of, 249
Self-determination theory of needs, 342-343
Self-efficacy, 322
Self-esteem, xviii

cognitive restructuring and, 39
  intimacy deficits and, 15-16
  responsivity to treatment and, 247-248
Self-regulation, xv, 7, 11, 12, 122
  disruption of, 122-123
  dysfunctional patterns of, 123-124
  effectiveness of, 123
  primary goods and, 26-27
  reference value/goal in, 124
  relapse process, approach/avoidance
    goals, 235-241
Serran, G. A., 53
Seto, M. C., 303
Sex offender classification models, xvi,
    154-155
  case formulation, 162-164
  child molester typology, 166-167
  functional analytic approaches to,
    161-164, 168
  nondiagnostic classification, 164-165
  offender heterogeneity, 168
  psychiatric diagnosis, 155-161, 167-168
  quadripartite theory and, 8-9
  rapist typology, 165-166
  See also Adolescent sex offenders
Sex Offender Risk Appraisal Guide
    (SORAG), 93-94
Sex offenders, xi, xii
  developmentally disabled, 24
  help-seeking by, 77-79
  life maps of, 143
  See also Empathy; Good lives model;
    Pathways model; Risk-need model
Sexual deviance. See Deviant sexual behavior;
    Sex offender classification models
Sexual gratification, 39-40
Sexual motivation, 11, 13-14
Sexual offending, xi, xvi, xvii
  assertiveness/hostility, discrimination
    of, 142
  belief schemas and, 147
  children-as-sexual-objects, 130
  cognition in, schema-based model, 145-
    147, 146 (figure)
  entitlement belief, 130, 137, 142-143, 144
  explanatory schemas, 143-144
  hostile masculinity and, 141-142
  multifactorial motivation of, 136
  offender self-perception, 143
  planning framework of, 11
  schemas in, 141-144

  stereotyping, role of, 146-147
  theory-of-mind deficits and, 127
  treatment, schema-based approach,
    147-150
  See also Child sexual abuse;
    Developmental antecedents;
    Empathy; Social cognition theory
Sexual scripts, 14-15, 18, 233-234
Shame, xviii, 249
  behaviors of, 249-250
  group therapy and, 255
  internal/external aspects of, 249
  personal characteristics and, 250-251
  sex offending and, 250
  therapist style and, 252-253, 255, 257
Shingler, J., 149, 150
Siegert, R. J., 58, 121, 132, 136, 248
Simon, L. M. J., 167
Sine, L. F., 91
Situational offenders, 8, 12
Smith, S. K., 95, 96
Smith, W. R., 192
Social cognition theory, xv-xvi, 138
  information processing, 139, 142
  memory structures, schemas, 138-139
  sexual offending, schema-based
    model of, 145-147, 146 (figure)
  See also Cognitive therapy theory
Social control, 277
Social learning theory, 51, 53, 56, 317
Social life, 26
Sockloskie, R., 141
Spence, J. T., 141
Spradley, J., 104
Static-99, 218, 219
Stermac, L. E., 139
Sternberg, R. J., 4
Stewart, C., 79, 287, 288, 306
Stoner, S. A., 281
STOP IT NOW! Campaign, 301,
    309-313, 311 (table)
Striving, 26-27, 33
Sturgeon, V. H., 92
Substance abuse, 66, 67-68
Suspiciousness hypothesis, 142
Symons, D., 58
Sympathy. See Empathy
Synthesized theory on rape, 51
  analysis of, 52-54
  forced copulation threshold, 52, 53-54
  learning theory and, 51, 53

propositions of, 51-52
sex hormones, brain function and, 52, 53

Tabachnick, J., 309, 310, 311
Tagney, J. P., 257
Tanaka, J., 141
Tapert, S. F., 289
Taylor, G., 249
Theory knitting process, xiii, 4
Theory of mind, xv, 47-48, 124-125
    deficits in, 125-126
    developmental nature of, 126-127
    mind reading and, 125, 127
    negative effects and, 126
    sex crimes and, 127
Therapist-client relationship, 246, 251-253
Therapy goals, xii, xiii-xiv
    avoidance goals, 79
    formula-based assessment/treatment and,
        xvii-xviii, 30
    good lives model and, 35-37
    offender rehabilitation, 23-24
    zero tolerance, 289
    See also Clinical practice; Cognitive
        therapy theory; Responsivity factors
Thornhill, R., 56-59
Thornton, D., 149, 150, 302
Tierney, D. W., 179, 246
Tooby, J., 50
Treatment programs, xi, xii, xvi, 226-227
    avoidance goals, 79
    behavioral economic approaches to, xiv
    child sexual abuse, 5-6
    conditioning strategies, 8
    delivery models for, xiii, 228
    developmentally disabled offenders, 24
    development/evaluation of, 303-304
    formulation-based approach,
        xvii-xviii, 229-231
    group vs. individual format, 253-255,
        256-258
    help-seeking, 77-79
    intimacy skill enhancement, 12
    manual-based approach, xvii, 30, 228-229
    open format, 254
    pathways model, 232-235
    schema-based approach, xvi, 147-150
    self-regulation model, relapse process and,
        235-241

social control definition of, 277
    See also Behavioral economics; Clinical
        practice; Good lives model;
        Rehabilitation; Relapse prevention;
        Responsivity factors; Therapy goals
Tucker, J. A., 66, 68, 77, 78

Uncontrollable world belief, 131, 137
Uniform Crime Report, 302

van Beek, D. J., 246
Vermont Treatment Program for Sexual
    Aggressors, 182-183
Victim Empathy Distortions Scale (VEDS),
    176, 177, 180
Victims:
    abuse by, 17
    blaming of, 250
    just-say-no programs, 298
    offender empathy and, 40-41, 164
    victim-specific empathy
        measures, 176-177
Violence and Sex Offender Risk Appraisal
    Guides, 218-219
Vogt, W. P., 90
Vuchinich, R. E., 66, 67, 68, 77, 78

Wacquant, L., 106
Wagner, C., 324
Ward, T., 23, 58, 79, 121, 126, 129, 132, 136,
    137, 139, 140, 161, 163, 196, 248, 250,
    287, 288, 306, 320
Webster, C. D., 302
Webster, S., 24, 42
Weekes, J. R., 326
Weinrott, M. R., 195, 196, 199, 201, 303
Well-being, xix, 16
    rehabilitation and, 25, 29-30
    See also Good lives model
Widiger, T. A., 159
Worling, J. R., 192, 197, 203
Wright, M. A., 178
Wurtele, S. K., 178

Young, J. E., 148, 149
Youth Risk Behavior Survey, 301

About the Editors

Tony Ward, PhD, DipClinPsyc, is the Director of the Forensic Psychology Program at the University of Melbourne. He was previously director of the Kia Marama Program for sexual offenders at Rolleston Prison, Christchurch, New Zealand. His research interests include the offense process in offenders, cognitive distortions, and models of rehabilitation. He has published more than 110 research articles, chapters, and books. These include *Remaking Relapse Prevention* (with D. R Laws & S. M. Hudson; Sage, 2000) and the *Sourcebook of Treatment Programs for Sexual Offenders* (with W. L. Marshall, Y. A. Fernandez, & S. M. Hudson, 1998). He is currently working on a book on theories of sexual offending and rehabilitation.

Address: Department of Criminology, University of Melbourne, 234 Queensberry Street, Melbourne 3010, Australia.

E-mail: t.ward@criminology.unimelb.edu.au

D. Richard Laws, PhD, was the director of the Sexual Behavior Laboratory at Atascadero State Hospital in California from 1970 to 1985; project director at the Florida Mental Health Institute, Tampa, from 1985 to 1989; manager of forensic psychology at Alberta Hospital, Edmonton, Alberta, from 1989 to 1994; and most recently a psychologist with Adult Forensic Psychiatric Services in Victoria, British Columbia, from 1994 until his retirement in 1999. Dr. Laws is known in the field of sexual deviation as a developer of assessment procedures and in program development and evaluation. He is the author of numerous articles and book chapters in this area and serves on the editorial board of several journals. He is the editor of *Relapse Prevention With Sex Offenders* (1989), coeditor with W. L. Marshall and H. E. Barbaree of *Handbook of Sexual Assault* (1990), coeditor with W. T. O'Donohue of *Sexual Deviance* (1997), and coeditor with S. M. Hudson and T. Ward of *Remaking Relapse Prevention With Sex Offenders* (2000). He is past president of the Association for the Treatment of Sexual Abusers. He is adjunct faculty at the University of Victoria and Simon Fraser University in British Columbia and is Honorary Professor at the

University of Birmingham (UK) and Cardiff University (UK). E-mail: drlaws@telus.net

Stephen M. Hudson, PhD, DipClinPsyc, was Director of Clinical Psychology at the Department of Psychology, University of Canterbury, Christchurch, New Zealand. He was instrumental in the establishment of New Zealand's first specialized treatment unit for child molesters at Rolleston Prison, Kia Marama, in 1989. His research work was grouped into three major areas: intimacy and attachment style, cognitive distortions, and offence pathways/relapse prevention models. The results of these research projects were published in more than 80 books, book chapters, and scholarly articles. He coedited a number of important books in the sexual offending area, including *Remaking Relapse Prevention* (with D. R Laws & T. Ward; Sage, 2000), the *Sourcebook of Treatment Programs for Sexual Offenders* (with W. L. Marshall, Y. A. Fernandez, & S. M. Hudson, 1998), and *The Juvenile Sex Offender* (with H. E. Barbaree & W. L. Marshall). Dr. Hudson died on November 1, 2001, after a short battle with cancer.

About the Contributors

Anthony R. Beech is a Senior Lecturer in Forensic Psychology at the University of Birmingham, U.K. Over the past 10 years he has been the lead researcher of the STEP (Sex Offender Treatment Evaluation Project) team. Here he has been involved in treatment evaluation and the development of systems to look at treatment need and treatment change in sex offenders. He has written widely on the topics of assessment and treatment and other related subjects.

Astrid Birgden is a Forensic Psychologist and Manager, Sex Offender Programs, CORE-the Public Correctional Enterprise, Department of Justice and Fellow, Criminology Department, Melbourne University. She has a history of working with offenders including clients with intellectual disability and/or mental illness. She is currently developing a framework to reduce reoffending for all offender types across the Victorian correctional system. She has a particular interest in the application of therapeutic jurisprudence in the criminal justice system.

Mark Brown, PhD, has been on the staff of the Department of Criminology at Melbourne University since 1995. In addition to academic duties, he has undertaken correctional consultancy work in Victoria, Western Australia, and New Zealand. His primary teaching and research interests lie in corrections and penal history. He has written extensively on the subject of dangerousness, risk assessment, and legislative measures to deal with serious offenders. He recently coedited with John Pratt *Dangerous Offenders: Punishment and Social Order* (2000), and is currently writing a history of colonial policing and punishment in British India. Contact: Department of Criminology, University of Melbourne, 234 Queensberry Street, Melbourne 3053, Australia. E-mail: mark.brown@unimelb.edu.au

Marie Connolly, PhD, is Head of the Department of Social Work at the University of Canterbury in Christchurch, New Zealand. Her research interests span two main areas: working with families in child protection, and the offending patterns of sex offenders. She is the author of *Effective Participatory Practice: Family Group Conferencing in Child Protection* (1999) and editor of

New Zealand Social Work: Contexts and Practice (2001). She is also the Director of Te Awatea Violence Research Centre.

Christopher Drake is a clinical psychologist working in a community-based forensic clinic. Most of his clinical work is focused upon working individually with sexual offenders who have been deemed not suitable for group-based treatment programs. His research work focuses on treatment of cognitive distortions and on sexually deviant behavior in the mentally ill.

William Glaser is Consultant Psychiatrist at the Victorian Institute of Forensic Mental Health and Visiting Fellow at the Departments of Criminology and Psychology, University of Melbourne. His research and clinical interests include sex offenders, mental health in prisoners, offenders with intellectual disability, and the assessment of personal injury litigants.

Stephen Hart is Professor of Psychology at Simon Fraser University. He obtained his PhD in clinical-forensic psychology at the University of British Columbia. His major research interests are assessment of violence risk, psychopathic personality disorder, and mentally disordered offenders. Together with Ron Roesch, he is Coeditor of the *International Journal of Forensic Mental Health.*

Robin Jones is a clinical psychologist who has worked in criminal justice settings in a range of countries over the past 12 years. Cross-cultural and ethnic issues have been an important dimension of her work throughout this period. After gaining a master's and Diploma in Clinical Psychology in New Zealand in 1989, she spent several years developing and implementing corrections-based sex offender programs, including contributing to a bicultural treatment approach for Maori offenders. She then worked for 7 years in community-based settings in New York City, directing first an alternative to incarceration program for jail-bound adolescent male sexual offenders, and subsequently a medium-secure residential program for severely emotionally disturbed adolescent females. Her work almost exclusively involved ethnic minority clients, their families, and communities. She also consulted to juvenile justice programs in New York at both city and state levels on subjects including cultural issues in treatment.

She moved to Melbourne 18 months ago and is now affiliated with Melbourne University Department of Criminology. She provides supervision and consultation to a range of correctional programs and, in her role as a consultant to CORE, continued to work on cross-cultural issues, with a current focus on indigenous programming within correctional settings in Victoria. She has published a range of book chapters and journal articles and has presented widely at international conferences on criminal justice, clinical, and cross-cultural issues.

Thomas Keenan is Senior Lecturer in Developmental Psychology at the Department of Psychology at the University of Canterbury, Christchurch, New Zealand. His main areas of interest are infant and early childhood cognitive development; children's theory of mind; and developmental issues in the etiology of sexual offending.

P. Randall Kropp is a clinical and forensic psychologist specializing in the assessment and management of violent offenders. He works for the Forensic Psychiatric Services Commission of British Columbia, Canada, is a research consultant with the British Columbia Institute Against Family Violence, and is Adjunct Professor of Psychology at Simon Fraser University. He has conducted numerous workshops for mental health professionals, police officers, and corrections staff in North America, Australia, and Europe. He has published journal articles, book chapters, and research reports, and he is a coauthor of two works on risk assessment, the *Manual for the Spousal Assault Risk Assessment Guide* and the *Manual for the Sexual Violence Risk-20.*

Ruth E. Mann is head of sex offender and domestic violence treatment programs for Her Majesty's Prison Service (England and Wales). She is responsible for designing treatment programs, training therapists, supporting implementation, monitoring treatment integrity, and evaluating clinical impact. She has worked with convicted sex offenders for 15 years, and has specialized in cognition and motivation as aspects of sex offender treatment.

Karen Owen is Forensic Psychologist and Manager, Sex Offender Programs, CORE-the Public Correctional Enterprise, Department of Justice and Fellow, Criminology Department, Melbourne University. Prior to working with sex offenders, she worked with clients with intellectual disability, particularly those with challenging behaviors. She has a particular interest in cognitive processes in sexual offending and is conducting research in the area.

Devon L. L. Polaschek is a Senior Lecturer in Criminal Justice Psychology and Director of Clinical Training at the Victoria University of Wellington, in New Zealand. A clinical psychologist, with a background in offender rehabilitation, her research program focuses on psychological assessment and management of rapists and other serious violent offenders.

Michael J. Proeve has a master's degree in Clinical Psychology from La Trobe University and a PhD from the University of South Australia. He has worked in forensic mental health, correctional, and community settings with a variety of types of offenders and has also worked as a full-time Lecturer. He is currently Director of the Sexual Offender Treatment and Assessment Program (SOTAP) in Adelaide, South Australia.

Bea Raymond is Psychologist and Coordinator, Sex Offender Programs, CORE-the Public Correctional Enterprise, Department of Justice and Fellow, Criminology Department, Melbourne University. Prior to working with sex offenders, she has worked with clients with sensory disability. She also has a particular interest in staff training and is conducting research in the area.

Richard Siegert is currently Associate Professor and Head of the Rehabilitation Teaching and Research Unit in the Department of Medicine at the Wellington School of Medicine of the University of Otago. He is a clinical psychologist and neuropsychologist with experience working in forensic and other clinical settings. His research interests range widely and include cognition in neurological and psychiatric disorders and psychometrics applied to clinical problems. His major theoretical preoccupation concerns the implications of our evolutionary past for understanding psychopathology. He welcomes any feedback on his chapter at rsiegert@wnmeds.ac.nz

Laura Sorbello is a registered psychologist who has completed 8 years of training in psychology at the University of Melbourne, Australia, specializing in the forensic/clinical domain. Throughout her training and employment opportunities, she has had widespread experience in individual and group therapy with offenders displaying a range of issues and dysfunctional behaviors associated with their offending behavior.

She also has a strong commitment to the development, design, and evaluation of offender rehabilitation programs. Notably, her adaptation of Linehan's (1993) Dialectical Behaviour Therapy program for suicidal and self-harming offenders, known as the RUSH Program (Sorbello & Eccleston, 2000), has gained recognition throughout Australia by forensic colleagues. Apart from extensive practical experience in various forensic settings, her research interests involve examining psychological factors associated with intimate violence; assessment, treatment, and rehabilitation of offenders; treatment and prevention of suicide and self-harming behavior in offenders; female offenders; and sexual offenders. She has recently been involved in the delivery of a range of training workshops and lectures on these topics to other psychologists and trainees in the field.

Claire A. Stewart, MA, DipClinPsyc, is a lecturer in Disability Studies at Deakin University, Melbourne, Australia. Her current research interests include rehabilitation theory; disability policy; and parent, professional, and interagency collaboration in the disability area. Contact details: Claire Stewart, MA, DipClinPsyc, Institute of Disability, Deakin University, 221 Burwood Hwy, Burwood 3125, Melbourne, Australia. E-mail: cstewart@deakin.edu.au